WORLD WAR II
TRUCKS
AND
TANKS

WORLD WAR II
TRUCKS
AND
TANKS

JOHN NORRIS

To my wife Elizabeth who has stood waiting for me in all weather
conditions while I photograph vehicles great and small.
Thank you for being so patient.

First published 2012
by Spellmount, an imprint of The History Press
The Mill, Brimscombe Port
Stroud, Gloucestershire, GL5 2QG
www.thehistorypress.co.uk

British Library Cataloguing in Publication Data.
A catalogue record for this book is available from the British Library.

ISBN 978 0 7524 6602 6

Typesetting and origination by The History Press
Printed in India

CONTENTS

ACKNOWLEDGEMENTS

The author would like to thank the many owners for allowing their vehicles to be used in illustrating this work, including Damien Horn who very kindly turned out his Stoewer R200 on Jersey, Rex and Rod Cadman's late-build Panzerkampfwagen IV Ausf. J tank, which is often on display at the annual War & Peace Show in Kent. Thanks to Adrian Snell with his M14 International half-track and also Tony Oliver at History on Wheels at Eton Wick near Windsor in Berkshire. Thank you to Steve Lamonby for his various vehicles at the many shows over the years. My thanks also to Preston Isaac for allowing access to the Cobbaton Combat Collection at Chittlehampton, Umberleigh. My sincere thanks also go to all the vehicle owners who are too many to list here but very kindly displayed their vehicles at events where they could be photographed. Finally, my gratitude to the Tank Museum at Bovington with its fine displays of some very rare vehicles.

INTRODUCTION

Many books have been written on the subject of trucks and tanks used during the Second World War, ranging from encyclopaedias to complete histories dealing with specific vehicles like some kind of mechanical biography. The war ended in 1945 but today there are many people who are fascinated with the vehicles used during that time and some are fortunate enough to own one or more examples of these wartime vehicles. These new civilian owners maintain the vehicles in running order and in some cases have completely restored them from piles of neglected metal that have been left to rust forgotten in a field or barn somewhere. Specialist societies have been established, such as the Invicta Military Preservation Society (IMPS) and the Military Vehicle Trust (MVT), both of which have created a support network for vehicle owners, and each society also organises a series of special gatherings where owners can display their vehicles. These events have an international following and owning and restoring lorries (trucks), motorcycles and armoured vehicles from the period of the Second World War is a very serious business. Specialist auction sites on the internet deal with the buying and selling of these vehicles and topical programmes highlighting the restoration of tanks and trucks have also appeared on television.

Several owners or more will sometimes arrange journeys to travel to historic sites where battles were fought using the type of vehicles they own and use them to drive to the location. These can cover many miles and the convoys are referred to as 'road runs' and include examples of many different types, which have been turned out to participate in these mobile displays. Motorcycles, Jeeps, trucks and wheeled armoured cars often take part and routes are planned to pass through towns and villages in France and Belgium along with other countries that were occupied by German forces during the war. Far from being upset by the appearance of these columns passing by, the residents in these towns frequently line the streets to watch the column drive past. It is all very reminiscent of those days in 1944 when similar parades passed along the same streets and roads to liberate these towns.

Many surplus vehicles were sold off after the war to overseas armies and some were sold to civilians and used in the post-war period for a range of duties including removals, carnivals and circuses, recovery and much more. This was not the first time such a move had been undertaken. After the First World War military vehicles were sold to civilian companies for haulage and recovery work. Many vehicles of the Second World War can today be seen at military vehicle gatherings, where they are probably already familiar to visitors either through war films or museums. Gatherings of these vehicles always attract thousands of people who come to see them being put through mobility displays such as the Trucks and Troops event at the National Motor Museum at Beaulieu in Hampshire, and at the Imperial War Museum at Duxford in Cambridgeshire. Larger events attract larger crowds and some of them feature battle re-enactments where the tanks and armoured cars participate in the set-piece action displays. For example, the annual War & Peace Show and Military Odyssey, both held in Kent, each feature battle re-enactments to show how armoured vehicles and trucks operated in war and the Bovington Tank Museum in Dorset also features vehicles in arena displays using tanks from its own collection along with privately owned vehicles that attend to support the event. Such displays serve to increase the interest in trucks and tanks at all levels, and visitors to these shows also include members of modelling clubs who enjoy recreating these vehicles in minute detail in a range of scales. To cater for this interest a range of manufacturers produce kits of almost every type of armoured fighting vehicle or truck ever built and used during the Second World War, in a range of scales and materials from plastic to metal and even radio-controlled versions.

This book is intended to be used as an introduction to provide background details on some of the more common types of vehicles involved in campaigns during the Second World War and to highlight some of the vehicles that are most likely to be seen at shows such as Military Mayhem in Kent or the Bunker Bash in Essex, or be on display in one of the smaller vehicle museums such as the History on Wheels Museum at Eton Wick near Windsor in Berkshire. Many vehicles participating in these events are original but some of the scarcer types, particularly the German designs, are recreations because so few of the originals exist outside of museums. It is also intended to explain to the reader the numbers of vehicles involved in some of the campaigns where more tanks were used in one battle than several European armies combined have in service today. Also, the numbers of tanks built will come as a surprise, especially those such as the Tiger, which were not nearly as numerous as some people might suppose.

Where possible the images in this book show the restored original vehicle but this is not always possible and in some cases recreated versions stand in as very good substitutes. These recreations have sometimes been built using 1:35 scale plastic models of the vehicle as reference points, such as the German SdKfz 222 or SdKfz 223, which were in turn produced by examining the original vehicle in museums or design drawings. Thus it comes full circle with the real design inspiring a model kit for a hobby that is then used to recreate a life-size model for another hobby related through interest in wartime vehicles. Obviously the recreated vehicles do not stand up to detailed scrutiny when compared to the real thing, but they are usually good enough to give a general impression and many have been used in war films and television documentaries. The number of recreations of wartime vehicles is growing and, in so doing, showcase designs that would otherwise only ever have been seen in museums because they are so scarce. Where images of these recreated examples are used it will be made clear in the captions.

Despite their advancing age, many of the original trucks and tanks still have many years of service left in them due to the unstinting efforts of their owners. It would be fair to say that as long as there are organised displays, people will turn out to see them. The background behind the design and development of these tanks and trucks is quite well known in many cases, but what is not so well known is the history of where they were used and in what numbers. This operational use puts an entirely different understanding on them, particularly when one takes into account the conditions under which they operated. Some vehicles are quite common, such as the Jeep used by the US Army and other Allied armies, with almost 640,000 being built. By comparison the German Army only received around 52,000 Kubelwagens, a light vehicle comparable to the Jeep that served mainly in liaison roles, but they were used in every theatre of war where the German Army fought. A selection of the vehicles profiled in this book are shown in colour and in some cases a number of original photographs have been included just by way of comparison. It will be noted that some vehicle types are absent, but it is hoped that those that do appear will compensate for this. Gatherings of military vehicles are busy and exciting events, and if the opportunity arises to visit them it is suggested that one does so, because the only disappointment would be in missing what is surely the ultimate in live-action displays.

1

SETTING THE SCENE

When war in Europe broke out in September 1939 reliable motor vehicles had only been in existence some fifty years, but already they had proved their worth on the battlefield by providing invaluable service during the First World War and in a host of other subsequent conflicts around the world. In 1914 Britain had gone to war with an army comprising 164,000 regular soldiers, 27,500 horses and only around 922 motor vehicles of all types, including 80 lorries or trucks, 827 motor cars and 15 motorcycles. Four years later the British Army had increased to more than 5,363,000 troops, almost 900,000 horses and the number of motorised vehicles had multiplied over 132 times to reach nearly 122,000 machines; a figure that included 56,000 motor cars and 34,000 motorcycles, the rest of the number being made up by lorries and a new development for the army known as the armoured fighting vehicle or AFV for short. This included tanks, armoured cars and the first self-propelled guns (SPGs), which had not been known at the start of the conflict and were only made possible by the power of the internal combustion engine. In the interwar years more designs appeared that had been influenced by conditions and roles on the battlefield and many of these had been tried in action. In the 1920s the vehicles for the British Army were sometimes tested first in Farnborough, Hampshire, before being sent for trials in Wales and Scotland, and then underwent further tests under extreme conditions in Egypt and India. Those that were good entered service and those that were not were abandoned. The same process of selection applied to lorries and motorcycles, which armies around the world had to have in order to move equipment and tow artillery.

The British Army referred to its transport vehicles as lorries, and the French called them *camion*, while the American armed forces called them trucks. The Germans used the term *wagen*, which was a generic term meaning wagon and was applied to all motorised transport whether armoured or unarmoured. The term used to describe such vehicles is largely immaterial and in the classic 1942 war film *One of Our Aircraft is Missing* the term 'truck' is frequently used in the dialogue. As far as the military is concerned, just as long as the vehicles could operate in the role for which they were intended, which was to transport men to the front along with supplies and ammunition, or in the case of the tank, to crush barbed wire and deal with machine-gun positions and other tanks, they were satisfied. The American term 'truck' has come into general usage and therefore for the purposes of this work this is the term that will be used. Among the different types of vehicles there were also motorised ambulances, which brought the

This truck built by Karrier in the late 1920s was used by the British Army to move the increasing loads needed by the armed forces.

wounded back to the hospitals in a seemingly never-ending flow. In four years of the First World War the British Army alone moved 3.25 million tons of foodstuffs, 5.25 million tons of ammunition and an incredible 5.43 million tons of fodder for the horses and mules. The other belligerent nations, including Russia, Italy, France and Germany, faced the same problem, and had to move similar loads of stores for their respective armies. In addition to this were the other items essential for the continued conduct of the war in Europe, which eventually stretched east from Russia, south into Italy and Greece and west to France and Belgium.

Depots for the distribution of war materiel were established in France, usually where railways and harbours could handle the bulk shipments. But these modes of transportation could only take the materiel so far before it had to be offloaded and put on to trucks for dispatch to various units. For example, an official record for the period of January to October 1915 reports that the depot at Calais alone issued to the British Army: '11,000 prismatic and magnetic compasses, 7,000 watches, 40,000 miles of electric cable, 40,000 electric torches, 3,600,000yd of flannelette, 1,260,000yd of rot-proof canvas, 25,000 tents, 1,600,000 waterproof sheets, 12,800 bicycles, 20,000 wheels, 6,000,000 anti-gas helmets, 4,000,000 pairs of horse and wheel shoes, 447,000 Lewis-gun magazines.' The war was barely one year old and already such demands were being placed on the supply systems. Other supplies were equally daunting in their sheer volume, such as 90 million lb of bread and the monthly meat ration, which rose from 3.6 million lb in 1914 to 67.5 million lb in 1918. Feeding an army on campaign in any period has historically always been difficult. In 1700, for example, it was calculated that an army of 60,000 consumed 45 tons of bread, and that it required sixty portable bread ovens and 200 wagons of fuel to bake this amount. To move such vast volumes of supplies, vehicles had to be available and the numbers in service with the armies had to increase. With motor vehicles this is reflected in 1918 by the fact that some 13 million gallons of petrol were being issued each month.

During the war there was an ongoing debate between the traditional army minds, which preferred horses, and progressive minds, which argued for the internal combustion engine. Traditionalists made the point that horses were in abundance and could be replaced from local sources such as farms or those animals captured from the enemy if necessary. The progressives maintained that horses had to be fed and cared for even when not working, while when the engine of a vehicle was turned off it used nothing. Furthermore, vehicles captured from the enemy could be put to good use; this would be demonstrated many times. One of the progressive-thinking officers to argue the case for motorised transport was Douglas MacArthur of the US Army, who in 1933 stated that: 'the horse has no higher degree of mobility today than he had a thousand years ago. The time has therefore arrived when the Cavalry arm must either replace or assist the horse as a means of transportation, or else pass into the limbo of discarded military formations.' MacArthur was probably better placed than some other officers to pass such judgement because he had seen at first hand just how vital motor vehicles and tanks were as war-winning components during the First World War and would be again for armies in the future. He would, in time, come to be proven correct, but

The German Army used hundreds of thousands of horses on the Eastern Front.

one cannot help but think his words were perhaps more than a little influenced by the opinions of J.F.C. Fuller who, five years before these comments were made, had written in his 1928 work *On Future Warfare* that: 'The probabilities are that in the future petrol-power will revolutionise the art of war as extremely as did the introduction of fire-arms.'

In an earlier age before the internal combustion engine and petrol, the Prussian officer and military theorist Carl Philipp Gottfried von Clausewitz, 1780–1831, wrote extensively on the conduct of war with his most famous work being *Vom Kriege* (*On War*). In this he states that: 'Everything is very simple in war, but the simplest thing is difficult.' He continued: 'War is the province of uncertainty; three-fourths of the things on which action in war is based lie hidden in the fog of a greater or lesser certainty.' Indeed, as he pointed out, it has never been easy to send an army on campaign and once deployed the difficulties do not stop, but rather only increase. The French had their equivalent to von Clausewitz in Swiss-born Antoine-Henri Jomini, 1779–1869, who theorised the term 'strategy', including thoughts on how troops should be supplied and supported with food, equipment, heavier weapons and reinforcements. Both theorists were writing in a time before the advent of the motor vehicle, when draught animals such as oxen, mules and horses were the only means of moving supplies either in wagons or as pack loads, but even so their comments were still valid in the age of the motor vehicle.

Typically an average horse could comfortably carry a load of up to 200lb but the animal required 20lb of fodder to eat per day to keep it healthy. This meant that one horse was needed solely to carry the food supplies for itself and nine other animals. The more animals that were used the more the problem was mul-

Pushing an ambulance through the mud in France during the First World War.

tiplied, which is why the amount of fodder transported by the British Army in the First World War outweighed the tonnage of ammunition by 180,000 tons. An army with, say, around 40,000 horses for cavalry and transport would require up to 500 tons of fodder each day. It was a problem that could not be ignored and as armies increased in size and the length of time spent on campaign was extended, the problem would only get worse, and these problems were still there during the Second World War. The distances over which supplies had to be transported could mean success or failure to an army on campaign. For example, one of the reasons postulated for Russia's defeat during the Russo-Japanese War of 1904–05 was that its supply lines, extending some 4,000 miles back to depots in Russia, could not maintain the volume of logistics and lacked the transportation needed to support the army.

The motor vehicle and the aeroplane had been developed by civilians during peacetime and it was not long before the military was investigating the war potential of these two inventions. It would be fair to say that had it not been for the war in 1914 the development of the motor vehicle and the aeroplane would have been much slower without military intervention and demand. The way in which warfare was conducted had changed dramatically since the start of the century and there was growing interest in new inventions in fields such as aviation. The military in many countries were very keen to adapt it but it would require some kind of practical display to convince the military planners of the true value of new innovations such as aircraft. One of the earliest demonstrations was a little-known event that took place on 1 November 1911 in the remote oasis area of Tagiura, near Tripoli in Libya. On that day Lieutenant Giulio Cavotti dropped four bombs during the course of Italy's colonial campaign to subdue local tribespeople and in doing so created another milestone in aviation history as being the first man to drop bombs offensively on an enemy. Although the attack was made against an enemy who had no means of retaliating, the point had been proved and history had been made. The episode came only two years after Louis Blèriot's historic cross-Channel flight, but it set minds thinking about future military applications for the aircraft. The following year French pilots dropped bombs on targets in Morocco. In 1913 Spanish pilots also bombed targets in Morocco to quell unrest among the local populace in Spain's colonial territory. Even the tiny country of Bulgaria got in on the act and used mercenary pilots to drop bombs on the Turkish city of Adrianople, modern-day Edirne, during the war of 1912–13.

The military had also long expressed an interest in motor vehicles and in 1898 Colonel R.P. Davidson of the Illinois National Guard experimented by mounting a Colt machine gun on to a Duryea motorised tricycle to produce one of the first mobile weapon platforms. Several years later on the other side of the Atlantic, the German company Ehrhardt produced a prototype of an armoured car equipped with a 50mm gun in 1905. From these early experiments the motor vehicle evolved

Pierce Arrow was used from around 1916 to carry supplies. It has solid rubber tyres. The driver of the
Pierce Arrow truck used in the First World War had rudimentary controls (above left).

into many different forms of AFVs during the First World War, which in turn led to
its most powerful expression – the tank. Vehicles to transport supplies and troops
would be in such great demand by the military during the First World War that
public events were organised to raise money to buy vehicles for the armed forces
in addition to those purchased by the government. These events produced a huge
response and trucks and other machines were bought with the proceeds and sent
out to France.

The greatest funds were raised in the big cities, where wealthy philanthropic supporters gave generous donations. However, even the smallest towns and villages did their 'bit for the war effort', which often produced surprises. The actual numbers of vehicles purchased in such a way may not have been huge or war winning, but the troops appreciated the motives. For example, in the tiny fishing port of Brixham in Devon, the local fishermen raised enough money to buy an ambulance, which they presented to the British Red Cross Society and St John Ambulance Association in 1916 just before the Somme offensive in July that year. Men from Brixham would have been greatly heartened to know they had not been forgotten, such as one NCO serving with the Royal Army Medical Corps, who wrote home: 'One of the Ambulance lorries we have here is a gift from the Brixham fishermen. Of course I salute it every time I see it. I will bring it home with me next year.' He was being optimistic, as the war was to last for more than another two years, but vehicles like the Brixham gift would add to the numbers required, and dependency on them increased as they were used to move everything from nails for horseshoes to shells for the artillery. The Queenswood School, Clapham Park, made a similar donation of an ambulance and the vehicle served with the British Army in the Salonika theatre of operations. Other countries organised their own similar schemes and the system was used again during the Second World War, with towns raising money to buy a fighter aircraft or a tank, and proved a popular morale booster.

It has been opined that logistics are '90 per cent of the business of war' and, considering the amount of war materiel absorbed on campaigns, this is correct. The word 'logistics' has several definitions, including speech and reason, but it also means 'ratio', denoting what an army is entitled to. In more specific terms, the Greek word '*logistiki*' defines the modern meaning of logistics as having an 'account and financial organisation'. In the Roman and later Byzantine military societies certain officers were appointed as '*logistikas*' to denote that they were responsible for the financial and supply distribution affairs of the army. Over the centuries the word '*logos*' has been adapted by many countries such as France, from which it derived the term '*logis*', meaning lodge or quarter in terms of billeting troops. The role of the troops serving in the units handling the supplies was not fully understood by those serving in the front line, who thought that those in the rear areas were having an easy time of things. Consequently they were given many undeserved and derogatory terms, such as '*Ettappenschweine*' (lines of communication pigs), which was used by the German fighting men in the First World War. This was rather unfair because the support troops faced dangers from artillery as they moved forward and suffered casualties as they did so. In addition, the front-line troops would have had no supplies had it not been for the likes of the Army Service Corps of the British Army, and without these essential supplies they could not have fought on. The actual units in which they served have come to be referred to as 'tail' arms as opposed to 'teeth' arms, which are the fighting forces at the front. The supporting units in some cases contained almost as many men as there were engaged in the actual fighting on the front line. In November 1918 the American Expeditionary Force had over 1 million fighting men in France, with more than 688,000 men with a fleet of 30,000 trucks to support them in what was termed 'services of supply'. By 1918, during the eighteen months that American fighting men had been in France they were supplied with more than 1.2 million weapons, including rifles, pistols and machine guns, over 67,800 horses and mules complete with saddles and harnesses, and some 1,000 artillery tractors, all of which had to be shipped from America and then transported to the front line.

In the first months of the war in 1914 the French Army had faced a crisis with a lack of reservists arriving at the front. The German Army was still advancing and in response Marshal Joseph Gallieni, as Minister for War, ordered the taxis from Paris to transport troops to the front. Gallieni remarked: *'Eh bien, voilà au moins qui n'est pas banal'* ('Well, here at least is something out of the ordinary'). Finding itself equally short of motorised transport to move the mass of troops quickly, the British Army had commandeered London buses to transport reinforcements to the front. Unconventional as such moves were, the tactics worked and showed how vital motor transport, even improvised, now was to a modern army. In February 1916 the French Army was determined to hold the town of Verdun against all German attacks, and poured thousands of troops into its defence. The 45-mile stretch of road leading to the town from the supply depots became known as the *Voie Sacreè* (Sacred Way) and 3,900 trucks on average traversed its length each day. On 21 February all horse-drawn transport was ordered off the road to make way for the more numerous and faster moving motorised trucks. In one week alone from 28 February some 190,000 troops and 25,000 tons of supplies were moved along the *Voie Sacreè* to save Verdun. The armed forces in all countries agreed that horses and motor vehicles would co-exist and continue to serve alongside one another in supporting their armies, for the time being at least. Military planners recognised that such a compromise was best, but over time it became inevitable that horses should ultimately give way to the ascendant power of the internal combustion engine.

By 1916 vehicles from cars to trucks and motorcycles had become a common sight within the armies, but on 15 September that year a new dimension was added to the battlefield with the appearance of a vehicle the likes of which had never before been seen. This was the tank, and numbers of them were built up in readiness for what would become the Battle of Flers Courcelette in the latter stages of the British offensive known as the Battle of the Somme, which had been launched on 1 July 1916. Tanks, like the aeroplane and motor vehicle, had begun life as a civilian project to produce agricultural machines that could cross soft, muddy fields using a system of continuous tracks. At first these had been steam-powered; one such was the design invented by the American designer F.W. Batter in 1888. This was followed by other designs that eventually arrived at the petrol-driven machine designed by David Roberts working for Hornsby & Sons in 1907.

Armoured cars such as the British Rolls-Royce had been used by the Royal Navy armoured car squadrons as early as 1914, but these were large lumbering machines covered in armour plate, with some weighing up to 28 tons. They were fitted with continuous 'caterpillar' tracks and were armed with machine guns and modified field guns, which meant that they could crush anything beneath their tracks. When the Germans saw the approach of these vehicles some cried out in terror that the 'Devil was coming'. Armoured cars had been operating since the early stages of the war and were used in Europe, Russia and the Middle East against Germany's Turkish allies, but the tanks were completely different because they were not only larger but they also carried heavier weapons, firing 6lb shells from their adapted naval guns. France and Britain led the way in developing their own tank designs and Germany responded very late with the huge A7V, but they also used tanks captured from the Allies. This was a trend they would return to in the Second World War. When the United States entered the war in 1917 France and Britain provided the US Army with tanks, which would have a profound influence on officers such as Lieutenant Colonel George S. Patton Jr and Brigadier General Douglas MacArthur. The first American operation involving tanks was conducted by the 344th and 345th Battalions on 12 September 1918 when they attacked St Mihiel as part of the 1st Provisional Brigade, Tank Corps, commanded by Patton. Further tank designs would lead to variants known as self-propelled guns being developed, and also created a specialist role in response to the threat for anti-tank guns, which would also be mounted on chassis in order to become mobile. Then on 11 November 1918 all this effort was made redundant when the armistice was signed and the fighting stopped.

For more than four years during the First World War, French ports and the French railway network had been burdened with carrying troops and war materiel and the Germans had experienced the same thing as their front lines were supplied. Finally, after many campaigns and the introduction of some of the most destructive weaponry that science and industry could develop, including poison gas and flame-throwers, the war had at last ended. The armies began to withdraw, and America, which had neither reason nor desire to remain in Europe, departed, leaving the control of any future military designs Germany may have up to Britain and France. In the post-war period America was left holding US$32 million worth of tanks and despite officers such as General Rockenbach arguing for an independent tank force, their opinions were ignored and the tanks were left in the control of the infantry. America could see no real need for tanks and the budget was severely limited. Twenty years after the end of the First World War, and with another war in Europe threatening to break out, the US Army in 1938 had only 300 light tanks in service compared to Japan's 2,000. At that time the only tank of any note in service with the US Army was the M1 combat car, a light tank by any other interpretation, but in order to get around the reluctance for tanks the military termed the vehicle 'combat car'.

Germany had left the battlefield in November 1918, abandoned the trenches and discarded vast amounts of war materiel. On 28 June 1919 in the French town of Versailles, the League of Nations, which had been formed only two months earlier in April that year, gathered to debate the future political and economic position of Germany and decide on the size and state of her armed forces. In what has become known as the Treaty of Versailles the Allies limited Germany to an army of no more than 100,000 men without conscription. In addition, Germany was forbidden to have anti-tank and anti-aircraft guns and no heavy field artillery, nor was it allowed tanks, aircraft or submarines. Naval vessels had to be under 10,000

The Rolls-Royce armoured car was armed with a single Vickers .303in-calibre machine gun and was used for patrolling and reconnaissance duties.

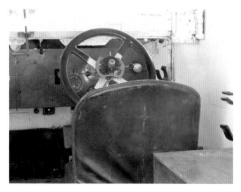

The driver's position of the Rolls-Royce armoured car was very basic like the civilian vehicles of the day.

The turret of the Rolls-Royce armoured car was riveted and had to be traversed by hand.

British crews of early tanks stand by a Whippet tank in France *c.* 1918.

tons and no General Staff was permitted. Outwardly Germany had no option but
to agree reluctantly to comply with the terms. Almost immediately and in secret
General Hans von Seeckt, who had served on the General Staff during the war, set
about circumventing the terms of the treaty. He served as the commander-in-chief
of the Reichswehr but for several years he negotiated with Soviet Russia to acquire
weapons, vehicles and training in their use in secret. Some weapons designers
left Germany to take up 'temporary' residency in countries such as Sweden where
they continued to design and develop weapons in secret ready for the time when
they could return to Germany. One of these was Joseph Vollmer, the designer
behind Germany's only operational tank of the entire First World War, the A7V,
which appeared in 1918. During his voluntary exile he helped design the LK I and
LK II tanks used by Sweden. To all intents and purposes, Germany was observing
the limits of the Treaty of Versailles. In response, the Allies began to scale down
their armed forces and research into new weapons development was curtailed. In
America too, the military budget was reduced and research and development into
new weapons was cut.

    The armies at the front in the First World War had been kept provisioned through
a system of logistics that had been used for many centuries, but it was the scale
involved in modern warfare that baffled the more old-fashioned military minds.
One of the more progressive post-war military thinkers who grasped the funda-
mentals of this new form of servicing warfare was General Archibald Wavell, later

Lord Wavell. He had long recognised the necessity of logistics, and in his Lees Knowle's lecture, presented to Trinity College in Cambridge in 1939, he expressed the importance of logistics by stating to his assembled audience: 'I should like you to always bear in mind when you study military history or military events the importance of this administrative factor, because it is where most critics and many generals go wrong.' Even after the Second World War there were still some who could not grasp the function of logistics and General Wavell was continuously having to try to explain the importance of this support through his writings, such his work *Speaking Generally*, published in 1946, in which he paid tribute to the troops engaged in bringing up the supplies when he wrote:

> The more I have seen of war, the more I realise how it all depends on administration and transportation (what our American allies call logistics). It takes little skill or imagination to see where you would like your army and when; it takes much knowledge and hard work to know where you can place your forces and whether you can maintain them there. A real knowledge of supply and movement factors must be the basis of every leader's plan; only then can he know how and when to take the risks with these factors; and battles and wars are won by taking risks.

Wavell referred to such administration as the 'crux of generalship'. He was supported in this opinion by the military historian and theorist Major General J.F.C. Fuller, who wrote of logistics: 'Surely one of the strangest things in military history is the complete silence about the problems of supplies. In ten thousand books written on war not one is to be found on the subject, yet it forms the basis on which rests the whole structure of war: it is the very foundation of tactics and strategy.' Both men were absolutely correct in their assessments and were updating the words of von Clausewitz and Jomini. Men such as Fuller and Wavell knew how vital it was to provide an army with good lines of supply and so too did Heinz Guderian, who had been quartermaster of the German XXXVIII Reserve Corps in May 1918 when it advanced 14 miles during the Spring Offensive. This was just one demonstration during the First World War but the importance of such would be taken to greater levels during the Second World War. For example, the amphibious landings undertaken by the Allies during the war, including Normandy, Salerno, Anzio, Sicily, North Africa and the island-hopping campaign in the Pacific against the Japanese, would not have been possible without the ships, trucks and aircraft to bring the supplies up to support the advances of the tanks and infantry. For the Axis powers, the difficulties experienced came with supplying armies in the field. For the German Army it was the great land distances, as it pushed ever deeper into Russia, and for the Japanese it was supplying the myriad island garrisons across the Pacific Ocean and the distances in China. It was a prodigious effort to put an army into the field and even more of an effort to keep it there and functioning at maximum capacity and efficiency.

INTO A NEW ERA

oday logistics is defined as 'the branch of military science relating to pro-
curing, maintaining and transporting materiel, personnel and facilities'.
Thus logistics covers everything an army needs to remain at a state of readiness at all times, but especially during time of war, when weapons, ammunition,
supplies and vast amounts of petrol, oil and lubricants (POL) would be the very
lifeblood for the trucks and tanks that allowed an army to operate. An army without fuel and oil was doomed, as the Germans would discover to their cost during
the campaign in North Africa and again in Russia. In 1935, when Italy invaded
Abyssinia, the trucks and tanks rolled on against an ill-prepared resistance force.
Sanctions against Italy were put in place but there was no embargo on oil and as a
result Italy was able to maintain its conquest of the country. Had the Italian forces
been denied the vital oil, the army's trucks and tanks would not have operated
and the aircraft could not have flown operationally for longer than reserves would
have allowed.

During the Second World War supplies of petrol were vital and armies often operated at distances away from depots where their vehicles could be provisioned. One
answer was to carry as much petrol as possible in containers on the vehicles. The
British Army used flimsy tin cans with either 'crimped' or soldered seams that
split easily during the rigours of transportation. These held 4 gallons of petrol and
General Sir Claude Auchinleck believed that the design fault in these tins led to the
loss of at least 30 per cent of the petrol during the journey from base to the vehicle
it was to provision. During the campaign in North Africa the British Army captured
stocks of German-produced fuel cans made from pressed steel and sealed with
welded seams. The design was far superior to anything in use and so impressed the
Allies that they copied it, with more than 50 million being produced by the end of
the war. The Germans had always been nicknamed 'Jerry' by the British Army and
it was only natural they applied the term to these fuel cans, which became known
as 'jerrycans'. It has been expressed that imitation is the sincerest form of flattery,
and if that is indeed the case then this was a prime example of that.

Hitler and German Rearmament

When Adolf Hitler came to power as Chancellor of Germany with his Nazi Party
in January 1933 he had to bide his time before he could make his first overt
move militarily. In fact, he had to wait until March 1935 to be provided with an
excuse to dismiss the terms of the Treaty of Versailles and begin openly to set

about increasing the size and strength of Germany's armed forces with a rearmament programme. Even before this denouncement, the first new armoured cars for the German Army, in the shape of the Kfz13 armed with machine guns, were unveiled in 1934 along with the first new tank design, the Panzerkampfwagen I. These were armed with nothing more serious than two machine guns and gave no cause for concern. Even when the next designs of German tank, known as the Panzerkampfwagen II and abbreviated to PzKw, appeared in 1936 armed with 2cm cannon in a turret with machine guns, the British and French did not seem unduly alarmed. The Germans called their tanks panzers and referred to them and their armoured cars along with other specialist vehicles by the prefix SdKfz, which stood for *Sonderkraftfahrzeug* (special motorised vehicle) followed by a unique number indicating the type of vehicle. This identification also extended to include the half-track range of vehicles, even down to the small motorcycle-style Kettenkrad, which was designated SdKfz 2. Even trucks, light cars such as the Kubelwagen and motorcycles all had designation numbers and lettering to identify them, right up to the largest projects. Various models would be referred to as *Ausführung*, abbreviated to Ausf., which literally meant 'model' or 'mark'. Thus, we have, for example, the Panzerkampfwagen I referred to as SdKfz 101 Ausf. B, meaning model B of the tank.

The PzKw I and PzKw II had the nomenclatures of SdKfz 101 and SdKfz 121 respectively, which denoted their special status as armoured vehicles. Both of them would continue to serve in the German Army until 1943, by which time more than 1,400 PzKw I tanks would have been built, along with other variants including supply vehicles and SPGs, and some 3,600 PzKw II would have been built and produced in six different models and all variants. While the PzKw II was not the most powerful tank fielded by the German Army in the Second World War, it was far more advanced than a number of designs in service with other armies at the time, such as the British Army's A11 Matilda I infantry tank. The Panzer II was a natural continuation from the design of the Panzer I, which had been introduced in 1934, but it was better armed and had a faster road speed. Despite its lack of power, the Panzer II's design was versatile enough to permit several variants to be developed from the basic design, including SPG, recovery vehicle and bridge-laying vehicle.

Even before Adolf Hitler came to power in 1933 the German Army was already readying itself for a rearmament programme that would replace or introduce into service all those forms of weaponry forbidden under the terms of the Treaty of Versailles, including anti-tank guns and tanks. Some work on tank design had already been undertaken in secret using factories and facilities in Sweden as early as 1932, but it would not be until 1934 that the designs of the first German tanks were revealed. The German Ordnance Department had laid out specifications for a tank that would have a battle-ready weight of around 10 tons because it was thought that anything heavier would wreck the bridges as the vehicles traversed them. At this time the PzKw I had already entered service and numbers of these vehicles together with their crews would gain invaluable experience during the Spanish Civil War between 1936 and 1939. At the time of the outbreak of this conflict the PzKw II was just entering service and would also be used in action in Spain. In fact, the Spanish Civil War was seen as a proving ground for the German Army, and for armoured vehicles and tank crews in particular. By 1939 the German armaments factories, such as MAN, had already built over 1,200 PzKw II tanks, which meant that in the invasion of Poland in September 1939 almost the total force was deployed for the campaign.

PzKw II Ausf. A

The first prototype PzKw II vehicles were sent to Spain where they gained their first combat experience; this identified the weaknesses in the design and led to improvements. Further field trials corrected minor flaws and improved on the design. For example, the armour protection was increased and changes were made to the suspension, which meant an increase in the weight of the vehicle of almost 2 tons. The power of the Maybach engine was increased by boring out the cylinders and the first production models were built in 1935 and entered service in 1936. This version was the Ausf. A (Model A), of which 100 vehicles were built, and it was this series that was the first to enter service with the German Army proper. The Ausf. A weighed 8.9 tons and was armed with a 2cm KwK30 L/55

PzKw II light tank c. 1939 armed with a 2cm gun and machine guns. Used in Poland and France.

cannon in a fully traversing turret with an MG34 machine gun of 7.92mm calibre mounted co-axially. There were slight variations in the design of the six main
models of the Panzer II but some features remained unaltered. For example, the
main armament remained the 2cm KwK30 L/55, the radio was always the FuG5
and the layout of the road wheels was also the same on all models. The Panzer II
had five road wheels with four return rollers; the idler wheel was mounted at the
front with the idler wheel at the rear.

Vehicle Name	Manufacturer	Production date	Armament	Weight	Max. Speed
PzKw II Ausf. A	MAN, Daimler-Benz, Henschel, Wegmann, Alkett, MIAG, FAMO	1937–40	2cm KwK30 L/55 cannon and an MG34 7.92mm-calibre machine gun.	8.9 tons	25mph

PzKw II Ausf. B & C

The Ausf. B version was produced from December 1937 and this type had improved
engine power, new reduction gears and new tracks, but there was also an increase
in the weight. The Ausf. C version of the Panzer II began to appear only six months
later and this had improved armour protection which increased the weight of the
tank to 9.3 tons. The additional armour was simply plates of some 20mm thickness bolted to the superstructure, and was as a result of lessons learned during
the Polish campaign, when it was discovered that anti-tank rifles could penetrate
the armour of the PzKw II. This increased the weight by more than 1,200lb from
the original design and about 70 per cent of the Ausf. C vehicles were ready in
this improved form in time for the campaign into France. The first three models of
the Panzer II – Ausf. A through to Ausf. C – were 15.7ft long, 7.2ft wide and 6.5ft
high, and were very compact vehicles ideal for reconnaissance and engaging light,
unarmoured vehicles. The engine was a Maybach HL62TR six-cylinder, water-
cooled inline petrol engine. This developed 130hp at 2,600rpm to produce speeds
of 25mph on roads, dropping to around 12mph cross-country with a combat range
of 120 miles. Armour protection was from 10mm in thickness to a maximum of
14.5mm, and the vehicles could ford water obstacles to a depth of 3ft, traverse
spans of 5ft 8in and climb vertical obstacles of well over 1ft.

Vehicle Name	Manufacturer	Production date	Armament	Weight	Max. Speed
PzKw II Ausf. B	MAN, Daimler-Benz, Henschel, Wegmann, Alkett, MIAG, FAMO	1937–40	2cm KwK30 L/55 cannon and an MG34 7.92mm-calibre machine gun.	8.9 tons	25mph
PzKw II Ausf. C	MAN, Daimler-Benz, Henschel, Wegmann, Alkett, MIAG, FAMO	1938	2cm KwK30 L/55 cannon and an MG34 7.92mm-calibre machine gun.	9.3 tons	25mph

PzKw II Ausf. D and E

The next series of PzKw II tanks were the Ausf. D and Ausf. E, which were built between May 1938 and August 1939. In total only forty-three vehicles were built, and these were deployed with a single Panzerabteilung (panzer battalion) that saw service during the invasion of Poland. The Ausf. D and Ausf. E had thicker armour and were slightly larger than the previous three models, and consequently weighed 9.8 tons. The maximum armour on these vehicles was 30mm, fitted to the hull and superstructure. A Maybach HL62TRM engine was fitted that had seven forward gears and one reverse gear, and this permitted the vehicles a road speed of 34mph. The D and E models were 15ft 3in long, 7ft 6in wide and 6ft 9in high. These versions had a slightly different superstructure, hull and suspension from the original versions, but the turret remained unchanged and was operated by a three-man crew. The entire series of these models was withdrawn in March 1940 and converted to flame-thrower tanks. These were then given the designation of SdKfz 122 Panzerkampfwagen II Flamm Ausf. A and B. They would be used in service on the Eastern Front from June 1941 when Germany attacked Russia.

Vehicle Name	Manufacturer	Production date	Armament	Weight	Max. Speed
PzKw II Ausf. D	MAN	1938	2cm KwK30 L/55 cannon and an MG34 7.92mm-calibre machine gun.	9.8 tons	34mph
PzKw II Ausf. E	MAN	1939	2cm KwK30 L/55 cannon and an MG34 7.92mm-calibre machine gun.	9.8 tons	34mph

PzKw II Ausf. F

The final version of the PzKw II proper was the Ausf. F, which virtually reverted back to the original design, with only a few differences. The armour was between 10mm and 30mm maximum thickness and the weight returned to 9.5 tons, with the overall length just over 15ft 9in. The width was slightly greater at almost 7ft 6in and the height slightly increased to just over 7ft. The HL62TR Maybach engine produced road speeds of 25mph and combat range remained at 120 miles. In total some 524 versions of the Model F were built between March 1941 and December 1942 and it saw much service, mainly in a reconnaissance role.

Vehicle Name	Manufacturer	Production date	Armament	Weight	Max. Speed
PzKw II Ausf. F	FAMO	1938	2cm KwK30 L/55 cannon and an MG34 7.92mm-calibre machine gun.	9.5 tons	25mph

The Panzer (PzKw) II

The Panzer II carried 1,425 rounds for the MG34 machine gun and 180 rounds for the 2cm cannon. The ammunition fired by the main armament could be either high explosive or armour piercing, but penetration against armoured vehicles was limited. However, against light vehicles or unprotected ground targets the effect could be highly effective out to ranges of almost 2,000yd. Attempts at producing further versions of the Panzer II in other models amounted to little or nothing and the programmes were dropped. For example, only twelve vehicles of the Ausf. G were built between April 1941 and February 1942, but as far as can be ascertained they were never deployed in a combat role. Similarly, only four vehicles in the Ausf. H and Ausf. M versions were produced and none of these are believed to have seen actual combat service. Other versions were adapted for specific roles, such as the Ausf. J which was produced in very limited numbers and served in the bridge-laying role. Other variants of the Panzer II were developed into SPGs armed with a range of artillery such as captured Russian weapons of 76.2mm calibre and at least fifty-five were converted into amphibious roles in preparation for the invasion of Britain.

The PzKw II had originally been developed for a reconnaissance role, a function it performed remarkably well during all major campaigns. It was never intended to serve in many of the combat roles into which it would be pressed. Some of these roles, such as the self-propelled version Leichte Feldhaubitze 18/2 auf Fahrgestell Panzerkampfwagen II, armed with a 10.5cm le FH18M gun, would continue in service until the end of the war. This version was designated as the SdKfz 124 or Wespe self-propelled light field howitzer. This version shows how, despite being a small vehicle, the Panzer II and all its variants gave a good accounts of themselves and far exceeded all expectations. This version of the vehicle was developed by Alkett early in 1942 using the chassis of the PzKw II tank as frame on which a field gun could be mounted. The vehicle was increased in length to more than 15ft 9in and the engine was placed in front of the vehicle (unlike the tank designs of the day, which had the engines at the rear). An open-topped superstructure was built up on the hull that provided the crew with sufficient operating room around the gun, which was the standard field howitzer, the 10.5cm le FH18M, which increased the vehicle's weight to 11 tons. The gun had a maximum range of 13,500yd and could traverse 17 degrees left and right of centre line and be elevated up to 42 degrees. The Wespe carried thirty-two rounds of ready-to-use ammunition and batteries of these SPGs were supported by munitions supply vehicles, also based on the PzKw II chassis, which carried an additional ninety rounds for re-supply. In total, some 676 Wespe and 139 munitions carriers were built between 1943 and 1944, and they were used by artillery regiments of armoured units serving in all theatres of operation. The Wespe remained in service until 1945 and was considered to be one of the best SPGs of the war.

British and French Armaments

The British and French believed their respective anti-tank gun capabilities could deal with the German vehicles and, besides, French tank designs such as the Renault AMC 35 light tank with its 47mm main gun were more than a match for such light vehicles. At the time the British Army had 136 infantry battalions, eighteen horsed cavalry regiments and only four battalions of tanks and two regiments of armoured cars. Tanks in service with the British Army included a number of older designs such as the Mk II medium tank armed with a 3-pounder gun in a turret, which had been in service since 1926. Another tank of similar vintage in service was the Vickers Mk VI light tank armed with a .303in-calibre machine gun, but later variants were armed with a .50in-calibre machine gun. This vehicle had started life during the 1920s when several types of light tanks and carriers were being considered for development for the British Army by Carden-Loyd. They were useful vehicles for the roles in which they were designed to operate, primarily reconnaissance duties, but the shape of the British Army was changing and so was the type of warfare in which they were to engage. In 1928 the Carden-Loyd company was acquired by engineering giant Vickers, and the design team wasted no time in scrapping all the designs that the company's engineers considered to be of no value. There was one Carden-Loyd design that they did consider valuable, however, and that was in an advanced state of preparation at the time of acquisition. This vehicle design was the Mk I light tank and it entered service with the British Army in 1929, just one year after the takeover. It was to be the first tank of a series in its type that entered service with the army. The vehicle incorporated a fully traversing turret that had been developed by Vickers, and featured a Horstman-type spring-coil suspension along with several other modifications to the original design.

The Mk I Light Tank

The Mk I light tank was to prove so successful that in time it would serve as the foundation for the several other light tanks that Vickers turned out at a rapid rate. All versions bore a number of similarities such as forward-mounted engines, twin or single bogies and either one or more return rollers. The series was to culminate in 1936 with the Mk VI light tank, which was to run to improved 'marks', ending with the Mk VIC. In fact, this last design was to be the heaviest, fastest and best-armed tank in the range and would see service with the British Army until 1941. Although the Mk VI was lightly armoured compared to other tank designs of the period, it was widely deployed and saw service in France during 1940, in Egypt during 1941 and was also used on the island of Malta. In Egypt the British Army used these tanks in the role of mobile artillery observation posts. The vehicles in the range that had been intended for the Indian Army were diverted and ended up

Crews of British Vickers light tanks.

Vickers medium tank Mk II *c.* 1926.

in Persia, modern-day Iran, when that country was occupied and taken over in a preventative move by the British, who made it a protectorate. The Mk VI light tank was also later used by the Australian, Canadian and South African armies.

The Mk I light tank of the 1929 period was not all that far removed from the Carden-Loyd Mk VIII light tank in appearance, in as much as it had leaf springs for suspension and a pronounced turret. Only a year later, the Mk IA made its appearance and featured proper coil springs and a turret slightly set off from the centre line. These two early versions were quickly followed in 1932 by the much-improved Mk II light tank, which was the first of its type to be fitted with a Rolls-Royce engine.

Vehicle Name	Manufacturer	Date Designed	Armament	Weight	Max. Speed
Mk I light tank	Vickers	1929	.303in Vickers machine gun	4.8 tons	31mph

The .303in-calibre machine gun mounted in the turret of the Vickers light tank.

The riveted construction of the hull and turret can be seen clearly and the 'slab-like' design of the armour plate.

Vickers light tank design *c.* 1930s with Carden-Loyd suspension.

The Mk II light tank

The fully traversing turret of the Mk II was rectangular in shape and mounted a single Vickers .303in machine gun. The turret featured sloping sides and a mantlet fitted over the machine gun with an armoured sleeve around the exposed portion of the barrel. The vehicle was operated by a crew of two men who served in the roles of driver and commander/gunner. The driver's position had a square hatch equipped with slits and glass vision blocks for use when driving closed down, which is to say with all hatches closed. The commander was provided with a square access hatch in the turret roof. A unique feature on the Mk II light tank, and not to be incorporated into any other design in the light tank range, was the two sets of twin bogies on either side, with a raised rear idler wheel. The Mk II was 11.7ft long, 6.2ft wide and 7.3ft high. It weighed 4,318kg and had armour protection from 4mm minimum to 12mm maximum. This particular version of the series was fitted with a six-cylinder Rolls-Royce water-cooled inline petrol engine, which developed 60hp to give it a maximum road speed of 30mph. The vehicle had the useful operational range of 240km, which allowed it to function in a reconnaissance role. The Mk IIA light tank from Vickers entered service with the British Army in 1933 and was essentially a slightly improved Mk II, retaining as it did the same level of armour protection, engine, range and speed. It still only mounted a single Vickers .303in machine gun in the turret, even though countries such as France and Japan were arming their tanks with larger calibre weapons.

Vehicle Name	Manufacturer	Date Designed	Armament	Weight	Max. Speed
Mk II light tank	Vickers	1932	.303in Vickers machine gun	4.3 tons	30mph
Mk IIA light tank	Vickers	1933	.303in Vickers machine gun	4.3 tons	30mph

The Mk III and Mk IV Light Tank

The Mk II and Mk IIA were followed in 1934 by the Mk III and Mk IV. These had armour protection to a maximum thickness of 12mm and still featured a single .303in Vickers machine gun in the turret. The turret of the Mk III was narrower and had a lower profile than on previous versions of the light tank series, and was fitted with a front grille to protect the radiator. Very few Mk III light tanks were built, presumably due to the fact that Vickers was beginning to produce the Mk IV light tank. The Mk IV was a major leap forward in light tank design and featured many improvements over the previous marks. For example, the hull was built over the tracks to provide increased internal space for the crew, and the turret layout was changed to a design that was circular when looked at in 'plan' view. The Mk III and Mk IV light tanks still had two-man crews, but some Mk III vehicles were fitted with either a Vickers .30in-calibre medium machine gun or a Vickers .50in heavy machine gun, which would be mounted in the turret in place of the Vickers .303in machine gun.

Vehicle Name	Manufacturer	Date Designed	Armament	Weight	Max. Speed
Mk III light tank	Vickers	1934	.303in or .50in Vickers machine gun	4.3 tons	30mph
Mk IV light tank	Vickers	1934	.303in Vickers machine gun	4.3 tons	30mph

The Mk V Light Tank

The Mk V light tank from Vickers appeared in 1935 and because of the increased space inside the vehicle it could carry a three-man crew, which distributed the work tasks more evenly. The length of the hull was increased and the track extended by adding a rear idler wheel. It was mounted in a unique way by attaching it to the single-wheeled bogie and springing it in the same way, which allowed it to double in purpose as a road wheel. The turret on the Mk V was larger than previous models to the point where it could be armed with both a Vickers .303in machine gun and a Vickers .50in-calibre heavy machine gun. To increase the ballistic protection of the vehicle the sides of the turret were sloped sharply. The commander of the vehicle was provided with a cylinder-shaped cupola. A smoke grenade discharger was fitted to the right-hand side of the turret and was fired by means of a Bowden cable. The driver's hatch was made smaller on the Mk V but the front decking was extended. Nearly two dozen Mk V light tanks were built, some of which were used as experimental vehicles to proof trial features that were to become standard on the final mark of light tank.

Vehicle Name	Manufacturer	Date Designed	Armament	Weight	Max. Speed
Mk V light tank	Vickers	1935	.303in and .50in Vickers machine guns	4.8 tons	35mph

The Mk VI Light Tank

From 1936 onwards the Mk VI, which was to prove to be the final light tank design from Vickers, began to appear. On its introduction into service with the British Army, before the outbreak of hostilities, it superseded all previous light tank designs. The Mk VI was the largest and heaviest model in the Vickers light tank series, with armour protection up to 14mm maximum thickness and a weight of 5.2 tons, which was nearly a quarter as much again as the Mk II light tank. The Mk VI was 12ft 11in in length, 6ft 9in wide and 7ft 4in high. Like the Mk V, this version was armed with both Vickers .303in- and .50in-calibre machine guns. As with the Mk IV, this version was fitted with a Meadows six-cylinder water-cooled inline petrol engine that developed 88hp. It could cross 5ft gaps, scale vertical obstacles more than 24in high and negotiate gradients of 60 per cent. The turret was slightly larger in order to accommodate a radio set for improved communications and the commander's cupola was changed to be hexagonal shape in 'plan' view.

The Mk VIA light tank had the position of its return rollers altered and the Mk VIB had cupolas fitted that were cylindrical in 'plan' view. These were relatively minor modifications to the vehicle's design. Some versions of the Mk VI light tank were equipped to carry .303in Bren guns mounted on special turret brackets for low-level air defence. The Mk VIC carried a BESA 15mm heavy machine gun and a co-axial 7.92mm BESA machine gun, which was a more powerful armament than had ever been imagined on previous marks. The commander's cupola in this version was omitted, which did limit his view, but in its place two domed hatches for improved headroom were fitted. The driver's position was better protected against the effects of 'splashing' caused by small arms fire by deflector plates that were fitted to his vision blocks.

Vehicle Name	Manufacturer	Date Designed	Armament	Weight	Max. Speed
Mk VI light tank	Vickers	1936	.303in and .50in Vickers machine guns	4.8 tons	mph
Mk VIA light tank	Vickers	1936	.50in and .303in machine gun	4.8 tons	35mph
Mk VIB light tank	Vickers	1936	.50in and .303in machine gun	5.2 tons	35mph
Mk VIC light tank	Vickers	1936	BESA 15mm heavy machine gun and a co-axial 7.92mm BESA machine gun	5.2 tons	29mph

Post-Dunkirk Re-evaluation

Following the retreat from Dunkirk in 1940 it became all too apparent that the design of the Vickers series of tank was inadequate, both in weaponry hitting power and armoured defence, and those vehicles left in Britain were consigned to training roles. The turret of the light tank design was not large enough to accept a heavier gun, and the armour protection was not sufficient to sustain heavy battle damage. As the vehicles used in training roles wore out due to mechanical failure they were scrapped and replaced by more modern designs that were purpose built to function in the reconnaissance role of the more fluid battlefields of the Second World War. In 1939 the Polish Army had the light TK-3 Tankette with a single machine gun, which had been in service from 1932. Another armoured vehicle was the 7TP light tank; both were based on a British Carden-Loyd design. The 7TP was armed with a 37mm gun, and on paper it appeared that it could match some of the new German designs. In the overall assessment on the eve of the outbreak of war there did not appear to be any European country dominating the armour race and if there was, then it was surely France with designs such as the Char B1 heavy tank, Renault R35 light tank and Char Somua S-35 medium tank. Even in 1936, when the Germans unveiled the Neubaufahrzeug (NbFz) Panzerkampfwagen V (new construction vehicle or experimental medium tank) armed with a turret-mounted 7.5cm-calibre KwK L/24 gun with a 3.7cm co-axial gun and four machine guns in two further turrets, the alarms still failed to sound with the British and French. As it transpired this vehicle never entered service but it was a marvellous propaganda scoop for the Germans. However, three of these tanks and about 100 other types were deployed during the invasion on Norway in April 1940. Three Panzerkampfwagen V tanks, almost certainly the three experimental models that were built, were photographed in Oslo and thus proved their worth for propaganda purposes.

German SdKfz 10

Vehicle Name	Manufacturer	Production Date	Armament	Weight	Max. Speed
SdKfz 10	Demag, Alderwerke, Bussing-NAG	1937	N/A	4.8 tons	40mph
SdKfz 10/1	Demag, Alderwerke, Bussing-NAG	1937	N/A	4.8 tons	40mph
SdKfz 10/2	Demag, Alderwerke, Bussing-NAG	1937	N/A	4.8 tons	40mph
SdKfz 10/3	Demag, Alderwerke, Bussing-NAG	1937	N/A	4.8 tons	40mph
SdKfz 10/4	Demag, Alderwerke, Bussing-NAG	1938	2cm-calibre FlaK 30 anti-aircraft gun	5.5 tons	40mph

The SdKfz 10 served in all theatres of fighting and was a versatile vehicle being configured to various roles.

The driver's position of the SdKfz 10 Demag half-track showing standard steering wheel layout. The SdKfz 10 was used in a number of roles including artillery tractor, light anti-aircraft vehicle and troop carrier.

SdKfz 10/5	Demag, Alderwerke, Bussing-NAG	1938	2cm-calibre FlaK 38 anti-aircraft gun	5.5 tons	40mph

Throughout the 1930s the German Army continued to become ever more mechanised, leading to an increased demand for vehicles in all categories, including half-track vehicles that could be used for troop transport and as prime-mover tractors for towing artillery. One of the smallest and yet most versatile half-track vehicles to be developed was the SdKfz 10, which entered service in 1938 and

remained in use throughout the war. It fitted all the roles asked of it, including towing artillery, carrying cargo and even serving as a mobile platform for
mounting anti-aircraft guns. It was also used as a specialist chemical warfare
decontamination system. Some sources state that 14,000 vehicles were built, but
others give that number as more like 25,000. Whichever figure one chooses, what
is certain about this vehicle is that it was built in five variants and served in all
theatres of the war, including Europe, Russia and North Africa. It was standard
practice for subcontractors to supply parts for vehicles and even actually to build
the vehicles if it looked as though deliveries might not be met by the main contractor. Indeed, the SdKfz 10 was one such vehicle, and was built by several different
manufacturers, including Adlerwerke (which turned out over 3,400 vehicles) and
Bussing-NAG (which built 750 SdKfz 10 half-tracks). Another manufacturer of the
series was Demag, with factories in Berlin and Düsseldorf, which had designed
the vehicle and would build some 1,075 SdKfz 10s.

The range prototype was built in 1934 and, following further research and development along with field trials, the SdKfz 10 went into production in 1937, with
Demag as one of the main manufacturers. The two variants of the vehicle, designated SdKfz 10/1 and 10/2, were configured for chemical decontamination roles. The
SdKfz 10/3 was equipped with nozzles to spray poison chemicals, but in the event the
few vehicles built for this purpose never operated in their intended role. The SdKfz
10/4 and SdKfz 10/5 were equipped with pedestal mounts to carry the 2cm-calibre
FlaK 30 and FlaK 38 anti-aircraft guns respectively. These were used by the army
and air force (Luftwaffe), and the army also made modifications in the field to adapt
some vehicles for towing anti-tank guns. Already realising that the vehicles could
be used in this way, some manufacturers strengthened them in order to cope with
towing the larger, heavier guns, including the le FH18 howitzer of 105mm calibre.

The basic version of the SdKfz 10 Ausf. B when used to tow artillery such as the
PaK38 50mm-calibre anti-tank gun, was known as a Zugkraftwagen 1T (prime-
mover semi-tracked vehicle). These vehicles could also be used to tow ammunition
trailers with which to re-supply the guns. In the basic role for gun crews, the vehicle was fitted out with seats to accommodate the driver, co-driver and six men in
the rear. Overall the vehicle measured 15ft 7in long, approximately 6ft 4in wide
and was 6ft 6in high when the collapsible canvas roof was erected. The vehicle
weighed 4.8 tons and was capable of reaching speeds of up to 50mph on roads.
Various design changes were made to the fuel tank capacity and by 1940 at least
a new standard tank containing around 24 gallons of fuel was being fitted, which
allowed the SdKfz 10 an operational road range of over 170 miles, reduced to
around 100 miles when operating cross-country. The type of engine fitted and its
rating depended on the manufacturer and the period of the production the vehicle
was built during.

Typically a Maybach six-cylinder petrol engine HL42TRKM of 100hp was fitted
but other models were fitted with a Maybach HL38TRKM engine. The tracked

layout comprised of five sets of double road wheels with torsion bar suspension and the drive sprocket at the front. The front wheels were fitted with leaf springs. If the type of manoeuvre being executed was gradual turns, the front wheels were used for steering, but for sharper turns braking was applied to the tracks. The service life of the SdKfz 10 lasted the entire war and it was among the last vehicles remaining in use in May 1945, during which time it had shown itself to be a useful and dependable vehicle in whichever role it was used.

The Spanish Civil War to the Invasion of Czechoslovakia

When Italy and Germany sent troops, tanks and artillery to support the nationalist forces of General Franco during the Spanish Civil War in 1936, France and Britain did not appear unduly concerned. Although such military aid was criticised it was not condemned wholeheartedly, and Russia did send 700 tanks, mainly Christie and Vickers types, to support the republican cause opposing Franco. Despite warnings from people such as Winston Churchill, who could see through this and other moves, the British government did not act. Rearmament was a contentious point in Britain and the government of the day under Stanley Baldwin read the mood of the people and realised that it was not the right decision. Prime Minister Baldwin stated: 'Supposing I had gone to the country and said that Germany was rearming and that we must rearm, does anybody think that this pacific democracy would have rallied to that cry at that moment? I cannot think of anything that would have made the loss of the election from my point of view more certain.' At the time, Britain had a budget of £842,000 for the design, development and construction of tanks. Five years earlier the budget had been £357,000, but had actually decreased in 1932. It was only in 1937 that this budget was given a substantial increase, when it was granted £3,625,000 to develop tanks, by which time several European countries had entered into a rearmament programme. It may have been a case of too little too late, but rather too late than nothing at all. If war had not broken out in 1939, Britain's rearmament programme would not have been completed until 1946. Churchill was not a prophet, but he was wise enough to see what was happening in Germany and predicted that: 'in the end it is certain that a regime whose victories are in the main due to machines will collapse. Machines will one day beat machines.' He would come to be proven correct when the might of the Allied armoured divisions smashed into the heart of Germany, whose once-powerful tanks lay either destroyed or abandoned through lack of fuel.

That image lay in the future, but in the meantime Germany was growing ever stronger militarily and German troops were gaining experience in the fighting in Spain: honing their weapons skills and developing tactics with tanks and vehicles under combat conditions. Russia sent tanks to support the republican forces, but other European countries, including Britain, did not send heavy military hardware. On 17 January 1936 Joseph Goebbels, the German Minister of Propaganda, addressed an audience and declared: 'We can do without butter, but, despite all our love of peace, not without arms. One cannot shoot with butter, but with guns.' Realising the growing threat posed by its neighbour, France began a rearmament programme in June 1936, knowing it had made the right decision when at the same time Herman Goering, the commander-in-chief of the Luftwaffe, reaffirmed Goebbels' earlier statement by declaring: 'Guns will make us powerful; butter will only make us fat.' Hitler was very much centre stage and continuing his political manoeuvrings. He made much of his experiences as a soldier in the First World War and constantly reminded all around him of the fact. During a tour to observe military manoeuvres at Kummersdorf he saw the first German tanks engaged in field exercises. Turning to Heinz Guderian, who was escorting him, he said: 'That's what I need. That's what I want to have.' Hitler may not have been a tactical genius, but it did not require the skilled training of a military academy to realise that this would be a decisive weapon on the battlefield.

Even before his involvement with Spain, Hitler had already flexed his international political muscles when in 1935 he ordered his troops to enter the region of the Saar on the border between France and Germany. This was a French-administered zone, but when France and Britain did not react Hitler went one stage further, and the following year German troops entered the Rhineland, which had been a 'demilitarised zone'. Still neither France nor Britain did anything to prevent the move. On 7 March 1938 German troops crossed into Austria in *Anschluss* to annex the country and create the 'Greater German Reich'. This move gave Hitler more manufacturing capabilities for weaponry and vehicles. Further emboldened, Hitler occupied the Sudetenland border region between Czechoslovakia and Germany in September 1938. Britain, France and Italy agreed to the move and war was averted through negotiations, for the time being at least.

Hitler made his next move on 15 March 1939 when he ordered his troops to march in and take over the rest of Czechoslovakia, making it a Reich protectorate as part of Germany's expansion plan and giving it the title Bohemia-Moravia. This gave Germany another 11,500 square miles of territory, but more importantly added factories such as the Škoda Works, which was already manufacturing tanks, vehicles and artillery. Czechoslovakia was now a nominal ally of Germany but would suffer as badly as any other occupied country during the war. Germany benefitted the most from the situation with the acquisition of the armaments manufacturers that were turning out weapons, the most important of which were the Škoda and CKD (Praga) factories, which were producing armoured vehicles and trucks, but especially tanks. Indeed, it would be Czechoslovakian tank designs, later to be designated the Panzerkampfwagen 35 (t) and Panzerkampfwagen 38 (t) that would form the backbone of the German armoured divisions from 1939 until 1941. These two designs were classed as light tanks and such was their versatility that they would later be adapted to serve in a variety of roles, including as ammunition carriers and SPGs. However, it was the Panzerkampfwagen 38 (t) that proved to

The SdKfz 138 Hetzer tank destroyer developed on the 38 (t) chassis and used during the Battle of the Bulge in December 1944.

The Czechoslovakian-designed 38 (t) which formed the backbone of the early German armoured units and on which many SPG and other designs were based.

be the most versatile of the two designs and in this tank design alone more than 1,600 were produced in eight different models and the basic chassis was used for thousands more vehicles operating as reconnaissance vehicles, SPGs, ammunition carriers and tank destroyers such as the highly successful SdKfz 138 Hetzer tank destroyer for example. In fact, it has been estimated that at one point early in the war the Panzerkampfwagen 35 (t) and 38 (t) formed almost a quarter of the German Army's armoured forces.

The Panzerkampfwagen 38 (t)

Vehicle Name	Manufacturer	Production Date	Armament	Weight	Max. Speed
PzKw 38 (t): Ausf. A	Bohmisch-Mahrische Maschinenfabrik (BMM)	1939	3.7cm KwK38 (t) L/47.8 gun and 2x MG37 (t) 7.92mm-calibre MG37 (t)	9.4 tons	26mph
PzKw 38 (t): Ausf. B	Bohmisch-Mahrische Maschinenfabrik (BMM)	1940	3.7cm KwK38 (t) L/47.8 gun and 2x MG37 (t) 7.92mm-calibre MG37 (t)	9.5 tons	26mph
PzKw 38 (t): Ausf. C	Bohmisch-Mahrische Maschinenfabrik (BMM)	1940	3.7cm KwK38 (t) L/47.8 gun and 2x MG37 (t) 7.92mm-calibre MG37 (t)	9.5 tons	26mph
PzKw 38 (t): Ausf. D	Bohmisch-Mahrische Maschinenfabrik (BMM)	1940	3.7cm KwK38 (t) L/47.8 gun and 2x MG37 (t) 7.92mm-calibre MG37 (t)	9.5 tons	26mph
PzKw 38 (t): Ausf. E	Bohmisch-Mahrische Maschinenfabrik (BMM)	1940–41	3.7cm KwK38 (t) L/47.8 gun and 2x MG37 (t) 7.92mm-calibre MG37 (t)	9.9 tons	26mph
PzKw 38 (t): Ausf. F	Bohmisch-Mahrische Maschinenfabrik (BMM)	1941–41	3.7cm KwK38 (t) L/47.8 gun and 2x MG37 (t) 7.92mm-calibre MG37 (t)	9.9 tons	26mph
PzKw 38 (t): Ausf. G	Bohmisch-Mahrische Maschinenfabrik (BMM)	1941–42	3.7cm KwK38 (t) L/47.8 gun and 2x MG37 (t) 7.92mm-calibre MG37 (t)	9.9 tons	26mph
PzKw 38 (t): Ausf. S	Bohmisch-Mahrische Maschinenfabrik (BMM)	1941	3.7cm KwK38 (t) L/47.8 gun and 2x MG37 (t) 7.92mm-calibre MG37 (t)	9.5 tons	26mph

The origin of the tank that would become known as the Panzerkampfwagen 38 (t) was in 1937 when the company CKD (Praga) built a prototype design, known as the Vz38 in a series known as TNHPS, which came out as the overall winner against rival designs during field trials held in 1938. An order for 150 of the tanks was placed but the political situation at the time led to a cut back in filling orders and it was not until March 1939 that the first vehicle was ready. By then Germany was in control of Czechoslovakia and the first tanks went to the Wehrmacht as the Ausf. A version, and the original production company of CKD (Praga) was now known as Bohmisch-Mahrische Maschinenfabrik (BMM). In total only the original order of 150 Ausf. A vehicles were built, with production ceasing in November 1939. This meant that the first models were able to participate in the attack on Poland and later some were deployed to support the attacks against Norway and some were used to equip the 7th Armoured Division under General Rommel during blitzkrieg against France in May 1940.

The next three versions of the Panzerkampfwagen 38 (t) were designated as Ausf. B, C and D and a total of 325 of these were built between January and November 1940, making them the first models available to participate in the blitzkrieg against France and Belgium in 1940. They would later serve in Russia from 1941 onwards, as indeed would all other versions of the tank. Variants of the Panzerkampfwagen 38 (t) were also deployed to participate in fighting in all theatres of the war, including Greece, but none served in the North Africa theatre of operations. The most numerous versions of the tank to be built were the Ausf. E and F, with production running from November 1940 until October 1941, during which time some 525 were built. There were two more models, the Ausf. G and the Ausf. S, with a production run of 321 and 90 respectively and the output of all versions finally ended in June 1942 after which time variants such as SPGs were produced.

In all of the cases there was little to distinguish one version from another and all eight models of the Panzerkampfwagen 38 (t) actually shared a commonality in a great number of automotive parts, including the engine, which in all models was a water-cooled 125hp six-cylinder petrol Praga EPA which developed 2,200rpm to give a maximum road speed of 26mph, but this dropped to only 9mph when operating in cross-country. Sufficient fuel was carried to permit a combat range of 250km, which was better than the Panzer II. The gearbox was fitted with five forward gears and one for reverse to permit manoeuvrability in all terrains. In each of the eight models the tank was equipped with four large road wheels with the drive sprocket at the front, idler wheel at the rear and two return rollers. All versions were served by a crew of four comprising driver, gunner, loader and tank commander who kept in touch by means of radio. The armour protection on the tank varied according to the model and this affected the weight. For example, the original Ausf. A weighed 9.4 tons but the later Ausf. E, F and G models all weighed 9.85 tons. The overall dimensions varied slightly, with the Ausf. F measuring 15.1ft long, 6.8ft wide and 7.8ft high. Armour protection varied in thickness and ordinarily the Ausf. F would have been only 8mm on the top of the hull and 30mm on the side of the turret, which would have been the most vulnerable area. However, experience in early campaigns such as Poland showed the necessity to provide additional armour protection and in this case it was achieved by adding another armour plate of 25mm thickness over the existing hull armour to give 50mm protection. The overall structure was riveted, which gave it a 'pimpled' effect, unlike the welded designs of the later tanks.

The Ausf. F version of the Panzerkampfwagen 38 (t) was armed with a 3.7cm KwK38 (t) L/47.8 gun as a main armament mounted in a turret with full 360-degree traverse. The lower case suffix letter 't' within brackets identifies

Czechoslovakia as the country of origin of the weapon and tank. The KwK stands for *Kampfwagenkanone* and the 3.7cm calibre in this case had a barrel length of 47.8 calibres, to give around 5ft 6in in length. The main gun, for which ninety rounds were carried in the tank, did not have a muzzle brake and fired armour-piercing shells weighing 1.8lb at a muzzle velocity of 2,469ft per second, which could penetrate 41mm of homogeneous armour set at 30 degrees at a range of 100yd but falling to 35mm penetration at 500yd. The main gun could elevate to +25 degrees and depress to -10 degrees with manual operation for the turret traverse. Two MG37 (t) machine guns of 7.92mm calibre, both of Czechoslovakian origin, were also carried, with one mounted co-axially in the turret and the other fitted in the hull and for which 2,400 rounds of ammunition was carried. They had limited traverse and elevation capability, but were useful for self-defence and for providing fire support for advancing infantry. The armament and optical sighting units carried on the tank remained the same for the entire fleet throughout the war.

The Panzerkampfwagen 38 (t) did not only serve with the German armoured divisions, but was also used to equip the armoured units of its allies, including the forces of Hungary and Romania, where they were deployed on the Eastern Front in Russia. The tank was compact enough to be transported by railway at the rate of two tanks per flat car. One of the earliest proper tanks to equip the German armoured divisions, the Panzerkampfwagen 38 (t) was still in service in late 1944, by which time those still in service were declared obsolete. Its war record was second to none and despite being out-gunned by Allied tanks, its longevity in battle, during which it was deployed in some heavy fighting, is a testament to its usefulness.

Italian Advances and the German Invasion of Poland

The German Army used resources such as these from Czechoslovakia and other occupied countries to increase their capacity to wage war. Meanwhile, Italy had not been idle, and although committed to providing military aid to Franco in Spain, since October 1935 Italian troops had been engaged in a ruthless war, including the use of poison gas, to suppress Ethiopia in East Africa. Finally, on 9 May 1936, the Italians declared the war to be at an end, and annexed Ethiopia. Mussolini made his next major military move on 7 April 1939, when he sent 100,000 troops into Albania, which was also annexed to Italy. The invasion was a one-sided affair with Italian troops supported by air cover and a fleet of vehicles. Several weeks later, on 22 May 1939, Italy and Germany entered into an agreement called the Pact of Steel, which made them allies in the event of war. At the time, Italy's armaments output in weapons and vehicles, including tanks, was very limited and the country was not prepared for full-scale war – a fact that Mussolini made Hitler aware of during a meeting in August. It was one thing to subdue an ill-prepared country like Ethiopia or Albania, but a war against a well-equipped European army such as that of France was something entirely different. Hitler then made his next demand: the reunification of East Prussia with Germany proper. The problem with this was that the two areas were separated by the Danzig Corridor, which was Polish territory. On 1 September German troops crossed the border and although Britain and France had pledged their support to Poland in the event of war there was little they could do but issue an ultimatum calling for the withdrawal of troops. Germany ignored the demands and two days later, on 3 September, France and Britain declared war on Germany.

At the time the British Army was short of vehicles and to make up for the shortfall it pressed into service some 26,000 civilian vehicles, including 5,000 private cars, 7,000 motorcycles and 14,000 trucks. This took the total number of soft-skinned vehicles up to 55,000 and by the end of the war there were 1.25 million soft-skinned vehicles in service. One company producing cars for the civilian market was the Rootes Group, which had factories in Birmingham and Coventry

Hillman Minx 10 as used by the Royal Air Force for liaison duties between air bases.

in the Midlands where they built a series of vehicles under the Hillman marque known as the Hillman Minx. Over the years several versions were built and it was a popular car for civilian use in the pre-war period. The RAF was one of the military users of the 4x2 Hillman 10, known as such from the horsepower of the four-cylinder (22kW) 1,185cc side-valve petrol engine, which allowed road speeds of up to around 65mph. The vehicle had a pressed-steel body with a wheelbase length of 12ft 7in, and it was perfectly suited to liaison duties around air bases or for travelling between air bases. Hillman had been producing vehicles since before the war and the Minx design was built from 1932 and 1938; in 1939 the company moved into building more vehicles for the military and the 'Tilly' design was ideal for home-service use. The actual numbers used in this role has not been accurately tabulated but the fact they were used for the duration of the war says something for the design's usefulness. Tilly cars were built by other companies such as Austin and Morris, and the Humber 'Snipe' was sometimes used for converting into 'Beaverette' armoured cars for use by Home Guard units.

The Polish Army fought as gallantly as any army could but under the circumstances it was no match for the German Army, which outnumbered them and was supported with modern tanks and aircraft that smashed anything the Poles sent against them. The Polish Army fought stubbornly and bravely but by 27 September the Polish capital of Warsaw had surrendered. The Polish Army had comprised thirty infantry divisions, twelve cavalry divisions and ten reserve divisions. Poland had almost 900 tanks, mostly small, light 'tankette' designs except for ninety-five larger 7TPjw tanks equipped with 47mm guns, but these and the armoured cars could do little against sixty German divisions with thousands of tanks and vehicles. These tanks would later be pressed into service with the German Army. The Germans suffered 40,000 casualties killed, wounded and missing, and lost 217 tanks destroyed or damaged. Following the conclusion of the Polish campaign the Allies faced the Germans in the west and entered into a period of inactivity that lasted several months, during which time they simply sat in trenches and bunkers staring at one another along the Franco-German border. The American senator William Borah referred to it as the 'Phoney War', a term adopted by the British. Neville Chamberlain, the British prime minister, called it the 'twilight war' and claimed that Hitler had 'missed the bus'. The French called the period *drôle de guerre* (funny or peculiar war) and the Germans knew it as *Sitzkreig* (sitting war). Whatever one chose to call it, everybody knew that it all rested on the Germans, and if they chose to play a waiting game the Allies would have no option but to go along with it. Some small localised manoeuvring on the part of the French did take place, but it was no more than a show and the troops returned to their positions. Because they did nothing positive, the consequences of their indecision would lead to catastrophe for the Dutch, French and Belgian armies. The British Army would be luckier, but only just.

When Germany began its rearmament programme in the mid-1930s almost everything an army otherwise took for granted had either to be replaced completely or introduced from scratch. This was the case with armoured cars, required by the German Army, which needed their vehicles to operate in the variety of roles that would be demanded of them in the new tactics that were being devised. Those earlier vehicles, such as the Ehrhardt E-V/4 armoured cars, had served in the 1920s and were now obsolete, while others like the Kfz13 were severely limited in capability, though their speed and operational range was acceptable. In 1934 the German Army High Command issued a contract to the Leipzig-based company of Bussing-NAG to develop a new armoured car with four axles and full 8x8 all-wheel drive. From time of request through to production of the first prototypes and the first vehicles entering service took only three years, and in 1937 the Schwerer Panzerspähwagen (Heavy Armoured Reconnaissance Vehicle) or SdKfz 232 was ready in time to take part in the first phases of Germany's expansionist operations, including the Polish campaign where it served in the reconnaissance role, which it reprised in France the following year.

The Schwerer Panzerspähwagen (SdKfz)

Vehicle Name	Manufacturer	Production Date	Armament	Weight	Max. Speed
SdKfz 231	Bussing-NAG, Daimler-Benz, Magirus	1932–37	2cm KwK30 cannon or 2cm KwK38 cannon and 7.92mm MG34 machine gun	5.4 tons	44mph
SdKfz 232	Deutsche Werke, Schichau	1936–42	2cm KwK30 cannon or 2cm KwK38 cannon and 7.92mm MG34 machine gun	8.3 tons	53mph
SdKfz 233	Schichau	1942–43	7.5cm StuK 37 L/24 and 7.92mm MG42 machine gun	8.7 tons	50mph
SdKfz 234	Bussing-NAG	1944–45	2cm KwK38 L/55 and 7.92mm MG42 machine gun	11.5 tons	50mph

The vehicle that was produced had a very advanced design with an impressive cross-country capability, which surpassed anything else then in service any-where. A rear-mounted Bussing-NAG L8V-GS eight-cylinder water-cooled petrol engine developing 150hp at 3,000rpm produced speeds of up to 53mph on roads and carried sufficient fuel to give an operational range of around 170 miles. The ability to cope with naturally occurring obstacles on the battlefields, such as fallen trees and ditches, is always desirable in armoured car designs and while some had limited capability, the SdKfz 232 was better than most, and was able to span gaps of over 4ft, negotiate gradients of up to 30 degrees and vertical obstacles of over 1.5ft were no barrier to this vehicle, which weighed 8.3 tons. The SdKfz 232 meas-ured 19ft 2in long, 7ft 3in wide and 9ft 6in high to the top of the turret, which had a full 360-degree traverse capability and mounted a main armament of either a KwK30 or KwK38 2cm cannon for which 180 rounds of ammunition were carried. The gun could be elevated to +26 degrees and depressed to -10 degrees, allowing it to engage a wide range of targets, from vehicles to low-flying aircraft. It was not the only eight-wheeled vehicle in the German Army's arsenal but it was the first, and it served through the entire period of the war, with some still being used in 1945. This was an incredible achievement for a vehicle that ceased production in 1943 with a total of around 1,235, a figure that includes other specialised variants that were being built, and it is a testimony to its utilitarian design. It was replaced by the SdKfz 234 'Puma', but those examples of the SdKfz 232 that were still in service continued to be used in their original role.

It was a complex vehicle with a highly advanced chassis design and, apart from some improvements to the hull and minor changes to the automotive design, it remained the same vehicle throughout the war. Armour protection was between 8mm and 15mm, set at varying angles to help deflect projectiles. However, this level of protection was not considered sufficient and an upgrading programme was begun to retrofit additional armour to the vehicle. This took the form of an angled plate fitted to the front across the bow and forming spaced armour across the glacis plate. This was called a Pakschutz and looked rather like the blade of a snowplough. As the term implies, it was meant to provide protection against anti-tank guns. This was only a temporary measure and the first Pakschutz may have been fitted to the SdKfz 231 in early 1940. Typically of the troops, they soon found that they could store extra kit and supplies in the space between the Pakschutz and the glacis plate of the vehicle. The device was fitted until after May 1942, after which armour protection was increased to a maximum level of 30mm thickness instead, resulting in almost 1 ton being added to the weight of the vehicle. The SdKfz 231 was served by a crew of four who could also rely on a secondary armament comprising of a co-axial mounted MG34 machine gun, for which 2,100 rounds were carried, for self-defence and fire support in an emergency. The vehicle and its later derivatives, such as the SdKfz 232 which was built from May 1942, were formed into heavy platoons serving with the Panzerspähwagen squadrons on the heavy Aufklärungs (reconnaissance) detachments. The vehicles served in all theatres of the war, from Western Europe to Russia and North Africa, which means that modellers have a wide choice of settings, colour schemes and even variants in which to depict the SdKfz 231, from armoured car to radio vehicle with its frame aerial and even the special add-on armour Pakschutz device.

Allied Equipment and Preparations for War

In 1939 the French Army was one of the largest in Europe and had a tank force larger than any other European country, as well as a fleet of trucks to support it. When war was declared Winston Churchill was appointed to the post of First Sea Lord and stated, 'Thank God for the French Army'. The French had a standing army of 900,000 men with a further 5 million trained reservists with a tank force of 3,500 vehicles comprising 2,700 light tanks, 500 medium and 300 heavy tanks along with a strong artillery force for support. By comparison

Searchlights were mounted on trucks to give mobility to these large and heavy pieces of equipment.

Britain had an armoured force of 600 light and medium tanks. The German Army by contrast had some 3,400 light and medium tanks that had been built up from nothing, and these were available for an attack in the west. France relied on the Maginot Line to protect its eastern border against attack by Germany. The Maginot Line was an impressive series of defences stretching 87 miles, and was heavily armed and armoured. However, it stopped 250 miles short of the Channel coast; serving the guns of this series of subterranean fortresses was a force of 250,000 men.

When war was declared the French Army mobilised and Britain prepared to send the British Expeditionary Force (BEF) to take up positions close to the Franco-German border. At the time there proved to be a shortfall of light vehicles in service and the British Army was obliged to press into service some 26,000 civilian vehicles, including 5,000 private cars, 7,000 motorcycles and 14,000 trucks. This emergency move took the total number of soft-skinned vehicles up to 55,000 and by the end of the war the army had 1.25 million utility vehicles in service. The BEF numbered just four divisions in 1939 but by May 1940 it had increased its strength to ten divisions. Initially some 24,000 vehicles, including tanks, trucks and supplies, were moved into operational areas and defensive positions were prepared. The tank forces included 229 vehicles of which 171 were light tanks armed with only machine guns. One type of truck used at the time was the Retriever, dating from the early 1930s and built by Leyland, which was fitted with a 6-litre, four-cylinder overhead cam petrol engine of a design built by Leyland.

The Leyland Retriever was a 1930s design but it was used throughout the war as a field workshop and other roles. The driver's controls were very basic for such a large vehicle. The Retriever was spacious and Montgomery used one as his tactical vehicle on campaign.

The engine was rated at 73bhp at 1,150rpm and, although the trucks were in widespread use, the fleet had actually been declared obsolete. The coming of war was a reprieve and the trucks were kept in use for the duration and served to transport supplies. The Retriever was also fitted out to serve in the role of field workshop and breakdown recovery vehicles; some were equipped to serve as searchlight pontoon trucks. A Leyland Retriever was fitted into use as a field caravan for Field Marshal Montgomery when on campaign and was spacious enough for his maps and for meetings.

Range of vehicles in use by the British Army in the 1930s showing from left to right: 5-ton Leyland heavy tender; Morris six-wheel ambulance and Leyland wireless tender with its support truck.

View showing the height of this Leyland truck from the 1930s which is over 6ft.

All the lessons concerning the tactics the German Army would come to use in combat were there for the Allies to read, but works such as *Infanterie Greift* (*Infantry Attack*) and *Achtung-Panzer!* (*Attention-Armour!*), written respectively by Erwin Rommel and Heinz Guderian, both of whom had been officers in the First World War, went largely overlooked. In Guderian's book, for example, were listed all the elements for modern armoured warfare, combined operations and support, and the blueprint for the new form of warfare that would become known as *blitzkrieg* (lightning war). The Germans almost certainly did not invent the expression and it is believed that the term may have been coined by a journalist reporting on the Polish campaign in 1939. Heinz Guderian would later state that: 'our [Germany's] enemies coined the word Blitzkrieg.' This was a first-hand opinion and one cannot argue with those who were there and knew the real story. The Allies had seen a demonstration of the German Army's new blitzkrieg tactics during the Polish campaign but nothing could prepare them for it, and they could not formulate a strategy to counter it in the time given. A handful of British officers had taken notice before the outbreak of war, one of whom was Captain Basil Liddell Hart, whose own writings on tank warfare had influenced a number of German officers such as Heinz Guderian, who presented a signed photograph of himself to Hart inscribed: 'To Captain B.L. Hart from one of his disciples in tank affairs.' Another of Hart's devotees was General Hasso von Manteuffell, and he too presented Hart with a personal photograph addressed to 'the creator of modern tank strategy'. One could hardly fail to notice the poignancy in the sentiments appended to the photographs.

Pre-war exercise moving searchlight on trucks *c*. 1937.

Russia and the Russo-Finnish War

While the eyes of the world were focused on Germany and Poland, Russia had meanwhile been consolidating its territorial gains in Poland, which it had invaded on 17 September. Two months later Russia turned its attention towards Finland, its northern neighbour, which it attacked in November. The assault by 1 million men supported by 1,500 tanks and 3,000 aircraft looked set to crush the Finnish Army. The Russo-Finnish War is often overlooked in the wider history of the Second World War, but it was far from being a sideshow. The Russians had an estimated 24,000 tanks from which force they brought up more reserves such as the massive KV-1 tank. More importantly, they had supplies in abundance. The Finns turned out to be a tougher opponent than the Russians had thought and the fighting lasted until March 1940, by which time the Finnish armed forces had inflicted some 200,000 losses and destroyed 1,600 tanks. The Red Army had killed 25,000 Finns and Russia gained all the territorial demands it made. Finland would return to fight against Russia once again as Germany's ally on 26 June 1941. This was referred to as the Continuation War. The Finns would fight for more than three years but by 20 September 1944 they sought peace negotiations with Russia and then, in an about-turn, took up arms against its former ally, Germany, on 1 October 1944. During the time they fought as Germany's ally, Finnish volunteers were formed into the Nordost Battalion of the Waffen-SS and the SS Wiking Division, both units that required armoured support and trucks for supply and transport. In the post-war period the country had to pay huge reparation costs to Russia, which also made further territorial claims against Finland until the last payment was settled. The Finns also uniquely used reindeer as transport animals which, being indigenous to the region, were better suited to the harsh conditions, unlike horses which suffered terribly from the cold.

Sweden and the Norwegian Campaign

The Norwegian campaign was begun by Germany on 9 April 1940 when they launched a combined naval and airborne strike force from Denmark. The British and French sent troops and warships to assist the Norwegians and the fighting was fierce. The type of warfare prevented the use of tanks, and motorised transport was severely limited. The Norwegians possessed no tanks, and all their artillery was horse-drawn. In view of events in France and Belgium the Allies withdrew their troops, and on 9 June, exactly two months to the day since the German invasion, the Norwegians surrendered. Lying inland to the east was Sweden, which was historically neutral and reaffirmed this status, which was honoured by the Allies and Germany. Even so, Sweden felt obliged to maintain a state of 'armed neutrality', the same as the position adopted by Switzerland. Sweden found itself in a unique position in that it continued to trade with both sides throughout the war but favoured the Allies. Because of its position, Sweden maintained border guard posts along its frontier with German-occupied Norway to the west and Finland to the east, which were later increased when Finland allied itself with Germany against Russia in June 1941. The size of the Swedish Army was nominal and there were a few armoured vehicles, such as the M39/40 armoured car, which had entered service in 1939 and was armed with a 20mm cannon and 8mm machine gun. Other vehicles included the Stridsvagn m/40 light tank based on a German design, and the Stridsvagn m/41, which was based on a Czechoslovakian design. There was also an SPG variant known as the Stormartillerivagn m/43, which was armed with a 105mm gun.

In the immediate aftermath of Germany's attack on Poland, the whole of Europe braced itself for the war into which every country must surely follow, and which would thereby engulf the continent. Several countries had a history of neutrality, including Switzerland and Sweden, but even these nations realised that they too had to be prepared, with their armies equipped, should the fighting spill over their borders. When Germany invaded Denmark in April and also attacked Norway, it took the fighting to the borders of neutral Sweden, which then found itself surrounded by occupied countries. Fearing the worst, it placed its armed forces in a state of preparedness in case of attack. Swedish troops manned frontier

An m/43 Stormartillerivagn as used by the Swedish Army. It is armed with a 105mm gun in a ball mounting, and shows the rivetted design of construction.

posts on the border between Sweden and Norway and patrols were conducted to ensure that there was no breech of protocol. Sweden had only a small army in 1940, but despite its limited size in manpower it was equipped with artillery along with a small number of armoured vehicles, such as the m/39-40 armoured car and the Stridsvagn m/40 light tank. Sweden had the necessary research and design engineering resources required to produce armoured vehicles, but the m39/40 armoured car design was really little more than a truck chassis on to which armoured plate had been fitted for protection. The Stridsvagn m/40 light tank was actually designed by German engineers and its appearance showed this German influence. Indeed, Germany and Sweden had a history of cooperation in weapon design that went back to the end of the First World War, when German technicians moved to Sweden to continue development of weapons that Germany was forbidden to possess under the terms of the Treaty of Versailles. One of these development programmes produced the 88mm anti-tank gun so feared by Allied tank crews.

Just before the outbreak of hostilities in 1939 the Swedish company Jungner had acquired the rights to build a limited production run of some fifty Czech-designed AN-IV-S tanks, which entered service with the Swedish Army as the Stridsvagn m/37. These were useful vehicles with a good road speed that led to a further order being placed with the Czech manufacturer. This was to be for the TNHP tank, but when war broke out hostilities prevented the delivery being made. However, as an alternative arrangement Sweden was granted the right to build the vehicle under licence from Germany, which by then controlled the Czech armaments industry. In fact Germany was using the TNHP 38-ton design for its own purposes and developed a number of fighting vehicles on the chassis, one of which would later be the Hetzer self-propelled tank destroyer. The Swedish company Scania-Vabis was given the contract to build a total of 238 vehicles in two versions between 1942 and 1944.

The first variant based on the versatile TNHP chassis was the basic Stridsvagn m/41 light tank, which was armed with a 37mm-calibre main gun mounted in a fully traversing turret. A small number of the Czech-designed vehicles were also used to produce a second rather unusual but fascinating SPG version, which only ever saw service with the Swedish Army. According to some sources only around thirty-six of these SPG versions were ever built by Scania-Vabis, and these were known as the Stormartillerivagn (SAV) m/43. Using the chassis and hull, a super-structure of riveted design was built up using armour plate up to 25mm thick. This gave the vehicle a box-like appearance not dissimilar to the German Marder III SPG, which was also based on the LT-38 chassis, but was armed with the lighter 75mm anti-tank gun. Fitted into the front of the hull of the Swedish vehicle was a large ball-type mounting that permitted a 105mm-calibre field gun to be installed. Originally, the SAV m/43 was to have been armed with a gun of 75mm calibre, but it was decided that the more powerful gun would be better suited to the needs of the Swedish Army in terms of providing fire support and counter-battery fire. The ball mounting gave limited traverse and the gun could fire out to ranges of some 10,000yd depending on the elevation of the barrel.

The SAV m/43 was fitted with a rear-mounted Scania-Vabis six-cylinder water-cooled petrol engine that delivered 140hp to give road speeds of over 25mph. It weighed 11.8 tons and records show that one of the first units to be equipped with the SPG was an artillery regiment stationed in Kristinehamn. In the event of Sweden going to war the m/43 would have been used in batteries of six vehicles to provide artillery support for infantry or counter-battery fire. The vehicle was fitted with four road wheels either side with the drive sprocket at the front and the idler wheel at the rear with two return rollers, as used on the German Army's Marder III. The SAV m/43 SPG was served by a crew of four and had an operational range of about 125 miles. The vehicle was just over 6ft 6in high with an overall length of 15ft and a width of almost 7ft.

Sweden's state of neutrality was recognised internationally and it had not been involved in a war since 1814. Even so, it was still capable of producing weapons and one of the country's leading armaments manufacturers was Bofors, which produced some exceptional designs, such as the 40mm anti-aircraft gun. These weapons were exported and used by armies around the world, including Britain and America. The Germans had their own comparable weapon in the form of the FlaK 18, 36 and 37 guns, which fired 3.7cm shells, but even they used captured examples of Bofors guns. The Germans had exploited Sweden's position of neutrality by sending engineers to the country to work for Bofors, and used the loophole for their own military gain. In fact, the relationship between Germany and Sweden led to the latter redressing its military imbalance and beginning a rearmament programme. Sweden also built tanks such as the m/21 and although only ten were built, the design set the foundations on which a number of tank designs would be laid over the coming years. Sweden purchased a number of tanks from Britain and France, including Renault NC27 light tanks from which they took certain features to provide ideas, reducing the amount of time and expenditure spent on development and leading to several useful tanks designs, each of which incorporated improvements.

One of the resulting designs was the m/38 tank, which was built exclusively for service with the Swedish Army. This vehicle was the culmination of several years of development and gave the country a weapon platform that would help it guard its neutrality. Although a sound design, the m/38 was quickly followed by the m/39, which was armed with a 37mm-calibre gun mounted in a fully traversing turret. This was actually a very advanced design for a country with no historic enemies. In fact, the calibre of the gun mounted on the m/39 tank was larger than the machine gun on the German Panzer I and the 2cm-calibre cannon mounted on the Panzer II, both of which were in service with the German Army at the time.

Recreated Swedish intantryman
c. 1939 carrying his rifle in the
position for riding his bicycle.

The Stridsvagn m/40 light tank
was in service with the Swedish
Army during the war even though
Sweden was neutral.

Notable Swedish Military Vehicles

Vehicle Name	Type	Manufacturer	Production Date	Armament	Weight	Max. Speed
m39/40	Armoured car	Landsverk	1939	20mm cannon and 8mm machine gun	7.6 tons	44mph
Stridsvagn m/37	Light tank	Junger	1938	2x 8mm machine guns	4.5 tons	38mph
Stridsvagn m/40	Light tank	Landsverk	1940	37mm gun and 2x 8mm machine guns	9.4 tons	30mph
Stridsvagn m/41	Light tank	Scania-Vabis	1942	37mm-calibre gun and 2x 8mm machine guns	10.3 tons	26mph
Stridsvagn m/42	Heavy tank	Landsverk	1942	75mm-calibre guns and 4x 8mm machine guns	22.2 tons	26mph
Stormartillerivagn (SAV) m/43	Light tank	Landsverk	1944	105mm field gun	11.8 tons	25mph
m/37	Light tank	Junger	1938	2x 8mm machine guns	4.4 tons	37mph
m/38	Tank	Landsverk	1939	37mm gun and 2x 8mm machine guns	8.5 tons	28mph
m/39	Tank	Landsverk	1938	37mm gun and 2x 8mm machine guns	8.7 tons	26mph
Stridsvagn m/40L	Tank	Landsverk	1940	37mm gun and 2x 8mm machine guns	9.3 tons	25mph
Stridsvagn m/40K	Tank	Landsverk	1943	37mm gun and 2x 8mm machine guns	10.7 tons	28mph

By 1940 the indigenous Swedish tank design reached its pinnacle with the prototype for a new project known as the Stridsvagn m/40, which was fitted with an
engine rated at 142hp and again more powerful than the engine fitted to either the
Panzer I or Panzer II tanks. The first production models of this new tank, termed
the m/40L, would be improved on in a later version. This was known as the m/40K
and would be fitted with better armour protection that increased the combat weight
to 10.7 tons; it was powered by an engine rated at 160hp. The m/40L version of the
new light tank was built in relatively small numbers and by 1945 there were only
180 in service with the Swedish Army. These were in service with light tank companies, and in 1941 their typical strength included three platoons, each equipped
with four m/37 light tanks and one m/40L tank. Sweden was never involved in
any action during the Second World War, but its armed forces nevertheless had to
be maintained. The number of troops serving with the armoured units numbered
around 6,500 and included seventy-six heavy tanks of the Stridsvagn m/42 type
armed with 75mm calibre guns.

The m/40L was 16ft long, 6ft 10in wide and just over 6ft 6in high to the top of
the turret. The maximum armour thickness was 24mm and its combat weight was
9.3 tons. A water-cooled Scania-Vabis petrol engine of six cylinders and rated at
140hp produced a road speed of 25mph and fuel capacity was sufficient for over
120 miles. Four road wheels were fitted either side with two return rollers, a drive
sprocket at the front and an idler wheel at the rear of the layout. This permitted

the m/40L to negotiate vertical obstacles of 2ft, cross open spans of over 5ft and cope with gradients of up to 60 per cent.

The m/40L was served by a crew of three men and included quite a formidable armament mounted in a turret capable of a full 360-degree traverse. A 37mm main armament was complemented by two 8mm machine guns that were mounted co-axially. This layout would have been useful in providing close fire support to infantry units and for engaging lightly armoured vehicles. While not in the same category as later German tanks such as the Panzer III and Panzer IV, in this tank the influences that led to its development can be seen, and it served the purposes of the Swedish Army quite adequately. However, had the country been invaded it is doubtful whether the lightly armoured vehicle would have stood up in battle against German guns. In the end, the country was not involved in the fighting and the m/40 series and later tanks such as the m/41 and m/42 were never put to the test in battle.

The End of the Phoney War

Finally, after eight months, the wait was over, and the German Army attacked along the Dutch border and at points along the Belgian and French border on 10 May 1940. That same day the British prime minister, Neville Chamberlain, resigned from office and Winston Churchill was invited to form a government. Churchill was made of sterner stuff than Chamberlain and his appeasement policies, and would prove tireless in his efforts to win the war. The weight of the attack was overwhelming, as 136 divisions of infantry and ten armoured or panzer divisions, supported by artillery, aircraft and engineering units, moved as a cohesive force to swamp the Allies. One of the leading vehicles was the SdKfz 247, built in very low numbers but produced in two distinct models that were important for reconnaissance missions. Designated the Schwere Geländegängige Gepanzerte Personenkraftwagen (heavy cross-country armoured passenger car), the first ten vehicles were 6x4 design and termed Ausf. A. They were built by Daimler-Benz, based on the Krupp L2H143 chassis in 1937, and were intended as an armoured staff car for commanders of reconnaissance units. This version was powered by a Krupp M305 57PS engine, giving road speeds of up to 43mph. It weighed 5.2 tons and had an operational range of 217 miles.

The Schwere Geländegängige Gepanzerte Personenkraftwagen (SdKfz)

Vehicle Name	Manufacturer	Production Date	Armament	Weight	Max. Speed
SdKfz 247	Daimler-Benz	1941–42	N/A	4.5 tons	50mph

Following the campaigns against Poland in 1939 and the blitzkrieg against France and the Low Countries, the German Army sought an improved version of the SdKfz vehicle. In the seven-month period between July 1941 and January 1942 a further fifty-eight vehicles of a similar design were built by Daimler-Benz and designated the Ausf. B. Such low production rates were hardly a drain on resources but the fact remains that the role for such a vehicle on the battlefield was thought to be on a small scale. In combat it was intended that the commander of each Aufklärung (reconnaissance unit) of either a panzer or motorised division should be equipped with such a vehicle. The Ausf. B version of the SdKfz 247 was markedly different from the Ausf. A version as it was a 4x4 vehicle based on the chassis of a heavy passenger car. The maximum thickness of the armoured body was 8mm and it weighed 4.5 tons, which was much lighter than the earlier version due to the third set of wheels being removed. The shape was changed and it measured 16.4ft long, 6.5ft wide and 5.9ft high. It was powered by a front-mounted, air-cooled, eight-cylinder Horch 3.5-litre petrol engine with five forward and one reverse gear, which gave road speeds of up to 50mph. It had an operational distance of 250 miles, which was very good for the role that it was intended to operate in. It appears from all reference sources that it was never equipped with any form of armament, not even for self-defence, apart from the personal weapons carried by the six-man crew. The SdKfz 247 remained in service until 1945, with some vehicles eventually being fitted with additional armour at the front to protect the engine. Some sources state that no radio equipment was fitted but this is contradicted by the fact that wartime photographs show examples of the Ausf. B with a 'star-shaped' antenna and it is unlikely that this feature would be fitted without a radio. However, despite all efforts at this time, the radio type that was fitted is still unknown. The vehicle was open-topped, which exposed the crew not only to the elements but also to shell splinters from overhead explosions. To protect the crew against inclement weather a canvas cover could be pulled overhead.

Motorcycles

Among the first vehicles to cross the borders, scouting ahead of the armoured columns to make sure the roads were clear and to report on the conditions of bridges over rivers, were fast-moving motorcycles. Throughout the war these machines would become one of the most versatile vehicles to be used by all belligerent nations. Every army used motorcycles and they were deployed to all theatres of fighting, from the desert wastes of North Africa all across Europe and the frozen steppes of Russia. The American company Harley-Davidson built some 90,000 machines for the American armed forces during the war and a further 30,000 for Russia under the terms of Lend-Lease. In 1942 Harley-Davidson also copied the German BMW R71 motorcycle to produce the XA model, but only 1,000 of these were produced because they proved too expensive to build. Throughout the rearmament period of the 1930s the German Army came to realise the usefulness the motorcycle would have as a military vehicle and how it would fit in with the new blitzkrieg tactics that were being devised, and a series of machines were developed accordingly. One of the leading manufacturers of motorcycles was Bayerische Motoren Werke (BMW), which would produce some of the most popular and enduring machines to become

Recreated SdKfz 247 radio vehicle equipped with 'star' aeriel. Built in small numbers, the vehicle
served well in its role. Here the SdKfz 247 radio vehicle looks very convincing at a re-enactment event
and shows style of construction.

workhorses on the battlefield, serving as they did in the reconnaissance role, or as
medical services, liaison and general communications vehicles.

Before the war the Munich-based BMW firm produced a range of motorcycles
such as the R12, which was used by the German Army between 1935 and 1941, and
the R61, which was also produced as a combination vehicle with sidecar. But it was
the Schweres Kraftrad 750cc mit Seitenwagen, better known as the R75, with its
Boxer OHV two-cylinder, 26hp, petrol-driven engine and sidecar that would become
the most popular machine and prove its versatility in many campaigns, including
Poland in 1939, France in 1940 and Russia in 1941. It was used in Greece and Italy

and saw service in many other occupied nations. By the end of the war in 1945, more than 16,000 R75s had been built by BMW. The design and layout of the conventional motorcycle precludes it from being armed, but the fitting of a sidecar to the right-hand side meant that a machine gun could be mounted and operated by the passenger in this unit. In the case of the R75 the weapon was invariably the MG34 with extra ammunition carried inside the sidecar unit. Additional equipment such as tools, tents and food could be strapped to the rear of the sidecar combination unit to allow the riders to operate with a certain degree of autonomy for days at a time when operating in the reconnaissance role. Typically the rifle brigade of a panzer division would include a motorcycle battalion comprising two motorcycle companies, a machine-gun company and a mixed company. The armoured reconnaissance battalion of a panzer division would also include a motorcycle company.

Motorcycles of the German Army

Vehicle Name	Manufacturer	Production Date	Features	Armament	Engine	Max. Speed
R12	BMW	1935–41	N/A	N/A	BMW 750cc	57mph
R61	BMW	1938–41	Sidecar and trailer	7.92mm MG34 machine gun	BMW 750cc	57mph
R75	BMW	1939 onwards	Sidecar	7.92mm MG34 machine gun	Boxer 750cc OHV two-cylinder, 26hp petrol	56mph
KS750	Zündapp	1940	Sidecar	7.92mm MG34 machine gun	751cc petrol	50mph

The German Army also used light cars such as the Kubelwagen and the amphibious-capable Schwimmwagen in the same roles as the motorcycle, but they lacked the advantage of the motorcycle, which could traverse bridges that had been rendered unusable for larger or heavier vehicles. For example, it was motorcycle riders that located the small, narrow bridge across the River Meuse just north of Sedan that allowed the first German troops to cross after all bridges had been destroyed by the French Army on 12 May 1940. With both sides of the river secured, the engineers could construct a bridge across the river to allow heavier vehicles to cross. Long before the bridge was finished the motorcycle units were moving ahead and scouting the ground before the tanks.

Almost from the very beginning of its rearmament programme in 1933, the German Army recognised the potential of the motorcycle. Indeed, as early as 1931 General Heinz Guderian, in command of a transport battalion, had conducted military exercises using motorcycles to represent tanks supplemented with obsolete armoured cars in order to formulate armoured warfare tactics that would later allow the panzer divisions to charge across Europe. His dictum would become 'Klotzern, nicht kleckern' (Smash, don't tap).

Riders of motorcycles remained vulnerable to rifle fire and during the campaigns of 1939 and 1940 they suffered heavy casualties. But it was the ability of

A replica example of a Germany army DKW motorcycle as used during the war.

BMW R75 motorcycle combination with two PzKw IV tanks in the rear, probably somewhere on the Eastern Front.

BMW R75 motorcycle combination.

Collection of various types of German Army motorcycles used during the war, including the light trailers for carrying extra supplies.

German Army BMW equipped as a medical support unit.

Replica BMW motorcycle combination loaded with three crew to depict how a reconnaissance unit would have operated.

Replica German Army motorcycle armed with MG42 as it would have been during the war.

Replica German Army motorcycle combination in action during a battle re-enactment scenario to show how it would have been used for real.

the riders to push their motorcycles across obstacles and maintain the impression
of a continued advance that favoured German tactics. The machine-gunner in the
sidecar could fire at targets and provide support for infantry as they advanced.
Even when the main roads were clogged with the debris of war, the motorcycles of
the panzer divisions could still fan out and reconnoitre ahead of the main columns.

The BMW R75 motorcycle combination weighed 0.7 tons and had an overall length of 7ft 10in. The air-cooled 750cc engine gave it a maximum speed of
57mph and the fuel tank had a capacity to allow a range of operations of more
than 200 miles, which was more than sufficient when deployed in the reconnaissance role. The vehicle was operated by the rider and a passenger was carried in
the sidecar, but an additional man, such as a radio operator, could also be carried
in order to relay information back to the main unit. The crew would be armed
with personal weapons, either rifles or MP40 sub-machine guns, so that between
them they could defend themselves. The motorcycle combination proved a robust
machine able to transporting enormous loads far beyond what it was understood
to be capable of. For example, wartime photographs exist that show a motorcycle
combination, presumably in France, transporting five men sitting on the machine,
which is also towing a PaK35/36 anti-tank gun of 3.7cm calibre – a remarkable
feat of endurance. Such a move would not have been standard operational proce-
dure, but it does show what could be achieved in an emergency.

The R75 was fitted with a four-speed gearbox and included a reverse gear, which
was good for getting out of the muddy quagmire on the Russian front. The layout was
conventional with hydraulic brakes on the drive wheels and mechanical braking for
the front wheel with telescopic front forks for suspension. An unusual feature about
the R75 was the fact that the wheel of the sidecar was also driven by the engine,
which proved invaluable in the deep mud of the Eastern Front in Russia. When operating with medical units, the R75 could both carry supplies forward and assist with
the evacuation of the wounded in the sidecar, making the combination one of the
most understated machines of the whole Second World War.

Other motorcycles that were also available to the German Army included the
Zündapp KS750, which, like the BMW R75, could be equipped with a sidecar combination for use in liaison and reconnaissance roles. The Zündapp KS750 had an
air-cooled 751cc petrol engine that drove the rear wheel and also that of the sidecar
when it was fitted. This model also proved its worth in the same range of duties as
other motorcycles and was deployed to all theatres of war where the German Army
fought. Because of their small size and manoeuvrability combined with their speed,
it could be said that motorcycles were the prying eyes of the attacking force.

The German Motor Industry

As early as 1934, Lieutenant Colonel Nehring wrote that in his opinion the German
motor industry should be supported by the army as a whole. In other words, he

believed that the German Army should become the main client of the country's motor industry, which would greatly benefit the industry and allow for expansion. Between 1933 and 1935 German military spending more than doubled from 5 million RM (Reichsmarks) to 11 million RM, and the German motor industry consolidated its position by becoming wholly autonomous. By 1937 German Ford vehicles were manufactured using only materials from Germany. After the *Anschluss* and the occupation of Czechoslovakia in 1938, Germany had a massive industrial power base at its disposal for the production of motor vehicles and armoured vehicles, including tanks. But it was a very mishmash organisation with much duplication and was wasteful with resources. In 1938 General Major von Schell proposed a new streamlining plan for the motor industry called the Schell Plan. Among the many changes suggested was a proposal to reduce the number of motorcycle designs from 150 different models to only thirty. It may have been due to being denied armoured vehicles, including personnel carriers, that prompted the German Army to place such emphasis on the motorcycle and experiment with them to move large units of troops. These trials began in the mid-1930s and culminated with a series of field exercises, one of which involved putting an entire battalion of infantry of a panzer division's rifle brigade on motorcycles for speed of movement. This planning allowed the German Army to have large numbers of motorcycles in service and available for the invasion of Poland in September 1939, for the blitzkrieg westwards into France, Holland and Belgium in May 1940 and again for the invasion of Russia in June 1941. In every area of occupation the motorcycle could be seen responding to all manner of situations, and among them was the Zündapp.

The Zündapp

Zündapp produced some 18,000 machines during the war, some of which were standard motorcycles, while others were a combination, fitted with sidecar units and used right up to the final collapse of the German Army in May 1945.

   The Zündapp motorcycle with sidecar was a useful and versatile vehicle in its role on the battlefield, which included the evacuation of wounded. Its unladen weight was less than 900lb and fully laden for combat it could weigh up to 1,800lb, which would amount to three men and their kit. In an emergency and over short distances the motorcycle could transport greater loads and, as with the BMW R75, there are photographs showing Zündapp motorcycles carrying loads that are evidently far in excess of what they were intended for. In combat, improvisation is a motivating factor and machines were operated beyond their capacity out of necessity. The ground clearance of these motorcycles was only 6in and, while it was set rather low, it was comparable to other motorcycles of the day. When the machine became bogged down in the glutinous mud on the Russian front the light weight and rear-wheel drive allowed it to be pushed out. The Zündapp motorcycle was rather a compact machine measuring less than 5ft 6in in overall width with sidecar and just over 7ft 9in in length. The machine had a good turn of speed and could reach speeds of around 50mph.

As with other motorcycle combinations, it only carried an MG34 7.92mm-calibre light machine gun armament for self-defence. It was usually fitted with a 'saddle drum' magazine because the ammunition belt could become snagged and prevent firing. As with the BMW R75 machine, extra ammunition would be carried in the sidecar unit; with a spare wheel on the rear of the unit and the crew's kit securely fastened, it was possible for such a combination unit to operate far ahead of the main unit in order to reconnoitre in front and bring back information regarding the enemy's movements. By using such versatile machines the German Army was able to maintain a stream of vital information through to the General Staff, which could then plan the next operational phase of an attack. In medical support and communications the motorcycle in all armies would prove essential at all levels on the battlefield.

The German Attack

The first victim of the German attack in 1940 was the tiny Dutch Army of 114,000 men, which surrendered on 14 May after the city of Rotterdam was bombed. In the five days of fighting, the Dutch Army sustained 9,779 casualties and its few armoured cars, such as the M39 Panserwagen had been no match for the German tanks or anti-tank guns. Those vehicles that were not destroyed in the fighting were taken into service by the German Army and the M39, for example, would be categorised as the Pz SpWg L202 (h). They were eventually used for internal security duties; the letter 'h' denoted Holland. The intensity of the German attack, which was spearheaded by columns of tanks with armoured cars and fast-moving motorcycle units scouting ahead, was more powerful than anything that they could have prepared against. Hitler later wrote an assessment of the Dutch Army, stating: 'They [the Dutch] put up a stronger resistance than we expected. Many of their units fought very bravely. But they had neither appropriate training nor experience of war. For this reason they were usually overcome by German forces which were often numerically very inferior.' For all his faults as a commander, including the fact that he never attended military college, Hitler gave credit where credit was due in his opinion. The Netherlands had been neutral in the First World War and the country believed that it could maintain this stance again, but circumstances dictated otherwise and the army was neither prepared nor equipped.

The rapidity with which the Germans advanced was startling. The XIX Corps, commanded by Guderian, covered a distance of 151 miles from the point of its initial attack to the Channel coast in eight days. This gave it an average advance rate of 19 miles per day, with the best performance being 56 miles in one day.

The speed of the advance led to Guderian being nicknamed 'Der schnelle Heinz' (Fast Heinz). Fuel consumption was a problem for the tanks with an armoured division requiring 1,000 gallons for every mile on roads and as much as double that figure when operating cross-country. German tanks were fuelled by petrol, which meant that in an emergency they could, in theory at least, refuel from commercial garages. Trucks carried fuel for the tanks and motorcycles in jerrycans, and tankers carrying fuel in bulk followed behind with the supply column. Much later, Guderian spoke about the campaign in France and commented that the commander of the 2nd Panzer Division believed his units were running out of fuel, stating: 'After regulating the fuel stocks in the hands of the troops it proved possible to continue the advance. One must always distrust the report of troop commanders [who say] "We have no fuel". Generally they have. But if they become tired, they have no fuel. This is a common experience of war with forward troops. During the campaign in France there was no lack of fuel; good staff work can avoid this calamity.' Regarding the same issue in later campaigns, he went on to state: 'Later in the war we often had a real scarcity of fuel because of the destruction of our industry. But in 1940 it was only a question of transport and easy to solve.'

This was Guderian changing his mind with hindsight because he knew it could be, and indeed was, vastly different, as he had witnessed first-hand during pre-war manoeuvres in 1938 when he was commanding a panzer division during the Anschluss between Germany and Austria. His tanks covered a distance of 400 miles in two days, which was an extreme test. On average there was a 30 per cent mechanical breakdown rate among the tanks and he noted at the time the 'inefficiency of maintenance facilities, particularly for the tanks'. He was also concerned about fuel supplies. The exercise taught the German Army many things about specialist recovery and support vehicles, supplies of fuel and maintenance problems. The 1939 Polish campaign and the attack against France, Belgium and Holland produced higher levels of mechanical failure among tank units, which reported on average a 50 per cent failure rate. This was only to be expected, as the stresses of combat are far greater than in peacetime manoeuvres. The mechanical failure could even be high among lorries, and pre-war exercises had shown that the army could lose up to 10,000 vehicles a year through breakdowns

Did You Know?

In 1941 a German armoured or panzer division was made up of a tank regiment with 150 to 200 tanks, a regiment of artillery with twenty-four guns of 150mm calibre, thirty guns of 105mm calibre, thirty '88mm' guns, which served in the dual role of anti-tank and anti-aircraft, and a light FlaK anti-aircraft battalion with 2cm guns. It also comprised a brigade of four battalions of Panzergrenadiers, a battalion of motorcycle and sidecar combinations, along with support units such as signals, reconnaissance, army air corps and supply detachments. In all it amounted to some 14,000 men and 4,200 vehicles.

alone. If the tanks were to be kept supplied then more supply lorries and specialist recovery vehicles had to be made available to the panzer divisions.

The other exponent in modern warfare involved in the 1940 campaign in France was General Erwin Rommel, commanding 7th Panzer Division, who covered a distance of 110 miles in the same time, with a daily average of 13.75 miles' advance per day; the unit was nicknamed the 'Ghost Division'. The entire column of an armoured division, including troops, supporting artillery and horses, could stretch along 70 miles of roadway and in some extreme cases would move at an average speed of 2.5mph, causing massive tailbacks and bottleneck jams at junctions. The tanks could move cross-country but the supply trucks were restricted to roads, which did not always run parallel to the axis of advance; they had to keep up as best they could. These supply trucks also needed to be fuelled in order to remain operational. The German Army had six standardised units (called *Kolonne* or 'columns') to transport supplies. The first was the Fahrkolonne, which was a horse-drawn unit with the capacity of transporting 29.5 tons. The second type was the Leichte Fahrkolonne, which was identical to the Fahrkollone but could only transport 16.7 tons. The Leichte Kraftwagen Kolonne was a motorised column capable of transporting 29.5 tons. The Schweres Kraftwagen Kolonne was the heavyweight unit capable of transporting 59 tons of supplies, including food, ammunition and medical supplies. The Leichte Kraftwagen Kolonne für Betriebstoff was the motor transport column responsible for fuel and had the capacity to move 5,500 gallons. Lastly, there was the Schweres Kraftwagen Kolonne für Betriebstoff, which had the capacity to transport 11,000 gallons of fuel. These transport columns would move the supplies as close as possible to wherever they were required in order to minimise handling.

Rommel and Guderian had given written warnings of what could be expected in future wars and now they were proving it in practice on the battlefield. The size of armoured divisions would vary during the war but it would always remain autonomous and this was the same in all armies.

Development of the British Army's A11 Matilda Mk I

Vehicle Name	Manufacturer	Production Date	Armament	Weight	Max. Speed
A11 Matilda Mk I	Vickers	1938	.303in machine gun or .50in-calibre machine gun	10 tons	8mph

Despite all the published material available and the actual demonstration of blitzkrieg tactics in Poland, the British and French still maintained their belief in their tactics for armoured warfare, which held that tanks should operate in support of the infantry. Indeed, many of the tank designs had the term 'infantry' as part of their designation. The British A11 Matilda Mk I 'infantry tank', for example, was deployed to France with the BEF in 1940 and the A12 Matilda Mk II was also classed as an infantry tank. The development of the A11 or Matilda Mk I can be traced back to the mid-1930s when the British Army sent General Sir Hugh Elles to Vickers with a view to ordering a new design of tank. The design was to be of a type referred to as an infantry tank, which meant that it had to have adequate armour protection, be armed only with a single machine gun and have a much reduced speed so as not to outpace the infantry, because it would be these troops that the tank would be supporting during an assault. These design stipulations were fine on paper and Vickers could certainly have produced a vehicle to meet these requirements; however, to add insult to injury, the British Army wanted the resulting vehicle to come in at a price of no more than £6,000 per tank, which was asking a great deal and would mean many compromises.

At the time, the usual practice when the army required a new tank was to send an experienced officer of senior rank to negotiate with the armaments manufacturer and to discuss the needs of the army. The officer concerned would outline what would be required of the vehicle and the armaments manufacturer would then produce a blueprint for consideration; any modifications would be highlighted and changes were made accordingly. That was the most sensible course of action because the company that was to produce the tank knew its own capabilities and what could be achieved. In this case there was a restraint on budget, and a manufacturer does not want to work at a loss. The British Army was adamant that they wanted to follow the trend in tank design in other countries such as France, where companies like Renault were producing light tanks of very good design. Field trials and military manoeuvres with tanks showed that vehicles operated with a crew of only two men were greatly limited in what they could achieve and that such designs were not that further advanced from the light tanks used during the First World War.

At the time of the request by the British Army one of the leading tank designers in the country, Sir John Carden, was working for Vickers, and so the responsibility fell to him to create this new tank. He, more than perhaps anyone else, realised that the army was asking for a grossly underarmed vehicle, and should have known better. The A11, or Matilda Mk I infantry tank as it was known, lacked a large-calibre main gun armament and was to be armed instead with a single machine gun of either .30in calibre or .50in calibre, mounted in a turret with a full 360-degree traversing capability. There were later plans to arm the tank with a larger gun but the turret proved too small to accommodate one. Sir John Carden was left with no other choice but to opt for a vehicle design that had a turret operated by a single man. To produce a vehicle that was no more than a mobile machine-gun post would not provide a battle-winning weapon, especially as the German Army was known to be arming more powerful anti-tank guns with increased hitting power, and ever-heavier projectiles were entering into service. Carden also had to be mindful of the reduced speed requirement, which he must have known would further risk the vehicle's survival on the battlefield.

Armed with only a single .303in-calibre machine gun, there was little the Matilda Mk I could do against heavier, more powerful German tanks in 1940.

The Matilda Mk I gave a good account of itself during the 1940 campaign in France but they were all destroyed or abandoned in the retreat to Dunkirk.

The Matilda Mk I was an old-fashioned design but it was compact; however, its road speed of 8mph was very slow.

The Matilda Mk I was operated by two men who served as driver and commander machine-gunner.

The British Army General Staff had asked for, and expected to receive, the vehicle they had in mind. Finally, in April 1937, the first production order was placed and the following year the 1st Army Tank Brigade took the first Matilda Mk I infantry tanks into service. At the time, Germany was rearming with advanced designs such as the Panzer II and armoured cars such as the SdKfz 231, SdKfz 222 and SdKfz 232, but the British Army stuck with the Matilda Mk I even though it appeared to have been outclassed already. It weighed in at just over 10 tons and was protected by armour between 10mm and 60mm in thickness. Overall the new tank was 15ft 11in long, 7ft 6in wide and 6ft 1½in high. A petrol-driven eight-cylinder Ford engine developing 70bhp at 3,500rpm produced a road speed of 8mph. It had an operational combat range of 80 miles, could negotiate 2ft-high vertical obstacles and span gaps of 7ft. It was outclassed in speed, range and hitting power by the Panzer II and the wheeled armoured cars it would soon be pitted against in battle.

The Development of the German Army's SdKfz Armoured Car

Vehicle Name	Manufacturer	Production Date	Armament	Weight	Max. Speed
SdKfz 221	Weserhütte	1935–40	7.92mm MG34 machine gun and later a 2.8cm sPZB41	4 tons	56mph
SdKfz 222	Bussing-NAG, Weserhütte, Schichau, MNH	1936–43	KwK30 or KwK38 L/55 2cm cannon and a 7.92mm MG34 machine gun	4.2–4.7 tons	53mph
SdKfz 223	Built by Auto Union and assembled by Schichau and Maschinenfabrik Niedersachsen	1935–44	MG34 machine gun	4.4 tons	50mph

The SdKfz 222 was one of the first of the series of new vehicles. It had a building programme that lasted from 1936 to 1943, during which time some 989 vehicles were produced. The first models of this new armoured car entered service with the German Army proper in 1938, and during its service life the range was deployed in all the major campaigns and used in the blitzkrieg tactics into Poland in 1939, France 1940 and Russia in 1941. In all, the design was produced in several versions with the entire production range being built by four main manufacturers, including Bussing-NAG. Although production stopped in 1943, those surviving SdKfz 222 vehicles continued to be used until 1945. The SdKfz 222, in keeping with other light reconnaissance vehicles, was developed to replace the earlier Kfz13 and 14 vehicles, which had only been lightly armed with a single machine gun and equipped with a radio. The SdKfz 222 was a more specialised vehicle with improved armour and heavier armament and, as such, equipped the Panzerspähwagen squadrons (armoured scout car units) of the Aufklärungs

Recreated SdKfz 222 armoured car showing faceted construction with armour plate, and 2cm cannon in the turret during a battle re-enactment. The design of this vehicle was built in very small numbers.

(reconnaissance) battalions. At the time only France had any credible vehicles that could be considered comparable to the new German vehicles, such as the Panhard AMD 178, which was armed with a 25mm cannon and a 7.5mm-calibre machine gun.

The SdKfz 222 was a compact design, 17ft 9in long, 6ft 5in wide and exactly 6ft 7in high to the top of the turret, which gave it a low silhouette. It weighed 4.2 tons, which increased to 4.7 tons when fully loaded. A three-man crew served the vehicle, which went ahead of the armoured columns in order to gather information. It was equipped with a short-range FuG Spr Ger 'a' radio set, which allowed details of the enemy's movement to be sent back to the

Recreated SdKfz 223 amroured car in action during a battle re-enactment (top). SdKfz 223 with frame-type aerial and armed with an MG34 machine gun (above).

heavier vehicles. The armament was sufficient to provide local self-defence and comprised a KwK30 or KwK38 L/55 2cm cannon for which some 220 rounds of ammunition were carried pre-loaded in magazines, and a 7.92mm-calibre MG34 machine gun for which 2,000 rounds of ammunition was carried. The weapons were mounted co-axially in a two-man turret that had a most unusual design in that it was decagon-shaped in plan view (meaning ten-sided). It was capable of a full 360-degree traverse to provide all-round covering fire, but being hand operated it was rather slow to bring on to a target; a well-trained crew and in battle conditions speed was all important. The main armament could be elevated to +87 degrees, which was an extremely high angle but meant that it could fire at low-flying aircraft; it could also be depressed to -4 degrees in order to engage all ground targets. In combat, the SdKfz 222 served well in the North

Recreated SdKfz 13 scout car and liaison vehicle armed with a single machine gun.

African desert and across Europe, but in Russia the harsh extremes of the cold reduced its operational capability, leading to it being replaced by other vehicles functioning in the reconnaissance role.

During its production run the vehicle was fitted with two different types of engine, but the speed remained around 50mph and the combat range of 187 miles was unaffected as the standard gearbox layout of five forward and one reverse was common to all types. The first SdKfz 222 vehicles were fitted with the Horch 3.5-litre engine, but those built after May 1942 had improvements to their design, which included the Horch 3.8-litre engine. At around this time the armour thickness protecting the front of the hull was also improved to 30mm, but the rest of the armour covering was unaltered. The turret was open-topped, which exposed the crew to the elements, but more importantly to the effect of shell splinters and hand grenades, which could be thrown into the interior at short range. To counter this threat a wire-mesh screen was fitted that could be folded back to allow the crew to operate the weapons and provide access and exit to the vehicle. The SdKfz 222 had good ground clearance and the armour was well sloped to deflect light projectiles; set into either side of the body were doors for driver access and for loading ammunition. Stowage boxes were carried externally on the left-hand side and a spare tyre was carried on the right-hand side.

A variant of the SdKfz 222 was the SdKfz 223, but perhaps as few as only 500 or so of these were built between 1935 and 1944, which amounted to an average of fifty vehicles per year. This may not have been a great burden on the armaments industry, but it may have been inconvenient to produce such small numbers when the workforce could have concentrated on other more important designs instead. The SdKfz 223 was not an original design but rather an adaptation of the SdKfz 221 armoured car, designed as a small, fast vehicle for carrying signals equipment and providing long-range communications using the Funkgerät 10 (radio equipment) and the Funksprechgerät 'a' (radio-telephone equipment). Production began in 1935, the same year as the SdKfz 221, with both vehicles designed by Wesserhutte Eisenwerk of Bad Oeynhausen. The chassis were built by Auto Union in Zwickau and assembled by Schichau of Elbing and Maschinenfabrik Niedersachsen in Hanover. The vehicle was fitted with a collapsible frame aerial, sometimes referred to as a 'bed-frame antenna' due to its similarity to that item. This could be folded flat over the rear of the vehicle when not in use, such as during routine maintenance or when parked in rest areas. The SdKfz 223 served with the Panzerspähwagen squadrons of light panzer and with motorised infantry divisions, providing communications for the armoured cars operating well in advance of the main column. Because it was never intended to engage directly in fighting it was only armed with a single MG34 machine gun with just over 1,000 rounds of ammunition for self-defence purposes. The weapon was fitted into a low-profile turret that was set further back than on the SdKfz 221 in order to provide space for all the radio equipment. The turret had a full 360-degree traverse capability using hand wheels for all-round defence.

The armoured 8mm-thick hull was well sloped and multi-faceted to give many angles with which to deflect light projectiles. The vehicle was based on the HOCH 801 heavy car chassis and was powered by a rear-mounted Horch 3.5-litre petrol engine of 90hp, which gave it a road speed of up to 50mph (25mph cross-country) with an operational range of 187 miles. The SdKfz 223 weighed 4.4 tons and was the same size as the SdKfz 222. A crew of three operated the vehicle, with the driver given good visibility through four armoured vision slits that could be opened. The turret was open-topped but a hinged wire-mesh screen was fitted to prevent hand grenades from being thrown into the vehicle. The SdKfz 223 underwent a series of modifications during its service life but these did not alter its appearance. The changes included the thickness of the frontal armour being increased to 30mm, the introduction of a new chassis, and the addition of hydraulic brakes and a more powerful Horch 3.8-litre engine, which increased the speed slightly to 53mph. It served right until the end of the war and, although not a fighting vehicle in the true sense of the term, its role within the panzer divisions as a reconnaissance and communications vehicle was undeniably important to the blitzkrieg tactics of all the major campaigns.

The German Army Attack

When war broke out in September 1939 the BEF, of which the 1st Army Tank Brigade was part, was deployed to France along with its complement of 139 Matilda

Mk I tanks. They took up positions and maintained a presence by passing time engaged in exercises. Apart from conducting reconnaissance patrols there was little to do in the way of operational activity. This inactivity was shattered when the German Army attacked in May 1940, overwhelming virtually everything in its path with the speed and ferocity of the armoured thrusts of their tanks. In the fighting retreat towards Dunkirk the 1st Army Tank Brigade lost all 139 Matilda tanks either through fighting or abandonment because they were unable to cope with the mechanical strain placed on them. The crews did put up a valiant effort in conducting a fighting withdrawal, but the German armour and anti-tank guns were just too powerful and ripped into the flimsy design of the Matilda. It has been estimated that up to 75 per cent of British tank losses were due to mechanical failure.

The armour of the Matilda Mk I provided protection against the lighter anti-tank guns such as the 3.7cm-calibre PaK35/36, nicknamed the 'Doorknocker' by the German troops because it was ineffective. Against the heavier-calibre anti-tank guns such as the PaK18 and 36, of 88mm calibre, there was little if any chance of survival. The main weakness of the tank lay in the almost skeletal appearance of the chassis and the exposed track, suspension and drive mechanism. In order to meet the constraints placed on him, Carden had been forced to employ components that were already in use on other tanks. For example, the chassis was ten years out of date, being based on the style fitted to the Vickers 6-ton tank, which had entered service in 1928. The engine was underpowered and had to be modified to drive the rear sprocket wheel through a basic transmission. It may have been pared down to the bare essentials but when put to the test in battle the Matilda did not go down without a fight.

When captured examples were examined by the Germans, they must have wondered what possessed the country that had developed the tank to pit such an obsolescent design against more modern models. The two-man crew in the cramped interior, the basic radio set and lack of offensive capability against vehicles meant that the Matilda was limited in its role on the battlefield. The British Army had to abandon its tanks in France but a number of Matilda Mk I tanks had been left in Britain and were used for maintenance training. The actual service life of this tank had only been two years, but during that brief period its deficiencies had become clear in battle tests, but from these deficiencies, lessons were learnt.

The British Army's A12 Matilda Mk II

Vehicle Name	Manufacturer	Production Date	Armament	Weight	Max. Speed
A12 Matilda Mk II	Vulcan (latterly sub-contracted to the North British Locomotive Works, the LMS Railway Works, Harland & Wolff and Fowler, Ruston and Hornsby)	1938 onwards	2-pounder gun and .303in-calibre Vickers machine gun (later a 7.92mm-calibre BESA machine gun)	26.5 tons	15mph

Fortunately for the British Army, it had the larger, more powerful A12 Matilda Mk II, which fared much better during the Dunkirk campaign. This had started life in the early 1930s when the British Army found itself desperately lacking in tanks with good armour protection and an armament with hitting power. The Matilda A11 infantry tank was entering its prototype stage, but even at that early point in its development there were already debates going on concerning the possibility of increasing the fighting capacity of the tank. This meant that there would have to be a major rethink concerning the new tank design and other future designs of infantry tanks.

One suggestion put forward was to equip the A11 Matilda tank with a two-man turret and arm it with a 2-pounder gun. The idea was simple and sounded good but the problem was that the tank was in service and crews had already been trained on it. The suggestion offered the simplest solution to the problem, but unfortunately those who proposed it had failed to take the narrow limitations of the A11's hull into account and the idea was scrapped. Another problem with the suggestion was the additional weight, which would have placed even greater strain on an already overworked engine. What was needed was an entirely new tank design. The request was put forward and the design department at Woolwich Arsenal was entrusted with producing the design for the new tank. The plans drawn up included strengthened suspension and twin commercial diesel engines, which had originally been suggested for the A7 tank of 1932. Thick armour would be provided in the form of a cast turret and bow plate. Unfortunately the heavy industry in Britain in the mid-1930s was limited in its capacity to produce large castings. This shortcoming was due to the fact that there was no demand for the large castings required by the new design because most British tanks were built using welding and riveting techniques. This was not the case in other countries such as France and America, where advanced casting techniques and welding processes were used to produce machinery and tanks.

In November 1936 the contract to produce the new tank was awarded to the Warrington-based foundry Vulcan, which produced a wooden model of the vehicle in April the following year. By 1938 the company had built a pilot model using mild steel to be used in feasibility trials. The project had experienced some delays,

The Matilda Mk I and Mk II served together in France in 1940, the Mk II having entered service in 1939 and later seeing service in North Africa. It was used as a flail tank to clear minefields and used as experiments to develop other systems for specialist units. The size difference and armament of the two Matildas was incredible. The 2-pounder gun on the Matilda Mk II was limited but in North Africa it took its toll on Italian vehicles.

one of which was caused by problems concerning the delivery of the Wilson gearbox. Trials with the pilot model were finally completed in 1938, but even before the trials had commenced the British Army had placed an initial order for sixty-five new tanks. On completion, an order for a further 100 vehicles was placed. It was fortunate for all concerned that the trials went well, otherwise there would have been a great many questions to answer. In fact, only main mechanical changes were suggested, and given the overall complexity of designing a new tank, they were relatively minor. Nevertheless, changes were ordered to the suspension and the engine cooling. The new tank was designated the A12 and was detailed as an infantry tank. It was 18ft 5in long, 8ft 6in wide and 8ft 3in high, with a weight of 26.5 tons. It was one of a series of heavier new tanks entering service with the British Army and followed in the same direction as many armies that were being re-equipped at the time. It was intended to support the infantry and a British Army General Staff policy document of the time stated: 'If tanks are to survive at infantry pace while supporting men on foot, they must [be able to] resist the fire of current anti-tank guns, and yet retain the ability to destroy hostile men and weapons, including enemy tanks.'

By 1938 talk of war was everywhere despite reassurances from politicians and the talks that defused the Munich Crisis. All across Europe, countries began to rearm. Britain was one of them and realised, rather late in the day, that more tanks were needed. An additional order for the new A12 was placed with Vulcan foundry, but the company realised that it could not meet the increased demand alone. Therefore, other companies were sub-contracted including the North British Locomotive Works; the LMS Railway Works; Harland & Wolff, the Belfast-based shipbuilders in Northern Ireland; and the engineering concern of Fowler, Ruston and Hornsby. Vulcan remained the prime contractor, however, and undertook much of the important casting process. The A12 tank was far from being an easy machine to put into mass production, because the size of the castings and other features had low tolerances and allowed little margin for error. The side skirts over the tracks, for example, were cast as a single unit. However, in a move to ease manufacturing processes, the number of mud chutes was reduced from six to five. The precise time limit required to produce all the components of the A12 is difficult to compute, but it has been calculated that it took some 2,000 man hours to assemble all the components on the production line.

In September 1939, when Britain declared war against Germany, there were only two of the new A12 tanks in service. Just six months later, in early 1940, the number of A12 tanks in service allowed for one battalion of the 7th Royal Tank Regiment to be equipped with the vehicle as were other units. The A12 gave a good account of itself in action during the retreat towards Dunkirk and fighting rearguard actions against German armoured units with superior numbers. A number of the new tanks were involved in mounting a counter-attack against German forces in the Arras region and while it was well intentioned, it did little to prevent the inevitable overrunning of France. At the same time as these events in Europe several units of the British Army in Egypt were being re-equipped with the new tank, which would be used in the early campaigns against the Italians. After the retreat from Dunkirk, the A11 Matilda was declared obsolete and withdrawn from front-line service. This led to the troops referring to the A12 as the Matilda Mk II, which was the title it remained known by until the end of the war. There are those believe that the nickname was referring to 'Waltzing Matilda', a popular tune of the time, but actually the name came from a cartoon duck called 'Matilda' who waddled.

During the early campaign in Libya in 1940–41, the Matilda proved itself to be virtually impervious to the Italian anti-tank guns, which were mainly of light calibre. Italian tanks such as the Carro Armato L6 and Carro Armato M13, sometimes

called 'tin coffins', offered little danger to the Matilda Mk II with its armour protection of between 14mm and 80mm. The Matilda's armour was actually thicker than
that on the German Army's PzKw IV Ausf. E, which was fitted with armour up to
60mm maximum. This one-sidedness would only last until mid-1941, however, by
which time the newly formed German Afrika Korps entered the theatre with their
powerful 88mm anti-tank guns. With this weapon they could engage the Matilda
Mk II tanks at ranges in excess of 1,000yd, which was far beyond the range of the
2-pounder gun. From this point on, the crews began to lose faith in the Matilda's
survivability on the battlefield.

A series of trials were conducted into the possibility of increasing the size of the
main armament from a 2-pounder gun up to a 6-pounder gun of 57mm calibre.
It proved a failure because the turret of the Matilda Mk II was already far too
cramped and small to accommodate the larger breech mechanism and the three
men required to operate the gun. This inability to upgrade the size of the main
armament was one of the deciding factors that eventually led to the production
of the Matilda Mk II being suspended. The last time the Matilda was committed
to battle as a front-line tank to engage enemy tanks in direct action was during
the First Battle of El Alamein in July 1942. The design of the A12 Matilda Mk II
was typical of the period, divided into the three hull compartments (driving compartment, fighting compartment and engine compartment) with a four-man crew.
The first version of the Matilda Mk II was armed with a .303in-calibre Vickers
machine gun but later models were armed with 7.92mm-calibre BESA machine
guns. There was no provision for a bow-mounted machine gun as on other tanks
such as the A9 Cruiser or Crusader tank. The turret was heavily armoured and
fitted with hydraulic power for traversing through 360 degrees, and it was capable
of absorbing most anti-tank fire and surviving. Indeed, the Matilda Mk II was the
first British tank design to incorporate hydraulic power for turret traversing. The
machine-gun armament was changed for the close support version of the Matilda
Mk II, which carried a main armament of a 3in-calibre howitzer and a BESA
7.92mm-calibre machine gun, but the configuration meant that internal space was
even less. The commander's position was equipped with a circular cupola, but
while it provided all-round vision it was limited in aspect. In fact, this was one of
the few poorly designed points of the tank.

A total of sixty-seven rounds was carried for the 2-pounder gun, along with 4,000
rounds of machine-gun ammunition. Two AEC six-cylinder inline diesel engines
were coupled together to produce some 174bhp and these were connected to a
Wilson epicyclic gearbox and a rear drive sprocket. The suspension was derived
from the A7 tank design and was known as either the 'scissors' or 'Japanese' type,
which had been used on the Vickers Medium C tank and some French designs
during the 1920s and early 1930s. This system comprised of bogies linked together
and operating against horizontally mounted compression springs. This layout
meant that there were four pairs of rollers with two link units and two springs to

each suspension point. The entire unit was supported by a single vertical bracket mounted on the side of the hull. There was one such complete unit mounted on either side of the hull with a four-roller unit and large idler wheel at the front. The track was supported at the top by a series of return rollers. The system sounded complicated and indeed it was, but it worked extremely well. However, the tank was severely limited in its top speed: only 15mph on roads and 8mph for cross-country. It had an operational range of 160 miles and could ford water obstacles of up to 3ft deep, scale vertical obstacles of 2ft and cross gaps such as trenches and ditches up to 7ft wide.

Some later versions of the Matilda Mk II tanks were fitted with a pair of Leyland six-cylinder inline diesel engines, which produced 190bhp at a power-to-weight ratio of 7.17hp/ton. This version was built in greater numbers than those models powered by AEC engines. Another version, known as the Mk V Matilda II was fitted with an air servo on top of the gearbox to simplify gear changing. But apart from these relatively basic modifications the Matilda Mk II would remain unchanged throughout the entire course of its service life. By the time of the First Battle of El Alamein in July 1942, the Matilda Mk II had earned a reputation that resulted in it being christened the 'queen of the battlefield'. But by 1942 it was being joined by American-built tanks such as the Grant and M3 'Honey', which were beginning to enter the North African theatre of operations in increasing numbers. In view of this it would be fair to say that despite the Matilda Mk II's magnificent operational success rate, its service days were numbered. As more American-built tanks came into service the question arose of what to do with the surplus Matildas, most of which were still serviceable. Many were still in excellent running order and the army was loath to write off so many otherwise sound tanks. For the time being, at least, no one could see how else they could be usefully employed on the desert battlefield.

As it transpired, a solution to the problem was not far off. The thick armour and battlefield survivability of the Matilda Mk II made the design ideal for development for use in some highly specialised roles such as flail tank mine clearance, an application for which at least twenty-four tanks were used at El Alamein. These were known as Mk I 'Scorpions' and were specialised tanks that would prove themselves invaluable in clearing minefields as the Allies continued their drive to Tunis. The Scorpions comprised an external compartment that was mounted on the right-hand side of the Matilda Mk II and housed a Ford truck engine and the operator for the equipment. The truck engine rotated a drum through the means of an extension shaft, which was mounted on a girder arm. The drum was fitted with a series of heavy chains that rotated at up to 70rpm, whipping the chains to beat the ground and detonating anti-tank and anti-personnel mines as it moved forward. A later variant on this mine-clearing flail device required the removal of the turret with its 2-pounder gun. This version was fitted with two motors that were mounted externally in special housings to the rear of the vehicle's hull and were used to power the flail drum. The motors rotated the chain drum at a rate of up to 80rpm and allowed the tank to move forward at the grand speed of 2mph. While this may not sound fast, it was a great deal faster, safer and more efficient than sapper units using mine detectors moving forward on foot. The invention of the flail device is generally accredited to being devised by an engineering officer from South Africa by the name of Major Du Toit.

The Matilda Mk II was also developed to serve in other specialised roles, including being fitted with a large heavy roller to clear minefields using pressure, while others were used to place demolition charges to clear obstacles such as concrete anti-tank walls or field positions such as bunkers. Even more specialist roles included laying bridges, moving earth with 'dozer-type' blades, flame-throwing and dropping fascines (large bundles of tightly bound wooden stakes) to fill the gap in ditches. There were other unconventional roles devised for the Matilda Mk II, and there existed a radio-controlled version although its purpose was never entirely clear and the project was dropped. One can only surmise that it may have been an attempt to emulate the German Schwerer Ladungsträger SdKfz 301 demolition vehicle, and intended to deliver an explosive charge against obstacles such as the defences of the Siegfried Line on the German border.

The CDL Experiment

One of the more unusual of the Matilda's uses was the Canal Defence Light (CDL) experiment, which was intended to illuminate the battlefield at night, allow river crossings to be made and prevent the enemy from responding by blinding them with intense beams of light. The CDL system was the code name for a device that was used in limited numbers to support the crossings of the Rhine and Elbe rivers in Germany. The system had been under development for some time and the Matilda was seen as an ideal platform on which to mount the lights. The CDL comprised of an arc lamp of extremely high intensity, the beam of which was projected at the target through a vertical slit in front of a special turret using a series of reflectors. When used, the CDL system was designed to 'dazzle' enemy gunners in much the same manner as the flashgun of a camera can temporarily blind people and disorientate their vision. In the case of the CDL, the dazzle effect could be multiplied by the operator opening and closing the shutter in rapid sequence, creating a flickering effect. In the end the CDL was fitted to Grant tanks, a design which better lent itself to the installation of the CDL equipment, and these were deployed with the 79th Armoured Division.

The Matilda Mk II was also supplied to the Australian Army, which used them in the Pacific theatre of operations against the Japanese. The Australian Army developed them into flame-throwing tanks known as 'Matilda Frogs', and used them to burn out enemy emplacements. They also used the earth-moving version to improve tracks through jungle terrain in order that wheeled vehicles could traverse the route. A number of Matilda Mk II tanks were also supplied to the Russian Army, which despite liking the heavy armour, did not consider the 2-pounder gun to be of any use against the more powerfully armoured German tanks. Indeed, the 2-pounder was a stumbling block, because despite the best efforts it could not fire a high-explosive shell. In the early days of the war the 2-pounder gun, with its calibre of 40mm, could penetrate the lighter armoured vehicles, but as the war progressed and heavier tanks appeared it was left behind in the gun/armour race.

In the final months of the war the Matilda was replaced even in its specialist roles by the more commonly available Sherman tank, which could be adapted to almost every role, including being used as a platform for launching rockets. Following continuous use throughout the war years, the remaining Matilda Mk II tanks were mechanically worn out and it was deemed too costly to start a rebuilding programme. A small number of battleworthy Matilda Mk II tanks were still in service at the end of the war, although not in the role of gun tanks, making it the only British tank to see service throughout the entire duration of the Second World War and be used against all belligerents in all theatres of operations.

Tactics

Other countries were also building new tank designs in their rearmament programmes; France, for example, began developing the Renault R35 light tank in 1936 for the specific role of supporting the infantry. The official French view for the role of tanks on the battlefield was that they were a 'subdivision of the infantry' in order to 'make it easier for the infantry to proceed'. The Japanese Type 95 Ha-Go light tank was also developed for infantry support roles, and they never thought they would encounter large numbers of tanks in opposition on the battlefield. The British and French had numerical superiority in tanks but this advantage was lost by committing them to battle in groups often called 'penny packets' because they were so small in numbers. In such weak forces they did not pose a serious threat to the Germans with either their anti-tank guns or the tanks themselves. Of these new designs only the Matilda Mk II would prove itself capable of withstanding anti-tank fire, except against the 88mm gun, which had started service life as an anti-aircraft gun but had been used in the anti-tank role since the Spanish Civil War.

The Germans, on the other hand, developed tactics that sent large numbers of tanks into battle to overwhelm defences and outnumber tank forces opposing them. Guderian was adamant that the tank had to be used as a concentrated force in order to maximise the best use of it as a mobile weapon of protected firepower. The tank crews were taught to halt and fire, which gave better accuracy, while the French and British method of firing on the move was less accurate. The German tactic did leave them vulnerable to anti-tank fire, but the Allies were limited in 1940 in the calibre of their anti-tank guns, which in the British Army was only a 2-pounder, a variant of which was fitted to many of the British tank designs. Blitzkrieg tactics were basic principles applied on a large scale and it was per- haps this that the Allies could not understand and fully come to terms with. The blitzkrieg tactic was broken down into phases or elements and was essentially an expression of combined operations using land and air forces working in close cooperation. The first phase involved deciding on the axis or line of advance to be taken by the advancing units of infantry and armour which had already been reconnoitred by advance vehicles such as armoured cars and motorcycles, which scouted ahead and reported back. Under cover of artillery bombardment and ground-attack aircraft, the infantry followed the armoured advance moving for- ward to make contact with the enemy. While the defending enemy was still reeling from the shock of the artillery and aerial assault, the armoured units attacked in heavy numbers and pushed their way through the defences. Having pushed through the enemy positions, the armoured units then moved out and circled around any points of resistance that were left for the follow-on infantry units to deal with. These armoured thrusts cut lines of communication and supply routes. In the fourth and last phase, the armoured thrusts continued to advance with air support from ground-attack aircraft, leaving isolated pockets of resistance to be dealt with by the infantry. British officers such as General Wavell and General O'Connor learnt from these tactics and in turn adopted them, which allowed them to defeat the Italians in North Africa. The Americans would also learn these tactics in time and even the Russians developed 'tank armies' to overwhelm the Germans at engagements such as the Battle of Kursk in 1943.

The French and British put up stiff resistance against such tactics as best they could, but the Germans dominated the battlefield with their air superiority. The Italians developed a similar strategy called '*guerra di rapido corso*', but it was nowhere near the level of German tactics in terms of strength of armour or coordi- nated airpower. Later in the war the Russians would develop similar tactics with far greater levels of manpower and overwhelming armoured units. The French Army had had tank tacticians such as General Jean-Baptiste Eugène Estienne, who was considered by many to be the 'father of French armour', and Colonel Romain, who unfortunately failed to convince the French Army of the power of armour en masse. He wrote that it was 'up to the High Command to make them [tanks] operate in mass and, as much as possible, by surprise wherever it has been decided to make a decisive attack'. Colonel (later General) Charles de Gaulle espoused the strategy of forming armoured divisions but such theories were not fully understood by the old- fashioned minds from an earlier age. General Maxime Weygand was one of those who acknowledged that France had 'gone to war with a 1918 army against a German army of 1939'. In other words France was twenty years out of date in armoured war- fare. The French relied on artillery, which resulted in the Maginot Line; however, this was effectively by-passed except for a few assaults against some positions such as Markolsheim near Colmar which covered the River Rhine crossing.

Tank engagements occurred throughout the German attack into France and Belgium before the campaign finally ended at Dunkirk. The only real credible attempt to use armour to spearhead a counter-attack was mounted by two battalions of the Royal Tank Regiment (RTR) with seventy-four tanks and two battalions from the Durham Light Infantry on 21 May. They were supported by elements of the French 3rd Light Mechanised Division. Their line of attack took them directly towards positions held by 7th Panzer Division, commanded by Rommel, and the Matilda Mk II tank gave a good account of herself in battle. The attack went in so determinedly that Rommel believed that he was being assaulted by five divisions. Major Fernie instructed Warrant Officer 3 Armit of the 4th RTR to attack the German guns. The NCO drove towards the German positions and later recalled that: 'The guns were not camouflaged, and their only cover was a fold in the ground. I got two of them before they realised I was into them – the range was about 200yd. The survivors turned on me and one hit the gun housing.' The action was close-range and some of the Germans, including the feared SS, were seen to run. Armit continued: 'I got my gun going and returned to the attack. They must have thought I was finished for I caught the guns limbering up, and revenge was sweet.' The attack had been planned hastily and although it inflicted 700 casualties on the Germans and destroyed twenty tanks, the cost was high, and the RTR lost forty-six tanks. However, it did serve to make the Germans wary of their adversary and show more concern for their flanks

The Belgian Campaign

On 27 May 1940 Belgium surrendered, at the same time that the BEF and French troops were fighting a rearguard action to cover the withdrawal of the main armies to Dunkirk, from where they were being evacuated to England. The decision to withdraw the remains of the Anglo-French armies from Dunkirk was code-named 'Operation Dynamo' and lasted from 26 May to 4 June.

Belgium, like its Dutch neighbour, had taken a neutral stance, but all that changed when Germany attacked on 10 May 1940. The Belgian Army had a peacetime strength of 100,000 men, which increased to 550,000 on mobilisation. It had machine guns and was supported with mortars, anti-tank guns and some armoured cars. The troops fought to the best of their ability but after eighteen days they too were beaten; their few armoured vehicles were either destroyed or captured and 23,350 men were killed and wounded. Sensing that the Belgians were on the verge of collapse three days before the Belgian Army actually surrendered, Hitler wrote his assessment of the Belgian soldier: 'The Belgian Soldier, too, has generally fought very bravely. His experience of war was considerably greater than the Dutch. At the beginning his tenacity was astonishing.' He went on (it should be remembered at this point Belgium had not yet surrendered): 'This is now decreasing visibly as the Belgian soldier realises that his basic function is

The Evacuation of Dunkirk

In total more than 338,000 troops were evacuated, a figure that included 113,000 French troops and troops of other nations, including some Belgian and Dutch troops, contrary to popular belief. The cost was massive in manpower and materiel (which had to be abandoned because there was no room on the ships and time ran out). One of the units to be brought out was the 1st Armoured Division, and from its return to the UK until August 1941 it was engaged in anti-invasion duties while it built up its strength. In August 1941 it was sent overseas to Egypt and the division was present for the Second Battle of El Alamein in October 1942. It took part in the later campaigns that liberated Tunis. The division had a strength of just under 15,000 men and 343 tanks along with other AFVs for reconnaissance duties, and included artillery and attached units such as signals and engineers. Among the brigades serving with the division were the 7th Motor Infantry Brigade and the 18th Lorried Infantry Brigade, both of which required vehicles of different sizes for transport and carrying supplies.

to cover the British retreat.' Hitler's assessment recognised the Belgian fighting capability but his view of the role is incorrect, as the Allies were all fighting the same retreat and the average Belgian soldier would have been unaware of any strategy at higher level. The Germans quickly distributed propaganda leaflets and posters showing the British preventing French troops from evacuating at Dunkirk, but those who got away knew this to be untrue.

Captured Military Vehicles in the German Army

The French Army lost 90,000 killed and 200,000 wounded, with the remainder of the army capitulating when the French government signed an armistice on 21 June, seventeen days after Operation Dynamo had ended. During that period, despite being outnumbered in troops and tanks, the French Army had fought on, more stubbornly in some cases than at any point in the campaign before Dunkirk. The surrendering French troops were disarmed and taken into captivity and all the remaining trucks and armoured vehicles of the French Army, including tanks, were eventually taken into German service and given specific titles. For example, the Renault AMC 35 light tank became the PzKw AMC 738 (f) and the Panhard AMD 178 armoured car became the SdKfz 178 (f). The letter 'f' was used to denote French origin and the fleet of French armoured vehicles would be pressed into service as SPGs, flame-throwers and ammunition carriers. Some of the older tanks, such as the Renault FT-17 light tank, which the Germans termed the PzKw 18R 730 (f), had their turrets removed and incorporated into defensive positions as armoured machine-gun posts at points along the French coast. Some of these captured tanks were later taken to the Channel Islands, where their turrets were removed and used in the fortifications across the islands. The chassis were then used as towing vehicles or ammunition carriers for artillery units.

French military vehicles taken for service in the German Army

Vehicle Name	Type	German Army Designation	Armament	Max. Speed
Panhard AMD 178	Armoured car	SdKfz 178 (f) or Panzerspähwagen Panhard 178 (f)	25mm cannon and a Model 31 7.5mm-calibre machine gun	45mph
Renault AMC 35	Light tank	PzKw AMC 738 (f)	3.7cm KwK 18 (f)	25mph
Renault FT-17	Light tank	PzKw 18R 730 (f)	8mm machine gun or converted to supply tractors	5mph
Renault UE (Chenillette)	Supply tractor	UE 630 (f)	Some fitted with 3.7cm PaK35/36 anti-tank guns and others equipped with machine guns or to fire rockets	18mph

The Panhard AMD 178

The prototype of the Panhard AMD 178 (Auto-Mitrailleuse Découverte) armoured car was ready for field trials in 1933. French Army observers watching the trials were suitably impressed by the vehicle's performance that an order was placed for the army. By 1935 the first AMD 178 armoured cars were entering service to replace ageing vehicles. The vehicle was a fairly standard design along the lines of similar vehicles entering service with Britain and Germany at around the same time. It was of an all-riveted construction, including the hull and turret. It was 15ft 8½in long, 6ft 7¼in wide and 7ft 7in high. Into this compact space was fitted a crew of four men and an armament comprising a 25mm cannon, for which 150 rounds were carried, and a 7.5mm-calibre machine gun, for which 3,750 rounds were carried, along with other kit and provisions.

The regular driver sat facing forward with the gunner and commander serving in the turret, but the fourth member of the crew sat facing the rear, ready to act as the reverse driver in the event of an emergency getaway being required. The petrol engine was fitted to the rear and comprised of a four-cylinder Panhard SK water-cooled model developing 105bhp at 2,000rpm to give road speeds of up to 45mph and an operational range of some 187 miles. These capabilities, coupled with the ability to climb vertical obstacles of over 12in, made the AMD 178 quite a useful vehicle, weighing 8.5 tonnes. With armour thickness from 13mm to 18mm, it was sufficiently protected against most small arms ammunition.

The turret was hand operated and had a full 360-degree traverse capability, and the 25mm cannon could depress to -12 degrees and elevate to +14 degrees, allowing a wide range of ground targets to be engaged, including being able to bring fire to bear against defensive positions and upper storeys of buildings. The

Model 31 7.5mm machine gun added to this firepower and could be used either for self-defence or to provide support fire to cover infantry advancing during an attack. An alternative armament layout comprised of two Model 31 machine guns mounted in the turret, while a third version of the AMD 178 was unarmed but instead equipped as a radio vehicle to serve in a reconnaissance role, scouting ahead of units. All three versions were used by the French Army but it was the 25mm cannon armed vehicle that was in service in the greatest numbers.

At the time of Germany's attack against France in May 1940 there were around 360 AMD 178 armoured cars in service with the French Army and most of these were engaged in the fighting. When France capitulated in June 1940, the Germans readily seized on the captured French armoured vehicles, including the surviving AMD 178s, and pressed them into service. In German use these vehicles were given the designation Panzerspähwagen Panhard 178 (f), although some sources claim they were designated SdKfz 178 (f).

Whichever title one prefers, the fact remains that the Germans considered this to be a rather useful vehicle and made extensive use of it. For example, a number were sent to the Eastern Front in readiness for Operation Barbarossa, the attack against Russia in June 1941. Indeed, it is understood that more than 100 of the vehicles were lost during the fighting, which points to the fact that they were heavily committed in the reconnaissance role. Wartime photographs show the AMD 178 in use with the Germans with the road wheels removed and replaced with railway wheels for use on the rail network. Records indicate that some forty-three vehicles may have been configured to this role. The Germans also converted a number into specialised radio vehicles, with some being fitted with the distinctive 'bed-frame' aerial, which curved forward over the turret. In 1943 a number of AMD 178 vehicles were converted to carry a heavier armament by having their turrets removed and fitting a 5cm-calibre KwK L/42 gun in an open-topped turret.

The Renault UE Supply Tractor

Another example of how the Germans utilised captured enemy vehicles to the fullest can be seen in the UE Supply Tractor developed by Renault in 1931. At the time of the invasion of France in May 1940 there were more than 6,000 of these vehicles in service with the French Army. Known as *Chenillette* (small tracked vehicle), Renault referred to it as *Tracteur Blindè* (armoured tractor), and it was used to transport almost 800lb of supplies, such as ammunition, on the vehicle in a cargo bay at the rear or to take additional cargo using a trailer towed by the vehicle. The UE was served by a crew of two, who sat in the front and were separated by the front-mounted four-cylinder Renault 85 engine, which developed 38hp to reach road speeds of up to 18mph. The noise caused by the position of the engine meant that the men could not even talk to one another.

The Germans used the UE carriers they had captured to transport ammunition and other supplies. The armoured covers for the crew of the UE Carrier of the French Army (above left). The Germans converted some captured UE carriers into rocket-launching vehicles (above right).

The vehicle weighed 2.5 tons, measured 5ft 9in wide, 4ft 1in high to the top of the armoured hoods for the crew, and had an overall length of 9ft 2in. It was protected by armour of between 7mm and 9mm in thickness and lacked both radio and armament. It had an operational range on roads of more than 100 miles and over 60 miles cross-country. The tracked vehicle had a wheel arrangement comprising three sets of double bogies, with a drive sprocket to the front, idler wheel to the rear and two return rollers. The tracked trailer was fitted with a double pair of large road wheels on each side and could be loaded with almost 1 ton of stores. When France surrendered in June 1940 the German Army captured numbers of these little vehicles and set about modifying them to serve in a variety of roles.

The Germans referred to the captured stocks of UEs as *Infanterie Schlepper* (infantry tractor) and designated them UE 630 (f) to denote that they were captured French equipment. Research shows that the vehicle was developed into several roles, including as anti-tank gun platforms, rocket launchers and even as the basis for decoy tanks. The Germans did retain some in their original ammunition supply role, and kept the two armoured hoods known as *calottes*; the first use of them in this role was probably in 1941. The leaf-spring suspension was retained and the 300mm ground clearance also remained unaltered.

Some UEs were converted to carry a single MG34 machine gun; these were called Gepanzerte-MG Träger and were used for patrolling airfields, again from around 1941. This involved removing the left-hand *calotte* or armoured hood, leaving only the driver's *calotte*, and this was replaced by a box-like superstructure for the machine to be mounted. A second version of machine-gun carrier saw the addition of a similar superstructure built at the rear of the vehicle over the internal cargo compartment and a traversing turret with an MG34 mounted. Considerable supplies of ammunition would also have been carried, making this a mobile machine-gun post able to deploy anywhere to provide fire support.

Some UEs had both *calottes* removed and were converted to tractors for light anti-tank guns such as the 3.7cm-calibre PaK35/36, with ammunition carried on the vehicle in the cargo compartment. The armoured hoods had visors that could be raised and lowered like giant medieval knights' helmets and which provided some overhead protection. However, when lowered, the field of vision was severely restricted (probably no better than peering through slitted fingers) and the headroom was very limited. A self-propelled anti-tank gun version was developed which saw a 3.7cm-calibre PaK35/36 gun mounted to the rear of the vehicle, again utilising the space around the cargo compartment. The gun shield was left in place and ammunition was carried on board the vehicle, ready to use. This version was issued to *Panzerjäger* (tank-hunting) units from 1941 and, like the machine-gun versions, was intended as a light mobile vehicle. The gun had a limited amount of manual traverse, as it was restricted to 30 degrees either side and could be elevated to +25 degrees and depressed to -8 degrees. Some UEs were used to tow larger guns such as the 5cm and 7.5cm anti-tanks guns.

From around 1943 a number of UEs were converted to carry launcher units for four 28/32cm Wurfrahmen, fixed to fire forward over the vehicle's length. This meant that the rockets fired in whichever direction the vehicle was facing and the crew had to vacate it before firing the rockets remotely by wire command. These vehicles were in service with Panzerpionier companies in France between 1943 and 1944. The launching frame was fitted to the rear of the vehicle and was elevated to give the desired range using a basic sight unit fitted to the front of the vehicle, and it could be folded away when not required. An alternative version of this role was to fit two rockets on either side of the vehicle in the same manner used on the larger SdKfZ 251 half-track. This would have given mobility to the rocket launcher but once fired it would have either had to withdraw to be reloaded or a supply vehicle, probably an Infanterie Schlepper UE 630 (f), would have had to come forward with extra rockets.

Another rather unusual role for the UE was to serve as a mobile base on which a dummy superstructure was built using canvas and wood to give the impression that it was a much larger tank. Wartime photographs show some very good results that include a turret and main armament along with false tracks. This version was called Panzerkampfwagen-Attrappe; it would have been unlikely to fool infantry for very long but aerial photographic reconnaissance might have fallen for the trick. It certainly is interesting to consider the small UE as a Trojan Horse. As a main front-line fighting vehicle, the UE would have been severely restricted and extremely vulnerable, and so its main duties with security units suited it much better. The rocket artillery version would have kept it back from anti-tank guns but even bazooka- or PIAT-armed infantry could have destroyed them. Rather than dismissing the small vehicle, the Germans saw in it something useful and developed some into support vehicles such as *Schneeschleuder* (snow ploughs), infantry carriers, radio and observation vehicles and even *Fernmeldekabel-kraftwagen* (cable-laying vehicles) for field telephones.

The Evacuation of Dunkirk

As with the Dutch and Belgian armies, Hitler wrote his assessment of the French Army, which he identified as containing some 'marked differences'. Overall, he noted that in the French Army:

> Very bad units rub elbows with excellent units. In the overview, the difference in quality between the active and reserve divisions is extraordinary. Many active units have fought desperately; most of the reserve divisions, however, are far less able to endure the shock which battle inflicts on the morale of troops. For the French, as with the Dutch and Belgians, there is also the fact that they know that they are fighting in vain for objectives which are not in line with their own interests. Their morale is very affected, as they say that throughout or wherever possible the British have looked after their own units and prefer to leave the critical sectors to their allies.

Again he was exhibiting some respect for some units of the French Army and, while not entirely dismissing them, knew that when an army recognises it is defeated it is impossible to motivate it. The French had lost 90,000 troops killed and 200,000 wounded in the campaign. The remainder of the French Army was taken prisoner and all war materiel, including ammunition, mortars, AFVs and artillery, would be absorbed into service by the German Army to supplement its existing stocks of equipment.

Hitler believed he understood the mood and characteristics of the British Army, of which he had direct experience from the First World War. He had only been a corporal in that war, however, and was now trying to use that knowledge to assess the British soldier, whom he considered to be: 'Very brave and tenacious in defence, unskilful in attack, wretchedly commanded. Weapons and equipment are of the highest order, but overall organisation is bad.' Some of his points were valid but his opinions were out of date and he was not taking into account the fact that a new generation of officers would emerge from the organised chaos of Dunkirk, such as Major General Bernard Montgomery and Alan Brooke (later to become Field Marshal Lord Alanbrooke). Lord Gort, commanding the BEF, wrote of his experiences facing the blitzkrieg in his dispatches saying: 'The speed with which the enemy exploited his penetration of the French Front, his willingness to accept risks to further his aim, and his exploitation of every success to the uttermost limits emphasised even more fully than in the campaigns of the past the advantage which accrues to the commander who knows how best to use time and make time his servant and not his master.' His words were testimony to the nature of this new warfare and other commanders would learn from his first-hand witnessing of it.

The operation at Dunkirk had cost the British Army dearly, with more than 11,000 killed and a further 14,000 wounded, along with 41,338 taken prisoner or reported missing. In terms of vehicles, out of the 68,618 sent to France with the BEF, some 63,879 were destroyed or abandoned, including tanks and trucks along with 20,548 motorcycles. Some sources put the figure much higher at 75,000 vehicles and also state that the BEF lost around 11,000 machine guns of all types and 90,000 rifles. The artillery regiments had taken 2,794 guns of all calibres to France for anti-tank and anti-aircraft roles, of which 2,472 were either destroyed in the fighting or had to be abandoned because there was no room for these weapons on the evacuating ships. When Operation Dynamo was declared at an end the country was relieved that the British Army had been saved. However, Churchill was under no illusion, knowing that there was worse ahead, and reminded people that 'wars are not won by evacuations'. The US radio journalist Ed Murrow was based in London working for the Columbia Broadcasting System transmitting to neutral America; he broadcast his opinions over the airwaves, and echoed those of Churchill when he stated that to call the Dunkirk withdrawal a victory: 'there will be disagreement on that point.' Churchill knew losses had to be made good and it would take time, which was a commodity in short supply. As the last remnants of the BEF returned to England, the army could only count 200 serviceable tanks. On 10 June Italy declared war on Britain, no doubt hoping to gain something from the campaign even in its closing stages. On 21 June thirty-two Italian divisions attacked but were halted by French mountain troops and suffered heavy losses. For the Italians, North Africa would become the main battleground against the British Army.

British Army Vehicles taken for Service in the German Army

Vehicle Name	Type	German Army Designation	Armament	Max. Speed
Bren gun carrier	Tracked carrier	Gepanzert Maschinengewehr Träger Br 731 (e)	MG08 machine gun or SPG	31mph
A12 Matilda Mk II	Tank	Panzerkampfwagen Mk II 748 (e)	Either 2-pounder original guns or later 5cm KwK L/42 (Sf)	30mph

Vehicles littered the roads leading to Dunkirk and one of the enduring images of the beaches was the rows of lorries that had been 'parked' leading to the water, where they served as makeshift staging for the troops to clamber on to the rescue vessels. These losses would leave the army weakened in transport and the numbers of tanks lost in battle or abandoned along with other weapons did nothing to help matters either. As with vehicles captured from other armies, the German Army would benefit as it absorbed the vehicles abandoned by the British Army along with 500,000 tons of stores including ammunition. One vehicle that would be pressed into service was the Universal or Bren gun carrier, which the German Army termed the Gepanzert Maschinengewehr Träger Br 731 (e), which was modified for a range of duties. Some even found their way on to the Eastern Front after Germany attacked Russia in June 1941. The suffix letter (e) denoted the English origin of the vehicle and was also applied to captured examples of the Matilda Mk II tank, which the Germans termed Panzerkampfwagen Mk II 748 (e). Some were used to mount a range of weapons such as the 3.7cm anti-tank gun, machine guns and even the 88mm Raketenpanzerbüchse anti-tank rocket launchers in a manner similar to the French UE supply carrier.

The Bren Gun Carrier

The British Army used a range of carrier vehicles during the Second World War including the Oxford carrier and the Windsor carrier, which was built in Canada. Some were basic and changed very little during the conflict, while others were built in a variety of designs to suit different roles. One of the carrier vehicles to be used throughout the entire war was a most surprising design and became a veritable workhorse not only for the British Army but for several other Allied armies as well. This was the British-designed Universal carrier, more commonly referred to as the Bren gun carrier, which served not only as a troop and cargo carrier, but also as the test bed for an SPG platform, a flame-thrower carrier called the Wasp and many other experiments. The wartime production run of this utility vehicle exceeded more than 84,000 built in Canada, Britain, Australia, New Zealand and America, where 14,000 were produced for the US Army as the T-16 with certain modifications.

The Mk I carrier entered service in 1938 and featured in many of the pre-war propaganda newsreel films screened at cinemas across the country to show the British public how well equipped the country's army was. It looked impressive as whole battalions of infantry charged around exercise areas carried into battle on the fleet of carriers. When the BEF was deployed to France in 1939 on the outbreak

Bren gun carrier in camouflage colours for North Africa. The smoke grenade discharger can be seen. The flimsy water container would be replaced by jerricans.

Bren gun carrier on the move loaded with fuel carried in jerricans.

Bren gun carrier with recreated South Wales Borderers Regiment. It carries a spare road wheel and length of track for repairs.

Carden-Loyd carrier on which the Universal or Bren gun carrier was based.

Universal or Bren gun carrier in 43rd Wessex Division with infantry section on board.

of war the carriers went with the infantry divisions so that when the Germans attacked in May 1940 and unleashed their blitzkrieg tactics the Bren gun carriers were there to provide extensive service. Among the many vehicles abandoned by the British Army during the retreat to Dunkirk were these Bren gun carriers.

The carrier can be traced back to a series of developments based on designs produced by the vehicle development team of Carden-Loyd during the 1930s. The idea of a specialised carrier vehicle actually dated back to the early 1920s, when a range of carriers was built for the purpose of transporting ammunition for the artillery batteries. From this concept it was only natural that such a vehicle also be used to transport troops across the battlefield along with the light weapons used by infantry battalions such as Bren guns, mortars and .55in-calibre Boys anti-tank rifles. The actual term 'Bren gun carrier' was applied to only one specific model in a range more correctly termed the 'Universal carrier'. However, the name was popular with the troops and it stuck, no matter what role the vehicle served in, even if it was towing 2-pounder anti-tank guns.

In essence the carrier was little more than an open-topped steel box mounted on tracks and powered by an eight-cylinder Ford V-8 engine. The engine was situated in the centre of the vehicle with rectangular spaces on either side of the cowling that allowed troops to be seated or cargo to be stored for transportation. The driver's position was to the right and a seat to the left allowed for a Bren gun or Boys anti-tank rifle to be fitted and operated to provide fire support. The Ford engine was water-cooled and developed 85bhp at 2,800rpm to give top speeds of more than 31mph. The basic Bren gun carrier was 12ft 4in long, 6ft 11in wide and 5ft 3in high, producing a compact vehicle with a very low silhouette, yet capable of tackling a wide range of obstacles likely to be encountered on the battlefield. For example, it could negotiate vertical obstacles of more than 2ft high, span gaps of over 5ft, ford water barriers and traverse gradients up to 60 per cent. Unfortunately the open-topped design of the carrier meant that the crew and any infantry being transported were vulnerable to small arms fire and the elements. While it could be seen as a design flaw, the open top did mean that cargo and troops could be loaded and unloaded quicker than with an enclosed vehicle.

The basic Bren gun carrier weighed around 4 tons and was protected along the sides of the hull by armour up to 12mm thick. This left it vulnerable to even the lightest anti-tank weapons, but the vehicle was versatile enough to serve as a platform on which to mount a range of weapons apart from machine guns. For example, the Australians experimented by mounting a 2-pounder anti-tank gun on the Bren gun carrier, but this was not very successful and did not enter service. Heavier guns, including the 25-pounder field gun, were mounted on the carrier as a self-propelled vehicle with varying results, while as a flame-thrower vehicle called the Wasp, the vehicle was able to give support to infantry advancing against defensive positions. A 2in mortar was sometimes mounted to allow the crew to fire smoke grenades to screen their movement across open spaces when natural cover such as trees and hedgerows were absent. Due to its low height the carrier could normally use such features to its own advantage. In the 1940 campaign in France inexperience in battle led to a high casualty rate among carriers as they faced heavy artillery and mortar fire from the Germans.

The carrier's running gear was based on a design by Vickers and Carden-Loyd and comprised three road wheels in a layout of a single road wheel and a further pair on a single bogie with a shaft connecting both sides together. The suspension used a Horstman-type coil spring to give a rather seesaw motion on the move, but nevertheless had good cross-country ability. The carrier was driven by means of a steering wheel and operators could be trained quickly and easily because of the similarity to driving a wheeled vehicle. Changing direction to follow the path of a normal road was achieved by 'bowing' the track, which could be done without the need to reduce speed. For sharper turns the driver used the vehicle's brakes to stop one track and permit the other to move and thus turned the vehicle. It was a method used on other tracked vehicles and, provided it was done correctly, it was a perfectly adequate practice of steering.

The carrier served in all theatres of operations from the Far East to north-west Europe, including Italy, and even in the Middle East where the dry desert conditions tested the vehicle to its limit. In all cases the vehicle had an average combat range of over 155 miles, which was noteworthy and better than tanks. When towing anti-tank guns other carriers operating with the group transported ammunition and the crew. Carriers served throughout the entire war and after D-Day in 1944; as the Allied armies fought across Europe, increasing pressure was put on the operational role of the vehicles. In fact, by the end of the war it was carrying loads far in excess of what it had originally been intended to transport. This it did with apparent ease and without affecting its operational performance. So much so was the carrying ability and versatility that the carrier continued in service until the 1950s.

German Army Consolidation and Occupation of the Channel Islands

The Germans may have captured huge stocks of supplies, ammunition and vehicles, but the campaign in the west had cost them 27,074 killed, 111,034 wounded and a further 18,384 missing. It is relatively straightforward to account for troops killed, wounded and taken prisoner but the term 'missing' is rather more ambiguous. It is applied to those troops whose disappearance on the battlefield cannot otherwise be explained. If a man is shot he remains intact as a corpse, but if he is caught in the centre of an explosion caused by an artillery shell or mortar bomb there would be very little, if indeed anything, that would allow a positive identification to be made, and if several men were caught in such a blast together it would be impossible to separate individuals; thus 'missing' is applied in such cases. The 1939 campaign in Poland and the blitzkrieg in the west had cost the German Army dearly in manpower, vehicles and equipment, but they had gained enough resources to more than compensate for the losses in materiel. Fresh troops would soon be trained to replace those lost in the recent fighting and they could be used to consolidate territorial gains, which also included the British Channel Islands. Occupation forces established garrisons, with divisions being assigned to specific areas. For example the 319th Infantry Division would be raised in November 1940 and posted to the Channel Islands, along with other attached units, where they would remain until the islands were liberated in May 1945. Equipment, vehicles and even captured tanks were sent to the Channel Islands and Organisation Todt built thousands of defensive positions across the islands and dug miles of tunnels into the hillsides. The German propaganda ministry under Joseph Goebbels wasted no time and distributed to cinemas all across occupied Europe, including the Channel Islands, the newsreel film *Sieg im Westen* (*Victory in the West*). The film was screened to show how Germany won the campaign and defeated the Allies, leaving Britain to continue the fight alone.

The Krupp-built Protze truck showing tools and tow-bar arrangement. It was a useful all-purpose vehicle which served in all theatres of operations.

German Army Vehicles used for Channel Island Fortification

Vehicle Name	Type	Manufacturer	Production Date	Armament	Weight	Max. Speed
'Protze' L2H 143	Truck	Krupp	1937–41	Some equipped to carry 2cm FlaK 38 anti-aircraft gun in self-propelled role	2.5 tons	44mph
R200 (KfZ series)	Light standard cross-country vehicle	Stoewer	1936–43	KfZ4 model armed with light anti-aircraft gun	1.6 tons	60mph

Between July 1940 and May 1945 the Channel Islands would be fortified out of all proportion to their military value and absorbed vast quantities of steel and concrete which were needed to build these defences. Hundreds of pieces of artillery of all calibre, including weapons captured from the French, were moved to the islands, along with thousands of tons of ammunition. Aircraft were used to transport essential items and high-ranking officers to the islands while ships brought in the heavy equipment and troops along with vehicles. As the occupation progressed so the Germans consolidated their position by bringing further equipment to the islands, including more military vehicles such as light cars and even some captured French tanks, including twelve Char B1s, were moved to Jersey along with five flame-thrower variants of the same vehicle. Jersey also received eleven SPG variants of the R35 tank armed with captured 4.7cm Czechoslovakian guns and at least eight FT-17 tanks that dated back to the First World War. Many civilian vehicles were commandeered and captured stocks of French and British vehicles were also brought to the islands. Neighbouring Guernsey received similar deliveries of weaponry and vehicles.

Many standard German Army vehicles such as the Krupp-built 6x4, 60bhp, air-cooled 'Protze' L2H 143 truck arrived on the islands. It could carry a payload in excess of 1 ton and was also used to tow light anti-aircraft guns, or carry troops or ammunition. The vehicle was fitted with independent coil-spring suspension all round and was originally built as the L2H 43 between 1934 and 1936 with a 55bhp engine. The later L2H 143 was built between 1937 and 1941 and was used as a searchlight truck and communications vehicle. Artillery was the dominant factor in the defence of the islands and, apart from half-tracks as artillery tractors, no heavy vehicles were required in the long term. Light liaison vehicles and motorcycles were very useful on the small islands, which could be traversed in only a few hours along the narrow, winding country lanes. One thing the Germans had to get used to was the fact that the local civilian population drove vehicles, including horse-drawn carts, on the left-hand side, the same as on the British mainland, which led to the inevitable casualties, some fatal, on both sides. In June 1941, after one year of occupation, the Feldkommandantur issued an order that all drivers should drive on the right-hand side of the road. As the occupation progressed and the fuel situation worsened, particularly after the islands were cut off after the Allied landings at Normandy in June 1944, the Germans were the main vehicle users and they had full control of the traffic.

French FT-17 tank deployed on Guernsey by the Germans during the occupation.

Among the light vehicles to be brought over were Stoewer R200s for use in liaison roles during the occupation. These vehicles were produced in four versions and were built by Stoewer between 1936 and 1943. All versions had four-wheel drive and the basic model served through the war and was deployed to all theatres of fighting. The design was configured for four main roles and each was given a 'KfZ' or Kraftfahrzeug title to designate their role as a military motor vehicle. The KfZ1 was a four-seat personnel carrier for liaison duties, the KfZ2 was equipped with radios for signals, the KfZ3 served in the light survey role and the KfZ4 was armed with a light anti-aircraft gun which could also engage ground targets. The Stoewer was but one design in a whole series of vehicles known as *Leichter Einheits Geländegängige* (light standard cross-country vehicles), which were used by the German Army. Weighing only 1.6 tons, the KfZ2 or *Funkkraftwagen* (radio-carrying vehicle) was much lighter than the comparable m E Pkw KfZ15. The vehicle measured 12.6ft long, 5.5ft wide and 6.2ft high with the canvas collapsible roof erected. It was fitted with the Stoewer 2-litre ohv, four-cylinder, water-cooled engine with 1,997cc producing 50hp. The vehicle had a fuel capacity of 13 gallons, which allowed an operational range of more than 300 miles, and it could achieve speeds over 60mph.

Production ended in 1943 and the Volkswagen Type 82 Kubelwagen took over the roles of the vehicle, but those versions of the KfZ2 still in service were used right up until the end of the war. Other vehicle manufacturers such as Hanomag also produced the vehicle, and between 1937 and 1940 BMW built some 3,225 models. In 1940 a version known as the Type 40 was also built by these three manufacturers. This version had front-wheel steering only and was fitted with the Stoewer 2-litre AW2 engine, but that is a different vehicle. It had a ground clearance of only 8in and a turning radius of 39ft, but these features combined with its good operational range made it ideal for service on the small islands. The Kfz2 was fitted with only one door to the right-hand side at the passenger's position. The left-hand side was fitted with two doors and seating was fitted to allow up to two passengers as well as the driver. The radio sets were fitted in the rear of the vehicle with the antenna mounted on the left-hand side at the rear. There was stowage capacity in the boot and tools such as shovels and pick axes were carried for use in an emergency to recover the vehicle if it became bogged down. The windscreen could be folded forward if required or erected to seal the vehicle off from inclement weather with the roof erected also.

The success of the Polish campaign and now the overrunning of Western Europe in ten weeks had strengthened the impression that the German Army wanted to project, which was that it was greatly motorised. The truth of the matter was

The Stoewer could drive the narrow routes of the roads on Jersey and Guernsey to keep in touch with units around the island. The Stoewer R200 radio vehicle was useful for communications throughout the five years of German occupation on Jersey.

Top left: Re-enactor depicting a Luftwaffe officer serving in the infantry role with Panzerfaust anti-tank weapons and a bicycle of the period. Top right: Recreated German infantryman with bicycle of the period armed with Panzerfaust anti-tank launcher. Towards the end of the war Luftwaffe personnel served as infantry. Above: This recreated scene shows re-enactors with Panzerfaust anti-tank weapons and bicycles of the period.

something entirely different. German propaganda neither admitted nor denied the levels of motorisation in the army and left it largely up to their enemies to reach their own conclusions, which were wide of the mark. In September 1939 only sixteen of the German Army's 103 divisions were motorised and even this level had only been reached by limiting the numbers of vehicles in service with other units. Typically an infantry division had around 950 vehicles but almost 5,400 horses, and the logistics to supply this disparity was worthy of First World War figures. The vehicle fleet required 20 tons of fuel each day while the horses needed over 50 tons of fodder to feed them even when not working. In 1938 the German Army had more than 100 different types of truck in service and even in 1939 there was still such a shortage of transportation that 16,000 civilian vehicles were commandeered. After the French Army had surrendered in 1940 the captured vehicles were distributed throughout eighty-eight infantry divisions so that by 1941 they were in service ready to be used in Operation Barbarossa, the German invasion of Russia, in June that year. Another mode of transportation utilised by the military was the humble bicycle. All armies in the war used bicycles, including the Japanese, and in June 1944 images from D-Day show Allied troops going ashore with bicycles. During the course of the war the German Army would use as many as 3 million bicycles, including civilian cycles commandeered for units of the Volkssturm, the home-defence volunteer units.

German Army Communications Vehicles

The German Army realised how important it was to maintain communications at all levels and for that purpose they developed a range of vehicles for this role, such as the SdKfz 260 and SdKfz 261, both termed *Kleine Panzerfunkwagen* (small armoured radio cars), which entered service with the German Army in early 1941 and remained in use throughout the remainder of the war. Both vehicles were 4x4 drive and powered by a front-mounted engine of either a Horch 3.5 litre or 3.8 litre fitted with a gearbox to give five forward and one reverse speed. The vehicles could reach speeds of over 50mph on roads and had an operational range of over 186 miles, which meant that they could serve over a wide-ranging area and keep in contact with armoured units. Being specialist radio vehicles they were operated by four-man crews serving with signals units. Armour protection was very marginal, being between 5mm and 8mm with an open-topped roof that left the crew very vulnerable to even small arms fire when in combat. The armoured body was built up in a method called 'faceting', which meant that the armour plates were set at angles from 30 degrees to 35 degrees to help deflect some light projectiles. The vehicles were unarmed and only the personal weapons of the crew would have been available for self-defence. Each version weighed 4.2 tons and measured 15.8ft long, 6.5ft wide and 5.8ft high to present a very low profile. The two types of vehicles were produced in four series, with production lasting from November 1940 until April 1943, during which time only 493 are believed to have been built. When serving in inclement weather conditions canvas roof covers could be fitted, but these would have afforded little in the way of protection. Indeed, during the cold winter months in regions such as Norway and Russia where the vehicles served the crews must have suffered terrible privations.

Vehicle Name	Type	Communications Equipment	Production Date	Armament	Weight	Max. Speed
SdKfz 260	Small armoured radio car	Funktrupp 'c' comprising Funkgerät 7 and Funksprechtgerät 'a'	1940–43	N/A	4.2 tons	53mph
SdKfz 261	Small armoured radio car	Funktrupp 'd' comprising Funkgerät 12 and Funksprechtgerät 'a'	1940–43	N/A	4.2 tons	53mph

Externally there was little to tell the SdKfz 260 apart from the SdKfz 261 except that the former was fitted with a rod aerial for the medium-range radio equipment, while the latter vehicle featured a collapsible frame aerial for long-range radio equipment. It was the communications carried on board that set the vehicles apart. The SdKfz 260 was fitted with the *Funktrupp* (troop radio) 'c' which comprised *Funkgerät* 7 (radio equipment) and the *Funksprechtgerät* (radio telephone equipment) 'a'. The SdKfz 261 was fitted with the Funktrupp 'd' which comprised the Funkgerät 12 and Funksprechtgerät 'a'. Both vehicles were deployed to serve with signals units attached to the headquarters of regiments, brigades and divisions of armoured units and the armoured radio companies of *Nachrichten* (communications) battalions. The operational life of these vehicles may have been relatively short compared to other similar vehicles but they did deliver an important service wherever they were deployed.

3

AFTER DUNKIRK AND TOWARDS LEND-LEASE

With Western Europe now under German occupation, the rest of the world, especially America, looked on, and Britain appeared to be standing alone. However, these free countries had not reckoned on the unconditional support of the dominion and Commonwealth forces of the British Empire, which meant that manpower was not a problem.

Canada

The burden of producing sufficient vehicles and weapons to equip the armies was a huge obstacle to overcome, but even that problem would be alleviated by countries such as Canada, which declared war on 10 September 1939 and would freely produce thousands of vehicles that supported the Allied war effort.

Canadian Vehicle Production

Vehicle Name	Type	Manufacturer	Production Date	Armament	Weight	Max. Speed
Mk I Fox	Armoured car	General Motors	1942	.50in-calibre and .30in-calibre machine guns	7.5 tons	44mph
Ford F30 truck	Truck	Ford		Used by LRDG and fitted with various machine guns	1.5 tons	
Chevrolet C8A	Heavy utility truck	Chevrolet	1939–41	N/A	0.4 tons	50mph
Otter	Light reconnaissance car	General Motors Canada	1942–45	Bren .303in machine gun and a Mk I Boys anti-tank rifle	4.8 tons	45mph
GM C15TA	Armoured truck	General Motors	1943–44	N/A	4.4 tons	40mph
Ram	Tank	Montreal Locomotive Works	1941–43	2-pounder gun and up to three .30in machine guns	28.6 tons	25mph
Kangaroo	Personnel carrier	Montreal Locomotive Works	1943–44	Either a 50in- or 30in-calibre machine gun plus a 30in machine gun	25 tons	25mph
Badger	Flame-thrower vehicle	Montreal Locomotive Works	1944	Wasp II flame-thrower	25tons	25mph

Military Police units used unarmed versions of the Fox. Gunner's position inside the Fox showing the .50 inch and .30 inch machine guns (top left).

Canada built over 1,500 four-wheeled Mk I Fox armoured cars, based on the British Army's Humber armoured car, at the General Motors production facility. Unfortunately it was not one of the better thought-out designs and it had problems with the steering that meant it was not well liked by the troops. Nevertheless, these vehicles were sent to serve in India, Italy and Britain, and some served in Holland during the closing stages of the war. The Mk I Fox had a crew of four, comprising commander, driver, gunner and radio operator, and was armed with a .50in-calibre machine gun in a fully traversing turret with a .30in-calibre machine

The driver's position of the Canadian Fox showing the standard driving wheel for steering (left). Turret and mid-section (right).

gun mounted co-axially. Fitted with a GMC six-cylinder petrol engine, it had a maximum speed of 44mph and an operational range of 210 miles. The Fox had armour protection to 15mm maximum and was 15ft long, 7ft 7in wide, and 8ft high to the top of the turret; it weighed just over 7.5 tons.

Indeed Canada's war effort is frequently overlooked but its output certainly helped the Allied cause tremendously. For example, the country also produced the Ford F30 truck, which served as the tractor for the Bofors 40mm light anti-aircraft gun, served with the LRDG and was also used as an ambulance. Canada produced some 13,000 Chevrolet C8A heavy utility trucks, which served in the role of ambulance, signal vehicle and troop transport. Another armoured vehicle design that Canada contributed to the Allied war effort was the Otter light reconnaissance car. The country never once shirked its responsibilities and, indeed, by the end of 1942 Canada had some 177,000 men serving overseas in the army. They would go on to participate in some of the hardest-fought actions of the war, including the raid on Dieppe in 1942, and would have the Juno beach assigned to them during the D-Day landings at Normandy in 1944. In fact from June 1944 until May 1945 the Canadian Army sustained some 48,000 casualties, of which over 12,500 were killed.

The heavy manufacturing bases in Canada turned out large numbers of other types of vehicles, including almost 4,000 GM C15TA Armoured Trucks for carrying troops, weapons and tanks, such as 1,400 Valentines, most of which went to Russia, almost 1,900 Ram tanks,

Did You Know?

Canada built more than 50,000 armoured vehicles and some 815,000 other vehicles for the British Army alone. In fact by the end of the war around 38 per cent of Canada's production had been for Britain and included 1.7 million small arms, 43,000 heavy guns, 16,000 aircraft and 2 million tons of explosives.

Canadian-built Chevrolet C8A.

Canadian-built Ford F30 used to tow the Bofors 40mm anti-aircraft gun.

The LRDG used a variety of weapons and vehicles such as this Canadian-built CMP Ford 30 (left) fairly bristling with machine guns. The LRDG used different vehicles for the arduos role of desert war including this CMP Ford F30 (30cwt) LRDG 'Y' Patrol Aramis (right). It is painted pink to blend in with the sandy terrain.

a Canadian design, and over 2,000 Sexton SPGs fitted with 25-pounder guns that were built at the plant in Sorel. On top of these came the production of thousands of other vehicles, including Kangaroo personnel carriers and the Badger flame-thrower vehicle. In addition to this output came aircraft and ships to replace losses and keep the shipping lanes across the Atlantic open to permit these supplies to be transported. One of the lesser known but no less important vehicles produced by the impressive Canadian armaments manufacturers was a vehicle referred to as the 'Car, Light Reconnaissance, Canadian G.M. Mark I Otter I'. Needless to say this was shortened to 'Otter' and was basically built to the same general specification as the British Humber Mk III light reconnaissance car. However, through the judicious use of components produced in Canada, the design resulted in a vehicle markedly differ-ent from the Humber. The engine bonnet was much shorter but higher, which gave the vehicle a more pronounced hull with a distinct hump-like appearance.

Originally it was intended that the Otter be equipped to carry the same armament as the Humber, and provision was made accordingly. But, as it transpired, a deci-sion was taken that the vehicle be armed with an entirely different complement of weapons. The compact turret could fully traverse through 360 degrees and mounted a Bren .303in machine gun, which, with its 500 rounds per minute cyclic rate of fire, gave all-round defence. Mounted in the hull front next to the driver was a Mk I

GM C15TA Armoured Truck, crew seats and driver's position.

Boys anti-tank rifle, which had restricted traversing capabilities. This weapon was operated using a bolt action to fire ammunition of .55in calibre from a five-round box magazine. It could penetrate 20mm of armour at 0 degrees impact at a range of 550yd. This weapon had been withdrawn from front-line units in 1941 because of its inadequacies against tanks with thick armour. In the case of the Otter, however, which was to operate in a mainly reconnaissance role, it was believed that the Boys anti-tank rifle would be sufficient for this purpose. After all, reconnaissance vehicles were not supposed to enter combat with anything larger than themselves, because they were only meant to be covertly observing developments of enemy movements from a distance. In fact, the Boys would have been capable of destroying light vehicles if the firer hit the engine with steel-cored bullets. Similarly, it could have been used against parked aircraft, which would have been rendered unserviceable if the engine took a hit. In some versions of the Otter, the Boys anti-tank weapon was replaced with a No. 19 radio to give improved communications for liaison and information purposes.

The Otter was fitted with a six-cylinder General Motors engine that developed 104bhp and a maximum road speed of 45mph. The three-man crew comprised the driver, commander and gunner, who also operated the radio. Access to the vehicle was through large doors set on the right-hand side by the driver's position and another on the left side for the gunner. It was adequately protected for its intended role with armour protection varying between 6mm and 12mm, which made it comparable to other vehicles operating in similar roles, such as the British Humber armoured car.

Not everybody was satisfied with the Otter, however, and some were quite disparaging in their overall assessment. One of the main areas of concern lay in the fact that the weight of the Otter was greater in relation to, say, the Humber light reconnaissance car, by being more than 1 ton heavier. Another fact that was pointed to was that the Otter lacked an auxiliary gearbox, leading critics to believe that its survival on the battlefield would be severely compromised. However, despite these elements of doubt the Otter went on to provide great service. In the grand scheme of things the wartime production of the Otter was not very large (only some 1,761 vehicles), but that does not detract from its importance. Each vehicle had to be shipped across the Atlantic in convoys of transports in order that they could be deployed to all those theatres of war where Canadian forces served. Some were operated by units of the British Army, which was not an inconsiderable achievement for a vehicle produced in so few numbers and about which some had their doubts.

Although there were no variants of the Otter developed, it was flexible enough to be modified either before deployment to the battlefield or when actually in the field. The Royal Air Force regiment also realised the usefulness of the Otter and employed a limited number for conducting patrols and assisting in airfield defence by patrolling the perimeter. The RAF converted some vehicles for these roles by fitting them with a different armament to what they were normally equipped with. The Boys anti-tank rifle was replaced with a 20mm cannon in the front of the hull. The Bren gun in the turret was replaced with twin Browning machine guns. The overall result was to improve the firepower of the Otter greatly, in keeping with the heightened importance of the role in which they were operating.

Australia

Vehicle Name	Type	Manufacturer	Production Date	Armament	Weight	Max. Speed
Sentinel	Tank	New South Wales Government Railways	1942	2-pounder gun and 2x .303in machine guns	28 tons	30mph

The Sentinel was developed for home defence after Australia was bombed by the Japanese Air Force (left). The Sentinel tank as developed by Austrlia in response to Japanese attacks (right).

Australia too showed how much it could do to help the Allied war effort by building around 5,600 Bren gun carriers and even went further by producing a locally developed tank called the 'Sentinel' which was used mainly for home defence. Although Australia as a country was isolated from heavy front-line action during the Second World War, when the Japanese bombed the port of Darwin on 19 February 1942 there was a very serious fear of further attacks and a possible invasion by Japanese troops seemed imminent. Indeed, Prime Minister John Curtain declared that 'Australia is facing the gravest hour in her history' and home-based troops were placed on alert. Australian troops had been fighting overseas in the Allied cause since the beginning of the war and had committed many fighting men to the Middle East. During the Second World War, Australia, like Canada, undertook to support the Allied cause by building extra numbers of much-needed vehicles, the designs of which had been developed in other countries. This helped ease the burden on Britain, which was trying to keep pace with losses incurred in battle. Australia built some 700 tracked AFVs based on British designs, for example. This may only seem like a small contribution in the grand scheme of things, but every little bit helped. Australia actually went even further and produced one locally designed tank, thereby proving the old adage that necessity is the mother of invention, and at the time the country's back was firmly against the wall.

Other Commonwealth Countries

Even remote New Zealand built 520 Bren gun carriers, all of which went towards helping Britain's war effort. Other Commonwealth countries such as South Africa also produced 2,694 Daimler armoured cars and 3,630 Marmon-Herrington armoured cars, and India produced a vehicle range known as Armoured Carrier, Wheeled, I.P. Mk II and another version called the AOV, building around 4,655 of these vehicles between 1940 and 1945. These vehicles from a country not used to producing such specialised equipment would be used in various theatres of war

Bedford MW truck could carry supplies or troops and the canvas cover gave some protection in bad weather. Bedford MW truck in 1st Armoured Division colour for North African campaign (top right) and in colours of 3rd Infantry Division (above).

but were especially useful in the Far East. On its own Britain produced 1,399 tanks during 1940 and many thousands of trucks and motorcycles. Indeed at one motor vehicle factory, Luton-based Vauxhall, a total of some 66,000 Bedford MW 15cwt (.75 ton) were built between 1939 and 1945. These trucks were fitted with 3.5-litre six-cylinder petrol engines to give a top road speed of 45mph with a fuel consumption of around 10–12 miles per gallon. The vehicles were used by all branches of Britain's armed forces but they were inadequately protected against the elements and early designs were known as 'pneumonia wagons' by the drivers because they were so cold. In 1940 Germany built 1,460 tanks, a number greater than Britain's effort by only a narrow margin. It also continued to produce trucks and motorcycles. Also, while Britain had its Commonwealth to add to its output, Germany had the factories in the occupied countries such as France that could build AFVs, trucks and motorcycles. There was also the captured stock of equipment including weapons and vehicles that would be pressed into service in various roles.

French Production under Occupation

Pre-war output of trucks in France had actually halved between 1930 and 1938, and these designs were based on civilian models. In 1936 the French defence minister, Edouard Daldier, ordered a rearmament programme calling for 3,200 modern tanks and 5,000 other tracked vehicles at a cost of 14 million francs and, although France had one of the most powerful armies in Europe, it still found itself going to war equipped with ageing vehicles such as FT-17 tanks and Berliet CBA trucks, which were both of First World War vintage. The main truck production companies of Renault, Citroën and Panhard, and others such as Berliet, produced vehicles that could carry troops and equipment but these were still essentially based on civilian models. When France surrendered the German Army used these factories to build trucks for itself. Louis Renault employed his workforce in this role and earned a reputation for being a collaborator. When the country was liberated in 1944 he was arrested by his countrymen, charged with collaboration and held in Fresne prison where he died under very suspicious circumstances. The company Peugeot built over 48,800 trucks and Citroën produced more than 15,000 trucks for the German Army, while the company of Latil built 4x4 heavy tractors, which were used during the Russian campaign. Citroën also built half-track vehicles such as the Unic Type P107 which could serve as artillery tractors, but pre-war strikes meant that only 3,276 were in service when war broke out. When the factory was captured some of the vehicles being produced were designed to permit them to carry light anti-aircraft guns but closer inspection revealed the mountings were suited to weapons used by the German Army rather than the Swiss-designed Oerlikon guns, which were in general service with the French Army at the time.

British Home Front Preparations and the Battle of Britain

Of course all that support for Britain lay in the future and would come over a period of time. In the meantime, all the vehicles and heavy weapons the British Army had lost at Dunkirk had to be replaced, especially artillery. At the same time the British Army had to be ready to defend the country against a very real threat of invasion. Replacing so much war materiel would take time and it was a slow process. In October 1939 an official call had been put out by the British government calling for volunteers to serve in a unit called the Local Defence Volunteers (LDV) who would guard vital points such as bridges and power stations in case of enemy sabotage. Former soldiers and retirees stepped forward and soon there were 250,000 men in the LDV which quickly earned itself the disparaging nickname of 'Look, Duck and Vanish' by comedians of the day. After the withdrawal from Dunkirk the LDV was renamed in July and became known as the Home Guard. The Home Guard would go on to increase in size to around 1.5 million men. There were river patrols in small boats, sections mounted on horseback and units all across the country, even in unlikely places such as the Bank of England and the House of Commons. They were armed with a range of standard weapons including rifles and machine guns, but also with some less conventional weaponry including devices such as the Northover Projector and Blacker Bombard, which were developed specifically for use by the Home Guard. Men in these units sometimes used their own vehicles but a range unique to Home Guard units were created called 'Beaverettes' after Lord Beaverbrook, the Minister of Aircraft Production who later became the Minister of Supply. These were often no more than commercial vehicles to which boiler plates had been welded and different designs were to be found all across the country. An estimated 2,800 Beaverettes were eventually built, mostly based on the standard 14hp chassis and there was also the 'Humberette' based on the Humber 'Super Snipe' commercial vehicle. Their usefulness in actual battle would have been questionable but for patrolling purposes they did show what could be produced in an emergency. An example of one of these vehicles is on display at the Cobbaton Combat Collection in North Devon. This is a restored example of a 1941 Mk III Standard Beaverette, weighing just over 2 tons and is based on a Flying Fourteen saloon car chassis and equipped with a Lewis machine gun in a rudimentary turret.

The country now readied itself for the invasion that must surely come given the successes of the German armed forces. All doubts of invasion were cast aside and defences were hurriedly erected and minefields laid at likely landing places on the coast. In some places obsolete tanks from the First World War were dragged into positions where they could be used as barricades on the roads. The recently formed Local Defence Volunteers may have been willing but they were far from ready and able, as they lacked any real armament. The defeated British Army was still regrouping and needed to be re-equipped. German plans for the invasion of England were code-named Sea Lion and involved an attacking force of 260,000 men that included a combined airborne and amphibious assault, supported by 62,000 horses and 34,000 vehicles. To make it happen the Germans needed mastery of the air and control of the sea lanes. The date for the invasion was set for 15 August. On that day aircraft of the Luftwaffe flew their first missions with the intention of destroying the Royal Air Force. This was the beginning of what is known as the Battle of Britain. As the fighting between the two great air forces continued throughout September and into October it became apparent to the Germans that they were not winning and they changed tactics to bomb Britain's cities in the assault known as the Blitz. The Royal Navy was still intact and controlled the waters around Britain and this, in addition to winter gales, reduced the threat of invasion. Germany was being held at bay but Hitler had moved his attention eastwards and was making plans to attack Russia. Britain's cities, in the meantime, were being bombed but the factories could produce tanks and lorries for the army and weapons to arm the infantry.

War with Italy in North Africa

When Mussolini declared war on Britain in 1940 the Italians had 300,000 troops in Libya supported by 1,811 pieces of artillery, 339 tanks, such as the dreadful M11/39 (which would later be replaced by the slightly improved M13/40), along with 8,039 trucks for transport and air cover provided by 151 aircraft. On paper it looked impressive enough and in Ethiopia, which Italy had seized in 1935, the Duke of Aosta as the commander-in-chief of the Africa Orientale Italiana (Italian Army in East Africa) had a force of 88,000 Italian troops with 200,000 colonial troops. Again, the force seemed impressive on paper but Aosta believed he could be expected to fight for six to seven months in the event of war. He was to be proved correct in his estimation when he surrendered four months after the British invaded Ethiopia in January 1941 and succeeded in destroying several major supply dumps of fuel and ammunition. In 1940 the Italian Army had 2 million men organised into seventy-three divisions, including three armoured divisions and two motorised divisions.

Italy's Motorised force in 1940

Vehicle Name	Type	Manufacturer	Production Date	Armament	Weight	Max. Speed
M11/39	Tank	FIAT-Ansaldo	1939	37mm gun and 2x machine guns	11 tons	20mph
M13/40	Tank	FIAT-Ansaldo	1940–41	47mm gun and 3x machine guns	14 tons	20mph
M14/41	Tank	FIAT	1941–42	47mm gun and 2x machine guns	13.8 tons	22mph

Britain had been forced to withdraw from mainland Europe but here in North Africa was the opportunity to keep in contact with the enemy. General Sir Archibald Wavell was commander-in-chief in the Middle East with a mere 30,000 troops in Egypt and more spread out across the region to protect the area that was vital to Britain for oil and to secure the Suez Canal, through which convoys could pass to transport supplies. The odds did not look favourable for the British forces, equipped as they were with Vickers light tanks which were obsolete. There had been clashes between the British and Italians during which it had already been demonstrated that machine-gun fire from British armoured cars and light tanks could penetrate the light armour of the Italian vehicles. The Italian commander Marshal Rodolfo Graziani, who had taken over when Italo Balbo, the commander-in-chief of the Africa Settentrionale Italian, ASI (Italian North Africa), was killed when his plane was shot down in June 1940,

Italian Vehicle Production

Italy's tank force at the time of declaring war comprised 1,000 light tanks mainly based on out-of-date designs and locked in with the infantry. Tank production would continue and numbers built up slowly with the development of designs such as the M14/41 light tank but Italy would never reach the same scale of output as its German ally. For example, by the second half of 1942 Italy had only produced 700 tanks, a figure that was less than half of its output of 1941. By the time Italy declared war its army already had five years of experience in fighting but it was still poorly prepared. Italy was famous for its pre-war sports cars and luxury motor vehicle models, but producing such items was a world away from building quantitative numbers of reliable lorries for the army. Motorcycles such as Moto Guzzi machines and even a tricycle design were built for liaison roles and light transportation, along with half-track tractors for towing artillery. Modern machines were produced for the army but there still remained old-fashioned types among the main designs and some vehicles fitted with solid tyres were not uncommon along with those fitted with pneumatic tyres.

This Moto Guzzi tricycle design was used to transport light loads such as medical supplies over short distances.

Italian Army Moto Guzzi motorcycles were used in North Africa and Italy for liaison roles and dispatch riders.

was ordered by Mussolini not to delay any further and attack, which he did on 13 September. Using a combination of motorcycles, lorries and horses to accompany the armoured units, the Italians advanced for four days covering a distance of 60 miles into Egypt and then, quite incredibly and for no logical reason, stopped to 'dig in' and prepare defensive positions around Sidi Barrani. By that time Wavell had received much-needed reinforcements including 154 tanks, forty-eight anti-tank guns, forty-eight 25-pounder field guns and twenty light anti-aircraft guns, but this was a token, and the question was when would more be coming? The answer was known in London, but it would take time and that was something of which there was precious little if a disaster was to be avoided.

Recreated Australian troops standing by a Valentine tank depicting Tobruk.

Nevertheless, Major General Richard O'Connor, commanding the Western Desert Force, ordered British patrols to be sent out, and these units were able to locate gaps in the Italian defences, leading to Operation Compass being planned. The operation involved Vickers light tanks and fifty Matilda Mk II tanks supporting the 4th Indian Division while the 7th Armoured Division moved round to a blocking position. On 9 December an artillery barrage opened the attack and Matilda tanks of the 7th Armoured Division destroyed twenty-five Italian tanks before moving their attention to the artillery. So complete was the surprise that the British took 38,300 Italians prisoner in only four days, by which time the older Vickers light tanks were almost worn out after continuous action. The momentum of the operation was maintained by the capture of supplies and 700 vehicles at Bardia, which provided transportation. Sensing a great victory, O'Connor pressed on and, using stocks of captured enemy food and fuel as improvised supplies, he was able to press forward. In two months the British had advanced 500 miles, capturing or destroying almost 400 tanks and 1,290 pieces of artillery, and taking 130,000 prisoners. In early February 1941 the Italians were pulling back. They launched an attack supported by armour but it was broken up with the loss of eighty tanks and a second attack similarly cost them another thirty tanks.

Before these operations started, events on the on the other side of the Mediterranean Sea would have an effect on the situation in Libya as the Italians opened up another theatre of operations when Mussolini ordered the attack of Greece with a force of 160,000 men on 28 October. They were badly mauled for their efforts by the Greek Army, which had only a limited number of vehicles at its disposal and was weak in anti-tank guns. The sub-zero temperatures caused further suffering among the Italians, who were finally pushed back by the Greek Army in November. The Germans moved in to support their Italian allies and attacked Greece, which caused the British to pull troops and an armoured force of fifty-two medium tanks out of North Africa to support Greece. General O'Connor believed that he could finish the campaign in Libya and Britain could then deal with the situation in Greece, but they could not deal with both situations at the same time. In the end the result was a disaster in Greece along with the fall of Crete.

In their weakened state, the British forces that had advanced into Libya from Egypt now looked more vulnerable than ever before. With Italian forces to the south-east in Abyssinia and the news that German assistance would shortly begin to arrive in Libya to the west, this meant that the British would be faced with the possibility of having to fight on two fronts. Bolstered with reinforcements in men, tanks and equipment, the Italians prepared to return to the offensive. The German officer chosen to command the specially created Deutsches Afrika Korps (DAK) was Erwin Rommel, who had proven himself during the campaign in France. He was an officer who got things done and the Allies knew he would not waste time. General Johann von Ravenstein, who would command the 21st Panzer Division and serve as Rommel's second-in-command, said of the desert that it was 'a tactician's paradise and a quartermaster's hell'. Sparsely populated, there would be no repeat of the high numbers of civilian casualties or lines of refugees clogging the roads in the way as there had been in the fighting in Europe, and armies would be able to manoeuvre great distances. As a theatre of operations it was a remote, hostile, harsh terrain where one mistake could cost a man his life and frequently did. Everything needed for both sides to continue the war had to be transported by sea to the region through the ports of coastal towns such as Tobruk and Mersa Matruh. The only way to achieve this was in convoys sailing across the Mediterranean Sea. For the Germans and Italians it appeared to be a simple matter of sailing from ports in Italy and southern France. For the British, their convoys had to sail the length of the Mediterranean, being attacked by aircraft all the way. The island of Malta offered some shelter but it too was soon under aerial attack. The Allies holding Tobruk during the German siege in 1941 would later come to consider a cargo ship with 5,000 tons of supplies to be worth the equivalent of twelve convoys.

The Italians in Ethiopia and Somalia may have appeared numerically strong but were weak in weapons, tanks and other vehicles, and much of their equipment was obsolete. Major General William Platt attacked from the north on 19 January 1941. Fighting was fierce and conditions were dreadful, with men reduced to 1 pint of water per day. Drinking water was also a problem, and clean, fresh supplies had to be brought to the troops in addition to food supplies. At the harbour of Sollum (sometimes written as either Salum or Sallum) in Egypt the Royal Navy landed almost 1.5 million gallons of drinking water from a convoy on one occasion. On 11 February General Alan Cunningham launched an attack from the south into Italian Somaliland. Colonial troops serving with the Italians began to desert. The first German troops began arriving in Tripoli on 12 February 1941, with Rommel arriving two days later and immediately setting about planning operations. Aware of these developments, the British nevertheless maintained the pressure from the north and south, determined to end the Italians; the fighting continued into March with conditions deteriorating all the while. On 27 March the British attacked with Matilda tanks from the Royal Tank Regiment supported by infantry in Bren gun carriers as the last of the Italian resistance was crumbling. By 6 April the British were in Addis Ababa, the Ethiopian capital, and after eight weeks, during which time Cunningham's men had covered 1,700 miles, the Italians surrendered. With the south-east now secure and the threat to the Suez Canal removed from the southern end of the Red Sea, the British could turn all their attention to the greater threat posed by the Germans and Italians in Libya. Tanks may have played a relatively small part in the campaign but their presence had been significant in bringing about the end of Italian aspirations of an empire in Africa.

Troop ship sailing through Suez Canal which had to be protected.

The Beginnings of Lend-Lease

In the eyes of the rest of the world Britain appeared to be standing alone, but actually the country was not forgotten. In America, President Roosevelt declared that the country must become the 'great arsenal of democracy' and to that end America began to mobilise its economy in May 1940, just as Operation Dynamo was unfolding in France. The first move America made to supply Britain was to

Armed with a 37mm gun and machine guns, the M3 Honey was a modern tank for the British Army in 1941. The M3 Honey light tank was used in the North African campaign by the British Army before America entered the war.

exchange fifty destroyers of First World War vintage for naval bases in the Atlantic. It may not have been much of a deal, indeed some saw it as an opportunity for America to rid itself of obsolete vessels, but at least it was something. Churchill was calling for America to sell Britain weapons and vehicles, but American newspapers carried features that called for the president to keep the country out of the war. Roosevelt responded by vowing to keep the US out of any war in Europe, which satiated the voting public who did not wish to enter such a war either. Behind the scenes, even as the last engagements of Operation Dynamo were being fought, British agents were already busy making arrangements to buy numbers of the M3 Lee-Grant medium tank. This was equipped with a 37mm gun in a fully traversing turret, but had a more powerful 75mm gun mounted in a side sponson. It was an unusual layout because at the time armaments manufacturers in America could not build a turret to take the powerful 75mm gun. The M3 was protected by armour up to 80mm thick, had a crew of six and was capable of speeds of up to 25mph. The negotiations secured a quantity of M3 tanks for the British Army but the first batches would not arrive in North Africa in early 1942. Other tank designs such as the M3 Honey light tank with its 37mm main armament would enter the North African theatre of operations sooner (the first would arrive in November 1941), but again all the final arrangements had to be made before deliveries could be organised.

The M3 Light Tank

The Development of the M3 Light Tank

Vehicle Name	Type	Manufacturer	Production Date	Armament	Weight	Max. Speed
M2A1	Light tank	Rock Island Arsenal	1935	37mm gun and 4x .30in machine guns	8.8 tons	45mph
M2A2	Light tank	Rock Island Arsenal	1935	37mm gun and 3x .50in machine guns	8.5 tons	30mph
M2A3	Light tank	Rock Island Arsenal	1938	37mm gun, 30in machine gun and 2x .50in machine guns	9 tons	40mph
M2A4	Light tank	Rock Island Arsenal	1940	37mm gun and 4x .50in machine guns	10.3 tons	35mph
M3	Light tank	American Car and Foundry Company	1940	37mm gun and 3x M1919A1 .30in machine gun	12.2 tons	36mph
M3A1	Light tank	American Car and Foundry Company	1941	37mm gun and M1919A1 .30in machine gun	12.7 tons	36mph
M3A2	Light tank	American Car and Foundry Company	Never Built	N/A	N/A	N/A
M3A3	Light tank	American Car and Foundry Company	1942	37mm gun, M1919A1 .30in machine gun, and a .30in machine gun	14.2 tons	36mph
M3A1E1	Light tank	American Car and Foundry Company	1943	37mm gun and 3x .30in machine guns	12.7 tons	36mph

The M3 light tank was one of the most widely used light tanks to serve with the British Army during the Second World War and was known as the 'Honey' by the armoured regiments that used it in the North African campaign. This particular armoured vehicle, which would eventually be built in three variants, began development in 1935 when it was known as the M2A1. The basic design featured a 37mm gun as the main armament and mounted in a turret capable of traversing a full 360 degrees, but the project passed through a series of variants that were intended to improved armour protection. Finally, in 1939, the series culminated in the M2A4 vehicle, a design of riveted armour-plate construction and weighing approximately 12 tons. Further changes were made to the design but by July 1940, the tank, by now designated the M3, was accepted as the standard light tank for the US Army.

At the time of the M3's acceptance into service, Britain was the only country actively fighting Germany and its ally Italy. The armed forces of Britain were stretched almost to breaking point as they set about recovering from the debacle of the retreat through Dunkirk in 1940, and troops, equipment and vehicles were all in desperately short supply. Finally in March 1941, Britain was provided overseas aid by America under the Lend-Lease Act, which permitted Britain to purchase 'war material', thus providing British forces with supplies of tanks and other essential supplies with which it could make good its losses.

Under the Lend-Lease Act all the M3 light tanks produced in the initial output were all scheduled for Britain, where they were destined for deployment to North Africa. Among the first units to receive the M3 light tanks were the 8th King's Royal Irish Hussars, closely followed by the 3rd and 5th Royal Tank Regiments of the 4th Armoured Brigade of the 7th Armoured Division. About eighty-four M3 light tanks were sent in this first batch in July 1941, almost one year to the day when they were accepted as standard for the US Army. This initial batch of M3 tanks was committed to battle for the first time in November 1941 at Babr Saleh as part of the Operation Crusader offensive.

The basic M3 light tank was built by the American Car and Foundry Company, which by August 1942 (by which time America was involved in the war and preparing for the invasion of North Africa) had produced more than 5,800 vehicles. By October 1943 the company had built over 13,800 M3 light tanks, but the design was declared obsolete only three months earlier. However, with such numbers in service it would not be withdrawn from the front line because to do so would leave units without any armour at all. Instead, the tank continued in service and was phased out gradually as replacement types became available. The M3 light tank was fitted with a Continental W-670 seven-cylinder, air-cooled, radial petrol engine, which developed 250hp at 2,400rpm, producing a road speed of 36mph and a cross-country speed of 20mph. The engine for the M3 had originally been fitted to the M2A4 and in 1941 it was in short supply, which led to some 500 M3s being fitted with Guiberson T-1020 diesel engines. The M3 had a combat range of around 70 miles on roads, but this could be extended by fitting two extra fuel tanks externally; these could be dropped for safety or for tactical reasons when the vehicle was entering combat. This feature came about from lessons learned during the North African battles.

The M3A1 was standardised in August 1941 but a number of new design features were introduced from the basic model. Firstly, the turret was made from homogeneous armour and also incorporated a power traverse for the turret and a turret basket. A gyro-stabiliser to allow the 37mm gun to be fired more accurately while the tank was moving was also fitted. The M3A2 version was to have been an all-welded design but in the event it was never built. The basic M3 design was 14.8ft long, 7.3ft wide and 8.2ft high. It had a combat weight of 12.2 tons and armour varying from 10mm to 44.5mm. For its size the M3 was quite remarkable, being able to ford water obstacles up to 3ft deep, cross 6ft-wide trenches, negotiate gradients of 60 per cent and scale vertical obstacles up to 2ft high. A crew of four served all versions in the M3 range. In all types the main armament was a 37mm gun in a fully traversing turret, with a co-axially mounted M1919A1 .30in-calibre machine gun. On the M3A3 version sponsons fitted to either side of the hull featured a further .30in-calibre machine gun. This made the M3 a virtual mobile gun emplacement, capable of providing fire support to infantry units.

With the British Army the M3 served to augment tank strength during the early battles in the North African theatre and it went on to serve in all theatres of the war including the Pacific, where the Americans used it to good effect against the poorly equipped and armoured Japanese tanks and also in destroying well-emplaced bunkers. Despite being thinly armoured and the lack of a heavy punch provided by the 37mm gun, the M3 was a well-liked tank, especially in the reconnaissance roles. Several series of trials to improve the automotive design of the M3 were conducted and the M3A3, which featured a number of these improvements, led to over 3,400 of this type alone being produced. A later experiment into producing an M3 with an all-welded turret and hull to replace riveting created the M3A1E1. While this never went into series production in its own right, the knowledge gained from the venture led to the M5 light tank being produced. For a tank that was declared obsolete halfway through the war the M3 'Honey' certainly did itself proud by being involved with some of the heaviest fighting and most memorable moments of the war, including the liberation of Paris and Antwerp.

The Lend-Lease Act

As the fighting in North Africa developed, American political figures such as the Republican Wendell Willkie took up the call to keep their country neutral. The pioneer aviator Charles Lindbergh, who had flown a solo transatlantic passage in May 1927, was a very public figure who also spoke out against America entering the war, but both Willkie and Lindbergh would come to change their minds about American involvement in the war after the Japanese attack on Pearl Harbor on 7 December 1941. Nevertheless, President Roosevelt continued to press to be allowed to supply Britain with more goods, arguing that lending equipment to any nation 'whose defense the President deems vital to the defense of the United States' was justified. Finally, in March 1941, the Lend-Lease Act was passed and America could openly provide materials to support Britain's war effort. Special freighters known as Liberty ships were built to transport the war materiel to Britain. These ships were prefabricated and in 1942 some 646 such vessels were built to move supplies to Britain. This meant vehicles, tanks, guns and ammunition, along with medical supplies and foodstuffs, ready for the build-up to defeating Germany. During the war Britain would receive about 25 per cent of its overseas aid from America alone, a debt worth some US$7 billion that would not be paid off until 2006, by which time it had been adjusted to be worth some US$30 billion. Britain was not the only one of the Allied countries to receive Lend-Lease support. China, which had been at war with Japan since 1937, received US$1.6 billion in aid; France received US$3.23 billion; and Russia received US$11 billion with oil, tanks, aircraft and vehicles. America supplied tanks, artillery and aircraft in vast numbers to Britain under the Lend-Lease agreement and to Russia after 1941. At the time, the strength of the US Army stood at around 1.4 million men with an armoured force of around 300 light tanks. By 1945 the US Army would have around 8 million men under arms, and the factories would have built many thousands of trucks and tanks for these troops and overseas Allied armies.

In the period 1939–40, for example, America produced 325 light tanks and only six medium tanks, and purchased 46,000 vehicles for the military. It would not produce its first heavy tank until 1942, but by the end of the war American factories had built more than 88,400 tanks. In addition, more than 41,000 other tracked vehicles were produced and 3,200,436 trucks and other wheeled vehicles were built. In the same period Germany would produce less than 28,000 tanks of all types. Germany could never hope to meet the output figures of American factories, even when those factories producing vehicles in occupied countries were taken into account, as evidenced by the numbers of RSO half-tracks built between 1942 and 1945, which amounted to 27,000 vehicles. The figures also show that the numbers of other vehicles entering service with the US Army also increased dramatically, and in June 1942 it took delivery of more than 62,200 vehicles for that one month alone. The strength of the combined US Army Air Forces would reach a peak of 2,411,294 servicemen and women, and between July 1940 and August 1945 it accepted into service more than 229,000 aircraft of all types, such was the capability of the nation. By comparison, between 1939 and 1945 the German output for aircraft of all types was less than 100,000 machines.

4

1941: A TURNING POINT

As the year 1940 ended, Britain still stood on its own but it had taken in large numbers of troops from countries now under German occupation, including Polish, French, Czechoslovakian and Dutch troops who had escaped and made their way to Britain. Some of these men volunteered for new units that were being raised, such as the commandoes and the parachute regiment. Mainland Europe was a no-go area in terms of any type of campaign and the only way of engaging the Germans was through nuisance raids to gain information and prisoners. The first commando raid was undertaken on the night of 23/24 June 1940 by No. 11 Independent Company, which sent a party to pick up information from the Boulogne and Le Touquet part of the French coast. Between July and September the same year, several further raids had been mounted, which included the island of Guernsey in the Channel Islands. It was only at sea with the Royal Navy or with Bomber Command that Britain could hit back at Germany. The German pocket battleship *Admiral Graf Spee* had been sunk in December 1939 and the Royal Air Force had bombed Berlin in late August 1940. Further air attacks against targets in Germany continued and it was only in North Africa that Britain could continue the fight in direct contact with the enemy. After the rout of the Italians from Somalia and Ethiopia in late April 1941 the position left a stand-off or stalemate in the west of Egypt as the British Army turned westwards to face the combined build-up of Italo-German forces. It was only a question of time before a campaign was launched.

Most British tanks at the time, such as the Matilda Mk II and the cruiser types, mounted a main armament comprising a 2-pounder gun, which the crews were reliably informed was the best weapon there was. As they would later discover, the weapon was useless against German tanks and it was only when the Valentine with its 6-pounder gun arrived that any parity was achieved. Rommel's forces included the 5th Light Division (later to become the 21st Panzer Division), which arrived two days before he landed and was followed by the 15th Panzer Division, which arrived in April. His tanks were mostly Mk II and Mk III Panzers armed with 2cm and 5cm guns respectively along with machine guns. He had other armoured vehicles and some older designs, and the Italian tanks were barely adequate, being lightly armed and armoured. The Italian M13/40 was armed with a 47mm gun and protected by 40mm of armour, but its speed of only 20mph and operational range of 125 miles limited its capabilities. By comparison the British Cruiser may have been armed with only a 40mm gun and protected by 40mm of armour but it could reach speeds of up to 27mph and had an operational range of 200 miles. Also, with 110 rounds of ammunition carried for the main gun and 4,500 rounds of ammunition for the two machine guns, the Cruiser could fight on for a lot longer than most Italian tanks. The Panzer III tanks were a different matter altogether but they had a limited operational range, and the Panzer II design suffered from a lack of hitting power. Deliveries of vehicles, whatever their vintage, continued to arrive to bolster the Germans in men and equipment and they built up their strength.

The nominal commander of the Axis forces was General Italo Gariboldi, the Italian commander-in-chief in North Africa, but Rommel had complete operational command and was answerable only to the German High Command in Berlin. The Italians had had a presence in Africa since sending troops into Libya in 1934 and following the invasion of Ethiopia in October 1935. The British Army had maintained garrisons in the region since the end of the First World War. This made the Germans the newcomers to desert warfare, but Rommel and his troops were fast learners and they quickly developed the skills necessary to operate in the harsh conditions. The Deutsch Afrika Korps (DAK) had been raised especially for the campaign and, together with the Italians, would be termed the Deutsch-Italienische Panzerarmee. It has been opined that the campaign in North Africa was really nothing more than a 'sideshow' for Hitler, who already had his mind on attacking Soviet Russia. As a result the Afrika Korps would always find itself short of supplies, replacement vehicles and tanks. In October 1940 Major General Wilhelm Ritter von Thoma told Hitler that in any future war involving German troops in the North African theatre, the 'overriding consideration' in his opinion would be one of logistics. Consequently they learned how to maintain their vehicles properly and kept them operational; their engineers had an enviable rate of recovering tanks from the battlefield. British veterans have often remarked how when the fighting stopped after a battle the Germans always remained on the battlefield to salvage what they could. For example, after Operation Battleaxe, the failed British attempt to relieve Tobruk in June 1941, the Germans recovered eighty-eight of the 100 tanks knocked out in the fighting. These would be cannibalised to repair other tanks or repaired and returned to the battle. The Germans also had transporter vehicles that brought the tanks forward, thereby saving wear and tear on the tracks.

By contrast the British had few transporters, which meant that their tanks had to move forward to the battle area on their tracks and then fight. The British had naval domination in the Mediterranean and air superiority with aircraft operating out of Malta, and the two forces could attack the German and Italian supply convoys between them. Such was the intensity of these attacks that only one vessel in four arrived with fuel and supplies. On average the Afrika Korps would receive some 47 per cent of the supplies and equipment that were sent. The remaining 53 per cent were sunk and in November 1941, for example, only 30,000 tons of an expected 70,000 tons of fuel and ammunition arrived. This severely limited the operational capability of Rommel's tanks. If not with total impunity, the British could certainly send their convoys with a good chance of getting through due to both naval escorts and good air cover. The Italians told Hitler that convoys sailing across the Mediterranean had to be suspended because: 'the British [RAF and Royal Navy] on Malta are slaughtering us!' Malta had to be supplied with fuel if air and naval operations were to continue and the Italian and German air forces bombed the island relentlessly.

Operation Pedestal

In August 1942, arguably the most famous convoy of the war arrived in Malta with much-needed supplies of fuel for the aircraft to continue the defence of the island. Operation Pedestal set out with a convoy of fourteen merchant ships escorted by destroyers and aircraft carriers on 2 August and eight days later passed the Strait of Gibraltar where it ran the gauntlet of the voyage to Malta. On 13 August three merchantmen arrived at the island but the fuel tanker *Ohio* was not with them. Two days later the battered *Ohio* entered the Grand Harbour at Valletta lashed between two destroyers. Five merchantmen arrived including the *Ohio*, which delivered 11,500 tons of fuel and oil. This allowed Malta to continue to be used as a base from where Rommel's convoys could be attacked. It has been estimated that 100,000 tons of shipping supplying the Afrika Korps was sunk in September 1942, including 24,000 tons of fuel, as a result of the *Ohio* delivering its cargo. In turn the losses meant that the Germans and Italians would be operationally restricted during the Second Battle of El Alamein which began on 23 October 1942.

The British Army was also learning lessons and began a programme of developing vehicles to serve in specialist roles on the battlefield. They also modified tanks to cope with the extreme conditions of desert warfare, such as a batch of 161 tanks that they received. These were the first in a series of specialised vehicles that would later lead to further developments for other theatres of operations.

Initially the British Army lacked the means to recover tanks in the desert and the engineers in the specialist support regiments such as the REME and Royal Army Ordnance Corps (RAOC) completed 'in-field' modifications by fitting winches and cranes to trucks. Things would continue to improve so that by the Second Battle of El Alamein, 23 October to 4 November 1942, more than 1,000 tanks and other AFVs belonging to X Corps were repaired in workshops and returned to battle during a three-week period. When the Lend-Lease Act was ratified in March 1941, specialised heavy 10-ton rated recovery trucks began to arrive from America to supplement the lighter 3-ton lorries that formed the backbone of the British Army's transport fleet. The heavier vehicles were produced by companies experienced in the manufacture of heavy-duty lorries for use on massive projects such as the construction of dams in America. These vehicles were also suitable for use in the desert with their four-wheel drive capability. In earlier wars food for troops and forage for the horses had formed the bulk of supplies being transported. Here in the desert and in other theatres this level would fall to an average of 10 per cent – petrol oil and ammunition took priority. The British understood the importance of their vehicles and veterans of the campaign reported: 'Your vehicle was your life, quite literally. We loved our vehicles and we'd do anything to keep them going.' They did too and marvels were worked in maintenance.

The one great universal fear that was common among tank crews of all armies was the dread of catching fire during a battle. If the vehicle exploded completely on being hit, the chances were that no one knew anything about it. When the vehicle caught fire it was terrifying. A tank crewman remembers:

> There was one particularly nasty form of ending one's days if one is trapped in a tank and the tank blows up and is on fire. Nobody who's been involved in this will ever lose the awfulness or the horror of screams of men trying to get out of their vehicles. If a tank is shot up and burning it didn't matter whose side it was on, the crew had to escape. Once they'd escaped from this tank I know of no occasion when they were ruthlessly shot down by machine guns. They had the elements to face, they had sand and thirst and hunger to face and the fact that they were out of their tank and couldn't make it back to their base was sufficient. If you could take them prisoner you would, but you wouldn't do anything out of hand.

Generally speaking the tank crews did not have the facilities to take prisoners and it was left to the infantry to sort and escort them back and put the captives into 'the bag'.

Rommel's orders were simply that he was to conduct an 'aggressive defence'. This went against his tactical and strategic battlefield policies, which embodied the much paraphrased principle that 'the best form of defence is attack', a doctrine that is sometimes attributed to Napoleon Bonaparte. This was the man, after all, who had written the book *Infantry Attack*: he wanted to come to grips with the enemy and the only way that could be done was by mounting an offensive. Rommel later wrote of his decision to launch an attack: 'There'll be consternation amongst our masters in Tripoli and Rome and perhaps in Berlin too.' He went on as though to take the blame in case things went wrong: 'I took the risk against all orders because the opportunity seemed favourable.' Wavell did not believe that the Germans were in any state of readiness to mount an attack and thought that they would need to spend more time organising themselves and building up their reserves. He was proven wrong when on 24 March Rommel made his first moves in what would be a three-pronged attack using the 5th Light Division and the Italian motorised division, which set out from a point 90 miles west of El Agheila. Tanks had never been subjected to such use and the toll on men and machines was punishing, as by the first day the distance to El Agheila had been covered using motorcycles and lorries to escort the tanks. The British began to retreat. The speed of Rommel's advance surprised even his superiors in Berlin as he kept up the pressure. By 1 April the Germans were approaching Agedabia and heading for Benghazi. Facing them were tanks of the 5th Royal Tank Regiment. Sergeant Jake Wardrop wrote of the situation: 'We sat behind a ridge and waited until they came, then popped up and let loose. There seemed to be nothing in front but tanks coming on, but we kept firing and they slowed down and finally halted and shot it out stationary.' It was a scene that would be repeated many times in the months to come.

Another unit facing the attack was the 2nd Armoured Division, which had been sent to Egypt as a reinforcement unit and would have the most unfortunate and short-lived history of any unit of the entire war. Raised in December 1939 it did not begin to receive vehicles, tanks or troops until March 1940, when the 1st Armoured Brigade took into service around 150 Vickers Mk VI light tanks, which were armed variously with either a .50in-calibre machine gun or a 15mm heavy machine gun mounted in a turret with a single .303in machine gun mounted co-axially. One of the reasons for the slow build-up was that priority in tanks and equipment was allocated to the 1st Armoured Division, which was serving as part of the BEF in France. When the 2nd Armoured Division was finally completed, its strength in October 1940 stood at 344 tanks (all of which were inadequately armed for the task that lay ahead) and 10,750 men. The tanks were predominantly Cruisers such as the A9, A10 and A13 Mk III, all of which were armed with 2-pounder guns in their turrets with short-range and limited penetrating capability. The 2nd Armoured Division landed in North Africa in early 1941 and was seen as a great boost to General Wavell who was pushing the Italians back. When Rommel launched his counter-attack in March 1941 the 2nd Armoured Division found itself heavily engaged and on 8 April was caught in a pincer movement between the Italian 10th Bersaglieri Regiment and the German 5th Light Division and 15th Panzer Division. Some men were lucky to escape and made their way to the port of Tobruk, which was being held against a German siege. The rest were either killed or taken prisoner at Mechili. On 10 May 1941, less than eighteen months after it was formed, the 2nd Armoured Division was officially declared disbanded and did not re-form again during the war.

The Cruiser tank design came about in the 1930s when Britain realised that it had to begin a tank rearmament programme in view of the developments being unveiled in Germany at the time. A number of new tank and other armoured vehicle designs by different manufacturers were investigated for the British Army. Some proved successful and were developed and introduced to service while others were rejected. Britain may have been instrumental in introducing the tank to the battlefield during the First World War, but in post-war years had lost any advantage it enjoyed and failed to maintain the impetus of armoured warfare. The new tank designs that were built in the 1930s, it could be argued, were too little too late. To add to the problem was the fact that those tank designs that did enter service were slow, had limited combat range and were armed with a main gun

that was less than up to the task of engaging enemy tanks. The gun was usually a
2-pounder of 40mm calibre, which was fitted to the likes of the A12 Matilda Mk II,
A9 Mk I Cruiser or the Crusader Cruiser tanks. Among the tanks to suffer from
inadequate armament and reduced combat range was the Cruiser Mk IV, which
entered service in December 1938 and was officially termed the A13 Mk II.

The Cruiser Tank

The tank design that was to become the Cruiser Mk IV or A13 got off to a shaky
start, but eventually it did enter service and was deployed to France in time to
oppose the German blitzkrieg in 1940. To begin with, because of a lack of suitable hull designs on which to base any future tank, the British were forced to
approach America for a vehicle, which was quite remarkable considering that at
the time America was only producing light tanks in very small numbers. In 1936
Morris Motors was asked to develop a new tank and was presented with a Christie-
designed vehicle straight from the drawing board on which to base their design.
The vehicle required modification in order to meet the needs of the British Army
along with original ideas as agreed on by the team of design engineers.

The Christie tank had a good speed cross-country and on roads could achieve
up to 50mph, but the British Army wanted changes if it was to meet their criteria for a vehicle capable of functioning in battle. For example, the speed, while
impressive, had to be reduced because high speeds meant that the crew would
be thrown about during any manoeuvring and could prevent them from operating at maximum potential. The speed reduction was achieved by using a Nuffield
Liberty V-12 water-cooled petrol engine of American design, which was originally
built for aircraft and dated back to the First World War. For use in the new tank
the engine was de-rated to deliver only 340hp, allowing speeds of up to 30mph,
but this was still better than the A9 Mk I Cruiser tank introduced into service in
1938 and better than the German Panzer III and Panzer IV. It was a reliable engine
and, even in its de-rated version, still permitted the Mk IV cruiser to scale vertical obstacles of some 2ft in height and to span gaps of over 7ft 6in wide, with an
operational range of 90 miles.

The first version of the of the new Mk IV Cruiser entered service in late 1938
and about 335 vehicles were built by the time the production run ended in 1939.
Some of these vehicles were used to equip units serving with the 1st Armoured
Division when it was deployed to France on the outbreak of war in September
1939 as part of the BEF, and they would remain there, abandoned, after the final
withdrawal was completed. The Mk IV had armour protection of between 6mm
and 38mm, which afforded protection against machine-gun fire but not against
anti-tank guns such as the PaK36 3.7cm or PaK38 5cm and certainly not against
the heavier guns. In all there were four variants of the Mk IV Cruiser and all

measured 19ft 5in long, 8ft 4in wide and 8ft 6in high. In addition to the main armament of a 2-pounder gun, the tank was armed with a co-axially mounted .303in-calibre Vickers machine gun and had smoke grenade dischargers on the turret. The turret sharply sloped with the intention of deflecting projectiles, but the lower half of the turret sloped sharply inwards towards the hull, which was a design fault that could allow anti-tank shells to become trapped or be deflected to the base of the turret. It was something that the crew had to live with and would prove to be the undoing of many Mk IV tanks during the fighting in France in 1940.

Vehicle Name	Manufacturer	Production Date	Armament	Weight	Max. Speed
Cruiser Mk IV (A13)	Morris Motors	1938	2-pounder gun and .303in-calibre Vickers machine gun	14.8 tons	30mph
Cruiser Mk IVA	Morris Motors	1939–43	2-pounder gun and BESA 7.92mm-calibre machine gun	14.8 tons	30mph
Cruiser Close Support	Morris Motors	1940 onwards	3.7in howitzer and 3x Vickers .303 machine guns	12 tons	25mph
Cruiser Mk VC	Morris Motors	1940–43	2-pounder gun and a machine gun	tons	

The layout of the running gear comprised four road wheels, with the drive sprocket at the rear and the idler wheel at the front. There were no return rollers and so the track often had the appearance of being too slack for driving. The second version of the Cruiser tank was the Mk IVA, which included some modifications to the gearbox and also saw the Vickers machine gun being replaced by a BESA 7.92mm-calibre machine gun. The third version was a 'Close Support' or CS tank, and was followed by the Mk VC. The Cruiser tank was deployed to the western desert where it went into service with some armoured units of the 7th Armoured Division. The Christie-type suspension served well in the desert conditions and overall the tank was useful, but was it finally withdrawn from that theatre of operations in 1942. In the fighting in France the tank fared poorly against German tanks, which were used more boldly and in greater numbers. Photographs from the campaign show Mk IV tanks badly shot to pieces. In the final stages of withdrawal from Dunkirk in June 1940, the British Army could not embark any of its heavy equipment such as artillery, trucks or tanks and all of this had to be abandoned. This included those Mk IV Cruiser tanks sent out in 1939 that had survived the campaign. While the Germans often pressed into service any useful vehicle or weapon, the Cruiser tanks do not appear to have been worth their while. Instead, they stripped captured vehicles of anything of use and what was left was consigned to the scrap heap. The withdrawal of the Mk IV from service in the Middle East also marked the end of the Cruiser's short but bloody service with the British Army.

The Rolls-Royce Armoured Car

Not all armoured vehicles used by the British Army in the Middle East were committed to the front line. Some had the vintage of their design going against them
and for that reason were deployed to other roles such as airfield security with the
Royal Air Force. One such vehicle was the Rolls-Royce armoured car, which dated
back to the First World War. In 1940 there were about seventy-five in service in
the Middle East. They had originally been built using the chassis of conventional
vehicles, on to which was built an armoured body formed from steel plates. The
armament comprised a Vickers .303in-calibre machine gun fitted into a fully traversing turret mounted mid-section above the crew compartment. These armoured
cars had been used as reconnaissance vehicles in the First World War and their
machine guns were for self-defence. The original Rolls-Royce designs from the
Derby factory were the progenitors of later designs and the service rendered was
so good that it led to an interwar design being developed that was directly based
on the first wartime vehicles.

Vehicle Name	Manufacturer	Production Date	Armament	Weight	Max. Speed
Rolls-Royce armoured car (1914–18)	Rolls-Royce	1914	Vickers .303in-calibre machine gun	3.5 tons	45mph
Rolls-Royce armoured car (1920 Pattern)	Rolls-Royce	1920	Vickers .303in-calibre machine gun	3.8 tons	45mph
Rolls-Royce armoured car (1924 Pattern)	Rolls-Royce	1924	Vickers .303in-calibre machine gun	9.1 tons	

The initial Rolls-Royce armoured car designs were strong, robust and capable of
withstanding the rigours of the Western Front between 1914 and 1918; they were
also quite capable of operating in the desert vastness of North Africa. The car
had a standard four-wheeled configuration with the rear axle fitted with twinned
wheels. The wheels were not protected, which left them vulnerable to punctures
caused by enemy small arms fire. For this reason two spare wheels were carried
to allow the three-man crew to keep the vehicle in operational order. A six-cylinder inline water-cooled petrol engine developing between 40bhp and 50bhp gave
the vehicle a maximum road speed of 45mph and it had an operational range of
180 miles. The vehicle had a deck area to the rear that could be utilised to carry
external loads including supplies of food and water, fuel, tools and spares for
maintenance in the field.

  The steel-plate covering was riveted into place and was between 8mm and 9mm in
thickness and extended to cover the engine. The driver's position had a steel plate to
cover the windscreen and this feature could be lowered or raised depending on the
situation. The radiator grille also had steel doors that could be closed when going

into action. Large headlamps were fitted over the front wheel arches in the manner of civilian cars. Another feature taken from civilian designs was the running boards, which were fitted along the length of the vehicle. The Rolls-Royce armoured car was 16ft 2in long, 6ft 4in wide and 8ft 4in high. The turret with its Vickers machine gun could traverse through 360 degrees using hand gears, and extra ammunition supplies could be carried on the rear deck area. The Rolls-Royce armoured car had served throughout the entire First World War, including duties in the Middle East and Russia, so it was only natural that the design was retained after the war, but with some modifications. The first post-war version of the Rolls-Royce armoured car appeared in 1920 as a result of a War Office request for eighty further vehicles and was virtually unchanged from the 1914 version. It weighed 3.8 tons, only 670lb heavier than the original vehicle, due partly to the fact that the wheels were of a more modern design, but the rest of the extra weight was made up by the fact that the turret was slightly larger and by other modifications that were made to the armour protection. Only four years later, in 1924, another version of the Rolls-Royce armoured car made its appearance. With its modifications, this model weighed 9.1 tons due to the fact that the turret was fitted with a commander's cupola, which also added to the overall height. The Vickers machine gun was now fitted into a ball-type mounting in order to provide for easier and smoother traversing when firing, and larger wheels with wider tyres were fitted to take the extra weight.

By the time of the early days of the Second World War in 1940 there were still approximately seventy-five of these vehicles in operational service in the Middle East and for home service in Britain. The Royal Air Force operated some of the Rolls-Royce armoured cars in Iraq in 1941, where they were used to help put down a revolt by local tribes and the 11th Hussars had used some during some of the earlier engagements against the Italians. Some modifications were made to the vehicles by the RAF to improve their operational role of airfield security, which involved removing the roof of the turret and replacing the Vickers machine gun with a Boys .55in-calibre anti-tank rifle. A smoke discharger was added and a Bren gun was mounted to cover the rear of the turret. The Rolls-Royce armoured car continued in service until 1945 when they were finally phased out. They may not have been much, but, as a way of using otherwise obsolete vehicles for rear-area security duties to free up more essential armoured cars for front-line service, they were ideal. The Germans had more modern designs and against these, such as the types armed with 2cm cannons, the Rolls-Royce armoured car would have stood little chance in a fire fight.

The German Invasion of Yugoslavia and the Attack on Tobruk

On 6 April five German panzer divisions with a force of around 1,000 tanks invaded Yugoslavia, which could only offer resistance with weapons and tanks that were out of date. Within two weeks the Germans had added another country to their list of blitzkrieg victims. On that night a German motorcycle patrol operating near Derna encountered a lone British light vehicle and took the passengers captive. The prisoners were Major General Richard O'Connor, commander in Egypt, and Lieutenant General Phillip Neame VC. It was quite a coup for the Germans, who sent both officers into captivity in Italy, but it would be short-lived as both men later succeeded in escaping. Germany appeared to be heading for a war on three fronts if it was not careful. The forces in Western Europe were garrisoning defences along the French coast and, although they knew that Britain could not mount an invasion of any size, they still had to be vigilant. The situation in Yugoslavia had absorbed troops and tanks but Hitler believed the situation was still within the capabilities of his armies. This, meanwhile, left North Africa.

While the situation in Yugoslavia was developing, Rommel's northern armoured column was advancing along the coast towards Barce and Derna, which gave him ports to receive supplies from. His second column moved inland and succeeded in capturing vital stocks of fuel and other much-needed supplies at Msus and Mechili on 7 April, thereby denying them to the British. The capture of the supplies was a windfall for Rommel and here he was now using the same methods to extend and supplement his offensive that the British had used against the Italians only months earlier. The second column then headed towards Gazala, to place themselves 40 miles west of Tobruk with its port installations, essential for the unloading of supplies. If Tobruk could be captured the Allies would no longer be able to send in supplies by convoy and would be forced to send them further back along the Egyptian coast. Defending Tobruk was the 9th Australian Division, commanded by Major General Leslie James Morshead, who, determined to hold the port, had ordered them to dig in and prepare for a siege. They constructed two concentric lines of defences that encompassed the area surrounding Tobruk and extending inland to a depth of almost 10 miles in some places. The outer defensive line was the 'Red Line', which ran from a point on the coast west of Tobruk and formed a wide sweeping arc to the east where it terminated on the coast. The inner defensive position was the 'Blue Line', forming an arc but not ending at the coast, which gave it the appearance of hanging in the air. Some of the defences incorporated some seventy positions built by the Italians and an anti-tank ditch that was up to 30ft wide in some places, but Rommel's third column had forged ahead in an even wider sweep to the south through Ben Gania.

By 11 April the Germans had taken Bardia and the 5th Light Division and 15th Panzer Division were to the east of the El Adem Road, a direct route leading north into Tobruk, which was now completely encircled. British Cruiser tanks of the 1st RTR and Panzer III tanks fired at one another across the anti-tank ditches surrounding the position like some land-based naval battle, and gave a foretaste of what was to come. The port had to be held if the Royal Navy was to escort convoys with the supplies for the British Army and Commonwealth troops. The Germans used the cover of darkness to probe the defences and in the late afternoon of 13 April they managed to penetrate the Red Line. The Australians resisted and during a counter-attack Corporal Jack Edmondson won a posthumous Victoria Cross for his action. The Germans still managed to advance and by 5 a.m. the next day their tanks were about half a mile beyond the Red Line, but the Australians were ready for them with anti-tank guns. As they negotiated the feature called the Pilastrino Escarpment, the panzers were fired on from the flanks, where the vehicles were weak in armour protection. British tanks joined in the melee and at close range the 2-pounder guns did some damage. After two hours of fighting the Germans withdrew, leaving behind seventeen destroyed tanks and many dead and wounded.

For the next two weeks the two sides faced one another off as the defenders prepared for the inevitable next round. The Germans had leant valuable lessons, and refined their tactics. They used the time to bring up more support in the form of '88' anti-tank guns. On the evening of 30 April the Germans made a limited attack and were repulsed. Alerted to the fact that an attack was imminent, the Australians positioned anti-tank guns, and several Matilda tanks were moved forward to cover the expected line of attack. The Germans were delayed due to fog and the attack was launched at 8 a.m. The panzers pressed past the anti-tank guns but in the process became entangled in a minefield. Fighting continued throughout the day but the Germans fell back, holding on to some small gains, but they had lost another seventeen tanks. The British moved their Matilda tanks forward only to be met by the 88mm guns. This was a tactic developed and favoured by Rommel and was effective. The Germans were always numerically weaker in tanks than the British and to counter this Rommel devised a method of luring unsuspecting tank crews into areas commanded by his anti-tank guns. This saved his vehicles for the main attack while taking a severe toll on the Allies.

Four days later Rommel called a halt to the attacks and his forces were left in possession of the 30-mile-long perimeter surrounding a besieged Tobruk. It was frustrating to be denied the port installations at Tobruk and the siege dragged on to December 1941, turning the defenders into virtual prisoners. The British received more urgent supplies with the arrival of a supply convoy code-named Tiger, which brought with it fifty Hurricane fighter aircraft and 400 tanks, which would allow General Wavell to mount an attack code-named Operation Brevity. So far the fighting had cost the Germans and Italian 300 tanks destroyed and 38,000 casualties. The Allies fared better with losses of approximately half that number.

On 15 May Wavell launched Operation Brevity, commanded by Lieutenant General William 'Strafer' Gott, with twenty-nine Cruiser tanks attacking the Italians at Fort Capuzzo while twenty-four Matilda tanks attacked German positions in the Halfaya Pass. The aim of Brevity was to consolidate ground from where another, stronger attack could be launched in order to relieve Tobruk. The British succeeded in capturing the Halfaya Pass but Gott became concerned about fighting in open terrain and the following day the operation was terminated. The Germans had lost only a handful of tanks and although they fell back from their positions in Halfaya Pass they

In total more than 5,600 PzKw III tanks were built during the war.

Recreated PzKw III showing how it looked armed with the short-barrelled 75mm gun. The plates along the side are protection against anti-tank weapons.

Recreated PzKw III to depict how the short-barrelled 75mm gun version would have looked (top left) and two modern recreated versions of the PzKw III to depict the long-barrelled 50mm version and the short-barrelled 75mm version (top right). The PzKw III was built in a series of models and also used as the basis for SPGs and assault guns such as the StuG. III.

spent time consolidating before making their next move on 26 May when 160 tanks were deployed in the direction of the Egyptian border. It would turn out to be a ploy but the British believed they would be caught in a flanking attack and began their withdrawal from the Pass. Seizing the opportunity, Rommel rushed his forces into the Pass and fortified it with artillery, including the 88mm gun. The Allies would soon come to call the position 'Hellfire Pass' with good reason, and Rommel would earn the nickname 'Desert Fox' because he was so cunning.

The next planned operation by the British was code-named Battleaxe and had the same intention as Brevity in that it was meant to relieve Tobruk. It began on 15 June but the Germans already knew of the plan through radio interceptions that referred to the operation by the code word 'Peter'. Both sides were experiencing troubles with their vehicles, especially their tanks, with sand entering the air filters and clogging the air intake. General Wavell noted: 'Our infantry tanks are really too slow for a battle in the desert, and have been suffering considerable casualties from the powerful enemy anti-tank guns. Our cruisers have little advantage in power and speed over the German medium tanks. Technical breakdowns are still too numerous.' The British attacked Halfaya Pass and lost a number of tanks in the process, including Matilda Mk IIs. Other objectives were taken and the operation continued through 16 June, but by 17 June the Germans were pushing hard. Wavell decided to close down the operation, having sustained 969 casualties, killed, wounded and missing, and a total of ninety-one tanks lost amounting to twenty-seven Cruisers and sixty-four Matildas. The German and Italians had suffered a combined casualty rate of 1,270 killed, wounded and missing, and had lost fifty tanks. However, they remained on the battlefield to recover what they could, including British tanks, and in the end they salvaged all but twelve vehicles that could be returned to the battlefield.

The reason that the Germans were able to keep one step ahead of the British is because they were receiving information about British intentions from the American military attaché in Cairo, Colonel Bonner Frank Fellers, whose coded messages were intercepted and deciphered by the Italians. Colonel Fellers was a conscientious officer and very capable in his position, but unknown to him or anyone else was that a member of the Italian Military Intelligence Service (*Servizio Informazione Militare* or SIM) working at the US Embassy in Rome had stolen the so-called 'Black Code' in September 1941, copied it and returned the original to the embassy. Fellers was privy to British military plans and was passing on details to the Military Intelligence Division in Washington; the Italians were intercepting these and decoding and sending the information to Rommel. At the time, America, not being in the war, still had diplomatic relations with Italy. It is almost impossible to calculate how much damage had been done by the time the leak was finally discovered in June 1942 and the stream of information was plugged. The British had broken the Black Code and when the Americans realised the security breach they changed it so that by the time Montgomery launched his offensive from El Alamein in October 1942 a new code was being used.

Five days later the main emphasis of the war shifted away from North Africa as Germany embarked on its next phase, which would see the true power of the blitzkrieg unleashed against a vast but largely unprepared enemy.

Operation Barbarossa

The war was twenty-one months old and still going in Germany's favour when Hitler ordered Directive 21 or 'Case Barbarossa', the code to launch the attack against Russia, on 22 June 1941. Suddenly all other aspects of the war seemed secondary. Although Hitler had never attended a military academy he did have a general grasp of military strategy, but in this instance he had no idea of the scale of the problems that lay before the German Army in this vast country. The distances covered with apparent ease during the early phase of the campaign led Hitler to believe that another victory lay ahead. The Russian Army was believed to have a force of some 24,000 tanks but as most of these were obsolete they did not pose any problem to the modern tank forces of the German Army. The Red Air Force would be overwhelmed as their out-dated aircraft were shot down by the Luftwaffe's modern fighters such as the Messerschmitt Bf 109. Within days of the start of the campaign German troops would advance deep into Russia with seemingly nothing to prevent them.

The German Tank Force in Russia

Vehicle Name	Type	Additional Features or Modifications	No. Vehicles Involved	Armament	Weight	Max. Speed
PzKw I	SdKfz 101	Armour 7mm–13mm	410	2x MG34 7.92mm-calibre machine guns	5.3 tons	23mph
PzKw II	SdKfz 121	Later developed as SPGs and flame-throwers	746	2cm KwK30 cannon and MG34 7.92mm-calibre machine gun	9.4 tons	25mph
PzKw III	SdKfz 141	80 used as diving tanks	1,440	Ausf. A to D: 3.7cm KwK L/45 and 2x MG34 7.92mm-calibre machine gun; later versions up-gunned to 5cm and 7.5cm guns	14.8 tons for Ausf. A, increasing to 21.9 tons for Ausf. N	20mph for Ausf. A, increasing to 25mph for Ausf. N
PzKw IV Ausf. E	SdKfz 161	Spaced armour applied to turret and side over wheels	Between 517 and 550 all types depending on source	7.5cm KwK37 L/24 and 2x MG34 7.92mm machine guns	21 tons	26mph
PzKw 35 (t)	S-11a	At least 12 developed for artillery tractors		3.7cm KwK34 (t) L/40 and 2x MG37 (t) 7.92mm-calibre machine guns	10.5 tons	21mph
PzKw 38 (t)	TNHPS or LT Vz38	Developed into tank destroyers and others into SPGs, including Marder III		3.7cm KwK38 (t) L/48.7 and 2x MG37 (t) 7.92mm-calibre machine guns	9.4 tons	26mph

The scale of the attack was unprecedented and included 3 million troops in 146 divisions supported by three air fleets with over 1,800 aircraft. Seven armies and four panzer groups with 3,580 AFVs, 7,184 pieces of artillery, 600,000 other vehicles for transport and liaison roles, and 750,000 horses were committed to the attack. The tank force included 1,440 PzKw III and between 517 and 550 PzKw IV, with the remainder being made up of 410 older PzKw I and 746 PzKw II tanks along with a number of PzKw 35 (t) and 38 (t) tanks. This was blitzkrieg on a grand scale and it looked as though the tactics that had worked so well in Europe and against Poland might just add another casualty to Germany's list of conquests. Some believed that Hitler may have taken on an enemy that was too strong for his armed forces; after all, the Soviet or Red Army was estimated to number around 3 million men. Other strategists thought the Soviets were too weakened by the army 'purges' of 1937–38 when Stalin had ordered the liquidation of around 35,000 officers and the army was left with only 10 per cent of its generals. One of the victims of the purges was Marshal Mikhail Tukhachevsky who had been an exponent of tank warfare and had not only predicted that Germany would attack Russia in a future war but had gone on to add that the country would survive because: 'In the final result, all would depend on who had the greater moral fibre and who at the close of operations disposed of operations disposed of operational reserves in depth.' Almost 200 years earlier Frederick the Great had recognised this and placed great emphasis on the provision of supplies for his own troops, while at the same time disrupting the enemy's lines of communication, which included their supply lines. Russia would come to show itself to be like a champion heavyweight boxer defending his title in the ring. The country would take enormous punishment and just when onlookers thought it was all over, like the boxer, it would come back with startling energy and reserves of strength.

Britain had stood alone against Germany for a year, during which time the threat of invasion had been very real; the German attack against Russia now gave Britain an ally. The Battle of Britain had been won by the fighter pilots of the RAF and the country had survived the Blitz against London and other cities such as Bristol, Birmingham, Coventry and other centres of war materiel production. The attack against Russia split Germany's forces and took the pressure off Britain. Only the day before the attack Winston Churchill, in conversation with his secretary John Colville, said to him: 'If Hitler invaded hell I would at least make a favourable reference to the Devil in the House of Commons.' Casting aside any differences, the Soviet ambassador in Washington went 'cap in hand' and asked the Americans for US$2 billion in aid. America was still neutral and Roosevelt could not give direct support but he did order that what assistance that could be provided was given in the circumstances.

The following day, on learning of Germany's attack, Churchill declared: 'No one has been a more consistent opponent of Communism than I have, but all this fades away before the spectacle that is now unfolding.' Admittedly, Churchill was not a supporter of communism but here he

Did You Know?

The river crossing at Pratulin was made by tanks that had been specially prepared to allow them to drive completely submerged by means of a flexible hose attachment on their exhausts. In total eighty Panzer III tanks were used in this role and as they emerged they caught the Russians unprepared. The method of driving a tank submerged had been trialled by the British Army using A9 Mk I Cruiser tanks in 1938 but the experiment had not been pursued.

The Opel Blitz truck was used as a troop carrier, supply vehicle and to tow light artillery for the German Army throughout the war. Opel Blitz truck fitted to carry a 2cm light anti-aircraft gun. (left)

knew that he had an ally in the common cause against a greater enemy and he continued in his statement to support Soviet Russia: 'Any man or state who fights on against Nazidom will have our aid.' Despite Russia's strength of arms on paper, Churchill sensed how unprepared the Russian Army would be in the face of the blitzkrieg and ordered that supplies be dispatched, with the first convoys sailing in August. By October Matilda Mk II tanks were being sent to Russia even though the British Army needed them for the fighting in North Africa. Marshal Joseph Stalin called for Britain to open a 'second front' and insisted that an attack be made against mainland Europe. Such a move was impossible, of course, because the British Army was fighting in North Africa and trying to produce enough war materiel for its own use, and now also trying to help Russia. Stalin could not believe that Germany had attacked, after all the two countries had signed a non-aggression pact in 1939, but the attack had happened. The Russian Army and tank force was large but, apart from an engagement against a Japanese tank force in Manchuria on the Sino-Russian border in August 1939, the Russian military had no experience in battle. The Russian commander General Georgi Zhukov had used his tanks with daring and imagination but it was not enough to help Russia in June 1941. The Germans, on the other hand, had several years' experience of fighting, including action in the Spanish Civil War.

Hitler was well aware of the severe purges that had cost the Russian Army so many officers, and he also knew that much of the Russian Army's equipment was obsolete. He told his generals that: 'We have only to kick in the front door and the whole rotten edifice will come tumbling down.' His generals urged caution and tried to warn him against fighting on two fronts. In typical fashion, which would become more commonplace later in the war, he dismissed their opinions. Hitler believed Britain was finished but would not admit it. He persisted in this belief even though British and Commonwealth forces were doggedly fighting in North Africa and more than holding their own. German troops in France were engaged in building fortifications along the coast that extended from the Spanish border to Norway. The attack against Russia was made along a front 500 miles wide and the panzers made good progress as they seized intact bridges across the River Bug.

Tanks and other armoured vehicles could be used to seize ground and force the enemy into retreat but it was the infantry that held it. Most armies understood that tanks could not move forward to their next objective until the infantry had advanced in sufficient strength to secure the area. Japan did not develop a large armoured force and most of their operations were artillery and infantry. As a consequence they did not fully develop integrated tactics and relied on manpower with their infantry, which adhered to 'sheer dedication to battle in tight obedience to a strict military code'. The British Army knew armour had to work with infantry and used the strategy even if it caused them to be criticised, as was the case during Operation Market Garden when the tanks of XXX Corps would not advance without infantry support as they battled toward Arnhem Bridge in September 1944. The German infantry was regarded as '*Königin aller Waffen*' or 'queen of arms' and was declared to be such in wartime recruitment posters. They could march to an objective or if there were adequate vehicles available they could be motorised and driven forward in trucks such as the Opel Blitz or specialised armoured personnel carriers (APCs) such as the SdKfz 250 or the larger SdKfz 251. The Opel Blitz was also used as a balance vehicle and later 2cm anti-aircraft guns were mounted on some to serve as mobile platforms.

The German Army's Half-Tracked Vehicles

Just prior to the outbreak of war in 1939, the German Army began to seriously investigate the use of half-tracked vehicles and the way in which they could be employed to suit a variety of roles on the battlefield. By the time they launched their blitzkrieg against Western Europe in May 1940, the German Army was equipped with several versatile designs of half-tracked vehicles, from which two main types would emerge with the primary role of transporting troops. These were the SdKfz 250 and the larger SdKfz 251, and both would prove to be exceptionally useful in a variety of roles, exceeding all expectations. In fact, by the end of the war in 1945 the SdKfz 250 had been developed into no fewer than twelve different configurations.

The German Army knew that light-armoured half-track vehicles could be used on the battlefield as a 'maid of all work', and for this purpose the Demag 1-ton half-track vehicle was chosen as the vehicle on which to base the army's requirement for a light multi-purpose vehicle. Unfortunately at the time of this decision the vehicle was not armoured and, in order for it to take the extra weight of the armoured protection, it became necessary to remove the last axle from the running system. The company of Bussing-NAG developed the armoured body and the resulting vehicle became known as the SdKfz 250. It was thoroughly tested in the field throughout 1939, so that by the outbreak of the war it was already in service, if in limited numbers, along with fully trained drivers.

Nevertheless, the SdKfz 250, originally referred to as the Leichte Gepanzerte Kraftwagen, did not properly enter service with the German Army until 1940, by which time it was known as the Leichte Schutzenpanzerwagen. Thus its delayed introduction into service meant that it was just too late for service during the 1939 Polish campaign, but it did serve in a number of roles in the attacks against the Low Countries, Belgium and France, including as a reconnaissance, command and communications vehicle. After this initial battle-proving deployment, the SdKfz 250 went on to see service on all fronts during the war, including the Western Desert.

The basic model was the SdKfz 250/1, which served as an APC; it had a crew of two (driver and commander), and was capable of carrying four fully equipped troops such as a mortar crew or machine-gun crew. In this role it usually mounted at least one machine gun such as the MG42, in the same manner as used on the SdKfz 251 Hanomag. The machine gun was fitted with an armoured shield and mounted to fire over the front of the vehicle. The basic version, SdKfz 250, was 15ft long, 6ft 4in wide, and 6ft 6in high, but this varied according to the role in which it was serving and the armament it carried. The standard version had a combat weight of 5.2 tons, but again this varied according to armament and other equipment. The armour thickness was between 8mm and 15mm, which was sufficient for the APC role.

The vehicle in all its variants was powered by a Maybach HL42TRKM six-cylinder, water-cooled, inline petrol engine, which developed 100hp at 2,800rpm and

Crew in a Steyr Kfz21 1500A truck, which could carry troops or supplies and even tow light guns or trailers.

Steyr Kfz21 1500A truck towing PaK43 75mm anti-tank gun and carrying the crew. The Steyr Kfz21 1500A was a utility vehicle serving in various roles.

gave a top speed of 37mph on roads. The front wheels were not 'driven' but were rather used for steering purposes only. The automotive power was to the front drive sprockets on the tracks and the suspension was of the FAMO type, and while the vehicle itself was efficient, it was somewhat complicated to maintain. This was a telling point in the sub-zero conditions on the Russian front after 1941. Among the variants developed from the basic version of the SdKfz 250 vehicle, which carried light machine guns, there was an anti-tank gun version that even served in specialist engineer roles, as signals vehicles, as ammunition carriers with ordnance troops and was even used by the Luftwaffe.

The anti-tank gun version was termed the SdKfz 250/8 and mounted a 75mm KwK L/24 gun in the open area just behind the driver's position. In this case the

The SdKfz 250 was a versatile half-track design which could serve in many different roles including radio vehicle and mortar vehicle. Some of the radio equipment carried on the SdKfz 250 half-track (above left) and the driver's positions (above right) of the SdKfz 250, which has all the controls to cope with roads and cross-country roles.

MG42 machine gun was often used for target ranging and engaging light vehicles and soft-skinned targets in the open. This version could attack vehicles larger and more powerful than itself, but if the crew missed with the first round the engagement could turn into a one-sided fight in the enemy's favour. Because the 75mm gun was not mounted in a turret it had limited traverse and in order to aim the gun accurately the whole vehicle had to be pointed in the direction of the target. In that respect, this version was really an ambush weapon against vehicles or to provide fire support along with other artillery.

Another outstanding version was the SdKfz 250/9, which was an anti-aircraft vehicle served by a crew of three. In this role it was armed with a KwK38 2cm cannon, fitted with the TZF3a sight unit, with 100 rounds of ammunition. This

The SdKfz 250 Range

The twelve main versions were termed:

SdKfz 250/1: Basic Infantry Carrier
SdKfz 250/2: Telephone Carrier
SdKfz 250/3: Radio Car
SdKfz 250/4: Anti-aircraft Vehicle
SdKfz 250/5: Observation Post
SdKfz 250/6: Ammunition Carrier
SdKfz 250/7: Carrier for 81mm Mortar
SdKfz 250/8: Close Support (75mm L/24)
SdKfz 250/9: Armoured Car (20mm KwK Cannon)
SdKfz 250/10: Platoon Commander (37mm PaK Gun)
SdKfz 250/11: Light Anti-Tank (28mm PzB41 Gun)
SdKfz 250/12: Survey Vehicle

was fitted into a turret with a high angle mounting, providing a full 360-degree traverse with elevation between -10 and +85 degrees, permitting the guns to engage ground targets and low-flying aircraft with equal effectiveness. This was actually the same type of turret as fitted to the SdKfz 222 armoured car, which meant that if necessary the combination could operate as an effective half-tracked armoured car to traverse terrain inaccessible by wheeled armoured cars. Originally thirty 250/9 vehicles were ordered but they proved so combat effective in Russia that the version eventually replaced the SdKfz 222.

Most, but not all, versions of the SdKfz 250 had open tops, and some were fitted with anti-grenade screens of wire-mesh covering, which could be folded over the rear compartment to prevent hand grenades being thrown in by attacking enemy infantry forces. This feature was particularly useful when engaged in close-quarter combat or partisan fighting. The vehicle had an operational road range of over 186 miles and it could scale a vertical obstacle of 15in and ford water obstacles of almost 2ft 6in and negotiate gradients of 40 degrees.

The basic SdKfz 250 range was used as a base for a series of true variants that were modifications of the standard design. These had their own 'SdKfz' or special-ist designation rather than a simple oblique stroke suffixed after the SdKfz 250 number. For example, there was the SdKfz 252, which could tow a small two-wheeled trailer and was used as an ammunition carrier for field artillery, SPGs and tanks. Another derivative was the SdKfz 253, which also served in the support role for assault guns, such as the Sturmgeschutze, and doubled up as an artillery observation platform. These two versions each had fully enclosed armoured hulls with access hatches in the roof and rear doors.

The whole range of SdKfz 250 vehicles were produced in huge numbers and served throughout the war. They were versatile vehicles with excellent mobility.

There were plans to build at least three other versions or up-models in the SdKfz 250 range, but these were shelved as the war continued to go badly for Germany and due to the continued disruption to factories caused by Allied bombing. The SdKfz 250 series was highly regarded; to give an indication of this, in a twenty-eight-month period between June 1941 and October 1943, some 4,250 vehicles were produced. There is no doubt that it was a true 'maid of all work' on the battlefield, but there were other designs that served the German army equally well, if not better, such as the SdKfz 251 half-track which was a larger version of the SdKfz 250.

The vehicle that was to become the SdKfz 251 weighed 8.7 tons in its basic APC version and could carry ten fully equipped infantrymen as well as the driver and co-driver. This complied with the requirements which called for an armoured vehicle capable of transporting infantrymen on the battlefield. In 1935 the *Gepanzerter Mannschraftstranportwagen* (armoured personnel carrier) as it was then known was beginning to take shape and in 1938 the prototype was ready for field trials. Produced by the companies of Hanomag and Bussing-NAG, which built the chassis and hulls respectively, the vehicle was given the title of *Mittlerer Schutzenpanzerwagen* (medium infantry armoured vehicle) with the designation SdKfz 251. The first production models were ready to participate in the campaign against Poland. Output was low at first – only 348 were built in 1940 – but they were used during the campaign in the west that year. The SdKfz 251 was fitted with a Maybach HL42TKRM six-cylinder, water-cooled, petrol engine which developed 100hp at 2,800rpm to give road speeds of up to 34mph, which was more than sufficient to keep up with the tanks in the armoured divisions.

The APC version was 19ft long, 6ft 10in wide and 5ft 9in high. The vehicle could cope with vertical obstacles of up to 12in in height and cross ditches of 6ft 6in wide and had an operational range of 200 miles on roads. Armour protection was between 6mm and 14mm but the rear crew compartment, where the infantry sat, had no overhead protection, exposing the troops to the elements and also to the effects of shells exploding overhead. Two machine guns of the standard type issued to the infantry were fitted to allow one to fire forwards from behind a small armoured shield, while the weapon at the rear was fitted to a swivel mount to provide fire support for the infantry as they exited the vehicle. Being open-topped, the infantry could jump over the sides to leave the vehicle or through the double rear doors. The machine guns, for which 2,000 rounds of ammunition were carried, could be taken from the vehicle when the infantry was deployed.

Like its smaller counterpart, the SdKfz 250, this version was developed into a range of different purposes from ambulance duties to anti-tank roles. Production continued to increase and by late 1944 around 16,000 SdKfz 251 vehicles had been built. In total there were twenty-two different roles for which the vehicle was adopted. They had different lengths of service life but if they were capable of continuing to operate they remained in use. Examples could be found in operation right until the last days of the war at a time when fuel was extremely scarce. The SdKfz 251/1 was the basic APC infantry carrier and the list continued.

The SdKfz 251 Range

SdKfz 251/2 carried the Granatwerfer 34 8cm mortar.

SdKfz 251/3 was a radio vehicle that carried a range of communications equipment.

SdKfz 251/4 was an artillery tractor and ammunition transporter.

SdKfz 251/5 was a radio command vehicle for engineering platoons.

SdKfz 251/6 was a command post vehicle armed with machine guns.

SdKfz 251/7 was a specialised pioneer vehicle.

SdKfz 251/8 was an armoured ambulance capable of taking two stretcher cases or four seated.

SdKfz 251/9 – about 150 were built armed with a 75mm tank gun for service in Russia.

SdKfz 251/10 was armed with a 37mm anti-tank gun and machine gun.

SdKfz 251/11 was a telephone and cable-laying vehicle armed with machine gun.

SdKfz 251/12 was an artillery survey vehicle with radio equipment.

SdKfz 251/13 was an artillery support vehicle.

SdKfz 251/14 was an artillery support vehicle.

SdKfz 251/15 was an artillery support vehicle.

SdKfz 251/16 was a flame-thrower vehicle.

SdKfz 251/17 was armed with a machine gun and 2cm anti-aircraft gun.

SdKfz 251/18 was an artillery observation vehicle.

SdKfz 251/19 was a telephone vehicle.

SdKfz 251/20 was an infrared searchlight carrier.

SdKfz 251/21 was an anti-aircraft gun carrier mounting three 15mm machine guns.

SdKfz 251/22 was a vehicle armed with a 75mm anti-tank gun.

There were at least three other versions in the planning stage by this time, but the war was drawing to a close. The vehicle had good cross-country abilities and proved itself useful in a variety of roles and against a variety of weapons but it was complicated to maintain and the steering was not easy to control. Nevertheless the half-track series gave good account of themselves in Russia, including those designated as prime-mover vehicles for artillery.

Tactics

With such vehicles and a fleet of trucks to move the infantry forward under the umbrella cover of full air support, the Germans penetrated quickly and with

Recreated SdKfz 251 based on a post-war Czech-built OT-810 which was a replica of the original. Here it is shown in its anti-tank version (top). The real SdKfz 251 in the standard personnel carrier version which served in all operational theatres of the war is also shown (above right).

better coordination they were able to push onwards. Tanks, trucks, motorcycles and other AFVs had advanced 20 miles within hours in some places. The Panzer III and Panzer IV tanks rolled on with trucks carrying infantry to keep pace, along with fuel and ammunition to keep them supplied for battle. One unit of the LVI Corps, commanded by General Eric von Manstein and operating in the north, had advanced 50 miles before darkness fell on the first day. This was part of Army Group North under the command of Field Marshal Wilhelm Ritter von Leeb, the combined weight of which smashed a gap 100 miles wide in the Russian defences and pressed towards Leningrad. This major city lay on a strip of land resembling an isthmus, being bordered as it was to the east by Lake Ladoga and the Gulf of Finland to the west. With German troops to the south and their Finnish allies to the north, the city would find itself isolated and under siege from early September. Italian troops would also be committed to the siege, which would last 872 days and was not lifted until 27 January 1944. The Russians did manage to establish a route to keep supplies flowing into the city and in the winter when Lake Ladoga froze it would prove to be a vital lifeline as trucks drove over the frozen surface.

From the initial results it looked as though Hitler's predictions had been correct after all, as the Russians appeared to crumble. At first, the Russians refused to believe that they were being attacked and through this denial they paid a heavy price for not responding to the threat more quickly. By the end of the first day's fighting almost 1,500 aircraft had been destroyed, mostly on the ground, and those machines that did take off were shot down. This was an extraordinary way to repay the country that had only recently sent Germany 1.5 million tons of wheat and 2 million tons of oil, and until only days before was still transporting goods to Germany by train. The Russians conducted a brave fighting retreat, hoping to buy time to allow them to consolidate, but the Germans were relentless and pressed onwards. Army Group Centre under Field Marshal Fedor von Bock pushed on towards Minsk as their primary objective, beyond which lay the greater prize, the city of Smolensk. Army Group South under Field Marshal Gerd von Rundstedt was temporarily slowed in its advance but it was soon on its way to lay siege to the port facilities at Odessa on the Black Sea and then to push beyond to the Crimea.

Just over a week after the commencement of Barbarossa German tanks were 200 miles into Russia and Army Group Centre was on the outskirts of Minsk; once that had been captured the way would be open to the Russian capital city of Moscow. Resistance in Minsk, however, was much greater than the Germans had anticipated and the city was not captured until 9 July. The Russians lost 324,000 troops captured along with 3,300 tanks and 1,800 pieces of artillery. Each delay in seizing their targets cost the Germans valuable time because they wanted to try to conclude the campaign before the onset of winter. They did not seem to recognise that the Russians were trying to buy time and as they fell back they left nothing for the Germans, who would have to fight hard for anything they wished to capture.

This was a policy the Russians had used before against the French when they invaded in 1812 under Napoleon Bonaparte. The difference was that Napoleon made it to Moscow, but at a severe cost: when he arrived in the city he found nothing there to support his troops. Everything had been destroyed in a policy known as 'scorched earth'. It was a ruthless principle that denied food and fuel to the local populace but also meant that the invader could not live off supplies obtained locally. Joseph Stalin went on the radio to broadcast to the Russian people on 3 July and declared a 'national patriotic war' calling for everyone, soldier and citizen alike, to do their duty; he called for a scorched earth to be left for the advancing Germans, saying that not 'a single railway engine, a single wagon, a single pound of grain' should nor would be left for the enemy. If the broadcast was not heard the words were published in newspapers and spread by word of mouth.

After this drastic measure the invader would have to bring everything forward or face the prospect of the campaign collapsing. It looked as though history was going to repeat itself. Every mile the Germans advanced was another mile further to bring food and fuel. It has been opined that the most inhibiting factor in the conduct of land operations, except the combatants' morale and fighting ability, was logistics. If a nation possessed enough space and could maintain its will to fight, then a point must be reached when deep penetration by invading enemy forces had to stop short of complete conquest due to logistical failure. Russia had the space to fall back and give the Germans the impression that they were winning. The political officers ensured that morale held even if it meant harsh punishments for those who failed. Officers who failed in their duty were expected to commit suicide, such as the commander of the air force, Lieutenant General Kopets, who shot himself. Lulled into a false sense of security, the Germans continued with their advance and captured huge numbers of prisoners and materiel, and destroyed tanks, trucks and artillery. The morale of the Russians and their will to fight still remained unbroken. As they withdrew the Russians knew that the autumn rains and winter freeze were approaching; this was called '*rasputitsa*', the time without roads, when vehicles could not move. Apart from the main routes, the country's road network comprised largely of unprepared dirt roads that would be rendered impassable due to the weather. Snow, rain and ice would turn the roads into muddy routes that sucked in everything and slowed vehicles to a grinding pace. The same conditions were a problem to the Russians, but they knew the terrain and conditions, and were more experienced in dealing with such hardship.

The Russian Force

The Russian tank force was estimated to have up to 24,000 vehicles, but it was also estimated that only 1,500 of these were modern designs and of that figure only 27 per cent were believed to be fully operational. True, the Russians were systematically destroying supplies and would lose tens of thousands of tanks, trucks and pieces of artillery, but their capacity to replace these losses astounded everybody from the Germans to the Western Allies, who also sent vast supplies to the Russians. For example, between 1941 and 1945 the Russian factories produced 100,000 tanks, the same number of aircraft and 175,000 pieces of artillery. Britain saw it as its national duty to support Russia as its ally against Germany, and convoys were sent with supplies to help in the war against the common enemy. The convoys sent to Russia were given the prefix 'PQ' to denote those outward-bound while those making the return voyage were coded 'QP'. The most infamous incident involving a Russian convoy was that of PQ17, which sailed in late June 1942 with thirty-five merchantmen escorted by destroyers, corvettes and other vessels including tankers. The convoy came under intense attack from U-boats and aircraft and was ordered to scatter. Of the thirty-five

America sent thousands of half-tracks to Russia for use to move men, supplies and artillery.

The Americans supplied Russia with hundreds of thousands of Jimmy trucks.

cargo ships in the convoy only eleven eventually reached port. Apart from the loss of the twenty-four ships, 153 sailors were killed and 430 tanks were lost along with 210 aircraft, 3,350 other vehicles and 100,000 tons of various cargo. By the end of the war Britain had sent seventy-eight convoys of which eighty-seven vessels and a further eighteen Royal Navy escort ships were sunk, costing the lives of 2,773 seamen. They delivered 7,000 aircraft, 5,000 tanks and millions of tons of fuel, medical equipment and other material. Impressive as it was, these figures would represent only a drop in the total number of vehicles sent to Russia by America under the Lend-Lease Act. Initially America could do very little, but things would change, and in 1943 alone America sent 210,000 vehicles, 3,734 tanks and 2 million tyres. By the end of the war more than 400,000 vehicles, not including tanks, had been sent to Russia. Russia may have been caught unprepared but it soon stirred itself into action that stunned the world. To prevent the armaments factories and other vital industries from falling into German hands the Russians vitalised their massive work force and moved 1,500 factories hundreds and even thousands of miles to relocate them east of the Ural mountains and out of reach of the Germans. The entire factory staff went with their machines and in total more than 10 million people moved along with their tools and equipment. A year after this upheaval the Russian factories produced 24,500 tanks in the second half of 1942 and in 1943 this figure peaked at 30,000 vehicles. Russia had forty-two factories dedicated solely to the production of tanks and between them they built 18,000 KV tanks and 40,000 T-34 tanks, along with many thousands of other armoured vehicles. These last two types of tanks would come as a major surprise to the Germans who did not know of their existence.

Allied Materiel Production

With vast reserves of coal to power the factories and sufficient supplies of iron, Britain, with its overseas colonies, produced a total of 700 warships, 135,000 aircraft of all types, more than 160,000 tanks and other AFVs, along with tens of thousands of trucks. To manage this huge output, between 1939 and 1945 Britain and its Commonwealth had 20 million factory workers, including over 6 million women, in the factories. Between 1941 and 1945 America produced 250,000 aircraft of all types, 90,000 tanks, 350 destroyers and 200 submarines. In the second half of 1942 the country produced 20,000 tanks, a figure that increased to 29,500 in 1943. The percentage of industry given over to war production in the USA was still only in the order of 40 per cent in 1944, not to mention the numbers of battleships and aircraft carriers also turned out in that period. The number of women entering the factories grew by 6.5 million during the war and at its peak in 1945 the female labour force had grown to 19,170,000, representing 36.1 per cent of the total labour force. This was the face of 'Rosie the Riveter', popular in recruitment propaganda. There was also a drive to promote women ordnance workers or WOWs, but it could just as easily have been 'Wanda the Welder' or any other girl's name prefixing a duty such as 'Lana the Lathe-turner'. At one Ford factory producing trucks they employed 42,000 workers, mainly women, engaged on the assembly lines. By contrast German factory output kept up production but when the men were conscripted the workforce fell from 25.5 million to around 13.5 million. German women were reluctant to enter factories although some did enter the workplace as welders, but even so the number of women in factories between 1939 and 1944 was less than 15 million. This led to foreign labourers from occupied territories such as France, Belgium and Holland, along with slave labour from the concentration camps, being forced to work in the factories. The numbers brought in from the occupied territories exceeded more than 7.5 million and although some were experts, this system did not give the best results and the quality of vehicles and armaments produced was inferior and often failed. Trains carrying supplies and replacement parts passed through occupied territories and as an act of sabotage resistance workers would sometimes be able to misdirect these and send them to the wrong destination. For example, vital stocks required for vehicle repairs in, say, north Russia, would be diverted to the south, thousands of miles away from where the equipment was actually needed.

The German Advance into Russia

As the German advance into Russia was across such a broad front it led to inter-unit rivalry as commanders tried to compete with one another to see who could capture the next target. Heinz Guderian, who had 'steam-rollered' into France, was one of these officers and was invariably to be found way out in front. His 2nd Panzer Group covered a distance of 413 miles from Brest Litovsk to Smolensk from the start of the campaign on 22 June to 16 July, giving an average distance covered of more than 16 miles per day. Breakdown rates for tanks was still around 30 per cent and in order to prevent this from reaching higher proportions armoured advances were often slowed or halted after 300 miles in order to carry out maintenance and resupply with ammunition and fuel. Any such delay allowed the Russians the opportunity to withdraw, regroup and prepare defences. As they withdrew the German commanders saw it as the chance to pursue an enemy they believed was retreating and forewent the vital maintenance needed to keep the vehicles operational.

Field Marshal Günther von Kluge, in command of the 4th Panzer Army, recognised Guderian's eagerness to press on with the aim of capturing the city of Smolensk, which at the time lay 200 miles farther east. He told Guderian, 'Your operations always hang by a thread', but he still allowed his subordinate to charge ahead. The calculated risk paid dividends and on 16 July Smolensk was captured. By 27 July the Germans had captured another 310,000 Russian troops along with 3,100 pieces of artillery and 3,200 tanks. The Germans had around 200 SPGs and a tank force of 3,200, comprising 1,440 Panzer III tanks and 517 Panzer IV tanks, with the remainder being made up of older designs, including Panzer I and II types. The German tank crews were experienced but the majority of the Russians had not been in action before. The only general officer with recent battle experience was Georgi Zhukov in the north defending the city of Leningrad. He had been engaged against the Japanese at the Battle of Khalkhin Gol on 20 August 1939, where he had enjoyed armoured and air superiority with 500 tanks against some 180 Japanese tanks. His 500 aircraft gave him air cover to support his tank force that comprised BT-5 and BT-7 designs that dated from 1935 and were armed with 47mm guns. These were Bistrokhodny Tank (BT) or 'Fast Tanks' and as such were capable of 45mph on roads and 33mph cross-country. Protected by armour plates 22mm thick, they were equal to the Japanese tanks they took on three years earlier, but against heavier, more powerfully armed German tanks they were no match. From the time of Germany's attack to December, the Russians sustained at least 17,000 tanks lost in battle compared to German losses of only 2,700 tanks in the same period. The larger KV-1 tanks (Klim Voroshilov) were heavier and armed with 76.2mm-calibre guns. These heavy tanks could hold their own against German tanks. Unfortunately the Russians only had some 500 such tanks in service, but they had larger numbers of the T-34, also armed with a 76.2mm main gun, entering service. The Germans had yet to meet these formidable tanks in combat and may not have even been aware of their existence.

As the war progressed the Germans took to deploying an increasing number of captured enemy tanks in the campaign, mainly French designs, such as the Char Somua S-35 medium tank which the Germans designated as the Panzerkampfwagen 35C 739 (f), but these and other armoured vehicles did not always prove suitable for such battle conditions. For instance, captured examples of the French AMC-35 light tank were designated by the Germans as PzKfpw AMC 738 (f) and would be pressed into a variety of miscellaneous roles, but even so they would prove to have a very limited service value to the Germans and on the Russian front they were next to useless.

Renault AMC Light Tanks

The AMC-35 entered service in 1935 and, along with other designs of armoured vehicles, would give France a tank force numbering some 3,000 tanks of all types on the outbreak of war in September 1939. This force was organised into three armoured divisions, three light mechanised divisions and five cavalry divisions, which meant that the French Army was actually numerically stronger in terms of tanks than the German Army. Yet, despite its numerical superiority in tanks, France lost the campaign due to poor command decisions, mishandling of armoured forces and the committing of tanks to battle in small numbers to counter armoured thrusts by the more daring German Army. Some designs of French tank were actually better than their German opposite number, being armed with guns of heavier calibre and having better armoured protection that was thicker than that applied to German tanks.

The basic Renault-built AMC-35 light tank was armed with a 47mm-calibre gun and the level of armour protection was only 25mm, which was actually greater than some of the early German designs. The first prototype of the light tank that would become the AMC-35 was built by Renault in 1933 and utilised a turret from another light tank design, also built by Renault, that mounted a 37mm gun as the main armament. Field trials of this model revealed that it had a number of design faults that needed to be remedied and this resulted in the AMC Renault 34YR. This light tank seemed promising enough, with a maximum speed of 25mph and a fully traversing turret operated by two men. Unfortunately the main armament of only 25mm calibre was lighter than the weapon on the original prototype, and it was thought that such a small-calibre weapon would only be useful against light targets such as trucks. However, it should be remembered that the vehicle was not intended to be used in a direct assault taking on other armoured vehicles, but rather to gather intelligence, and that the light weapon was intended only for self-defence. At the time Renault was committed to developing other armoured vehicles for the French Army and, although the company had a highly experienced workforce and manufacturing resources, it could only stretch these so far while developing other vehicle designs for the French Army.

The company learnt a number of valuable lessons from the trials involving the AMC 34YR vehicle. One of these was the fact that even with its experience, the company did not know everything and designers acknowledged that further developments were needed, such as increasing the calibre of the main armament. These lessons were acted on and this led to the AMC-35 (standing for Auto-Mitrailleuse de Corps de Cavalrie), sometimes referred to as the ACG 1. Production actually ran to about 100 of these vehicles, with Renault only building a relatively small number, while the remainder were produced by the company of Atelier de Construction d'Issy-les-Moulineaux and incorporated a cast turret designed and built in Belgium. At the time, Belgium, a neutral state, acquired twelve, leaving the remaining eighty-eight tanks for the French Army. The version taken into service by the Belgian Army in 1937 was armed with a 47mm main armament and a co-axial armament of a 13.2mm-calibre heavy machine gun.

Vehicle Name	Manufacturer	German Army Designation	Production Date	Armament	Weight	Max. Speed
AMC-35 light tank	Renault	PzKpfw AMC738 (f)	1935	47mm main armament and co-axial 7.5mm-calibre machine gun	14.3 tons	25mph
AMR-33 VM light tank	Renault	PzSpWg VM701 (f)	1934–35	7.5mm machine gun	4.9 tons	37mph
AMR-35 ZT light tank	Renault	PzSpWg ZTI 702 (f)	1936–39	7.5mm-calibre machine gun, or either a 13.2mm Hotchkiss machine gun or a 25mm cannon	6.3 tons	34mph

The final design of the AMC-35 light tank which entered service with the French Army in 1935 was served by a crew of three. This comprised the driver, the commander and a gunner to operate the 47mm main armament and co-axial machine gun of 7.5mm calibre mounted in the turret with a full 360-degree traversing capability. In previous French tank designs the vehicle commander had been required to serve the main armament but with this design for the first time he could concentrate on his primary role of commanding the vehicle and assist with weapons firing as a secondary task. The turret was cast but the hull and superstructure was of a riveted construction, with a maximum level of 25mm thickness. It measured 15ft in length, 7ft 4in wide and 7ft 8in to the top of the turret. The AMC-35 weighed 14.3 tons and was powered by a Renault four-cylinder petrol engine developing 180hp, which gave it speeds of up to 25mph on roads; it also had an operational range of 100 miles. Suspension was of a type known as 'scissors', fitted with horizontal springs with the road wheels laid out with two sets of double bogies and a single set of further road wheels attached to the front of the layout to give five road wheels either side. The drive sprocket was set to the front with the idler wheel to the rear and a series of five return rollers. The vehicle could cope with vertical obstacles over 1ft 9in in height and span gaps of more than 5ft 9in.

Another Renault vehicle captured by the Germans was the AMR-33 VM light tank, which had been used throughout the French campaign in 1940. The term AMR in the title of AMR-33 VM stood for *Auto-Mitrailleuse de Reconnaissance* (machine-gun reconnaissance vehicle) and was used in this role to gather information on enemy movements to feed back to other, more powerful units to respond and engage the identified forces. The AMR-33 VM weighed only 4.9 tons and was very compact in design: 11ft 6in long, 5ft 3in wide and only 5ft 8in high. These reduced specifications were mainly due to the fact that the armament comprised only a single 7.5mm machine gun in a fully traversing turret of riveted design rather than a heavier-calibre main gun. This was considered suitable for a reconnaissance vehicle never intended to fight against more heavily armed tanks, and in effect made it a mobile machine-gun post comparable to the British Army's Matilda Mk I. The AMR-33 VM had a hull of riveted design with levels of armour 13mm in thickness and a road speed of 37mph, which was much faster than the

Matilda Mk I. Furthermore, the French light tank had a more rugged appearance than the Matilda Mk I and the Reinastella eight-cylinder, water-cooled, petrol engine developed 84bhp to permit the high road speed and power the vehicle over obstacles such as vertical surfaces over 2ft in height and to negotiate trenches spanning more than 5ft wide.

The road gear of the AMR-33 VM was quite complicated but it did ensure good mobility because of it, which was excellent for the reconnaissance role in which it operated. A pair of road wheels in a double bogie was fitted either side with a single further road wheel forward and another to the rear of the double bogie arrangement, to give four road wheels either side to distribute the vehicle's weight. The idler wheel was placed to the rear and the drive sprocket to the front with four return rollers. It was a handy little vehicle and a crew of two men operating as driver and as machine-gunner/commander was sufficient for the vehicle in a similar manner to the Matilda Mk I.

A variant of the AMR-33 VM was fitted with an 85hp Renault engine that gave a road speed of 34mph and, combined with other modifications, produced a vehicle weighing 6.3 tons. In all, a total of 200 of these tanks were built and entered service with the designation AMR-35 ZT. A two-man crew also served this vehicle, which could be armed with either a standard 7.5mm-calibre machine gun, a 13.2mm Hotchkiss machine gun or a 25mm cannon, also of Hotchkiss design. The Germans pressed into service those examples of the AMR-33 VM and AMR-35 ZT that had not been destroyed in the fighting, giving them the designation PzSpWg VM701 (f) and PzSpWg ZTI 702 (f) respectively, until they became worn out and had to be replaced by other vehicles. When the vehicles were declared obsolete the turrets were removed, along with their armament, and used as extemporised armoured machine-gun posts set on to a concrete base as static defences. Some examples of the light tanks after removal of their turrets were converted into mortar-carrying vehicles to provide mobile fire support to infantry units. As a fast light tank for reconnaissance roles the range was very good and for the remainder of their service lives the AMR-33 VM and other captured French armoured vehicles continued in service with the Germans, who made full use of them when weather conditions allowed and this way extended their service life a little bit longer.

Barbarossa Continues

The initial phase of Barbarossa had gone in Germany's favour but after several weeks of continuous combat, the tanks were beginning to show signs of wear and tear with mechanical breakdowns requiring serious maintenance. The German High Command had estimated that the main bulk of the fighting would be over after six to eight weeks and the way would be clear to advance on the strategic centres of Moscow, Leningrad and Kiev. In the first day of the attack the Luftwaffe had conducted air strikes against sixty-six airfields and destroyed 2,000 aircraft on the ground. On 3 July the army chief of staff, Colonel General Hans Halder, wrote: 'It is no exaggeration to say to say that the campaign in Russia has been won in 14 days.' He was, of course, being frightfully over-optimistic. On 8 July Field Marshal Fedor von Bock made his own report on the successes of the campaign so far, which at the time was less than three weeks old. In his report he listed that Army Group Centre had destroyed four Soviet armies comprising thirty-two infantry divisions, eight armoured divisions and many other elements including three cavalry divisions, which resulted in hundreds of thousands of Russians killed and more than another 287,000 taken prisoner. The Russians had lost over 1,500 pieces of artillery and 2,500 tanks, mainly in actions such as the engagement where 200 Russian tanks, including twenty-nine KV designs, were destroyed by the *Panzer-Abwehr Kanone* (PaK) (anti-tank guns). Tank forces in the Soviet or Red Army were made up of the light T-26 and BT designs and the heavier Klim Voroshilov or KV-1 and KV-2 designs. But even the heavy weight of these tanks with their thick armour could not protect them from German anti-tank guns, especially the 88mm. German tanks were also being equipped with increasingly heavier-calibre guns and the PzKw IV was being deployed with 75mm-calibre guns.

Two weeks after the first situation reports had been filed, the Germans calculated they had captured or killed 3 million Russian troops and destroyed 12,000 tanks and 8,000 aircraft, but the cost to them was also great. Specialist vehicles such as the Panzer-Bergegerat SdKfz 179 were developed to help recover damaged tanks from the battlefield. The Germans were to become masters of this operation and established field workshops. Each tank regiment had its own workshop company, which comprised two repair platoons, one recovery platoon and several sections that specialised in different aspects of repair. There were repair sections right down to tank company levels. If repairs could not be undertaken in the field the damaged vehicle would be towed back to the workshop company, which might be located up to 20 miles to the rear, and the vehicle was expected to return to the front in twelve hours. In theory and when spares were available that level could be achieved, but as the advance moved further into Russia and as winter set in, things became more complicated. The campaign had begun with a fleet of 200,000 trucks to support the supply routes but this figure consisted of more than 200 different types of vehicle, including those captured from France, Belgium and Poland. When these broke down it was almost impossible to locate spares for even the simplest of repairs.

On 11 July, while the generals were delivering their verdicts, their armies were still 10 miles short of Kiev and a halt had to be called for vehicle maintenance and to allow re-supplies to be brought forward if the attack was to continue. The tanks had covered hundreds of miles and on 28 June one unit had advanced an incredible 72 miles in one day. The lighter trucks and motorcycles were covering thousands of miles as they traversed backwards and forwards along the supply routes carrying orders and moving supplies. Engines had to be overhauled and repairs made, but all the time they were expected to keep up the pressure and attack. Army Group North was moving to invest Leningrad in a siege planned to reduce and capture the city. Stocks of ammunition and fuel continued to run low and, lacking suitable numbers of supply vehicles with good cross-country abilities to reach units in the remote areas, things were slowing down to allow the supplies to be brought forward. Even so, the Germans managed to capture the important centres of Bialystok, Minsk and Smolensk on the route towards Moscow. The southern flank of Army Group Centre moved towards the city of Kiev, which the Russians had designated as the Kiev Special Military District with a defence force of fifty-six divisions supported by almost 5,600 tanks, including 1,000 of the new KV-1 and T-34 types that the Germans met for the first time on the battlefield. At Smolensk, General Guderian had encountered a tank force some 100 strong made up of T-34s and KV-2s, the heavier version of the KV-1. Following one engagement against the KV-2, Major General Walther Nehring, commanding the 18th Panzer Division, stared in awe at the size of the tank, which had survived eleven direct hits. Fortunately for the Germans the Russian tank crews were not experienced in fighting as a cohesive unit and their gunnery was slow. On 12 September the city was finally surrounded but the battle continued to rage for another six days. Cut off from reinforcements and with ammunition and supplies running out, the Russian defenders surrendered. This left the Germans with 600,000 prisoners of war to deal with. They had to be marched back under escort, which meant that troops had to be diverted away from front-line duties at least until they returned to their units. The campaign against Russia was now 100 days old, 3.5 million men had been taken prisoner and by all estimates the bulk of the tank, artillery and air force had been smashed. The campaign had cost the Germans 400,000 casualties but it was still looking favourable for them.

The front-line troops had their own opinions of the campaign. Tank crews discovered that their guns were not powerful enough to penetrate the armour of the heavier tanks and so they devised a method to deal with them. The tactic was radical and called for them to move in very close and very fast with the intention of shooting off the tanks' tracks, thereby crippling the KV and T-34, which could then be dealt with by anti-tank guns. This realisation that their tank guns were not sufficiently powerful to destroy the latest Russian tanks led to the Germans fitting ever more powerful guns to their tanks and investigating methods of improving on the ammunition.

On 1 October Hitler ordered Operation Typhoon, the all-out advance against Moscow. The Germans committed 200,000 men in seventy-eight divisions but the armies were weakened by tank losses of up to 56 per cent on average and ammunition supplies were depleted to a level that was only sufficient for four days' fighting. At the start of the campaign there had been ammunition stock for sixty days' continuous fighting, and the consumption rates should give an indication of how tough the fighting had been. The operation went ahead all the same and two weeks later German tanks were on the outskirts of Moscow.

The weather now began to change and the first autumn rains washed out the roads and the advance slowed to a crawl. On 10 October the Russian leader Joseph Stalin appointed Marshal Georgi Zhukov to the task of defending Moscow. The Russians used the delay caused to the Germans by the weather to their advantage and built up reserves, so that by 1 November Zhukov had eighty-four divisions to defend the city comprising 1.25 million men, 10,600 pieces of artillery, 930 aircraft and 850 tanks, including more units equipped with the new T-34 and KV tanks. Over the following two weeks more reinforcements were sent into the city with over 100,000 men arriving along with another 1,000 pieces of artillery and a further 300 tanks. The railway system serving Moscow was intact, despite receiving the attention of the Luftwaffe's bombers, and supplies and reinforcements flowed into the city. On their return journey they took out vital manufacturing equipment from factories along with non-essential personnel.

On 7 November Stalin addressed the defenders of the city who were assembled in the Red Square outside the Kremlin. He declared: 'The German invaders want a war of extermination against the peoples of the Soviet Union. Very well then! If they want a war of extermination, they shall have it.' The country had a manpower reserve of 16 million men of military age that it could call on to commit to the fight and in the east there were fifty divisions and 3,000 aircraft to guard against an attack by Japan. When the Japanese bombed Pearl Harbor on 7 December 1941 and turned their attentions to Singapore and Malaya, the Russians, realising they were not at risk of attack, released these forces to reinforce their western front. As they arrived in Moscow all available civilian transport, including taxis and buses, were commandeered to move the troops to the western front in a scene reminiscent of London and Paris in the First World War. The workers and civilians of Moscow were also mobilised into work details numbering 450,000 and between them they dug 60 miles of anti-tank ditches and 5,000 miles of trenches. Finally the ground had frozen sufficiently to allow the German tanks to move once more but there were other complications. The temperatures frequently plummet to -30°C (even lower temperatures have been recorded) and the Russians refer to this as 'General Winter', one of their greatest defending officers. Radiators burst, water pumps froze and fuel and oil solidified in the tanks and sumps of the fleet of 27,000 vehicles supporting the advance. The Germans had never experienced anything like it and had made few if any preparations for these extreme conditions. Men froze to death and frostbite weakened units. The weather was causing more casualties and destroying more vehicles than actual fighting and General Winter was living up to its reputation. Fodder could not be brought forward for the horses and they died in their thousands.

Conditions in the summer created dust that clogged the air filters of the 60,000 transport vehicles as they passed along the compacted earthen Russian roads. This was bad enough, but when the rain came otherwise perfectly service-able vehicles had to be abandoned because they had sunk deeply into the mud, which sucked at everything. Then the sub-zero conditions in some cases dropped to -40°C and nothing could be salvaged. Under these conditions the Germans somehow still managed to advance so that on 27 November they were less than 20 miles away from the centre of Moscow. On the same day General Eduard Wagner, Quartermaster General of the German Army, stated: 'We are at the end of our resources in both personnel and materiel. We are about to be confronted with the changes of deep winter.' The advance rate was little more than a crawl and on 4 December the last operational tank in service with the 1st Panzer Division, nicknamed 'Antony the Last', finally broke down. Field Marshal Fedor von Bock also voiced his concerns and on 16 December reported: 'it is doubtful if the units can hold a new, unprepared defensive line is clear – because of the shortage of fuel and because of icy roads I am not getting my motorised units back; I am not even getting my horse-drawn artillery back because the horses cannot manage the weather.' Russians tanks had wider tracks and the trucks had higher ground clearance than the German vehicles, which meant that they could cope with the snow and mud better than the German designs.

The Russian Counter-Attack

On 5 and 6 December the Russians launched their counter-attack along a front 600 miles wide. Weapons were frozen solid and could not fire. The Russians, sup-ported by T-34 tanks, some of which came straight from the factories and were not even painted, attacked in overwhelming numbers and forced the Germans back, leaving in their wake the abandoned vehicles that were useless in any case due to the weather. The attack was continued until March 1942, and pushed the Germans back 90 miles on average, and in some places more than twice that distance. One Russian soldier wrote: 'We sped forward, slowed only by the terrain.' Thousands of villages and towns had been recaptured but, more importantly, by early spring 1942 the Germans had lost 500,000 men, 1,300 tanks, 2,500 pieces of artillery and 15,000 other vehicles including transportation trucks. The only major failure was at Demyansk where they had hoped to encircle the 96,000 troops of II Corps, part of the Sixteenth Army. The Russians were on three sides but they could just not manage to close the gap at the rear to cut off the unit. The Luftwaffe proved to be the saving force and over a period of ten weeks they flew up to 150 flights per day to transport 65,000 tons of supplies in and to evacuate 34,500 wounded. The men at Demyansk were finally relieved at the end of April 1942 but by then the threat against Moscow had been removed. A similar but smaller action had taken place at Kholm, south of Leningrad, where between 23 January and 5 May 1942 the Luftwaffe managed to support 5,500 troops by air supply after they were cut off for 105 days. At this early stage in the campaign the Germans were still capable of achieving such actions because they had the resources, but it could only last for so long as demands increased. The Russians had achieved a great deal in pushing the Germans back as far as they had but they were far from being defeated. In April 1943 the Russians hoped to regain the city of Kharkov, and Marshal Semyon Timoshenko, commander of the Red Army's south-west front, made plans for its recapture. Stalin ordered that it be taken and Timoshenko committed the Sixth Army to attack from the north while the Twenty-Eighth and Thirty-Eighth Armies attacked from the north-east and south-east respectively. Altogether he had deployed 640,000 men and 1,200 tanks, including the new T-34 with its 76.2mm main gun. The Russians attacked on 12 May but, unknown to them, the Germans, under the command of Field Marshal Fedor von Bock, were also planning an offensive called 'Fridericus' using their own Sixth Army in the north supported by forces to the south. The attack pre-empted the German attack by six days and the Russians managed to break through the German lines. The Germans responded by putting in a full-scale attack and even though Russian officers on the spot realised the danger, Stalin ordered things to be left as they were. On 17 May von Bock launched Fridericus in strength and within a week had moved to cut off the Russian Sixth and Fifty-Seventh Armies. By 28 May it was all over and was another resounding victory for the German Army, which had killed or captured more than 277,000 Russians and destroyed more than 2,000 pieces of artillery along with 1,250 tanks. Hitler now began looking at the oil fields in the Caucasus region and in particular the great city of Stalingrad.

Manufacturing in Russia

Being a communist state there was no private enterprise in Soviet Russia because the state owned everything including all manufacturing. There was a motor industry to produce vehicles for a range of purposes including the military, but like the collective farming policy that controlled agricultural output, there was a Five-Year Plan governing how the industry should operate. The first of the Five-Year Plans ran from 1928 to 1933 and during that period the AMO factory near Moscow was engaged in building Italian-designed 1.5-ton trucks. Another factory was built at Gorky and this was the GAZ, which covered an area of 256 acres and employed a workforce of 12,000, making it the largest plant of its type in Europe. It built 1.5-ton American-designed trucks called the Model AA and together these two factories increased production from 50,000 vehicles in the first Five-Year Plan to more than 200,000 by the second Five-Year Plan. Other factories were also built, such as the ZIS (Zavod Imieni Stalin) and YAG (Yaroslav Automobilini Zavod), and these added to the output of trucks.

Russian Trucks

Vehicle Name	Type	Manufacturer	Production Date	Armament	Weight	Max. Speed
AAA	Truck	GAZ	1934–43	Some fitted with quadruple 7.62mm machine guns and towed anti-tank guns and artillery	2.5 tons	35mph
ZIS-6	6x4 truck	Zavod Imeni Stalina	1933–41	Mounted the Katyusha 'Stalin Organ' rocket artillery	4.1 tons	34mph
GAZ-67	4x4 truck	GAZ	1943–44	N/A	1.3 tons	56mph

Because of the German-Soviet non-aggression pact agreed in 1939, Russia had felt secure from attack. In the weeks and months after the attack of 22 June vital manufacturing facilities such as the GAZ, AMO, ZIS and YAG factories would all be relocated beyond the Urals along with all of the workers. There the factories would be established in new centres of industry such as Sverdlovsk, Magnitogorsk and Chelyabinsk and would produce tanks, trucks and guns. Yet it seemed that no matter how many trucks and cars were built there was never enough to replace the thousands lost in battle. The vehicles sent by America bolstered the output and the contribution by Britain also helped the situation. As with other armies, some of the Russian trucks, such as the 2.5-ton AAA built by GAZ, were adapted to mount armaments such as quadruple machine guns for the anti-aircraft roles. Other trucks including the 6x4 ZIS-6 were adapted to carry the rocket artillery systems that were the famous 'Stalin Organs' which terrified the Germans with the shrieking noise as the rockets were fired. Russia produced 2.5-ton half-tracks for use as artillery tractors and between 1933 and 1940 well over 1 million trucks were built by the GAZ and KIM factories. The Americans supplied vast numbers of vehicles including Jeeps, which the Russians promptly copied at the GAZ factory and produced as the 4x4 GAZ-67. This was a heavier vehicle than the Jeep and some 92,000 were built between 1943 and 1953, which was still only a fraction of America's production figures for the Jeep. As impressive as all this was, it was Russia's output of AFVs, especially tanks, which bolstered the army and gave it the fighting force to take on the Germans.

War on Three Fronts

Hitler's forces were now engaged on three fronts – something that no logical commander ever wants. Russia was absorbing more resources in manpower and weaponry than could be afforded but Hitler refused to acknowledge the fact. In France the Germans realised that they must begin constructing defences against an Allied landing and this absorbed millions of tons of concrete, steel and guns. In North Africa, things were looking slightly better, but the campaign was still only being viewed as a sideshow. The oil fields in the Middle East were a tempting prize

Recreated SAS with Jeep fitted with machine guns to show how the vehicles appeared.

but those in the Ukraine were within Hitler's grasp and Army Group South was foremost in threatening this region. Operations in North Africa had been continuing meanwhile, with both sides receiving vehicles, supplies and more troops. The problem facing Rommel was the shortage of fuel as the British continued to sink the supply ships carrying fuel for his vehicles. On the Russian front, millions of men and thousands of tanks were being engaged in battles and by comparison the fighting in North Africa was small scale, but to the British it was important because it was weakening Germany's ability to fight and showed Russia that its ally was doing its best. By now, though, some of the vehicles and tanks used in the campaign were of considerable age and were only kept operational by the resourceful efforts of the engineers and mechanics on both sides. Fighting continued and specialist units such as the LRDG gathered information and the Special Air Service (SAS) sent out raiding groups to destroy fuel dumps and airfields. All the while the armies were trying desperately to build up resources for an attack, defence or counter-attack.

The harbour town of Tobruk was still under siege by the Germans but the garrison of Australian and British troops was holding on. While they held this port facility they could receive supplies. The British received a new commander-in-chief when Churchill appointed General Sir Claude Auchinleck to replace General Wavell. Diligently, he built up his resources in readiness to attack Rommel in what was being regarded as round three; to the ordinary soldier it was another part of the 'Benghazi handicap' or 'Benghazi stakes', so-called after horse-racing terms. The British had already advanced almost 500 miles against the Italians between December 1940 and February 1941, until Rommel arrived and pushed them back almost to their starting point. Now, in November, the British were poised to advance once again and cover the same old ground. This time, though, things would be different because the British had new tanks in the form of the American-built M3 Stuart light tank which the troops nicknamed 'Honey' because it was well liked. Later on more American-built tanks would be sent to the theatre, including the M3 Lee-Grant medium tank which would also be sent to Russia under terms of the Lend-Lease Agreement. Factories in America were now producing hundreds of tanks and between July and December 1941 some 2,000 Lee-Grant tanks were built. In fact, these designs and other American equipment would be tested in battle by the British many months before America entered the war. Lacking supplies and replacement equipment, Rommel's armoured forces had to press captured British tanks such as the Matilda Mk II and Marmon-Herrington armoured cars into service.

Non Lend-Lease Vehicles from the USA

The American government may not have been supplying arms and equipment to Britain before 1941 but that did stop individual private companies such as the Indianapolis-based company of Marmon-Herrington from selling a range of automotive components, including four-wheel drive conversions for Ford trucks, which were sent to South Africa in 1939. This allowed engineering companies to modify chassis of 4x2 trucks to produce 113 armoured cars that became known as Mk I Marmon-Herrington and entered service in 1940. The Mk II was built on a 4x4 chassis in 1940 and 900 were produced, some of which were deployed against the Italians in East Africa in March 1941. The Mk II Marmon-Herrington armoured car weighed about 6 tons and was 14ft 9in long. It had armoured protection between 6mm and 12mm and was fitted with a Ford eight-cylinder engine rated at 95hp, achieving speeds of up to 50mph. Armed with a Boys .55in anti-tank rifle and two .303in machine guns and served by a crew of four, the vehicle had an operational range of 200 miles. Successive modifications produced the Mk III and Mk IIIa versions and some of these had their weaponry changed on the battlefield to fit heavier-calibre weapons, including captured examples of enemy weapons with 20mm and 47mm calibres taken from Italian and German vehicles. The Germans captured Marmon-Herrington vehicles and pressed them into service and some wartime photographs show some of these vehicles fitted with wheels to permit them to run on railway tracks.

The series continued to be produced leading to the development of the Mk IV of which 2,116 were built in two versions. These were the Mk IV and the Mk IV F, which incorporated a mixture of Marmon-Herrington and Canadian Ford components. Both designs were armed with a 2-pounder (40mm-calibre) anti-tank gun mounted in a turret and a .30in-calibre machine gun mounted co-axially with the suspension, rear-mounted engine and transmission all bolted to the hull. The design had no direct affinity with Marmon-Herrington and although built in large numbers the requirement for the vehicle had largely passed by the time they began to enter service in 1943, unlike the earlier Mk II and Mk III vehicles that had been used extensively against the Italians, and consequently the Mk IV saw no combat service. After the war the Mk IV Marmon-Herrington armoured cars would be sold to overseas armies including the Greek Cypriot National Guard but with the original Ford V-8 engines replaced by Perkins six-cylinder diesel engines.

The Marmon-Herrington Armoured Car

Vehicle Name	Type	Manufacturer	Production Date	Armament	Weight	Max. Speed
Mk I Marmon-Herrington	Armoured car	Marmon-Herrington	1940	2x Vickers .303in-calibre machine guns	5.6 tons	45mph
Mk II Marmon-Herrington	Armoured car	Marmon-Herrington	1940	Boys .55in anti-tank rifle and two .303in machine guns	5.8 tons	50mph
Mk III Marmon-Herrington	Armoured car	Marmon-Herrington	1941	.55in-calibre Boys anti-tank rifle and .303in-calibre machine gun	5.6 tons	55mph
Mk IIIa Marmon-Herrington	Armoured car	Marmon-Herrington	1941	2x Vickers .303in-calibre machine gun	5.6 tons	55mph
Mk IV Marmon-Herrington	Armoured car	Marmon-Herrington	1943	2 pounder (40mm-calibre) anti-tank gun and a .30in-calibre machine gun	6.6 tons	50mph
Mk IV F Marmon-Herrington	Armoured car	Marmon-Herrington	1943	2 pounder (40mm-calibre) anti-tank gun and a .30in-calibre machine gun	6.1 tons	50mph

While the earlier armoured car designs had been useful with good turns of speed and endurance for desert warfare, they had lacked heavy armament, which was why the Mk IV had been developed with its 2-pounder gun fitted into a fully traversing two-man turret. The gun was the field-pattern type because it was felt that the recoil of a tank-pattern weapon would be too powerful. Even so, a recuperator was fitted under the barrel and this was a prominent feature of the design. The secondary armament was a .30in-calibre machine gun and a further machine gun could be fitted on the turret roof. Either side of the turret a smoke grenade discharger was fitted to help screen the vehicle's movement over open group. Both the Mk IV and Mk IV F versions were served by a three-man crew, with the Mk IV F retaining the Ford V-8 engine. This version was 15ft long and measured 6ft wide and 7ft 6in to the top of the turret. It weighed 6.1 tons and had a fuel capacity of 46 imperial gallons, which gave an operational range of 200 miles. Carried on the vehicle were all the ancillary items necessary to maintain it in the field and sand channels to help recover it in the event of it becoming bogged down in deep sand. Positions were also provided for the stowage of kit on the outside rear of the vehicle. The driver's position was well equipped with an opening to provide good visibility and an armoured screen that could be lowered for his protection. Steering

The crews had to live out of their vehicles as shown in this reproduction of a Marmon-Herrington Mk III armoured car which is of the type used in North Africa.

Reproduction Marmon-Herrington Mk III armoured car as used in North Africa. The reproduction is as close to the real thing as is possible.

was achieved by a standard steering wheel mounted in the middle and facing straight ahead. To permit driving with the screen lowered a vision block was fitted. Large side openings allowed the crew to enter and also gave visibility to the sides. Access to the vehicle could also be achieved through the hatch in the turret roof.

Operation Crusader

Finally, after months of waiting and preparation, the British made their move and Auchinleck ordered Operation Crusader to commence at break of day on 18 November 1941. Churchill broadcast a speech to the troops saying: 'For the first time British and Empire troops will meet the German with an ample equipment in modern weapons of all kinds. Now is the time to strike the hardest blow ...' It was stirring stuff and a force of 10,000 vehicles and 100,000 men attacked with the intention of driving the Germans back and relieving the 23,000 men in the garrison at Tobruk, which had been isolated for seven months. The British armoured units of XXX Corps had 453 Cruiser tanks, 287 Crusaders and 166 Stuarts along with armoured cars. In addition the 1st Army Tank Brigade attached to XIII Corps had another 135 tanks comprising Matilda Mk IIs and the newer Valentines, which were fast but still lacking heavy guns. The two main German units – the 15th and 21st Panzer Divisions – faced this with only 272 tanks comprising PzKw III and PzKw IV tanks, but British intelligence estimated that around a third of these were not battleworthy. Despite the rain the British advanced and made good gains. The following day the 22nd Armoured Brigade equipped with Crusader tanks engaged the Italian Ariete Division at Bir el Gubi and in the fighting they lost twenty-five tanks but destroyed thirty-four Italian vehicles. The brigade lost a further thirty tanks due to mechanical failure and were forced to retire. At Sidi Rezegh the Crusader tanks of 7th Armoured Brigade took the Italians by surprise and their gunfire destroyed a large number of their aircraft on the ground. The Italians quickly rallied and prevented the British from linking up with the garrison at Tobruk.

In a separate action at Gabr Saleh, less than 50 miles south of Tobruk, the German battle group known as Kampfgruppe Stephan, with eighty-five

Did You Know?

It is understood that the suffix letter 'F' in the Mk IV F version refers to the Ford components that were used on the vehicle. Indeed, it was Canadian Ford F 60L 3-ton four-wheel drive trucks with their driven front axles that provided the basis for the design. These components were brought in when there was a shortfall in supplies coming from the USA. The earlier versions of the Marmon-Herrington armoured cars with their lightweight weaponry were often converted to carry heavier weapons using captured stocks of enemy weapons, but with the appearance of the Mk IV there was no need for such in-field modifications. Although the fighting had finished before the vehicles could be deployed they were kept in service and deployed to other regions such as Batavia where the Royal Air Force used Marmon-Herrington Mk IV armoured cars to restore and maintain the peace between the fighting factions of Indonesian nationals and colonial authorities in police actions. South Africa did retain some vehicles for its own use and although there were plans to develop a Mk VI version it did not progress very far and the programme was cancelled. The planned Mk VII and Mk VIII variants did not go beyond the prototype stages and they too were cancelled.

tanks, engaged the 4th Armoured Brigade, equipped with Stuart tanks, in the first large-scale tank battle of the desert war so far. The Germans had artillery support and anti-tank guns and although each side claimed a victory the British withdrew having lost twenty-three tanks, while the German losses were minimal. On 23 November Rommel turned his attention against Tobruk and the day before had ordered the 15th and 21st Panzer Divisions to concentrate on Gabr Saleh and move on to Sidi Rezegh, which was what the British wanted. Unfortunately it did not turn out the way the British would have liked because Rommel had made better preparations and virtually destroyed the 7th Armoured Brigade, which was left with only ten tanks capable of fighting. General Ludwig Cruwell headed to Bir el Gubi where he joined forces with the Italian Ariete Division. Together they exploited a gap in the line between XXX Corps and XIII Corps but he found his way barred by the 5th South African Infantry Brigade. In the fighting that followed, the South Africans lost 3,400 killed or taken prisoner. The remnants of the 22nd Armoured Brigade with only thirty-four tanks and some artillery were also in the gap and they made a stand. Cruwell had 160 tanks and a further 100 Italian tanks, and with such superior numbers he charged recklessly at the British positions. It cost him dearly, with the loss of seventy tanks, but the action had also caused the British to spend their last reserves and they were forced to withdraw. Night was falling and Rommel was watching events at Sidi Rezegh and wrote: 'Visibility was poor and many British tanks and guns were able to break away to the south without being caught. But a great part of the enemy force still remained inside.' He went on to conclude: 'hundreds of burning vehicles, tanks and guns lit up the field.' He called the scene '*Totensonntag*' (Sunday of the dead).

Lieutenant Cyril Joly, serving as a tank commander with the 4th Armoured Brigade, wrote of the fighting at Sidi Rezegh, summing it up generally as a whole:

> It was a frightening and awful spectacle – the dead and dying strewn over the battlefield, in trucks and Bren-carriers, in trenches and toppled over in death, other vocal with pain and stained by red gashes of flowing blood or the dark marks of old congealed wounds. Trucks, guns, ammunition, odd bits of clothing were smouldering or burning with bright tongues of fire. Here and there ammunition had caught fire and was exploding with spurts of flame and black smoke. Tanks of all kinds – Italian, German and British – littered the whole area.

It was a scene that would be repeated many times, not just in the desert but all across Europe.

The AEC Armoured Command Vehicle

Vehicle Name	Type	Manufacturer	Production Date	Armament	Weight	Max. Speed
AEC 4x4	Armoured command vehicle	AEC	1940 onwards	N/A	7.7–12 tons	35mph

Operation Crusader was still in action and the fighting continued while losses on both sides mounted. Rommel arrived just outside Tobruk where he met General Cruwell, who believed that most of the British forces were destroyed. Among the vehicles seized by the Germans were some British AEC 4x4 armoured command vehicles, two of which were used by Rommel and his staff and nicknamed 'Max' and 'Moriz', but the design as a whole was referred to as 'Mammut' (Mammoth). They were not armed but they were large and spacious, and if equipped with radios were perfectly suited to the role of command vehicles. They weighed 7–12 tons and were fitted with an AEC diesel engine rated at 95bhp, which allowed these vehicles to reach speeds of up to 35mph. The next four days were an anxious time and it tested men's nerves to the limit. One of those who gave in under the strain was Lieutenant General Sir Alan Cunningham, who was evacuated to a hospital in Cairo suffering from severe mental exhaustion. Major General Neil Ritchie was appointed in his place. Orders were issued for Major General Sir Bernard Freyberg VC and his tough 2nd New Zealand Division to push on to Tobruk. The beleaguered garrison did not wait for their relief to arrive and, jumping into anything that moved including Bren gun carriers and trucks, they took the initiative and fought their way south-east to link up with the New Zealanders who were now only 4 miles distant. They joined in the fighting along the Sidi Rezegh ridge, which was held by the Italians, and the position was captured.

Rommel's Retreat

Rommel knew the campaign was over and realised that although he may have lost the battle the war was not yet finished. Gathering his forces together and with only forty operational tanks, he conducted a well-organised retreat despite being strafed by aircraft virtually all the way back to Libya and his starting point. He was not only beaten on land, but also at sea, where his supply ships bringing fuel and other supplies were being sunk. In November alone the Royal Navy and RAF had sunk sixteen supply ships with a total of 60,000 tons of fuel, ammunition and other equipment vital to the Afrika Korps. Round three of the Benghazi Stakes had been won and on 10 December Churchill announced to the House of Commons that: 'The enemy, who has fought with the utmost stubbornness and enterprise, has paid the price for his valour, and it may well be that the second phase of the Battle of Libya will gather more easily the fruits of the first than has been our experience.' Operation Crusader had cost the British and Commonwealth troops 17,700 killed and wounded and more than 800 tanks destroyed, battle damaged or broken down. The Germans and Italians had suffered more than 38,000 killed, wounded and captured along with 340 tanks destroyed or damaged. Three days before Churchill's speech, the war had taken another direction when on 7 December Japanese naval aircraft bombed the American naval base at Pearl Harbor.

Pearl Harbor

By 1941 it was becoming increasingly clear to many people that it was only a question of time before Japan entered the war as a full signatory of the Tripartite Pact
alongside its allies Italy and Germany. Japan had actually been engaged in hostilities against China since the invasion of 1937 and fought brief but bloody border
engagements with the Russians. Relations between America and Japan had been
deteriorating for some time and finally, on 7 December 1941, Japan used aircraft
flying from aircraft carriers to bomb the US Navy base at Pearl Harbor, thereby
showing the world what it was capable of. Japanese forces rapidly expanded
across the Pacific to invade other territories such as Borneo, Timor and Malaya.
Japanese aircraft bombed the British colonies of Singapore and Hong Kong in the
early hours of the morning of 8 December. President Roosevelt condemned the
attack on Pearl Harbor and on 8 December addressed Congress and called it 'a
date which will live in infamy'. Britain reacted to the attacks by declaring war on
Japan later the same day. Four days after the Pearl Harbor attack, 11 December
1941, Hitler and Mussolini declared war on America. Hitler had unwittingly made
an enemy of this mighty industrial nation. He would have done well to heed the
prophetic words spoken by the Japanese Admiral Isiroku Yamamoto, who said
after the Pearl Harbor attack: 'I fear all we have done is to awaken a sleeping giant
and fill him with a terrible resolve.' America would indeed become the 'arsenal of
Democracy' as Roosevelt had declared, and in terms of the armoury of the Allies, it
would change the entire course of the war.

   When Winston Churchill first heard the news of the attack on Pearl Harbor he
could scarcely contain himself because he knew that with America as an ally the
defeat of Germany was almost certain. In February that year Churchill had broadcast an impassioned speech calling for America to 'Give us the tools and we will
finish the job'. As he later wrote after the war in the multi-volume work *The Second
World War*: 'So we had won after all!' He continued in the same work by writing:
'No American will think it wrong of me if I proclaim that to have the United States
on our side was to be the greatest joy.' It had taken a dreadful act of war to push
America into the fray, but he knew that it also meant survival. Churchill travelled to
Washington, where between 24 December 1941 and 14 January 1942 he conducted
a series of talks with Roosevelt in what is referred to as the Arcadia Conference.
Here they agreed to combine all resources at their disposal to make the defeat of
Germany their main priority. The effect was almost immediate as the great industrial might of the country shifted into producing tanks, guns and planes for the
battles that lay ahead. America's entry into the war also gave Britain, which had
been standing alone against Germany for eighteen months, another much-needed
ally. Over the years America has been unfairly criticised for not entering the war
sooner, but the plain fact of the matter was that until Japan's act of aggression
and the declaration of war against the country by Italy and Germany, it was not
America's problem. But as the year 1941 ended, it had become her problem.

5

THE WAR WIDENS: THE CAMPAIGNS OF 1942

In 1941 the strength of Japan's army stood at 1.7 million men in fifty-one divisions. By 1945 this figure had increased to 5 million men in 140 divisions. At the peak of its expansion Japan controlled an area measuring 3,000 miles by 3,500 miles, much of it spread out across the Pacific Ocean with garrisons established on islands. Japan probably had the worst trouble of any belligerent country when it came to trying to produce armaments. The country, comprising of a range of islands, had a population approaching 73 million, but it had few natural resources of its own to speak of and no raw materials, which meant that everything from oil to iron ore had to be imported and later the Allied submarines took a huge toll on the convoys. The Japanese working population was around 33 million in 1944 working an average eleven-hour day and while the country produced some remarkable warships it only managed to build 70,000 aircraft between 1941 and 1945. The US Navy would by comparison accept 75,000 aircraft into service during the same period. The workforce of Britain and the Commonwealth numbered 20 million, worked a sixty-hour week and produced 135,000 aircraft and more than 160,000 tanks and other AFVs, mainly due to better production methods and access to raw materials. From 1931 until 1938 the Japanese only built 1,700 tanks and during the entire war they only built around 6,000 AFVs of all types, illustrating the Japanese military preference for warships and aircraft. For example, in the second half of 1942 Japan only built 500 tanks, fewer than Italy and only 10 per cent of Germany's output of over 5,000 for the same period. Most of these were inferior designs but there was rumour of a 100-ton tank that never appeared, but had it been built the problem of how to move it and even for what purpose could never have justified the resources for its deployment.

The Anglo-American decision to defeat Germany first would lead to the European theatre of operations dominating the war as it had done in the First World War, but that is not to say that the war in the Far East was any less important. Japan occupied vast tracts of land in China along with Burma, Thailand and Malaya. Capturing the larger islands of Sumatra, Borneo and Mindanao gave them more land and occupying the greater northern end of New Guinea and Timor allowed them to operate aircraft from where multiple-engine bombers such as the 'Betty' G4M, with a range of 3,000 miles, could threaten Australia. The Pacific War was mainly conducted at sea with engagements on islands such as Saipan, Tarawa, Iwo Jima and Okinawa during the American island-hopping campaign of amphibious landings as they leap-frogged towards the main Japanese islands. Tanks were used in all theatres and those used by the Allies in the Far East were identical to those used in Europe and North Africa. The Japanese tended to use small, light tanks with low armour protection and small-calibre guns, which were used as infantry support. Although allied to one another in the so-called Pact of Steel, Japan was separated by thousands of miles from Italy and Germany and consequently they were unable to support one another's campaigns directly. In fact, on several notable occasions each acted without informing the other of its intentions. For example, Hitler attacked Russia almost certainly without informing Italy or Japan, and Italy did not inform Germany of its intention to attack Greece. The Japanese attack at Pearl Harbor may have been guessed at by Germany but it is almost certain that they had not been told officially.

The Japanese Threat to Australia

Port Moresby was threatened and the Japanese landed on the island of Papua New Guinea; it seemed that an assault against Australia would be the next move by Japanese forces. Australia was becoming ever more isolated and the supply routes to and from the country were becoming increasingly vulnerable. This meant that essential war materials both to and from Australia, including armoured vehicles, could not be guaranteed. Further islands were occupied by the Japanese and on 19 February aircraft flying from bases on the Celebes islands bombed the harbour installations at Darwin. It was to be the first of sixty-two air raids that would be launched against the port and its environs over the next twenty-one months. Five days earlier the Japanese had parachuted 360 troops into southern Sumatra and naval activity pointed to the likelihood of an invasion of Australia. The threat was very serious but in the end it never materialised. Prior to the outbreak of Japanese hostilities the Australian military authorities, probably sensing the growing hostile attitude of Japan, had decided that they must produce their own tank design that would be built in Australia and be meant only for use by Australian troops. For this purpose an engineer was sent to America in early 1940 with a view to studying tank-building methods. By November that year the first specifications for the Australian tank had been drawn up. The vehicle was to be called the Australian Cruiser I ACI, which had guidelines concerning the weight limits that were to be within 16 to 20 tons imperial weight. The new tank was to be armed with a 2-pounder gun, comparable to many British-designed tanks at the time, had a road speed of at least 30mph and carried armour 50mm thick.

Australian Sentinel Project

The Sentinel project began with incredible speed and by January 1942, with little or no previous experience in these matters, the first designs for a wholly

Australian-built tank had been drafted. The tank was a completely new design and the idea of Colonel W.D. Watson, a tank designer from Britain. The concept, although an original design, was actually a hybrid that had been conceived with the intention of building a tank within the capabilities of Australia's wartime resources. Indeed, the first Mk I tanks went into production in August 1942, but eventual numbers built were never great.

The turret was a single one-piece casting which in itself was a remarkable feat of engineering given the fact that Australia lacked the heavy engineering plant to achieve this work and the experienced workforce to undertake the production. The hull was to be produced in the same manner, which further stretched an already strained manufacturing industry. In fact, at the time this work was being undertaken the country did not even have the ability to manufacture a motorcar. The casting method for hull and turret was chosen because it was considered to be a faster process than rolling armoured plate. The engine for the new tank also posed another problem, because all such automotive components had to be shipped in. The problem was solved by linking together three Perrier Cadillac '75' V-8 cylinder petrol engines, along with American-built transmission, to provide a single unit with an output rating of 330hp at 3,050rpm. The power plant was mounted in the rear section of the hull, typical of tank design of the day, with two of the engines lying side by side and the third mounted behind them. The power from the engines was transferred forward through a Carden-style shaft to the clutch and a five-speed gearbox. This layout placed the drive sprockets at the front and the idler wheels at the rear. The vehicle could reach top speeds of 30mph on roads, as laid out in the specifications, and had an operational range of 200 miles, which was more than adequate for Australia's needs for home defence.

The tracks used on the Australian Cruiser I AC1 were supplied by American manufacturers and were identical to the type used on the US Army's M3 Lee and Grant medium tanks. The suspension had been intended to be of the type also used on the M3 tank, but in the end was a spring design using a horizontal-volute form, not unlike the type used on the French Hotchkiss H35 tank, except that at the top of each of the three sets of bogies with their two wheels, there was a small return roller to support the track. This gave a total of six road wheels on either side with three return rollers, in a configuration similar to the Canadian-built Ram II tank.

The project came to be known by the informal name of Sentinel and although Mk I to Mk IV would be listed, a Mk II Sentinel was never produced. The Mk I was armed with a 40mm-calibre 2-pounder main armament mounted in the turret, which had a full 360 degrees traversing capability. A Vickers .303in-calibre machine gun was mounted co-axially and while such a layout had produced poor results against German tanks, it was thought to be sufficient against those from Japan, which were very poorly armoured. A second Vickers machine gun was carried in a mounting in the centre of the glacis plate, firing forwards. The

Mk I Sentinel was 20ft 9in long, 9ft 1in wide and 8ft 5in to the top of the turret, which gave it a higher silhouette profile than most Allied tanks in service at the time except for the US-built M3 medium tank.

Vehicle Name	Manufacturer	Production Date	Armament	Weight	Max. Speed
Cruiser Mk I AC1 (Sentinel)	New South Wales Railway Company	1942	40mm-calibre 2-pounder gun and a Vickers .303in-calibre machine gun	27.5 tons	30mph
Cruiser Mk III AC3 (Sentinel)	New South Wales Railway Company	1943	87mm-calibre 25-pounder gun and a Vickers .303in-calibre machine gun	29 tons	30mph
Cruiser Mk IV AC4 (Sentinel)	New South Wales Railway Company	1943	17-pounder gun and a Vickers .303in-calibre machine gun	30 tons	35mph

Despite being quite literally cobbled together from resources available, the Mk I Sentinel had armour protection that also met planning requirements and varied between thickness of 25mm and 65mm, which made it comparable to the Churchill Mk VIII and greater than the armour fitted to the Crusader Mk III, which had a maximum armour thickness of only 51mm. The Mk I Sentinel had a combat-ready weight of nearly 28 tons and was served by a standard tank crew of five men. However, the Mk I was not without its operational problems and, to put it politely, gave less than reliable service. Despite this, a total of sixty-six Sentinel Mk I tanks were built. The next model in the series should have been the Mk II, another light Cruiser-type tank, but mechanical problems with the prototype Mk I led to a delay and the project was abandoned in 1941, the same year that it was proposed. The Mk II was studied but it was considered too complicated and with the additional delays it never entered production. Thus production went straight from Mk I to Mk III, beginning in mid-1943. At this stage in the war the fighting in the Pacific was taking a distinct turn in favour of the Allies and some American-built tanks were being shipped to Australia. Despite this the Australian military decided to press ahead with the development of the Mk III Sentinel in July 1943.

The automotive equipment as fitted to the Mk III Sentinel was basically unaltered from the Mk I, and this eased production and avoided retooling in the factories. But obviously some alterations were made to the original design in order to create the Mk III. This centred mainly on changing the structure of the main armament and its layout. In place of the 2-pounder, the new Mk III was armed with a 25-pounder gun that was fitted into a modified turret that had the capacity to accept such a dramatic increase in size of weapon. Trials on this combination had been undertaken as early as June 1942 and it was the success of these that led to the Mk III. The turret was well designed, being well sloped to deflect anti-tank rounds and it was very spacious, which allowed the fitting of the 25-pounder while retaining a full 360-degree traversing capability. A Vickers .303in-calibre machine gun was mounted co-axially to the left of the main gun as on the Mk I.

The bow-mounted machine gun was removed, however, in order to make room for stowage of the much larger shells fired by the 25-pounder. An earlier suggestion had mooted the idea of arming the Mk I with the 6-pounder anti-tank gun, but at the time all these weapons were urgently required by the troops fighting in the Middle East and none were ever made available even for trials and the suggestion was dropped.

On the Mk III the arrangement of the three Cadillac engines was changed to a semi-radial pattern and the layout was altered and made more compact. A further improvement was to fit a link to the single common crankcase. Following the introduction of the Mk III into service the Mk I Sentinels were either up-gunned or used for training and experimental armament improvement trials. Some of the tanks were modified to be fitted with the 17-pounder gun, comparable to the Sherman Firefly, and these were designated Mk IV Sentinels. The changes created a heavier and larger vehicle than the original design and as a result the version was never put into production. In March 1943 the tank served as a platform for further trials with a range of other weaponry, including the possibility of mounting two 25-pounder guns in a turret. This was to conduct recoil trials during firing and was never pursued beyond this experiment. The actual calibre of the 25-pounder is 87mm and, combined with the size and weight of the gun, it could not have been an easy task to fit one such weapon into a turret let alone two. Indeed, one is inclined to speculate how successful a version of the Sentinel with two 25-pounder guns would have been on the battlefield. Firing trials proved the feasibility of the project but it almost certainly would not have operated in the role of a standard tank but rather like an SPG but with a limited ammunition capacity.

The Mk III and Mk IV Sentinels were built in relatively small numbers by the New South Wales Railway Company at Chullora, where the Mk I had also been built. The entire production of the tank may have been very much an irregular affair and entire output never reached anywhere near the figure of 700 that records show was the number considered to be the force required by the Australian Army at the time to counter any Japanese invasion. Except for home service and experimental trials, no Sentinel tanks ever entered operational service proper and none were ever deployed overseas into battle against Japanese tanks. In fact, it would have been an interesting situation and no doubt a very much one-sided contest, especially with those Sentinels armed with 25-pounders engaging the much lighter Japanese tanks. As the American forces gathered strength and forced the Japanese back, so the pressure on Australia and the likelihood of invasion subsided. American-supplied tanks were sent to Australian forces serving in the Pacific theatre of operations and the need for the Sentinel tank passed. As a stopgap measure it had worked and provided the Australian forces with its own armoured vehicles. They had been shown to be comparable to some Allied armour at the time, but lacking proper resources and manufacturing facilities the design was left behind by improved developments. Despite that, they would undoubtedly have held their own against Japanese tanks, which were never built in great numbers or great quality, lacked heavy armament and had a limited range.

Japanese Vehicle Production

Within months of the attack on Pearl Harbor the Japanese appeared to be every-where at once and the Allies were forced to retreat in order to avoid further mass surrenders such as that of the 80,000 British and Commonwealth troops when Singapore fell in February 1942 and the 76,000 American and Filipino troops when Bataan was taken in April the same year. Japan's tank designs were largely obso-lete, being consigned to the infantry support role. For the assault against Singapore, Lieutenant General Yamashita Tomoyuki with the Twenty-Fifth Army had 60,000 troops in three divisions supported by over 600 aircraft but only eighty tanks and forty armoured cars. In 1942 the Japanese tank forces were formed into three divi-sions but deployed in small 'penny packet' groups, and their tactics and design meant that they were unsuited for supporting any amphibious landings. During the fighting in the Philippines the American tanks had been destroyed by anti-tank guns, but elsewhere Allied tanks proved more than a match for the lightly armoured and armed Japanese tanks. The dense jungle and steep terrain was wholly unsuitable for tank movement, which restricted them to operations along roads or being used in ambush tactics, and by the end of May 1942 the Allies had no credible armoured force in the region. Like its German ally, Japanese troops seized abandoned vehicles and pressed them into service, including armoured vehicles if they had not been properly disabled. Troops on campaign simply took civilian trucks for transportation from plantations along with any military trucks they captured intact.

If Japanese tank production was not up to supplying vehicles then the motor industry was not much better for providing an expanding army. The Japanese motor industry did produce a full range of vehicles for the military, including 6x4 trucks with a 1.5-ton capacity such as the Isuzu Type 94, along with staff cars and half-track vehicles such as the IKEGAI Ko-Hi 5-ton, which were used as artillery tractors. In the 1920s and 1930s most vehicle production in Japan was undertaken using American technology. For example, in 1929 Japanese companies produced 437 cars but American companies built 30,000. In 1936 the introduction of the Motor Car Manufacturing Enterprise Law meant that half of all holdings in vehicle production plants must be Japanese. By 1939 the Foreign Exchange Control Law banned the production of foreign vehicles, which meant American vehicles. At the time Japan was almost entirely dependent on America for scrap metal for use in the production of vehicles, but as relations between the two countries worsened so this trade dried up.

Japan had invaded Manchuria in 1931 and further expansion into China in 1937 gave some access to raw material, such as coal, but Japan would always struggle to get sufficient supplies and this would have a telling effect. In the first year of the war against America, Japan produced 45,433 trucks between 1941 and 1942, of which half were designated for civilian use. Compared to other countries where vehicle production increased, Japan's output actually declined year on year. Between 1942 and 1943 production of trucks dropped to 36,483 vehicles. From 1943 to 1944 output was down to 25,672 vehicles and a year later this had dropped to 21,743, which was less than half the figure at the start of the war. In the last five months of the war from April to August 1945 Japan's truck production was 6,726 vehicles. To make up for this shortage the troops were compelled to use huge numbers of captured civilian vehicles and military trucks, which caused them the same problems in maintenance and spare parts as the Germans experienced.

United States' Vehicle Production

By contrast, American industry brought new innovations in production and ideas to extend the service life of components. The introduction of rubber blocks and rubber-jointed tracks for tanks meant 3,000 miles of service compared to 600 miles for the all-metal jointed tracks as fitted to the German PzKw IV. The Americans also learned quickly and from the early riveted designs on the M3 Stuart light tank and M3 Lee-Grant medium tank they developed the M4 Sherman with a welded and cast construction, which would become the mainstay of the Allied tank force. The M5 light tank was an improved version of the M3; with its welded design and improved layout it would go on to serve to the end of the war after its introduction in 1942. The Americans also introduced a whole range of trucks and utility vehicles in a series called 'WC'; these were designed and built by Dodge, which was based in the city of Detroit in Michigan. Some thirty-eight different types were developed, each with an identification code and intended for roles varying from the WC9 ambulance to the WC7 command car. The initials had specific meanings, with the letter 'W' standing for the year 1941 and 'C' being the 0.5-ton rating. In fact, the letter 'C' code was kept for the 0.75-ton and 1.5-ton 6x6 Dodge trucks.

Dodge

Dodge was established in 1914 and gained a reputation for building reliable trucks for a range of uses in all categories. It was in 1939 that the company produced its first prototype of a purpose-built military vehicle in the form of a 4x4 ½-ton vehicle in what was then the 'VC' series. Some designs were built in very small numbers while others were produced in their thousands, and between 1940 and 1942 the company produced some 79,771 ½-ton trucks. When America entered the war in 1941 the series became 'WC' and one of the truly outstanding features of the designs was the high degree of inter-changeability of its parts, which meant that maintenance was easier, and that spares could fit many vehicles. The designs varied in weight and size according to the intended role and served in all theatres and all branches of the US military. The WC56 was a 4x4 vehicle similar to the Willys Jeep but it was heavier and did not prove so popular with the troops, although it was still used in limited numbers. The WC56 measured 13.8ft long, 8.1ft high and 7.1ft wide. It weighed 2.5 tons and had a payload capacity of over 0.8 tons. The WC57 was designated as a command car and measured 14.6ft long, 6.8ft high and 6.5ft wide. The WC57 weighed 2.5 tons and had a weight capacity of more than a 0.75-ton payload; over 6,000 were built and used in Europe and the Far East.

Vehicle Name	Type	Manufacturer	Production Date	Armament/ Payload	Weight	Max. Speed
WC51	Weapon Carrier	Dodge	1942–45	0.75 tons and .30in-calibre machine gun	2.5 tons	54mph
WC52	Weapon Carrier	Dodge	1942–45	0.75 tons and .30in-calibre machine gun	2.6 tons	54mph
WC54	Ambulance	Dodge	1942–45	0.75 tons	2.5 tons	54mph
WC56	Command car	Dodge	1942–45	0.75 tons	2.5 tons	54mph
WC57	Command car	Dodge	1942–44	0.75 tons	2.5 tons	54mph

One of the most widely used of the WC series of vehicles was the design referred to as 'weapon carrier', of which some 182,655 were built between 1942 and 1945. This was produced in two types known as the WC51 and WC52, both of which were 4x4 with a ¾-ton load rating classification and the only difference in design was that the latter version was fitted with an integral winch over the front bumper. Apart from this feature they were identical when one takes into account the additional weight of the winch on the WC52 version. The WC51 was produced in greater numbers, with 123,541 being built. The WC51 measured 5.6ft in height with the canvas cover removed but this increased to 7.1ft when it was erected. The vehicle weighed 2.5 tons and could carry a cargo payload of up to ¾ ton. When transporting troops it could carry six to eight men, including driver and co-driver, with weapons and personal kit. The WC52, of which

The WC54 ambulance served across Europe and Italy. The double doors at the rear made it easier to handle stretcher cases.

Dodge WC21 light cargo vehicle with a payload capacity of 1,300lb; it was one of the large range of utility trucks used by the US Army.

The WC51 and WC52 weapons carriers could carry heavy loads for their size or a squad of infantry. Weapons carriers were used across France and into Germany during 1944 and 1945.

Weapons carrier in the markings of the British 3rd Infantry Division.

59,114 were built, was slightly heavier at 2.6 tons and measured 14.7ft long due to the front-mounted winch.

Both vehicles were powered by a six-cylinder Dodge petrol T214 engine rated at 76hp at 3,200rpm, giving a road speed of around 54mph and an operational range of more than 130 miles. Transmission was four forward gears and one reverse and, being American designed, the vehicle was left-hand drive. Even when the larger 6x6 trucks entered service the WC51 continued to be used, mainly to carry supplies, leaving the larger vehicles to carry troops and heavier cargo loads as part of the specialist convoy systems that were developed to supply troops in Europe after the Normandy Landings in June 1944. The WC51 and the WC52 were versatile and could be armed with machine guns and other devices. They were used by other armies during the war, with Russia alone receiving 25,000 weapons carriers, where they were assigned to such duties as towing the ZIS-3 76mm calibre anti-tank gun.

Another of the most numerous WC designs was the purpose-built ambulance, designated as the WC54, with around 26,000 being built between 1942 and 1944. This was just one of the standard military ambulances used during the war and it served with the US Army Medical Corps in all theatres of operations. Its capacity to transport either four wounded as stretcher cases or seven seated casualties plus a medic made it an

The WC56 was used for liaison duties in the UK and after D-Day in Europe. The driver's position of the WC56 command car was the same as commercial vehicles for ease of use.

indispensable vehicle for the movement of casualties from the battlefield to rear areas and better hospital treatment. Indeed, wartime photographs show it on the beaches at Normandy and later during the campaign to push inland after the landings. The WC54 replaced the WC27 ambulance and some other older designs. It measured just over 16ft long with a wheelbase of 10ft 1in. The body was built from sheet metal and the vehicle measured 6ft 6in wide and 7ft 6in high, and weighed around 2.5 tons. During its production run the vehicle underwent some very minor design modifications, but all featured a heater for the comfort of the casualties. The vehicle had a fuel capacity of 30 gallons, the engine was the Model T214 six-cylinder petrol and it had a gearbox with four forward gears and one reverse.

The WC56 command car was used close to the front line to gather information. Probably the most famous person to travel in this type of vehicle was General Patton in the European campaign 1944. The WC57 command car. Another of the Dodge range of WC wheeled vehicles (above right).

The Friendly Invasion

The USA would supply hundreds of thousands of trucks and tanks as the war progressed, but in January 1942 it was still coming to terms with the fact that it was now involved in a global war. With the decision to defeat Germany having been made between Churchill and Roosevelt at the Arcadia Conference it was vital that US troops, equipment and aircraft were sent to Britain. The first troops arrived in April to be joined later by aircraft that would take part in the bombing campaign against Germany. The USAAF built its bases across Britain, with the main concentration in the Suffolk and Norfolk areas, and the army personnel were billeted in specially constructed camps. Large country estates were also commandeered and troops were billeted in the grounds, which were vast enough to serve as vehicle parks for the trucks and tanks. The 28th Infantry Division, the 'Keystone' Division, was sent to Wales where they took over various locations including Margam Park near Port Talbot and used the more than 800 acres surrounding the large manor house to practise training. The grounds of Dunster Castle in Devon were also taken over for the same purposes, as was the land around Bowood House in Wiltshire. Littlecote House in Berkshire would be used by the 101st Airborne Division; Braunston Park in Leicestershire was used by the 82nd Airborne Division; and at Saltram near Plymouth in Devon the estate, owned by the Parker family, was used by a number of specialist units along with the 4th Infantry Division and other

Littlecote House near Newbury in Berkshire, which was used by the 101st Airborne Division in the build-up to D-Day.

Saltram House near Plymouth in Devon which was
used during the build-up for D-Day.

Tank inspection pit at Saltram House. It has been
filled in but would have been deep enough for a
man to stand in to look under a tank parked on the
concrete.

infantry units. The grounds of Saltram were also used as a vast vehicle park and
maintenance facilities were built to service the tanks and trucks. This was called
the 'friendly invasion' by the British and they welcomed their American allies. Over
the coming months millions of American service personnel arrived in Britain, with
some based in Northern Ireland for training, and hundreds of thousands of trucks,
tanks and artillery were brought over, along with millions of tons of supplies.

Continuing German Operations in Russia

In Russia, where the German Army was still reeling from the powerful counter-
attacks that had pushed it back from the outskirts of Moscow, Stalin was calling
for the Western Allies to open a 'Second Front' by invading Europe. The Russians
believed they were bearing the brunt of the fighting and would not accept that
such a campaign could not be mounted until sufficient equipment and troops had
been assembled to make it a success. The Western Allies, Britain in particular, wondered how much longer Russia could last after losing so much in the way of men

and equipment. Forced to withdraw from its primary objective, the German Army was far from being defeated and proved as much by tightening its grip around Leningrad in the north, while in the south units of Army Group South had made the first moves in November 1941 to invest the city of Sevastopol in readiness for another siege. In December the Eleventh Army of General Erich von Manstein had attacked and forced the defenders back from their first line of defence, which comprised 2 miles of trenches, anti-tank ditches and minefields. The city lay on the coast in the Crimea, which itself was virtually an island, being attached to the Ukrainian mainland by only a narrow strip of land to the north. In such a position the city and its population, which included a defending garrison of 100,000 troops, had their backs to the sea. German operations against Kerch to the east led to the capture of 170,000 Russian troops, 250 tanks and 1,100 pieces of artillery, which could have been used to support Sevastopol. Manstein built up his forces, which included bringing forward railway-mounted guns including the massive 800mm calibre known as 'Dora', to shell the city. The city's defenders had 600 pieces of artillery, thirty-eight tanks and only fifty-five aircraft. The Germans had 600 air-craft to bomb the city, artillery backed by rocket launchers called Nebelwerfers, and the support of their Italian allies along with Bulgarian and Romanian troops. Three rings of defences surrounded the city with minefields, pillboxes and concrete bun-kers, all of which had to be broken through before Manstein's forces could enter the city properly. The fighting continued until 3 July when the last of the city's defend-ers surrendered, giving the Germans another 100,000 prisoners. The engagement had lasted 247 days and the Germans had fired 46,000 tons of artillery shells in addition to the aerial bombs dropped on the city.

The Dora and the Gustav

The Dora, along with the Gustav, was the largest-calibre railway artillery piece ever built and had originally been developed by the Krupp company with the specific inten-tion of bombarding the French Maginot Line. In his book *Lost Victories*, Field Marshal Erich von Manstein, who commanded the German Eleventh Army in the operations against Sevastopol, described Gustav as: 'A miracle of technical achievement. The barrel must have been 90 feet long and the carriage as high as a two-storey house. Sixty trains had been required to bring it into position along a railway specially laid for the purpose. Two anti-aircraft regiments had to be in constant attendance.' He went on to say of the Gustav railway gun: 'The effectiveness of the cannon bore no real relation to all the effort and expense that had gone into making it.' In other words, the whole thing was a ghastly drain on resources.

The Gustav railway gun had been developed by Krupp in response to a query raised by Hitler in 1936 in regard to what size calibre artillery pieces would be required to reduce the French defensive fortifications of the Maginot Line. The German Army High Command had also enquired of Krupp as to the size of weapons required to pound the Maginot Line and Krupp had postulated weapons in the calibre of 70cm, 80cm and even 100cm. Despite the fact that no orders had actually been placed, the design team assumed that the weapon was required and set about designing the Gustav and Dora. Drawings were prepared and presented to the Army Weapons Office in 1937, which approved them and the building programme started. No one could have foreseen the difficulties in producing such massive weapons, but there were so many that Krupp's production schedules for standard weaponry went awry. Instead of having the guns ready for 1940, as promised, it was 1941 before they could be assembled and test fired for proof. Adolf Hitler was present at one of the field trials, accompanied by Heinz Guderian and Dr Muller of Krupp, who informed Hitler that the 80cm-calibre Gustav could be used against tanks. To this statement Guderian was stunned and later stated: 'For a moment I was dumbfounded as I envisaged the mass-production of "Gustavs".' He quickly explained to Hitler that the gun could be fired, but could never engage an individual target because it required forty-five minutes to reload after firing. In fairness, what Dr Muller probably meant was that Gustav could be used to break up massed armoured attacks by tanks, rather than being used as a true anti-tank gun.

The Gustav gun was dispatched to Sevastopol in 1942 to participate in the siege of the city. It required a crew of more than 1,400 men for its operation and defence, in addition to the anti-aircraft units. The Gustav was formally known as the '80cm K (E)' and was built in sections to allow it to pass the railway loading gauge. The fully assembled weapon was over 140ft long, 33ft wide and 38ft high, and weighed 1,328 tons. It took some three weeks to assemble the weapon and prepare it ready for firing. The Gustav was assembled using a four-rail double track, with two outer tracks for the assembly crane. The two halves of the bogie units were placed into position and the gun carriage was built up on top. The barrel, which came in two sections, was assembled by inserting the rear half into the jacket, and connecting the front half by means of an enormous junction nut, and mounting the whole assembly on the cradle. The gun was dismantled into breech ring and block, the two barrel sections, jacket, cradle, trunnions and trunnion bearings. All of these sections were transported on special flatcars. The mounting was split longitudinally for movement and dismantled from the top downwards. The sections were transported on additional flatcars hauled by trains.

The Gustav fired two types of shells, one of which was the 4.7-ton high-explosive shell and had a range of around 29 miles. The second type of shell was the 7-ton concrete-piercing shell, which could be fired out to ranges of over 23 miles. During its deployment at Sevastopol the Gustav fired between sixty and seventy rounds and one of the concrete-piercing shells penetrated through some 100ft of rock at Severnaya Bay and destroyed a Russian ammunition stockpile. The Gustav was later moved to Leningrad, but the siege there had been lifted by the Russians before it could be made ready.

At the other end of Russia at the same time the campaign against the city of Leningrad was bogged down in stalemate with 300,000 Germans holding the southern end of the isthmus and the Finns holding the northern end. The Finns and Germans had not joined their front lines to cut off the southern edge of Lake Ladoga, which left the Russians in possession of Lednevo with its railway links and Novaya Ladoga with road links from where supplies could be transported into the besieged city. The Finns may have been allies of Germany but as far as they were concerned they had re-conquered the territory they had lost in 1940 during the war against Russia and they were satisfied. They were not prepared to go any further and this left open the water route into Leningrad. The Russians had built defences but with a population of 3 million the problem was feeding the people. In October 1941 the city was being supplied with 1,000 tons of food daily brought in by ship from Novaya Ladoga, but when the waters froze in November that rate dropped to half the capacity. The problem was compounded when a German attack captured a stretch of the rail link at Tikhvin and severed the route into Lednevo.

The Communist Party secretary in Leningrad, Andrei Zhdanov, ordered that a route be cut through dense forest so that trucks could carry supplies from the railhead at Zaborye to Novaya Ladoga, from where convoys could continue to Lednevo and across the waters of the lake. The route that was hacked through the forest to connect Zaborye to Novaya Ladoga covered a distance of 50 miles and had been created in just over four weeks, from 9 November to 6 December. It was a prodigious feat of work by labourers, many of whom were on the point of collapse from hunger. The terrain was so steep in places that the trucks had to be physically pushed up the inclines. Even so, the best distance they could manage to cover was 25 miles per day. There was some news when a Russian counter-attack seized back the railhead at Tikhvin, which shortened the route the trucks had to take and, with the waters of Lake Ladoga frozen, the trucks drove across the icy surface. By January 1942 there were up to 400 trucks daily driving the treacherous 20-mile route across the frozen surface of Lake Ladoga from Lednevo to Osinovets from where they could continue overland to Leningrad or the rail-head could take supplies direct to the city. The civilians called it the 'Road of Life', but to the drivers who risked crashing through the ice it was the 'Road of Death'. Only seven months earlier some fifty-four trains had removed almost 1.2 million works of art and national treasures from the city in a month-long operation to prevent them from being captured by the Germans. By the time of the first thaw in April 1942 some 53,000 tons of supplies such as fuel and ammunition and a further 42,500 tons of food had been driven across the Lake Ladoga ice road. The siege of Leningrad would last for a total of 890 days and would not be relieved until 13 January 1944. The suffering of the people and the military defenders was enormous, with an estimated 1.5 million being killed or dying of starvation. The struggle to save the city and keep it supplied was one of the greatest examples of logistics during the war, but it was overshadowed by events at Stalingrad where entire armies would be wiped out. Andrei Zhdanov declared that 'We must dig Fascism a grave in front of Leningrad'. The cost to the German Army and its Italian and Finnish allies is not known, but the fact that the operation tied down so many troops, tanks, trucks and other equipment certainly assisted by preventing them from being deployed elsewhere.

The Capture of Tobruk

Two weeks after Manstein's troops had captured Sevastopol, Rommel and his Afrika Korps in North Africa were adding to the German Army's victories by capturing the defensive positions of El Duda and Belhamed outside the town port of Tobruk. He also captured British supply depots near Bardia and the airfield at El Adem. Sensing the victory that had eluded him several months earlier, he wrote:

> Evidence of the British defeat could be seen all along the roads and verges ... Vast quantities of material lay on all sides, burnt-out vehicles stood black and empty in the sand. Whole convoys of undamaged British lorries had fallen into our hands, some of which had been pressed into service immediately by the fighting troops, while others were now awaiting collection by the salvage squads.

Some of the vehicles that fell into German hands would have been trucks such as the Morris CS8 built by Morris Commercial Cars based in Birmingham. There were about 26,000 of these useful little vehicles built in three main versions, with production beginning in 1937. Nicknamed 'Gin Palaces' by the troops, they were used as radio vehicles by the Royal Corps of Signals. They were also used to transport supplies and troops (for which purpose they were fitted with wooden slatted seats) and even to evacuate the wounded. The CS8 was fitted with a petrol 3,498cc six-cylinder engine rated at 60hp. Two fuel tanks, each with an 11-gallon capacity, gave the vehicle an operational range of 220 miles on roads. Some were produced with a very basic roof and doors of canvas, while later versions were fitted with steel doors. The rear body was built up from wooden slats with a tailgate that dropped down to make loading and unloading easier.

British Vehicles used by the German Army in North Africa

Vehicle Name	Type	Manufacturer	Production Date	Armament	Weight	Max. Speed
CS8	Truck	Morris Commercial Cars	1937	N/A	0.9 tons	37mph
4x2 PU 8cwt	Truck	Morris Commercial Cars	1936	N/A	1.8 tons	50mph

Other abandoned vehicle types captured would have been the 4x2 Morris PU 8cwt, many of which had already fallen into German hands at Dunkirk in 1940. They should have been wrecked to prevent their being used by the Germans, but such actions were not always totally destructive and beyond draining the sump and running the engine until it seized up not much else could be done to render them useless. To good mechanics and engineers it would not have proved much of a problem to get the vehicle back on the road. In the desert, vehicles were pressed into a variety of roles, some for which they were never intended and invariably carried loads far exceeding their design limitations. The Morris PU 8cwt was used by the British and Australian troops as radio trucks and supply trucks, and those captured intact by the Germans were put to the same use. The basic PU 8cwt was 12ft 9in long and 6ft 3in wide. Built between 1936 and 1941, with Canada producing many, they were also used in India. The vehicle weighed 1.8 tons and the six-cylinder 60hp engine gave a road speed of around 50mph. Like other military vehicles it was versatile and could carry troops, supplies and even tow light anti-aircraft guns. With so many of their own vehicles being delivered by convoy, the Germans eagerly seized on the opportunity to supplement their fleet of vehicles, which by then were in great need of replacement or extensive servicing.

It had taken Rommel almost six months to reach this point having started his offensive on 21 January at El Agheila, which was where Operation Crusader had pushed him back to. In typical fashion Rommel had not wasted time and effort but acted swiftly and although he had only 560 tanks, of which 332 were German (the rest being Italian or captured vehicles), he mounted his offensive. The British Eighth Army, commanded by Lieutenant General Neil Ritchie, was equipped with 850 tanks including Matilda Mk IIs, Valentines and M3 Stuarts, but also, more importantly, 167 M3 Grants armed with 75mm guns, which would prove to be invaluable to the British. The Free French garrison at the defensive position of Bir Hakeim (sometimes written as Bir Hacheim) was held by troops of the French Foreign Legion commanded by General Pierre Koenig. German sappers worked to clear a way through the minefields and the Luftwaffe pounded the position with some 1,300 sorties. On 3 June the Italian Trieste Division and the German 90th Light Division attacked the position but the French held. Over the next week the Germans allowed the French no respite and attacked or probed the defences day and night. Bir Hakeim was virtually surrounded except for a narrow corridor. The British had been ordered by Ritchie to support the French defenders and on the evening of 10 June, under cover of darkness, General Koenig led his command of 2,700 men out of the position and through the desert to rendezvous with a fleet of British trucks that had been sent out to bring them back to safety. When Rommel's troops entered Bir Hakeim on 11 June all he found were 300 men who were too seriously wounded to be evacuated and the graves of 600 other defenders. On the same day he attacked east out of the position known as 'the Cauldron', which lay to the north of Bir Hakeim and from where on 5 June he had launched

The Morris Commercial 15cwt truck was a general-purpose
vehicle for carrying supplies and troops.

Driver's position for the Morris Commercial 15cwt truck with
basic controls.

an attack that had inflicted 6,000 casualties on the British and destroyed 150
tanks. This latest attack forced the British to retreat and over the following week
Rommel's Afrika Korps and the Italians captured more ground so that by 17 June
he was threatening Tobruk itself.

Tobruk, so essential for supplying the Allies, had eluded Rommel the year
before, but was now at his mercy. The garrison at Tobruk comprised 35,000 men,
including Indian, South African and British troops, with sufficient supplies of
food and ammunition to last for at least ninety days. On 18 June, aircraft of the
Luftwaffe began to bomb the positions, sappers cleared the mines and tanks of the
21st Panzer Division attacked defences held by the 2nd/5th Mahrattas. Lacking
anti-tank guns and heavy support, the Indians were overwhelmed but the survivors fought on with the Cameron Highlanders until they were forced to surrender.
Realising that they could not hold, Major General Henry Klopper, commanding
the Tobruk garrison, ordered supplies to be destroyed. Fuel, oil and ammunition

were blown up but even so, when the garrison finally surrendered on 21 June, Rommel reaped a rich harvest including 5,000 tons of supplies, 2,000 vehicles and, most importantly, 500,000 gallons, amounting to over 2,200 tons, of much-needed fuel. It was shattering news to the Allies and Churchill in particular, who confided to Roosevelt that its loss was 'one of the heaviest blows I can recall during the war'. Hitler promoted Rommel to the rank of field marshal and the way was open to Cairo and the Middle East with its oil supplies. Roosevelt reacted to the news by immediately sending 300 of the new Sherman tanks to help the British and Commonwealth troops.

Morris Commercial truck used by the British Army in North Africa but the Germans also used captured vehicles for their own transportation of supplies and troops.

Morris Commercial truck with 7th Armoured Division badge. This vehicle was used throughout the North Africa campaign.

The British forces in North Africa did not collapse as might have been expected, but instead, under General Sir Claude Auchinleck (nicknamed 'the Auk' by the troops), as commander-in-chief Middle East and also as the field commander of the Eighth Army, took up positions called 'boxes'. There were several of these strongly defended positions, so called because of their all-round defence, and the largest of these enclosed El Alamein in a wide sweeping arc that ran from the coast east of the town, continued south and then ran west before moving northwards back to the coast. Cairo, and Rommel's prize, lay 150 miles farther east, but first he had to smash these boxes. He sent in the 15th and 21st Panzer Divisions to attack the Deir el Shein box on 1 July. This was held by the 18th Indian Brigade and the German tanks captured the positions the same day. The 90th Light Division followed a feature known as the Miteirya Ridge to the south of El Alamein, skirted the defences and advanced towards the box held by the 4th Armoured Brigade. The Germans became tangled in a minefield, and artillery fire from the El Alamein defensive perimeter added to their losses. Auchinleck had sent 155 tanks of the 7th Armoured Division to positions south of the Deir el Munassib box, held by the New Zealand Division. In the centre the 1st Armoured Division was positioned to counter any attacks there and the 6th New Zealand Brigade held the Bab el Qattara box.

The Italian Ariete Division attacked the New Zealanders' positions on 3 July but rather than wait for them to come close the New Zealanders moved out and forced the Italians back. Over the next week both sides made thrusts, such as the Australian attack on 10 July against positions held by the Italian Sabratha Division, which fell back. The next day was no better for the Trieste Division, which abandoned its position at Tel el Eisa when the Australians attacked. By 14 July Auchinleck still had 400 tanks he could commit to battle while Rommel was down to only thirty serviceable tanks. With so much armour the British had the advantage in firepower. Even so, the German tank crews fought on determinedly. Rommel's artillery had run out of ammunition and his Italian allies were crumbling fast and so could not be relied on for support. On 21 July Auchinleck mounted a night attack but at Deir el Shein, formerly held by the 18th Indian Brigade, his tanks ran into an ambush and anti-tank guns and mines claimed eighty-seven Valentine tanks either destroyed or damaged, which had to be abandoned. The fighting continued until the end of July, with Rommel receiving supplies and reinforcements, but Auchinleck was reluctant to engage in another battle so soon. He wanted to wait for his reserves to build up but Churchill saw this as weakness and decided that he would replace 'the Auk' with someone who was more aggressive and willing to take risks. For the time being, at least, the war in the desert was at a stalemate once more. Meanwhile, the war continued in Russia.

The M3 Medium Tank

The M3 Lee, or Grant, was another American-built tank, like the earlier M3 Honey light tank, which had been battle-proven before America entered the war proper and demonstrated to the US Army what their tanks were capable of achieving in combat. America was not involved in the war in Europe in 1939 but that did not prevent military observers from taking an interest in developments and sending reports to various departments. One such observation from 1939 reported that tank guns at the time were proving inadequate, especially those in the 37mm-calibre bracket. Events of 1940, with the overrunning of Western Europe spearheaded by panzer divisions, confirmed this, and American designers began to examine ways of fitting guns of 75mm calibre into tanks. The problem was that turret designs of the time were not capable of supporting such a large-calibre gun and so an alternative method was devised. This alternative was known as a sponson mounting, a design more commonly used on warships, but while this solved the problem of getting a large gun into a tank it raised the problem of how to traverse the weapon. By their very design, sponson mountings permit only a limited traverse, whereas a turret can traverse through 360 degrees for all-round protection.

In July 1940 the US Ordnance Committee, which advised on such matters, designated that a new tank design using the sponson method for mounting a 75mm gun should be developed and termed it the M3 medium tank. Previous contracts for other tank designs were cancelled and the Chrysler Corporation of Michigan was awarded the contract to produce the M3 tank. The company already had experience of building vehicles for the military and for this project it acquired a site on which to build a purpose-built tank factory at Warren in Michigan. By the end of the war the company had produced around 25,000 armoured vehicles, including 3,352 of the new M3 tanks.

A British tank commission sent to America in June 1940 faced obstacles in purchasing tanks because American producers believed that Britain was about to surrender following the country's defeat at Dunkirk. They were therefore reluctant to build a tank to British specifications. Undeterred, the British delegation decided that the M3 medium tank would suit the needs of the British Army and an order was placed with the Pullman Company and the Pressed Steel Company. These companies would eventually build 500 and 501 M3 tanks respectively. Other companies such as Baldwin would produce a further 1,220 and Alco built 685 M3 tanks. Not all of these were destined for Britain and Canada, and later Russia was also supplied with the tank. What did make a significant difference was that for the first time the same mass-production methods used to build civilian cars were applied to building tanks. This greatly eased assembly and speeded up the production rate.

Vehicle Name	Manufacturer	Production Date	Armament	Weight	Max. Speed
M3 (Lee I)	Pullman Company and the Pressed Steel Company	1940	75mm M2 or M3 gun in sponson, 37mm gun and up to 3x .30in-calibre machine guns	27.5 tons	21mph
M3A1 (Lee II)	Pullman Company and the Pressed Steel Company	1942	75mm gun, 37mm gun and 3x or 4x .30in-calibre machine guns	32 tons	26mph
M3A2 (Lee III)	Pullman Company and the Pressed Steel Company	1942	75mm gun, 37mm gun and 3x or 4x .30in-calibre machine guns	27.2 tons	26mph
M3A3 (petrol) (Lee IV)	Pullman Company and the Pressed Steel Company	1942	75mm gun, 37mm gun and 3x or 4x .30in-calibre machine guns	30 tons	29mph
M3A3 (diesel) (Lee V)	Pullman Company and the Pressed Steel Company	1942	75mm gun, 37mm gun and 3x or 4x .30in-calibre machine guns	30 tons	26mph
M3A4 (Lee VI)	Pullman Company and the Pressed Steel Company	1942	75mm gun, 37mm gun and 3x or 4x .30in-calibre machine guns	29 tons	30mph
M3A5 (Grant II)	Pullman Company and the Pressed Steel Company	1942	75mm M2 or M3 gun in sponson, 37mm gun and up to 4x .30in-calibre machine guns	28.6 tons	25mph

The M3 was built in several versions, including the standard M3A1 design through successive models to reach the M3A5, and then afterwards was used on other variants to produce the M7 'Priest' SPG, a vehicle recovery model, workshop vehicles and even vehicles for use in mine-clearance roles. In service with the British Army the M3 was known by two names: the 'Lee' after General Robert E. Lee and the 'Grant' after General Ulysses S. Grant, who had been commanders during the American Civil War. The M3 was the Lee I; the M3A1 the Lee II; the M3A3 as the Lee IV; M3A3 (fitted with a diesel engine) the Lee V; and the M3A4 the Lee VI. These versions kept the original small cupola-type turret mounting a .30in-calibre machine gun on top of the turret of the 37mm gun. This was the design also used by the US Army but the British did not much care for a tank with such a prominent profile at 10ft 3in high. The M3A5 version had machine-gun cupola removed and this design was called the Grant II. The Grant I was produced by Pullman and the Pressed Steel companies using a turret of British design and it was this version that was used at the Battle of Gazala on 27 May 1942, where for the first-time tanks of the Eighth Army stood anything like a chance against the German PzKw IVs.

Jake Wardrop was serving with the 5th Royal Tank Regiment and remembered: 'new tanks were arriving now and they were super, the finest things we had ever

seen. They had a nine-cylinder radial engine, were quite fast and had a crew of six
... The gun was a 37mm and the bottom one a 75mm ...' In action the tanks acquit-
ted themselves well, being able to dish out punishment to the German tanks and
withstand the fire from anti-tank guns. The crews were concerned about being
resupplied with fuel and ammunition to keep up the fight. One tank commander
recalled how relieved he was when 'The ammunition and petrol lorries duly
reached us, after a fairly adventurous journey. All the Grants were refilled with
ammunition, and the light squadron was brought in a troop at a time to fill up with
petrol.' The troops called the battle the 'Gazala Gallop' and of the 167 Grants committed almost half were knocked out, mainly by the powerful 88mm anti-tank gun.
By October 1942 a further 350 M3s were in the theatre where 210 were present at
the Battle of El Alamein, along with 270 M4 Sherman tanks.

The basic M3 had armour protection between 13mm and 37mm and was
18ft 6in long, 8ft 11in wide and 10ft 3in high. This would be reduced by 3in when
the upper machine-gun cupola was removed. Typically a Wright Continental
R-975-EC2 nine-cylinder petrol engine developing 340hp at 2,400rpm was fitted
at the rear. This gave a road speed of up to 26mph and 16mph cross-country with
an operational range of 120 miles on roads. Armament comprised either an M2
or an M3 75mm-calibre gun fitted into a sponson mounted on the right-hand side
of the tank and, while elevation was good, the ability to traverse was restricted.
The upper turret mounted either an M5 or M6 37mm-calibre gun with a co-axial
.30in-calibre machine gun, both of which were good against light vehicles, which
left the 75mm gun for the tanks. The upper cupola was also fitted with a .30in-
calibre machine gun for other light targets or infantry. Some versions, such as
the M3A4 Lee VI, were equipped with two additional .30in-calibre machine guns
in the front glacis plate to make the tank an armoured weapons platform. When
the M4 Sherman tank became available in greater numbers they replaced the
M3, which the British removed from North Africa and deployed to India and the
Far East where they in turn replaced the Matilda Mk II, Valentine and lighter M3
Honey. The M3 medium tank was declared obsolete in early March 1944 but it was
still useful in other roles such as for training purposes.

The German Panzerkampfwagen IV (SdKfz 161)

Until the deployment of the American-built M3 Lee-Grant and M4 Sherman tanks
to the desert the Germans had the most powerful tank in the theatre in the shape
of the Panzerkampfwagen IV. The prototype Panzerkampfwagen IV had appeared
in 1937 and, built in various models, it would remain in production throughout
the war. Indeed, it has the distinction of being the only tank to continue to be built
and serve in action from 1939 to 1945. In all some 8,540 gun tanks were built
of which around 3,774 Ausf. H were built, making it the most numerous model

produced. In addition there were hundreds more chassis produced for other roles such as the Sturmpanzer assault gun, which was armed with a 150mm gun and the *Panzerbeobachtungswagen* (observation post tank). The Panzer IV had the specialist designation of SdKfz 161 and the Ausf. H was produced by three companies – Krupp-Gruson, Vomag and Nibelungenwerke – between April 1943 and July 1944. There were a further 161 chassis completed for the Ausf. H tank that are understood to have been used on other projects including SPGs. The company of Nibelungenwerke on its own built a further 1,758 Ausf. J tanks between June 1944 and March 1945, which made them among some of the last tanks to be produced in a collapsing Germany. The Ausf. J had a larger fuel tank but it was still armed with the 7.5cm-calibre KwK40 L/48 for which eighty-seven rounds of ammunition were carried.

Vehicle Name	Manufacturer	Production Date	Armament	Weight	Max. Speed
SdKfz 161 Ausf. H	Krupp-Gruson, Vomag and Nibelungenwerke	1943–44	7.5cm-calibre KwK40 L/48 and 2x MG34 machine guns	25 tons	25mph
SdKfz 161 Ausf. J	Nibelungenwerke	1944–45	7.5cm-calibre KwK40 L/48	25 tons	25mph

The basic Panzer IV Ausf. H measured around 23ft long, 9.4ft wide and 11.5ft to the top of the turret. It was fitted with a rear-mounted Maybach HL120TRM V-12 diesel engine with six forward and one reverse gear, which developed 300hp at 3,000rpm to give road speeds of up to 25mph on roads and 12mph cross-country. The Panzer IV had a combat range of about 125 miles when operating on roads and could cope with verti-cal obstacles 2ft high, span gaps of over 7ft wide and ford water obstacles more than 2ft deep. It was armed with a 7.5cm KwK40 L/48 gun for which eighty-seven rounds of ammunition was carried. Secondary armament comprised of two MG34 machine guns, one mounted co-axially with the main gun and the other in a ball mount fitted to the right-hand side of the hull with 2,800 rounds of ammunition carried.

Among the characteristics that identified the Ausf. H from earlier versions was an increase in the level of armour plate to a maximum of 80mm and other internal modifications that were not immediately obvious. Externally, a cupola mount for a machine gun was fitted on the turret and the four return rollers were changed to an all-steel design. There were eight road wheels with the drive sprocket fitted to the front and the idler wheel to the rear. The turret had a full 360-degree capabil-ity and was powered by an electric motor. The gun could elevate to +20 degrees and depress to -8 degrees, allowing it to engage a wide range of ground targets.

The Ausf. H was fitted with brackets to allow sections of armour plate to be attached to the sides to protect the road wheels from anti-tank projectiles. These armour plates were called *Schurzen* and had been used on the Ausf. G and were also used on the Ausf. J version. Similar attachments were fitted around the sides of the turret; these were permanently attached, but did not hinder traverse. It was explained that the side plates were often lost in battle and certainly one of the

This Ausf. H version of the PzKw IV is armed with the 75mm gun and is of the type used in France and Russia.

This is the late-build Ausf. J of the PzKw IV armed with 75mm gun.

plates on the left-hand side was invariably left off the vehicle where the fuel filling point was. This would have been a tactical decision because to remove and replace the plate would have increased refuelling time and so it was usually left off the vehicle. Versions of the Panzer IV served in all theatres of the war, from Poland in 1939, France 1940 and Russia from 1941 onwards, along with the campaigns in

The PzKw IV was used by several armies after the war including Middle Eastern forces and had a crew of five. It served on all fronts and was supplied to Germany's Romanian and Hungarian allies fighting in Russia.

North Africa and Italy. It is believed that when the Allies landed in Normandy on 6 June 1944, most of the estimated 748 Panzer IV tanks in service with the nine panzer divisions in France were Ausf. H. During the war versions of the Panzer IV were also supplied to Germany's allies, including Hungary and Bulgaria.

The M4 Sherman Tank

The M4 Sherman was the third American-built tank to be used by the British Army in North Africa, where it was given its baptism of combat experience before America had committed troops to any theatre of war proper. The Sherman entered service in 1942 and by the time of what was to later become known as the First Battle of El Alamein, which began on 23 October 1942, there were some 270 in service with the British Eighth Army along with 210 M3 Lee-Grant tanks. These were among the first vehicles built and the British would go on to take into service a total of 17,000. Other Allied armies such as the Canadians, Free French and Polish would all be equipped with the Sherman and even the Russians took delivery of 4,102, some of which they fitted with the 76.2mm gun, which was also fitted to the T-34. The Sherman tank was built by three main manufacturing plants, Ford, Chrysler and General Motors, and by the end of the war they, along with subsidiary factories, had produced some 49,234 tanks between them. The M4 was produced in fourteen different versions and was used on various experimental concepts, not all of which were developed to service stage. Using the same technique to build tanks as commercial motorcars on the assembly line using prefabricated parts, it has been calculated that a Sherman tank could be assembled in thirty minutes, compared to the tens of thousands of hours for German tanks.

Selected Models of the M4 Sherman Tank

Vehicle Name	Manufacturer	Production Date	Armament	Weight	Max. Speed
M4 Sherman	Ford, Chrysler and General Motors	1942	75mm gun and 3x machine guns	29.8 tons combat weight	24mph
M4A2 Sherman	Chrysler and General Motors	1943	75mm gun and 3x machine guns	30.8 tons combat weight	29mph
M4A3 Sherman	Chrysler and General Motors	1944	76mm gun and 3x machine guns	29.8 tons combat weight	26mph
M4A3E2 Sherman 'Assault Tank'	Chrysler and General Motors	1944	7in gun	37.5 tons combat weight	22mph
M4A4 Sherman	Chrysler and General Motors	1943	75mm gun and 3x machine guns	34.8 tons	26mph
M4A6 Sherman	Chrysler and General Motors	1943	75mm gun and 3x machine guns	31.7 tons combat weight	30mph

Tank production in America was beginning to get under way in mid-1940 at around the same time that the Armoured Force, commanded by Brigadier General Adna R. Chaffee, was being created. The 1st Armoured Corps was activated in early July and comprised the 1st and 2nd Armoured Divisions based at Fort Knox, Kentucky, and Fort Benning, Georgia, respectively. More units followed so that by 1943 sixteen armoured divisions had been formed, each with their own tank battalions, infantry battalions and artillery support. Most would see action in north-west Europe and serve in many campaigns. The 2nd Armoured Division, nicknamed 'Hell on Wheels', served in North Africa, Sicily and all the European campaigns. There were also separate 'non-divisional' tank battalions and these tended to serve in the Pacific theatre, although some did serve in Europe. Among the new tank designs being considered was a project known as T-6, which incorporated a 75mm gun fitted into a new cast turret, which would allow a full all-round traverse capability of 360 degrees. The M3 Lee-Grant was being produced but this new design had a number of benefits and after consideration it was standardised in September 1941 as the M4 medium tank but commonly known as the 'Sherman'.

The Sherman tank was an evolving and changing design, and this affected its weight and dimensions, which changed to meet the variants being developed from the original basic model. The first production M4 weighed 29.8 tons but the later M4A6 weighed 31.7 tons and the M4A3E2 'Assault Tank', armed with a 7in gun in a turret, weighed 37.5 tons. Some 254 of these heavyweight versions, nicknamed 'Jumbo', were built and ready in June 1944. The basic M4 Sherman measured 19ft 4in long, 8ft 7in wide and 9ft to the top of the turret. It was armed with a 75mm gun, for which ninety-seven rounds of ammunition were carried, with a .30in-calibre machine gun co-axially mounted. An additional .30in-calibre machine gun was mounted in the front of the hull and a removable machine gun, either a .30in- or .50in-calibre machine gun could be mounted on the turret roof. Different engines were fitted to various models and this affected the speed accordingly; for example, the original M4 was fitted with a Continental R-975-C1 nine-cylinder radial giving road speeds of up to 24mph, while the M4A6 was fitted with an Ordnance RD 1829 nine-cylinder radial, which produced speeds of up to 30mph.

To deal with the heavier German tanks the Americans had proposed fitting a 90mm gun on to the Sherman but that would have meant designing a completely new turret. The British approached the problem by investigating the possibility of a 76mm-calibre gun firing a 17lb shell fitted into a modified turret. In October 1943 engineers at Woolwich succeeded and once other technical details had been sorted it was decided to fit 600 M4A4 Sherman tanks with the Mk IV L/55 76mm gun for which seventy-eight rounds of ammunition would be carried inside the tank. The Americans had initially resisted the idea of using the Firefly but some 160 vehicles were made available to them and the design was in service with crews trained in readiness for the Normandy Landings on D-Day, 6 June 1944.

The Firefly weighed 32.7 tons and measured 25ft 6in long and 9ft 4in to the top of the turret. Armour protection was 13mm to 75mm and an operational range of 125 miles with a road speed of 22mph, which made it a match for the Tiger tanks in the hedgerows of the Normandy countryside known as the Bocage. One of the most famous of all German 'tank aces' to fall victim to the Firefly was Michael Wittmann, who met his fate in close action during the Normandy campaign in 1944. One of the variants to be based on the chassis of the M4 Sherman was a design that became known as the M7 SPG and this served extensively across Europe and also in North Africa, to a lesser degree. The pilot models for new M7 SPG were produced by the American Locomotive Company in June 1941 with the project number T-32 appended and sent to the army for trials at the Aberdeen Proving Ground in Maryland. These trials were successful and proved the system to be workable with remarkably few design faults, and led to the army placing an order for 600. The only real criticism levelled at the T-32 design was that the configuration lacked an anti-tank capability. This was rather unfair because the design was intended to be what the artillery classified as a howitzer, which meant that it was to be used to provide fire support, with the weapon firing ammunition at high angles of trajectory. The barrel of the weapon could be depressed to a sufficiently low angle to engage enemy tanks, but this would be of little purpose when tanks would be in support to protect it against attack; furthermore, one would suppose that anti-tank guns dedicated to the role of destroying enemy tanks would be contained within the unit structure. As a weapon the SPG was nothing new in service, but it was the flexibility that the design gave to the artillery that made it important during the Second World War. In fact, all fighting nations would deploy their own form of SPGs that were based on the chassis of existing and proven tank designs. The advantage of the newly developed American design, however, was the speed it was produced, which made it quite extraordinary. In fact, within only eight months of the pilot models of the T-32 appearing the new weapon was standardised as the M7 Howitzer Motor Gun Carriage and accepted by the US Army in February 1942. Five months later a batch of 100 of these new vehicles was dispatched to the British Eighth Army in North Africa, but unfortunately the ship carrying them was sunk by a U-boat, and it looked as though the British Army would be denied the opportunity of giving another American AFV its baptism of fire.

The M7 Howitzer Motor Gun Carriage

The American Locomotive Company had already tooled up its factory to begin building the M7 and using the assembly-line technique had produced sufficient vehicles to allow another ninety to be sent out as replacements for those lost on their way to the British Army. These guns were sent by convoy and in September 1942 were handed over to units in the front line, including the 11th Regiment Royal Horse Artillery, which was serving with the 1st Armoured Division. Only two months later, in November, the 5th Regiment Royal Horse Artillery, also serving with the 1st Armoured Division, deployed their M7 SPGs and used them to engage and destroy German anti-tank guns, which had been well dug in to fire at British tanks during the final battles of El Alamein. The gunners of the Royal Artillery were impressed with the new American guns, and, typically for the British Army, nicknamed the gun 'Priest' because of the pulpit-like mounting for the 12.7mm heavy machine gun. In view of its success in battle the British Tank Commission in America requested that a further 5,500 M7 Priest SPGs be delivered by the end of 1943. Even with all its industrial might this was an optimistic request for America's armaments industry and it was realised that there was no way that this number of guns could be supplied to the British Army as well as those of the US Army, especially after events in December 1941. In the end the actual numbers entering service with the British Army would fall short of the requested amount.

Other Adaptations of the Sherman M4

The Sherman was not the best tank used during the war but it was certainly the most
numerous and was very important for a number of reasons. It was adaptable and was
used in all theatres of the war from Europe to the island-hopping campaigns in the
Pacific against the Japanese, where the temperatures and humidity were greater than
even the desert of North Africa. The Sherman 'Crab' was a development into a specialist role being fitted with large cylinders or rotating drums with heavy chains at the front
of the tank which rotated to beat the ground as the vehicle advanced to pound a path
through minefields. This was used during the Normandy campaign in 1944. Rocket-
launching frames were fitted above the turret and these were known as 'Calliope', but
probably the most unusual concept was that used by the 1st Coldstream Guards in
1945 when they fitted their Sherman tanks to fire 60lb aircraft rockets from either side
of the turret. This was called 'Tulip' and was certainly used during the Rhine crossing.
Extemporised launching rails were fitted to the turret and, although not accurate and
with a range of about 800yd, the rockets would have demoralised the enemy.

   The M4 chassis was used by the Canadians to produce the RAM and Kangaroo carrier, and other projects based on the same chassis design resulted in the M7 SPG
with a 105mm gun, known by the British Army as the 'Priest'. A flame-thrower version,
known as the 'Adder', of the Sherman was developed and it influenced a number of
overseas designs including the Australian 'Sentinel' and the Argentinian 'Nahuel'. The
British Army did use the M7 for a time but later went on to adopt a Canadian-developed
SPG that used the 25-pounder field gun and was known as the 'Sexton'. This was built

The M4 Sherman tank influenced many designs and was itself developed in many variations.

initially at the Montreal Locomotive Works in Canada and was another design based on the M4 chassis. One of the powerful versions of the Sherman was a British design called the 'Firefly' and fitted a 17-pounder anti-tank gun in replacement of the 75mm gun. The original gun could defeat most German tanks but against the heavier types such as the Tiger and Panther it was ineffective. It was for this reason that the British developed the Firefly.

The Sherman served as the backbone to many armoured units. The Germans called it the 'Tommy Cooker' because it caught fire easily, often killing the crew. It was armed with the 17-pounder anti-tank gun to become the Firefly which could destroy the heavy German tanks such as the Tiger I.

The Sexton SPG armed with 25-pounder field gun was used in Italy and across Europe during 1944.

Vehicle Name	Manufacturer	Production Date	Armament	Weight	Max. Speed
M7 Howitzer Motor Gun Carriage	American Locomotive Company	1942 onwards	105mm howitzer and a .50in-calibre machine gun	22.6 tons	26mph
M7B1	Pressed Steel Car	1944–45	105mm howitzer and a 50in-calibre machine gun	22.3 tons	25mph
M7B2	Federal Machine and Welder Company	1945	105mm howitzer and a .50in-calibre machine gun	21.6 tons	26mph

SPGs had been proven in earlier battles, but what made the M7 Priest so special was the fact that it was the first such design of any significance to enter service with the Allies. The M7 had actually come into being as a result of experiments to mount a 75mm howitzer on the chassis of a light tank in order to produce an SPG. This was very much the same way that Germany had produced the anti-tank Panzerjäger 1 SPG, with a 47mm gun mounted on the chassis of a PzKw I in 1940. Another series of trials involved a 105mm-calibre gun being mounted on the chassis of an M3 Lee-Grant medium tank, which was in series production at the time and was used by the British Army. From these trials it was decided to develop the M7 using the chassis of the M4 Sherman as opposed to the lighter M3 medium tank. During the development phase the basic system initially comprised an M1A1 105mm howitzer on its standard field mount being mounted on to a modified M4 medium tank with an open top and high-sided superstructure. The early production run of the M7 was based on the M3 medium tank chassis but it was supplanted by using the chassis of the M4A3 Sherman.

The M7, as based on the M4 chassis, was 19ft 9in long, 9ft 5in wide and 9ft 7in to the top of the machine-gun mounting in the 'pulpit'. To the right-hand side of the superstructure was a ring mount for a .50in-calibre machine gun. This stood proud from the hull and, with its armoured covering, looked not unlike the pulpit in a church, thereby leading to the term 'Priest', which soon gained widespread use. The M7 was powered by a Continental Model R-975-C1, nine-cylinder radial petrol engine which developed 350hp at 2,400rpm to produce a maximum road speed of 26mph and 15mph cross-country. It had an operational range of 125 miles on roads and could scale vertical obstacles of 2ft high, cross gaps of over 7ft unaided and ford water obstacles of 4ft deep.

The entire series of M7 vehicles, including variants, was armed with a single 105mm howitzer for which sixty-nine rounds were carried ready to use. For close defence and protection against low-flying aircraft, there was a single .50in-calibre machine gun, for which 300 rounds were carried. The main armament could elevate between -5 degrees and +35 degrees and had a traverse capability of 15 degrees right of centre line and 30 degrees left of centre line to give a 45-degree traverse in total without the requirement of having to move the vehicle's position. The problem causing the limited amount of traverse to the right was due to the fact that the driver's position to the left of the hull was in line with the breech mechanism as the weapon was moved. The M7 was protected by armour varying in thickness between 12mm and 60mm, and the vehicle had a combat-ready weight of 22.6 tons. It was served by a crew of seven men who operated in an open-topped fighting compartment and only the driver's position was under armour in the front of the hull.

With the introduction of the M7B1 version, and as production numbers increased, the Pressed Steel Company was engaged to maintain output, but the American Locomotive Company remained the main producer and built 3,314 M7s. The Pressed Steel Company produced 826 M7s of which around 450 were the M7B1 version. The only real difference between the original M7 and the M7B1 version was that the later design was slightly lighter. Some of this was due to the different engine, a Ford GAA V-8 that developed 450hp at 2,600rpm and achieved slightly reduced road speeds. The M7B1 version had a combat-ready weight of 22.3 tons and obstacle clearances were virtually identical to those capable with the M7. The traverse and elevation of the main armament was unaltered and could fire high-explosive rounds out to ranges of almost 11,000yd and other types of ammunition to ranges of around 11,500yd. The M7B1 was still served by a crew of seven men, as was the third version, known as the M7B2. Only 127 versions of this model were built by the Federal Machine and Welder Company, giving a total wartime production of 4,267 M7s of all types. The only real difference between this last version and the two preceding versions was the fact that the machine-gun 'pulpit' stood slightly higher. When in service with the British Army the 105mm gun was not without its problems and some M7 Priests were modified to remove the armament and the distinctive 'pulpit', and this led to them being nicknamed 'defrocked priests'. These unarmed versions were used for transport and observation roles for other artillery batteries. The British Army eventually developed a comparable SPG based on the Canadian-built Ram Cruiser tank, which mounted a 25-pounder gun and was known as the Sexton SPG. This break in use allowed the Americans to be supplied with all stocks of 105mm ammunition and in turn made logistical re-supply in the British Army much easier. The Americans did develop a trial programme of their own using the 25-pounder gun and produced the T-51 GMC in July 1942. The experiment was not a success and the programme was dropped.

The Valentine Tank

It could be said that the Valentine tank was made for the war in the desert because that is where many of them ended up serving with the British Eighth Army in North Africa. It was not much to look at and was certainly not a heavyweight in armour or weaponry, but it was capable of remarkable feats of endurance. For example, after the Battle of El Alamein in November 1942 some Valentine tanks in service with the 23rd Armoured Brigade were driven 3,000 miles on their owns tracks as they pursued the Afrika Korps westwards.

Vehicle Name	Manufacturer	Production Date	Armament	Weight	Max. Speed
Infantry Tank Mk III (Valentine)	Vickers	1940 onwards	Mk I to Mk VII: 2-pounder gun and .303in machine gun	16 tons	15mph

The 2-pounder gun was not very powerful but the Germans still used them against the British when they captured examples of the tanks. The Valentine was also fitted with a new superstructure and 25-pounder field gun to serve as an SPG called the Bishop. It was used in North Africa but its 2-pounder gun was limited.

The Valentine was used to develop some specialist vehicles, including 'swimming tanks' or duplex drives for D-Day.

Valentines in North Africa travelled 3,000 miles on their tracks after El Alamein.

In the mid-1930s the British Army realised that two types of tank would be necessary in any future war: a fast cruiser and a slow-moving infantry tank. The Vickers
company went it alone and developed their own infantry tank, which was moder-
ately well armoured but faster than the War Office type. The design was submitted
for approval on 14 February 1938 (St Valentine's Day), from which came the name
Valentine. The War Office did nothing for over a year but then in July 1939, sensing the impending outbreak of war, ordered Vickers to build 275 of the new tanks
without delay. The first tanks, officially designated Infantry Tank Mk III, entered
service in May 1940 and were among the first vehicles to make good some of the
losses of tanks abandoned at Dunkirk. Production continued until early 1944, by
which time 8,275 had been built. The Canadian Pacific Railway workshops built
1,420, most of which, along with 1,300 British-made tanks, were sent to Russia.
In British service the Valentine saw action in North Africa, Madagascar and the
campaign in the Far East. Even after it was replaced as a battle tank the chassis
were serviceable and these were converted for use as the basis for a number of
specialist vehicles such as bridge-layers, flame-throwers and swimming tanks. It
was also used for the Bishop self-propelled 25-pounder gun and the Archer self-
propelled 17-pounder gun.

   The Valentine layout was conventional, with the driver at the front, engine at
the rear and fighting compartment in the middle. Suspension was unusual in
that it employed six road wheels on each side in two three-bogie units. The final-
drive sprocket was at the rear and had a characteristic centre reduction unit that
revolved backwards at high speed when the tank was moving. The turret design
changed throughout its service from the early model which was operated by a
two-man crew and then later a three-man crew, but it would always be cramped.
The main armament was originally a 2-pounder gun, but the tank was up-gunned
with later versions being armed with a 6-pounder (57mm calibre) and then to a
75mm gun. The Russians believed the 2-pounder guns of the Valentines sent to
them were better suited to shooting sparrows and replaced them with 76mm guns,
a move that must have made the turret more cramped than ever.

   The Valentine weighed 16 tons and measured 17ft 9in long, 8ft 7in wide and 6ft
8in high. The early versions were fitted with an AEC A190 six-cylinder engine of
131hp to give road speeds of 15mph and an operational range of 110 miles. The
design went through a succession of changes in specification during its production life, and depending on the type, was served by a crew of either three men or
four. The Mk I and Mk II both had a two-man turret and the Mk III had a three-man
turret with all types being armed with a 2-pounder gun. And this remained the
same until the appearance of the Mk VIII, which was essentially a modified Mk III,
but armed with 6-pounder gun mounted in a two-man turret. The Mk IX and Mk X
Valentines were also armed with a 6-pounder gun but the Mk XI was armed with
a 75mm gun. Secondary armament was usually a single 7.92mm-calibre machine
gun but some versions armed with the 6-pounder gun omitted this weapon. The

amount of ammunition carried on the tank depended on the armament but typically some seventy-nine rounds were carried for the 2-pounder gun and 1,500
rounds for the machine gun; armour protection was between 7mm and 65mm.

Führer Directive 42 and Operation Blau

Things were about to change in the North African desert and thousands of miles
away in Russia decisions were also being made that would alter the whole course
of the war. At the time that changes in command were being made in the British
Army, Hitler was ordering a change of strategy in Russia, where his armies spread
across the country's vastness. There had been some reverses but on the whole
the war was still going favourably for Germany, and Hitler had plans for Army
Group South, and set for it a huge target, which if successful, could have weakened Russia's ability to fight. In April Hitler announced Führer Directive 42 or
Operation Blau (Blue), and ordered preparations to be made. From the rear ech-
elon he ordered huge troop movements to the south along with fifty-one divisions
supplied by his Bulgarian, Italian and Romanian allies. Italian support amounted
to 229,000 troops and 1,100 pieces of artillery along with an alpine corps complete
with 20,000 mules for the operation. When the movements had been completed
there were nine of the nineteen panzer divisions in Russia under Field Marshal
Fedor von Bock's command, along with four of the ten motorised divisions and
half of all infantry divisions. In other words, Army Group South had 50 per cent of
all the German Army's resources at its disposal.

With so much weaponry, equipment, troops and support available for the
campaign ahead, senior officers believed it would be successful. Any doubts
they may have harboured about turning south instead of pushing on eastwards
appeared to be without foundation and failure was never considered an option.
The opening moves saw a wide sweeping pincer movement against the city of
Voronezh, some 300 miles to the south of Moscow, and other sizeable towns such
as Staryy, Oskol, Millrovo and Morovsk were captured as the Sixth Army continued
its advance towards its Operation Heron target of Stalingrad. From here Hitler
could launch Operation Edelweis, the strike towards the oilfields of the Caucasus.
He had every faith in the Sixth Army under General Friedrich von Paulus, after all
they had been successful in every campaign in which they had participated so far.
The Sixth Army had been victorious in Poland and marched through Paris in 1940
and in 1941 they had been present when Operation Barbarossa was launched. If
the Sixth Army could help capture the vital resources, the Russian Army would be
crippled by lack of fuel while the Germans would have enough to be self-sufficient.
From early July to early August the Germans moved forward to try to encircle the
city of Stalingrad. During that time they had captured the city of Rostov with its
massive industrial centre. The advance was opposed by the Russians who put up
enough resistance to cover a planned, orderly withdrawal. Hitler was jubilant,

proclaiming: 'The Russians are in full flight! They are finished!' But it was to prove the undoing of the Germans in Russia and would change the course of the war.

The city of Stalingrad proper stretched for about 15 miles along the western bank of the River Volga, but its environs extended much farther. At its widest point it spread out over 4 miles and so its shape was linear, which would force any attacker to spread his forces wide. That is exactly what von Paulus did and although his troops would eventually capture some 90 per cent of the city it never made any incursions across the Volga and the east bank of the river remained in Russian hands. The city had a number of factories, including three that were very important: the Barrikady, the Red October and the Tractor Factory. The distances the Germans expected to cover were enormous and placed great strain on supply lines, men and machines. The 4th Panzer Army, commanded by General Hermann Hoth, had to cover more than 20 miles to help support General Ewald von Kleist's 1st Panzer Army, and faced fierce Russian resistance in the Don Basin. The two forces met but the Russians had withdrawn, leaving nothing of any consequence to be captured. Kleist later remarked that in his opinion, 'Fourth Panzer Army could have taken Stalingrad without a fight at the end of July, but it was diverted to help me crossing the Don. I did not need its aid, and it simply got in the way.' In fact the amount of traffic on the roads was so heavy that it caused congestion and traffic jams leading to delays as each unit tried to get its vehicles through on less than perfect roads. Hitler then ordered Hoth to return to the thrust on Stalingrad, adding to the mileage that was to be covered, and Kleist continued southwards towards the oilfields.

The Russians were not entirely unaware that a major offensive was about to be launched because they had come into possession of a full set of detailed plans outlining Operation Blau. They had gained the papers when the aircraft in which Major Reichel, chief of operations for

Italians used thousands of ponies and mules to move heavy loads such as this artillery unit.

the 23rd Panzer Division, was in made a forced landing close to Russian lines. The capture of such sensitive documents seemed too convenient to Stalin, who held the belief that the Germans still planned to attack Moscow. Despite their appearance to the contrary, Stalin dismissed the captured plans as a plant to deceive the Russians by subterfuge. Nevertheless, when the German attack came and the Russians realised what the object of the attack was they immediately mobilised the one resource they had in ample supply – manpower. A civilian labour force initially made up of 90,000 was put to work between August and September, and was set the task of building defences. The work continued day and night without pause, such was the urgency to halt the Germans. More workers joined and eventually they constructed 100,000 defensive positions including 70,000 pillboxes, using concrete and bricks. They dug 500 miles of anti-tank ditches, 200 miles of anti-infantry obstacles and 1,000 miles of trenches for their own infantry. Roads and mountain passes were blocked. The tanks and infantry of von Kleist were stopped and the Caucasian oilfields were safe.

General von Paulus and his Sixth Army with twenty-five divisions, 2,000 pieces of artillery and 500 tanks supported by the VIII Fliegerkorps, capable of flying 1,000 sorties per day, were at the gates of Stalingrad. Facing them, the garrison commander, Lieutenant General Vasili Chuikov, who had replaced General Alexander Lopatin, had a force of 54,000 men in the Sixty-Fourth Army supported by 900 pieces of artillery and mortars and 110 tanks. On taking up his command he reported to his superior, General Andrei Yeremenko, that 'We shall hold the city, or die there'. The city had been invested ready to be besieged and from 24 August heavy fighting patrols were being sent out to probe the Russians' defences, but the first serious attack was not made until 14 September. The combined weight of the attack with Hoth's troops brought the total strength to 200,000 men. Tanks entered the city in support of the attack and the Russians defended every building, street and cellar. The Germans were not used to fighting in such conditions and tanks are totally unsuited to fighting in built-up areas with buildings all around. Once they had entered the city the Germans did not withdraw and poured more men and reserves into capturing it. The Russians did not evacuate the civilians and they were able to bring reinforcements and supplies into the city by ferry across the River Volga. These boats were attacked by German aircraft and bombarded by artillery but the supply lines into the city kept operating. By the end of the battle these boats, known as the Volga Flotilla, had made 35,000 crossings to bring in supplies and 122,000 men and had evacuated the most seriously wounded. The fighting continued throughout the rest of the month by which time the Russians had lost 80,000 men killed and wounded.

The Beginnings of a Second Front

As the Germans were approaching the outskirts of Stalingrad, the Western Allies were putting a plan in action to launch a limited attack on the French coast. On 19 August an Anglo-Canadian force including fifty-one US rangers and some French commandos landed at Dieppe in an action called Operation Jubilee. The object of the operation was to make an assault in order to gain experience in trying to capture a port installation, which would be needed to support an amphibious landing. The Western Allies had been harangued by Stalin to launch a second front by attacking in the west, but they just did not have the supplies or specialist vehicles and equipment to undertake such an assault in 1942. Furthermore, they had no experience in large-scale amphibious landings. The attack against Dieppe was designed to give the Allies experience at all levels, including how important it was to get armour ashore from the landing craft. The bulk of the force was infantry and was made up by 4,963 troops from the Canadian 2nd Infantry Division supported by a squadron of twenty-eight Churchill tanks. The Germans later remarked that they considered the attack to be serious because it was too large to be an ordinary commando raid, and when they saw that it was an attempt to land a force on a beach they knew it was too small to be the anticipated invasion. The infantry managed to move inland away from the beach and fighting was fierce, but against defensive positions held by superior numbers, and even with air cover, they could only do their best. The operation collapsed as the casualty rate among the British and Canadian infantry mounted and the Royal Navy lost more vessels.

The first landings had been made before 5 a.m. but by 9 a.m. it was becoming clear that the operation was foundering. Major General Roberts, commanding the Canadians, organised for the RAF to provide air cover to allow the infantry to withdraw. At 11 a.m. the landing craft approached the shore to embark the men and by midday the operation was all but finished. It was an unmitigated disaster, with the Canadians losing 900 men killed and a further 3,367 wounded and taken prisoner. The British lost 275 killed, wounded and taken prisoner. Two of the tanks had sunk in deep water as they were landed, a number became bogged down in the shingle and fifteen made it to the sea wall and began to move off the beach before being halted by obstacles. The Germans lost 519 killed and wounded. In the grand scheme of things, compared to events on the Russian front, the Dieppe raid was a small pinprick. The Allies had learned many lessons from the mistakes made at Dieppe and they would correct some by the time of their next attempt at amphibious assault. The Germans had learned not to underestimate the Allies' resolve to invade Europe. Indeed, the Allies came to realise the limitations of ordinary armour and recognised the importance of developing special armoured vehicles to break through defences and also that a port installation was vital for supplies to be ferried in to support the assault. The episode was a failure but it demonstrated to Stalin that his Western Allies were making some kind of effort.

The Defence of Stalingrad

At Stalingrad the populace was mobilised to build barricades, women soldiers served on anti-aircraft guns and to a man they were resolved to defend the city come what may. The German situation looked strong but in reality they were at the end of a very long and consequently very fragile supply line. Furthermore, they had no reserves of anything to speak of. In their advance to invest the city, tanks and other AFVs had spearheaded the attack followed by the supply con-voys with the infantry bringing up the rear. Even so, the advance had been so fast that it had outpaced some of the supply columns. The Russians continued to fall back, avoiding battle and this further added to the Germans' false sense of victory and they pressed on ever deeper into Russia. Hitler asked General Kurt Zeitzler, a specialist in logistics, for his assessment of the situation and was given the cautionary notice to take care of the positions held to the north of Stalingrad where the Italians, Hungarians and Romanians held the line. He also pointed out that the southern sector and the Sixth Army's right flank was also exposed. The Germans had never before had to fight in such conditions where men hid among the ruins of buildings, and the battle was costing them 20,000 killed and wounded per week. The streets were strewn with rubble, which reduced the tanks to a crawl and exposed them to anti-tank weapons.

Stalin proclaimed a policy of 'Not one step backward' and that there was 'no land beyond the Volga'. In other words the Russian Army had to stand and fight where it was. Snipers took their toll and battles ebbed backwards and forwards, with build-ings changing hands many times. Using the ferries the Russians were able to move 122,000 men into the city to carry on the fight but this was only the tip of the iceberg as the greater proportion of men, vehicles, supplies and weapons amount-ing to twenty-seven infantry divisions and nineteen armoured divisions were sent to assembly areas in readiness for the attack. When the River Volga froze, the ice bridge allowed more traffic to flow, like Lake Ladoga at Leningrad. The build-up continued until mid-November, by which time the Russians had built up a force of 1 million men, 900 tanks, thousands of trucks and 13,500 pieces of artillery sup-ported by 1,100 aircraft. The Germans were running out of fuel to the degree that between September and November the tanks of the 22nd Panzer Division could not operate. Finally, the preparations were complete and the Russians launched Operation Uranus on 19 November, attacking the Romanian positions to the north of the city, just as Zeitzler had predicted and tried to warn against. The powerful T-34 tanks, which the Germans had already encountered, were used in large numbers; the Romanians had no defence against them and fled their positions. The collapse left a 50-mile-wide gap in the German lines and the Russians poured through.

The attack to the south of Stalingrad was equally powerful and the Russians streamed through the German lines. Their advance was so fast that German Army military police directing the flow of traffic became confused and could not tell the difference between friend and foe. Russian troops on trucks seized bridges and secured them. On 23 November the two arms of the Russian pincer movement met up 30 miles west of Stalingrad and the Germans inside the city were surrounded and cut off. The Russians believed they had trapped 75,000 men but the figure was much higher; they had actually succeeded in cutting off 250,000 men. There was no chance of moving reinforcements into the city to support them but the Russians could move with almost total impunity and they were getting stronger every day. Three days after the attack von Paulus made an assessment of his situation and estimated that he had food for only six days and fuel and ammunition stocks were running critically low. Von Paulus signalled Hitler asking that he be allowed to fight his way out of the city. Hitler forbade such a move and told him

The Churchill was capable of speeds up to 15mph on roads. The British Churchill armed with 6-Pounder main gun. It was used in the flame-thrower role as the 'Crocodile'.

that supplies would be flown into the beleaguered city. This was a monumental task but Herman Goering believed his Luftwaffe could do it. The trapped Sixth Army needed at least 120 tons of fuel and 250 tons of ammunition each day to continue. Other supplies such as medical aid and food would push this figure up to 600 tons needed by each army.

The Luftwaffe would have to fly from bases at Tatsinskaya and Morozovsky, a three-hour round flight, which meant aircraft could only fly one mission per day. There were 225 Ju 52 transport aircraft but they were slow and lumbering, which made them vulnerable to attack by fighters. To support the operation He III bombers were pressed into service and although they were faster than the Ju 52 aircraft they could only carry 1.5 tons of supplies. The claim that the trapped Sixth Army could be supplied by air depended on all aircraft being serviceable and airfields inside the city being held by German forces. The best they could achieve was eighty serviceable aircraft per day and when the Russians captured the airfields the amount of supplies that could be flown in fell to less than 60 tons per day. The attempt to airlift supplies cost the Germans 488 aircraft shot down or crashed. Field Marshal Erich von Manstein, now commanding the newly formed Army Group Don, formulated Operation Winter Storm, which was intended to break into the city to relieve the Sixth Army. By now the Russians had pushed 80 miles west past Stalingrad but General Hoth with his 4th Panzer Division began his mission on 12 December. In his column he had a convoy of trucks carrying 3,000 tons of supplies. They battled on against Russian attacks, worsening weather conditions and rugged terrain. His progress slowed and finally on 23 December Hoth was ordered to withdraw. He was 30 miles short of his destination and the Sixth Army was effectively abandoned to its fate. The distance between the German front line and Stalingrad grew longer each day as the Russians continued to advance. The Sixth Army, now depleted, somehow continued to fight on but groups were surrendering. Finally the Germans surrendered on 31 January 1943. The fighting had cost the Germans 150,000 killed and the Russians took a further 100,000 prisoner. The Germans had lost so much equipment it was calculated that it could have supplied 25 per cent of the German Army in the field. They had suffered their worst defeat but there was more to come as the Western Allies mounted operations before the fall of Stalingrad. It had been a costly demonstration of how important good logistical support was to a modern army.

Developments in Europe and North Africa

The lesson of Stalingrad and how important it was to supply ammunition and fuel to an army was not lost on the Allies but the Germans did not appear to have learnt anything from the experience. No army could continue to lose weapons, vehicles and troops in the same way as Germany was and still expect the army to function. Yet here was Hitler still urging his forces to go on with depleted resources and minimal supplies reaching them. Production of trucks and tanks was a problem for Germany and the shortfall affected deliveries of supplies of food and fuel for the tanks. During 1942 the German factories produced 59,000 trucks for an army of 8 million deployed to three fronts: Russia, Western Europe and North Africa. By comparison, in the same period over 400,000 horses were sent to Russia, which explodes the propaganda myth of the motorised German Army that was widely broadcast at the time. Another move made by the Western Allies as the events at Stalingrad were being fought out was Operation Torch, an amphibious force to land a mainly largely American force on the North African coast of French Morocco and Algeria. This was launched on 8 November, eleven days before the Russians launched Operation Uranus at Stalingrad, and it would show Stalin what they were capable of achieving, and should have also served as a warning to Hitler of what to expect in Europe.

The forces comprised 65,000 American troops who had never been in combat before and other forces including Free French took the number of troops to 107,000 with tanks and trucks and supplies. Convoys to support the operation sailed from America direct to North Africa and maintained the supply line. Supplies, especially fuel, were vital for the army to continue to operate. To highlight this, as one American general remarked: 'My men can eat their belts, but my tanks gotta have gas.' During the Torch Landings several commanders emerged such as General George S. Patton and Mark Clark, both of whom had seen service in the First World War, and Omar Bradley who was too late to see action in the First World War but was very active between the wars. In fact Torch was his first front-line command and other generals would become prominent in other theatres and campaigns such as Mark Clark in Italy and Patton in North Africa, Sicily and Europe. The Americans had hoped for a quick campaign but after a week of fighting the French Vichy troops had put up a resistance and killed almost 1,400 American troops. They had 210 ancient tanks that were no match for the modern American designs, which included the Sherman and anti-tank guns. With the success of these new landings in North Africa the Germans were now faced with an improbable situation of fighting on two fronts on two separate continents, with each having to be supplied. The Germans responded to the Torch Landings by sending 17,000 reinforcements with General Jürgen von Arnim to the area, along with supplies and the first of the new Tiger tanks armed with the deadly 88mm gun. When Rommel was informed of the Allied landings he wrote in his diary that 'This spells the end of the army in Africa'. As usual he was correct but he still fought a hard campaign right to the end.

Four months before the amphibious landings of Operation Torch the month of July started badly for the British Eighth Army, which was on the back foot and waiting for Rommel to make his next move, surely the knockout blow. With minimal resources he had achieved the seemingly impossible, to the delight of Hitler who promoted him to field marshal. It was all very different from his position in May when he was within twenty-four hours of surrendering due to lack of water, but he had only been able to achieve these latest results by using the huge stocks of supplies he had captured at Tobruk. However, he was down to only fifty-five German tanks and thirty Italian tanks. The British had made preparations and Lieutenant General Eric Dorman-Smith oversaw the construction of defensive positions just outside the railway junction of El Alamein, which lay a few miles inland from the Egyptian coast. The British had lost 138 in the fighting of 13 June and after the Battle of Mersa Matruh on 26 June they had around seventy-five tanks capable of engaging in battle and had retreated to take up their positions at El Alamein. It was these and the prepared defences that the wave of Rommel's attack would break. The Russians were fighting on a single front but the British Army was stretched to its limit trying to maintain a defensive force in Britain to protect against any threat, and, along with the Americans, had to fight a completely separate war against the Japanese in the Pacific and try to stem the advance into India. These forces in all of these theatres had to be supplied with everything from troop reinforcements to vehicles, tanks, weapons, fuel and ammunition.

Rommel ordered the attacks to be halted and on 2 July, under concentrated artillery fire and harrying by the RAF, they retired. Like their counterparts in Russia, the Afrika Korps was at the end of a very long and fragile supply line that was being attacked by units of special forces, such as the LRDG and Special Air Service, which penetrated deep behind his lines. Rommel was strengthened by the arrival of reinforcements and 260 tanks. Auchinleck launched a number of attacks mainly directed against the weaker Italian forces, which made Rommel divert his tanks to support them. This put a strain on his vehicles and used up fuel, which was in short supply. By 11 July both sides were exhausted and stood facing one another like two boxers in a ring, each knowing that one of them had to make a move.

In August Churchill flew to Cairo and replaced General Auchinleck with General Harold Alexander, and when Lieutenant General William 'Strafer' Gott, the first choice for taking over the Eighth Army, was killed on 7 August, General Sir Alan Brooke, Commander Imperial General Staff (CIGS), suggested that General Bernard Montgomery be appointed to the position. The British were also receiving reinforcements, replacement tanks, supplies and the new, more powerful 6-pounder anti-tank gun. The Germans were still facing difficulties with their supplies getting through and on one occasion a convoy of six tankers was intercepted and four were sunk. Even though greatly reduced, Rommel was still able to make preparations and his tank force totalled 203 battleworthy vehicles. Each side began to lay vast numbers of mines, which claimed many victims such as an Italian force that became entangled in a British minefield. Eventually the Germans laid almost 250,000 anti-tank mines with 14,500 anti-personnel mines, which took a toll on the infantry who referred to these minefields as the 'Devil's Gardens'. To clear paths through these minefields the British used Matilda Mk II tanks called 'Scorpions' which were fitted with chain flail devices to explode the mines. Some M3 Lee-Grant medium tanks were also converted to this role and were also known as Scorpions. Infantrymen using their bayonets to probe the ground to locate the mines were used and specialist Royal Engineers using mine-detector devices identified where the mines were laid.

On 30 August the Germans attacked using the 15th and 21st Panzer Divisions supported by the Italians, including the Littorio and Ariete Divisions. Things did not go well and they sustained heavy losses. Rommel was very ill but he still remained active, and on 1 September he visited the forward area to see how the battle was progressing. He witnessed air attacks on his forces by the RAF and the destruction caused him to make the decision to retire. He had been promised an emergency airlift of fuel but he needed much more than could be flown in if he was to keep up his offensive. The fuel crisis was his main problem, which he pointed out on 27 August when he said that 'The whole battle depends on it'. Montgomery had more than 700 tanks available to him, of which 400 were in his defensive positions supported by screens of 6-pounder anti-tank guns, and all this blunted Rommel's attack. By the evening of 2 September the Germans only had sufficient fuel for 60 miles of operational service. The Battle of Alam el Halfa had cost him fifty tanks and 400 trucks along with fifty-five anti-tank guns. The British had lost sixty-seven tanks and seventeen anti-tank guns. Montgomery had only been in Egypt for two weeks and here he was blunting the Germans in his first action against Rommel.

Montgomery was pleased with the way his men had fought at the Battle of Alam el Halfa and seeing that his foe was not going to advance further he called off the battle. Montgomery may have been pleased but he was far from satisfied and spent the coming weeks training his army and building up his resources ready to deliver the knockout blow that would put the Germans into full retreat. Rommel's health was deteriorating and, believing that the British would not be in a position to attack until December, he took the opportunity to return to Germany on 23 September, leaving matters in the hands of General Georg Stumme, who had arrived in Egypt on 19 September. Lieutenant Colonel Friedrich von Mellenthin, serving on Rommel's staff, summed up the position by describing the battle as 'the turning point of the desert war'. He continued by saying that it was the 'first in a long series of defeats on every front which foreshadowed the defeat of Germany'.

Montgomery now set about planning his attack, which would be a three-pronged assault in three phases. The main attack would be made in the north, with diversionary attacks in the south; dummy tanks, trucks and fuel dumps all made from inflatable models, canvas and empty crates gave the impression of a build-up there. Radio signals added to this and kept the Germans guessing where the main thrust would come. In the north the British moved the XXX Corps forward, supported with artillery, trucks, engineers and all the attendant supplies. Finally, on 23 October at 9.40 p.m., two months earlier than Rommel had predicted, Montgomery launched his attack with an opening artillery barrage from 1,000 field guns. On average his forces were twice as strong as the German forces. He had 195,000 troops compared to a combined Italo-German Army of 104,000. He had more than 1,000 tanks, around 422 of which were M3 Lee-Grant and M4 Shermans, and in anti-tank guns he had over 1,400 of all calibres. The Germans had about 600 tanks, half of which were Italian and only thirty-eight PzKw IV capable of matching the Sherman. Artillery comprised 800 anti-tank guns, of which only eighty-six were of the powerful 88mm calibre and a further 500 field guns. The two sides were almost on parity in aircraft, with the RAF having 530 to the Luftwaffe's 500. The difference came in the fact that the Germans had only 350 serviceable aircraft and their fuel shortages restricted the operational readiness, which actually meant that the RAF had air superiority.

While moving between locations in his staff car on 24 October, General Stumme was attacked by aircraft. Stumme was uninjured but died a few days later from a heart attack. Rommel returned to the front line but by that time his forces had taken a terrible mauling by tanks, artillery and particularly air attacks. For example, by the evening of 25 October the 15th Panzer Division was down to only thirty-one tanks, having lost eighty-eight in the fighting in only forty-eight hours. Montgomery kept up the pressure and units were entering the battle as his strategy unfolded. At an engagement at Tel El Aqqaqir on 2 November British artillery contributed to the 117 German tanks destroyed in the fighting. Rommel assessed the situation and declared it hopeless, ordering his troops to withdraw. They fell back 60 miles to Fuka. On 4 November he informed Hitler of his decision, who immediately exploded in a rage and forbade any retreat. The Germans conducted a fighting retreat and beat off an attack by 200 tanks, and then Hitler changed his mind and allowed the Afrika Korps to retreat. The Italians were short of food, water and ammunition, and surrendered in their tens of thousands. The Germans commandeered the Italian vehicles so that they could withdraw, all the while being pursued. Rommel had nothing to turn and fight with and his forces were now in headlong retreat. Over the next few days the rearguard units, including the 21st Panzer Division, destroyed their last tanks. The weather broke and torrential rain turned tracks into a sea of mud so that the trucks carrying the infantry could only trundle along at little more than walking pace. Their saving grace was that the weather grounded the RAF and Montgomery kept in contact but maintained a distance just in case Rommel could muster a counter-attack. Passing through Sidi Barrani, another 80 miles back, German sappers destroyed bridges and roads in the rear. The Battle of El Alamein was over and had cost the Germans 50,000 killed, wounded or taken prisoner. They had lost hundreds of trucks and 450 tanks, the Italians had been forced to abandon seventy-five tanks through lack of fuel, and over 1,000 pieces of artillery had been destroyed or captured. Montgomery had lost 13,500 killed and wounded, 500 tanks knocked out and 100 pieces of artillery destroyed. Figures for the loss of British tanks vary, with some sources claiming that of the 500 tanks lost only 150 were beyond repair. Other sources claim that 600 were knocked out, of which 350 could be repaired, and a third source claims that 200 tanks were destroyed and 300 were repaired. A more accurate amount can probably be gained by drawing an average from the three figures.

In a speech he made in November 1942 Winston Churchill said of the Battle of El Alamein: 'Now this is not the end. It is not even the beginning of the end. But it is, perhaps, the end of the beginning.' He could have been speaking for all of the Allies, including Stalin and Roosevelt, as together the campaigns and operations were forcing the Germans back on all fronts. Even so, the leaders realised that there was still a long way to go before Germany was beaten. Montgomery knew the Germans had lost the battle but had not lost the war in North Africa, but he was determined to complete his orders from Churchill, which were to 'Destroy the German-Italian Army commanded by Field Marshal Rommel'. It would take time, but with Allied forces in the west waiting to receive the retreating Afrika Korps he was confident that the outcome was inevitable and Churchill's orders would be fulfilled. The opposing sides had 'see-sawed' back and forth, east and west, across the desert five times, covering thousands of miles. The vehicles were worn out and the troops exhausted.

6

1943: MORE LESSONS ARE LEARNT

The year 1943 started well for the Allies with the Germans in retreat in North Africa and the Russians also forcing them back and inflicting heavy casualties. Churchill and Roosevelt met at Casablanca on 14 January and held discussions to plan the next stages of the war. Stalin did not attend but General Charles de Gaulle for the Free French was present. Among the subjects for debate was the air war against Germany and the bombing of strategic targets. At the start of the war the RAF had been reluctant to bomb factories in Germany, even though they were producing tanks and artillery, on the grounds that they were privately owned. Three years on and attitudes had changed. The Germans had bombed cities and armaments centres in Birmingham and Coventry, and although the attacks had temporarily disrupted production, the bombing never halted the factories and they

Daylight bombing raid over Berlin by 8th USAAF to disrupt factory production.

remained centralised. The RAF had mounted the first so-called 1,000-bomber raid against Cologne on the night of 30–31 May 1942. With American bombers such as the B-17 and B-24 of the USAAF now arriving in Britain in ever greater numbers, the weight of aircraft sent against targets in Germany was huge. The bombing offensive was discussed and it was decided that it would be continued in order to achieve 'the progressive destruction and dislocation of the German military, industrial and economic system and the undermining of the morale of the German people to a point where their capacity for armed resistance is fatally weakened'. It was decided that the RAF would bomb by night and the USAAF would bomb by day, thereby allowing the defence measures no respite. The bombing campaign on its own did not halt production, but it had the effect of making the Germans decentralise, which slowed production and reduced output as parts had to be transported for assembly. America was unaffected by bombing and Canada too could carry on as normal.

The War in the Air

The RAF had already demonstrated the power they could unleash in bombing raids but in July 1943 the combined weight of the RAF and USAAF showed that they were unstoppable. On 24 July the first air raid in a series of attacks known as the Operation Gomorrah sorties was flown against the city of Hamburg, which was an industrial and military centre. U-boat pens, oil refineries and armaments factories made it an important target to attack in order to cripple the German ability to produce materiel for the war effort. For a total of eight days and seven nights the combined Allied air forces flew thousands of sorties and dropped tens of thousands of tons of bombs. Thousands of people were killed in the attacks and whole housing districts were destroyed. The bombing also destroyed 183 out of 524 large factories, 4,118 smaller factories out of 9,068 and a further 580 premises producing ammunition, vehicles and weapons. After the war German officials stated that had the Allies conducted further such raids, the country would have been forced out of the war. The Allies were unable to maintain such a weight of attack but continued air raids did force the Germans to decentralise their production centres. Even so, in early 1943 the Germans were producing 760 tanks a month but by the end of the year they were building 1,229, despite decentralisation. The bombing campaign against Germany would cost the RAF 10,123 aircraft lost between September 1939 and May 1945. The USAAF lost 5,548 bombers between 1942 and 1945, and between them the two air forces dropped an estimated 1,576,921 tons of bombs on targets in Germany and occupied countries.

The War at Sea

At sea the losses of supplies due to ships being sunk even in convoy had a telling effect on the armies. The Allies were able to reduce greatly Rommel's mobility by using submarines to sink his fuel tankers. The German U-boats were a problem and they claimed many victims. Churchill remarked: 'The only thing that ever terrified me during the war was the U-boat peril.' He was right to be concerned, as the figures showed. Between 1941 and 1942 U-boats and surface raiders sank 1,459 vessels, amounting to 7,619,000 tons of shipping. To put the losses into context, Britain received 55 million tons of imported food before the outbreak of the war but by 1940 the U-boats had reduced this level to 12 million tons. A whole campaign was fought at sea in order to defeat the U-boat and eventually the Allies won it with technology and tactics. During the whole of 1942 1,664 ships were sunk and Britain was on the verge of being starved if such losses were maintained, while fuel supplies were also becoming critical. In March 1943 a total of 108 vessels were sunk, but aircraft with extended range provided air cover and helped keep the U-boats at bay. In May the same year fifty supply ships were sunk but the use of specialist weapons, improved tactics and technology such as ASDIC and radar allowed the Allies to sink forty-one U-boats. They would continue to menace supply routes but their ability to range at will, largely unmolested, had been stopped. The build-up for the invasion of Europe continued and the numbers of tanks, trucks and other specialist vehicles, along with the troops and other supplies, arrived in British ports such as Liverpool and New Haven, from where they were taken to storage depots or transit camps. England was becoming one vast military camp. One joke doing the rounds at the time was that it was only the barrage balloons, used in air defences, that prevented the island from sinking under the weight of all the materiel arriving. Where to keep it all was another problem and remote country lanes in the south-west of England were used as temporary vehicle parks. The overhanging trees provided natural camouflage to screen them from any prying German reconnaissance aircraft.

The American Forces

After the Torch Landings the Americans realised that the fighting in the North African desert was unlike anything they could have prepared for and they came to understand what a vast and unforgiving area the battleground was, covering as it did many thousands of square miles. The British, Italians and Germans had learnt many lessons and now it was the turn of the Americans. For example, there were few roads maintained to a level that allowed travel apart from the main arterial highways that connected the larger towns. Minor routes were unreliable as they could often be blown away during violent sandstorms and to traverse the area with military forces a form of navigation known as 'dead-reckoning' was used, and without any landmarks it was like navigating at sea. Accuracy was all-important and the slightest margin of error could lead to the destination being missed. Without doubt the most experienced units operating in the region were the reconnaissance patrols. The Germans sent out their patrols, which covered vast areas, but it was the British that excelled in the role and created specialist units, the most famous of which was the LRDG. They were an irregular force and used a range of vehicles, such as Canadian-built CMP F30 trucks, Chevrolet and even captured German and Italian vehicles. The CMP, standing for Canadian Military Pattern, and the F30, standing for the weight (30cwt or 1.5 tons), it was a 4x2 truck with a payload of over 1 ton. It was fitted with a 239 C1 Ford/Mercury petrol engine, which gave an operational range of 6 miles to the gallon so that the twin fuel tanks, with a combined capacity of 24.5 gallons, allowed distances of up to 150 miles to be covered. Canada built around 400,000 CMP trucks out of a total of 815,729 built during the war. In fact, Canada on its own built more trucks than Germany for the same period. There were other specialist units raised such as the Special Air Service, which was formed by David Stirling of the Scots Guards, and the group known unofficially as 'Popski's 400,000 CMP Private Army' under the command of Lieutenant Colonel Vladimir Peniakoff. These also used a variety of vehicles including the American-built Willys Jeep. They also used whatever weapons they had, including captured enemy types, which helped extend their ability to operate for extended periods.

Vehicles of the Specialist Units

Vehicle Name	Type	Manufacturer	Production Date	Armament	Weight	Max. Speed
CMP F30	4x2 truck	Ford	1940 onwards	Various machine guns	1.5 tons	
Willys Jeep	Jeep	Willys MA, Ford GP, Willys MB, Ford GPW	1941 onwards	Various according to role	1.4 tons	65mph

Heading the American forces was an officer by the name of Dwight David Eisenhower who had never held a combat command. He was a relatively unknown factor but soon the whole world would recognise him and know him by his more familiar nickname of 'Ike'. Eisenhower had graduated from West Point in 1915 and during the First World War held various training posts and proved himself to be a very capable and skilled organiser. He was refused service overseas and one of the positions he held was to train tank crews. He had been promoted to the rank of brigadier general in October 1941 and his administrative capabilities were widely recognised. His first post when America entered the war in December 1941 was to be appointed deputy chief in charge of Pacific defences. In May 1942 he arrived in England with Lieutenant General Henry Arnold, but earlier Eisenhower had been assigned to the General Staff in Washington, where among his many duties, he was responsible for drawing up plans for the defeat of Germany and Japan. In June 1942 he was appointed commanding general European theatre of operations. Five months later he was appointed Supreme Commander Allied (Expeditionary) Force of the North African theatre of operations for the Torch Landings, during which period he strengthened his command skills. Further promotions and changes in his appointment came during 1943 and by the end of the year President Roosevelt appointed him Supreme Allied Commander in Europe.

The Pacific Theatre

The Pacific theatre could not be ignored but it did require an entirely different approach due to the vast distances involved. Following their massive defeats at Singapore and the Philippines the Allies knew they could not continue to fall back in the face of the Japanese onslaught the way the Russians had in the wake of Germany's attack. The British retreated back to the borders of India, covering around 1,000 miles in over five months, fighting all the way and losing over 10,000 men killed and wounded, and having to abandon much equipment including trucks, artillery and armoured vehicles. The Japanese kept up their pursuit until July 1942 when unconventional British long-range forces began to slow them down by striking at their supply lines with various units that were organised into a force called the 'Chindits', created by Brigadier Orde Wingate.

The Americans had also been busy fighting a major naval battle in the Coral Sea and winning a costly victory in another naval battle at Midway between 4 and 7 June 1942, which broke the Japanese naval dominance in the Pacific. American planners decided to invade the Solomon Islands and in order to do so they would first have to capture the island of Guadalcanal, which lay to the east of the Solomon Islands. To defend the islands in the group made up of Tulagi, Florida Island and Guadalcanal the Japanese had deployed almost 4,000 men and 100 aircraft. The Americans assembled seventy-five warships and transports to carry the invasion force, which included 16,000 US marines for the assault. America had no combat experience of amphibious landings and this force had been assembled very hastily; the men had only sufficient ammunition for ten days and their supply levels had been reduced from three months to only two months. The first wave of marines landed at Lunga Point on Guadalcanal on 7 August 1942, by coincidence the day before the US troops landed in North Africa during Operation Torch. The fighting in the operation lasted until 7 February 1943 and cost the Americans 1,752 killed and 4,359 wounded. The logistic support for the operation had been confused but eventually it was resolved and much was learned from the experience. The landings had been supported by M3 Stuart light tanks. The Japanese had little to oppose the tanks directly, which literally crushed everything beneath them as they attacked the Japanese positions. Major General Alexander Vandegrift, commanding the 1st US Marines on Guadalcanal recorded how the 'rear of the tanks looked like meatgrinders' from the bodies they had driven over with their steel

Chevrolet C60L transport truck with white star identification markings used for the Normandy campaign June 1944. It carries a bicycle for emergencies and there is a position on the cab roof for a machine gun.

tracks. It was the first operation in the 'island hopping' campaign and every shell, vehicle, gallon of petrol and soldier had to be transported in readiness for each amphibious landing.

Victory in North Africa

The reinforcements arriving in North Africa were only a fraction of what the Afrika Korps needed, but with the new Tiger tanks they could fight hard even with such reduced levels. The Tiger was formed into battalions comprising thirty vehicles and the Germans sent two battalions of Tiger I tanks to the North Africa theatre of operations between November 1942 and March 1943. This was an incredible move because the Germans were fighting a desperate war on the Russian front and they knew that it was only a question of time before an Anglo-American invasion of Europe was launched. Hitler may have rated the campaign in North Africa as a sideshow, but it was not going to be abandoned without a fight. Of all the varied tank types to be produced by Germany during the Second World War, the one design that stands out from all of them is the Tiger. The very name struck fear into Allied infantry and tank crews alike. The Russians had already encountered the Tiger and now the Western Allies were about to meet it for the first time in North Africa.

The forces making up the Operation Torch landings comprised the Western Task Force of 25,000 men commanded by Major General George S. Patton. The

Central Task Force of 39,000 men was under the command of Major General Lloyd Fredendall and Major General Charles M. Ryder commanded the Eastern Task Force, comprising 23,000 British troops and 20,000 American. Using the coastal route they moved on Algiers, which quickly capitulated. In the east Montgomery had succeeded in pushing the Afrika Korps all the way back to the Tunisian border by late January 1943, but this allowed Rommel to join forces with von Arnim. The forces of the Torch Landings took up positions along the Dorsal Mountains, a vast natural barrier that could only be penetrated through a series of natural passes.

On 14 February forces under the command of Fredendall began to move forward but they were unwittingly stumbling into an elaborate trap. Under cover of a sandstorm, the Germans had moved armoured units forward, including Tiger tanks, through the Faid Pass. The 10th Panzer Division and 21st Panzer Division linked up to surround an American force of 2,500 men. The next day the Germans attacked, and with air support they destroyed forty-six tanks and only 300 Americans managed to escape. The rest of the American force fell back towards the Kasserine Pass through the Dorsal Mountains, which had to be held in order to prevent a large supply base at Tébessa from falling into German hands. Rommel wanted to pursue the retreating Americans, no doubt with a view to capturing supplies that he could have used, but von Arnim, who was technically superior to him and also had experience in fighting in Russia, was cautious and did not want to take the risk given their limited resources and shortage of supplies. The difference of opinion was only resolved when Field Marshal Albert Kesselring flew in from Rome to assess the situation and gave his support to Rommel's plan. German tanks entered the Kasserine Pass on 19 February in pursuit of the Americans. The natural feature is barely 1 mile wide at its narrowest point and the Americans were able to make a stand and halt the German tanks. The next day the Germans renewed their attack using artillery and rocket artillery called Nebelwerfers, forcing the Americans to fall back again. The British gave support to their Allies and sent eleven tanks from the 2nd Lothian and Border Horse, but they were destroyed in the fighting.

The way appeared to be clear for the Germans to move into Algeria, advancing through Tébessa, with its prize of stocks of fuel and other supplies, and then through Thala. Rommel experienced a rare moment of caution and expected the Allies to mount a counter-attack and hesitated in making his move, choosing instead to assume a defensive stance. When no attack came he renewed his advance, but the Allies had taken the opportunity of the pause to strengthen their positions. The Americans held fast and defended Tébessa but the 10th Panzer Division with its Tiger tanks forced the British to fall back to Thala, where they established defences. The following day they received artillery support from the US 9th Division, which had covered the 600-mile distance from Oran in just four days. On 22 February the German advance was halted but the Allies preferred to hold their positions rather than putting in a counter-attack. The Germans began

to withdraw from the Kasserine Pass and Rommel, realising the weight of reinforcements and supplies reaching the Americans, knew he did not stand a chance
against their superior numbers and equipment, and did not mount an attack. Even
so, it was another twenty-four hours before the Americans discovered that he had
pulled off a masterstroke and completely melted away. The Americans had been
unprepared for such a frightening initiation into war and the fighting had cost
them 6,500 killed, wounded and captured. The British lost 2,500 men and the
whole effort had cost the Allies 183 tanks destroyed. The Germans and Italians
had lost 2,000 killed, wounded and captured and thirty-four tanks destroyed.

Italian Armoured Vehicles

The range of armoured vehicles used by the Italian Army during the Second World War
was not among the best designs fielded by any of the belligerent nations. There are many
reasons for this and, apart from the Semovente, which is generally regarded as the best
Italian armoured vehicle of the war, the remainder of the Italian designs were not well
thought out. Italy had been engaged in military campaigns since 1935 when it invaded
Ethiopia and in Spain from 1936, where Mussolini deployed more troops than Germany
and fielded light tanks such as the M13/40, which were later sent into action during the
disastrous Greek campaign of 1940. The inadequacies of these tanks were highlighted
in these campaigns and the Italians realised, somewhat late, that better designs were
required if they were to stand a chance on the battlefield. In 1941 the Italian Army finally
developed and put into production a light tank design that did show some promise of
being useful on the battlefield, but even so it was a classic case of too little too late.

Vehicle Name	Type	Manufacturer	Production Date	Armament	Weight	Max. Speed
M13/40	Light tank	FIAT	1940–41	47mm and 2x 8mm machine guns	14 tons	21mph
Carro Armato M14/41	Light tank	FIAT	1941–42	47mm-calibre gun and two Modello 38 8mm-calibre machine guns	13.7 tons	20mph
Semovente 90/53	Self-propelled gun	Semovente	1941	90mm gun	16.7 tons	22mph

The new tank was the M14/41, served by a crew of four and armed with a 47mm-calibre
main armament gun with 104 rounds of ammunition carried; this placed it slightly better
than the British 2-pounder 40mm-calibre gun fitted to many tanks such as the Matilda
Mk II, but it was still lower than the 50mm guns fitted to the German Panzer III tanks.
The M14/41 promised to be better than the earlier Italian tank designs, but in the later
phases of campaigns in North Africa it fared no better when it encountered anti-tank

guns or was engaged by British units using American-built tanks such as the Sherman. The Italian Centauro Armoured Division used M14/41 tanks in action at the Kasserine Pass in 1943 and lost many during the heavy fighting against the American forces.

Built by the motor manufacturing company FIAT, the full title of the new tank was Carro Armato M14/41, the designation 'M' standing for 'medium', '14' being the weight of the vehicle in tonnes and '41' the year of its introduction into service. Despite being termed a medium tank, the M14/41 was actually a 'light' tank and an improved version of the earlier M13/40, also a light tank. The improved version was fitted with a SPA 15-TM-41 eight-cylinder petrol engine developing 125hp to produce a top speed of 20mph. It weighed 13.7 tons and measured just over 16ft long, 7.2ft wide and 7.8ft high. Armour thickness varied from 6mm to 42mm, which was comparable to other tanks in service with Germany and Britain. It had an operational range of 125 miles, which was much less than many of its adversaries in North Africa. The M14/41 was constructed using a riveted design and looked old-fashioned when compared to other designs, which were constructed of welded hulls and cast turrets. It was fitted with vertical volute suspension with two sets of double-bogie wheels fitted on either side with the drive sprocket at the front, the idler wheel to the rear and three return rollers for the tracks. The main armament was a 47mm-calibre gun mounted in the turret that could traverse 360 degrees by hand and elevate to +25 degrees and depress to -15 degrees. The tank also carried two Modello 38 machine guns of 8mm calibre as secondary armament. One was mounted co-axially to the main gun with the second mounted in the hull, and over 3,000 rounds were carried.

The M14/41 may have been based on the M13/40 but the armour protection was much better than that design. It was produced from 1941 until 1942, during which time some 800 vehicles were built, but even despite its upgrades over earlier vehicles, the M14/41 could be considered obsolete even before it entered service. The flaws in its design became apparent when it was deployed in the North African theatre of operations. It had a ready tendency to catch fire easily when hit and many were destroyed in tank battles, with others being picked off by the anti-tank guns. When the Italian forces withdrew they abandoned many of their tanks, usually due to lack of fuel, and this included those M14/41 tanks not destroyed in the fighting. These were later recovered and refuelled and absorbed into use by the German Army, which designated them M14/41 736 (i). These were placed in service with Sturmgeschutz units and some went to the Panzerabteilung Adria. Those vehicles captured by the British Army were pressed into service for a short time but as there was no shortage of tanks they were soon abandoned. Some M14/41 tanks were deployed by the Italian Army to serve on the Eastern Front and these ended up being used by the Germans in this theatre of operations; there are photographs showing examples of the tank having been destroyed by Polish resistance fighters in Warsaw during the uprising in 1944. Although limited in service and with a less than impressive record in battle, the M14/41 later went on to be used as the chassis for the Semovente 90/53 heavy tank.

Eighty miles to the east, the Germans had established a defensive line of bunkers, tank traps and minefields known as the Mareth Line. In essence it was a stopgap measure from where they could launch an attack and that is just what Rommel intended to do, by attacking the British-held town of Medenine. Fortunately for the British, they had intercepted German radio messages and decoded them, giving warning of the impending attack, and were ready for it. So precise was the decoding that they knew the date of the attack, and when it came on 6 March the anti-tank guns were ready and waiting. The British had learned much in two years of desert fighting and allowed the German tanks to come within 400yd before opening fire and destroying fifty-two of the Germans' ever-diminishing tank force. Rommel flew to Berlin on 9 March to request personally that Hitler allowed him to evacuate North Africa. The request was denied and Rommel remained in Germany while von Arnim took over command of Army Group Africa.

The British had improved their tactics to make the artillery more flexible in providing support and the Americans would come to learn from such experience. General Fredendall had not lived up to expectations, and Major General Ernest Harmon, commanding the US 2nd Armoured Division, reported his unflattering opinion of his fellow officer, stated to Eisenhower: 'This is Rommel and tank warfare at its latest.' He continued by adding that it was 'way above poor Fredendall's head'. On 6 March Fredenhall was replaced by General Patton, who took up command and arrived with more Sherman tanks. For three weeks he attacked the passes through the southern end of the Dorsal Mountains at El Guettar and Maknassy with little to show for the effort. However, it did have the effect of forcing the Germans to take tanks out of the defences making up the Mareth Line. This served to help Montgomery, who ordered the New Zealand 2nd Division, some 25,000 men under the command of Major General Bernard Freyberg, to attack south-west and then swing behind the Mareth Line. The division covered a distance of 200 miles following a route that had been plotted by the LRDG. Linking up with other elements of the British Eighth Army, they moved over the vast distances all the time heading northwards towards their goal of Tunis. The weather worsened and the rain turned the roads to a muddy quagmire that slowed the Allies' progress. The Germans were still capable of turning to attack their pursuers and Montgomery was forced to keep changing his tactics to meet each situation. Through April the British continued to battle forwards even after they had linked up with the US II Corps on 7 April as they advanced north towards Tunis. By now the Germans were using up all their reserves and conducting a fighting withdrawal to take up defensive lines sweeping in a wide arc on the tip of Tunisia.

On 22 April British artillery joined American units to pound positions prior to an attack. General Omar Bradley, replacing Patton who was preparing for the next operation (the invasion of Sicily), ordered an attack by seventeen Sherman tanks to support an infantry attack against a feature known as 'Hill 609' from its height measured in metres. The Germans, literally with their backs to the sea, had only 175,000 men to oppose an Allied force of 380,000 men with 1,200 tanks, 1,500 pieces of artillery, 3,000 aircraft and unlimited supplies. The Germans had 400 aircraft, 130 tanks and ammunition supplies sufficient for three days if the 400 guns they had left were careful. A massive artillery barrage by 600 guns pounded the German positions on 6 May, which further weakened them. The next day the Americans were only 15 miles outside Bizerta and elements of the British 11th Hussars entered Tunis. Disparate fighting continued during which engagements the tanks of the 10th Panzer Division ran out of fuel. By 12 April the Germans and Italians had expended everything and Lieutenant General Hans Cramer sent a message to notify Berlin that 'Munitions expended, weapons and war equipment destroyed'. On 13 May General Alexander sent a signal to Churchill to report that the campaign in Tunisia was finished and the enemy had surrendered. North Africa was clear and the Allies could now concentrate on enemy forces in Europe from France to Italy.

The losses sustained by the Germans at Stalingrad and the surrender of their forces in North Africa were huge by any standards. They had lost thousands of trucks, tanks, artillery, millions of tons of war materiel and, most importantly, manpower. However, despite these losses the German Army still had some 10.3 million men under arms in the field in mid-1943, including allies and volunteers from occupied territories. There were millions of forced labourers producing vehicles, weapons and uniforms, and according to General Field Marshal Wilhelm Keitel these people were 'working for Germany', which implies that they were doing it of their own free will, when it was anything but the case. This workforce allowed the German armaments industry to increase productivity to supply the army by 80 per cent, which was made all the more remarkable when one considers the disruption to factory output caused by round-the-clock bombing by the RAF and USAAF.

Focus on Europe and Russia

The main fighting in North Africa was over and the onus was now put on the occupying forces in France to begin preparing defences to counter an Allied invasion of Europe, which Hitler and his generals knew must surely come. In Russia the fighting never stopped for a day and there was always movement and engagement somewhere across the vast expanse of territory; the German Army stripped men and equipment from France to redeploy in the east. Russian partisan groups attacked motorised convoys, blew up railway tracks and generally disrupted the rear areas through which passed the logistics to support the army. The railways were being used to transport tanks, ammunition, artillery and troops to the front, and these extended routes were particularly vulnerable. For example, in January 1943 some 397 attacks were recorded against railway targets, which resulted in damage to 112 locomotives and bridges. Some of the bridges were significantly important such as the one spanning 330yd over the Desna River on the Bryansk-Gomel railway line. To repair such damage required specialist engineers and equipment along with building material including replacement tracks, sleepers and points. In February the German General Directorate of Railways (East) reported 500 attacks, which rose to 1,045 incidents in May. By June there were 1,092 attacks against the railway, increasing to an alarming 1,460 incidents in July 1943. In the rear of the Army Group Centre, Russian partisans destroyed forty-four bridges, 298 locomotives and 1,223 wagons and carriages so that movement by rail was widely disrupted. A soldier reported that: 'With us trains move for one day and three days have to be spent repairing the track since the partisans blow everything up.' He continued by recounting how on one occasion a collision had been caused between a supply train and a troop train, which caused chaos on the over-burdened railway system.

The Russians were laying minefields at the rate of 2,400 anti-tank mines and 2,700 anti-personnel mines per mile and it has been calculated that they dug more than 3,100 miles of anti-tank ditches as defences against the German tanks. Using a workforce of 200,000 civilians the Russians also laid new railway tracks, such as the 50-mile stretch between Stary Oskol and Rzhava, built 250 new bridges and constructed 1,800 miles of new roads to ferry supplies to the front. All the while the Russians were building up their reserves and making good the deficiencies that had beset them in 1941 and 1942. Marshal Georgi Zhukov, who had defended Moscow and rescued Stalingrad, was created Deputy Supreme Commander and in 1943 he began to formulate plans that would crush the German Army in the east. Tank

Praying Mantis machine-gun carrier based on the Universal carrier. Never entered service.

armies, artillery and troops were all being assembled so that when the time was right he could strike in overwhelming force. Operations were still being conducted to hold down the Germans and on 2 February the Russians, fresh from their success at Stalingrad, launched an offensive and penetrated the German lines.

By 1942 the Germans had sustained losses of 1.9 million men killed, wounded or captured. By January 1943 they were down to fewer than 500 operational combat tanks and were under strength by almost 500,000 men. They were receiving replacement vehicles, and supplies were getting through, but they were losing a lot to partisan activity. The Germans had captured the city of Kharkov in early March and as the fighting continued in the latest offensive the Russians headed towards the city with the intention of recapturing it. This was entering a phase known as the Third Battle of Kharkov and between January and April the Russians poured in 500,000 troops in the Veronezh-Kharkov Offensive. They had already managed to capture the city of Rostov on 14 February but despite their best efforts Kharkov could not be taken. The fighting saw each side committing the usual tank types such as Tiger I and T-34 engaging in combat along with SPGs, including the StuG. III, anti-tank guns and half-tracks such as the SdKfz 7, which towed the deadly 88mm anti-tank gun. By the end of the fighting the action had cost the Russians 80,000 killed, wounded and captured, but they had fought hard and inflicted 56 per cent losses on the SS Panzer Corps committed to the battle. Even so, by 14 March the Germans still had the city of Kharkov and were determined to hold it. General Erich von Manstein claimed that he had destroyed 1,140 tanks and 3,000 pieces of artillery. These figures are questionable and probably greatly exaggerated and have been questioned by historians since then. After the battle the Russians held the line with a bulge, known as a salient, projecting forward of their own lines into the German front line. This was over 160 miles in width and the position was totally unacceptable to Hitler, who wanted to eliminate it. The Russians had pushed the Germans back some 300 miles in places, which extended their supply route and shortened the Germans' supply lines. For the Russians this was not a problem because they were in their own country with friendly local populace. The journalist Alexander Werth covering the war in Russia for *The Sunday Times* newspaper reported on the Russian morale in the aftermath of Stalingrad, and saw 'Horses, horses and still more horses blowing steam and with ice around their nostrils were wading through the deep snow, pulling guns and gun-carriages and large covered wagons; and hundreds of lorries with their headlights full on ...' The German supply lines remained a mess and were being attacked by partisans in the rear and the regular army in the front.

Vehicle Name	Manufacturer	Production Date	Armament	Weight	Max. Speed
PzKw V SdKfz 171 Ausf. D also known as 'Panther'	MAN, Daimler-Benz, MNH and Henschel	1943	7.5cm KwK42 L/70 and 2x MG34 7.92mm machine guns	43 tons	26mph

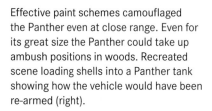

Effective paint schemes camouflaged the Panther even at close range. Even for its great size the Panther could take up ambush positions in woods. Recreated scene loading shells into a Panther tank showing how the vehicle would have been re-armed (right).

The Panther and the bicycle stand in stark contrast to show how the fortunes of the German Army changed towards the end of the war when fuel was not available to power the tanks and it was a man on a bicycle. With armour protection up to 120mm thickness, the Panther had little to fear on the battlefield. The Panther or SdKfz 171 with its 75mm gun could destroy most tanks at ranges of 1,000yd.

In mid-April the Germans began formulating plans to deal with the Russian salient and this was to be known as Operation Citadel. Hitler would commit more than 2,700 tanks to the coming battle, which represented around 63 per cent of the German Army's armoured forces in Russia, including the new PzKw V or 'Panther'. In 1941 the range at which German tank crews engaged Russian tanks was around 500yd and Russian tank crews engaged targets at 400yd. By 1943 each side had improved their tank gunnery due to more powerful guns on tanks and the range had increased to over 1,000yd for both sides. The Russians too were putting new vehicles into the field for the first time in preparation for the battle they knew was coming because their spy network, known as the 'Lucy Ring', was keeping them informed of German intentions. Among the new vehicles was the SU-122, which weighed 30 tons and mounted a 122mm-calibre gun on the T-34 chassis. The SU-152 was the KV-1 chassis on to which was mounted a 152mm ML-20S gun nick-named the 'Zverobody' (beast killer) and could destroy the heavyweight German tanks such as the Tiger, Panther and Ferdinand. The 44-ton SU-152 carried twenty rounds of ammunition for its main gun and was served by a crew of five. It had a top speed of 27mph and measured 29ft 4in long, 10ft 8in wide and 8ft high. Russian troops were reckless in their methods of tank hunting and infantrymen would often approach tanks to place demolition charges or mines directly on the vehicle, always with devastating effect. The tactic was suicidal but it achieved results.

Russian SU Tank Series

Vehicle Name	Manufacturer	Production Date	Armament	Weight	Max. Speed
SU-122	UZTM	1942	122mm M-30S gun	30 tons	34mph
SU-152	Chelyabinskiy Kirovskiy Zavod	1943	152mm ML-20S gun and DShK 12.7mm machine gun	44.8 tons	27mph

The Tiger Tank

By now the Western Allies and the Russians had engaged the formidable Tiger tank in battle and they had needed to rethink their tactics concerning tank fighting. The first Tiger I tanks had entered service with the 1st Platoon of the 502nd Schwere (heavy) Panzerabteilung and went into action in the Leningrad area in Russia. Ever since Germany began its rearmament programme in earnest in the mid-1930s, the military had been considering a number of designs for heavy tanks. In 1937 one of the suggestions proposed the idea that a version of the 88mm anti-tank gun be mounted on a heavy hull and chassis to produce an undisputed tank capable of destroying any challengers before they came close enough to open fire with any effect. The whole heavy tank programme kept changing direction and the requirements governing the final design of the tank kept being changed for no apparent reason. This led to delays, wasted materials and occupied factory space. Finally in 1942 a step in the right direction came when the armaments

manufacturing company Henschel was awarded the contract to produce the design
of a heavy tank on which all quarters agreed was the right one. The project was
given the specification VK 4501, and when it appeared it was like nothing else
ever deployed before on the battlefield. It was given the official designation of
SdKfz 181, but the name Tiger became the identifying title to friend and foe alike.

Vehicle Name	Manufacturer	Production Date	Armament	Weight	Max. Speed
Panzerkampfwagen VI (Tiger I)	Henschel	1942	KwK36 L/56 88mm gun and 2x MG34 machine guns	55 tons	23mph

The Tiger I or Panzerkampfwagen VI was undoubtedly a remarkable fighting
machine and yet it was a basic tank design except for the armour thickness, which
made it virtually proof against all but the most powerful ammunition. It was the
armour protection that varied from only 25mm in less vulnerable areas, such as
the engine deck, to 100mm in thickness over the frontal portion of the hull and
turret and the gun mantlet where it was 110mm in thickness, which almost guaranteed its survival on the battlefield. The best an Allied anti-tank gunner could
hope for was to disable the Tiger by hitting the track or the vulnerable engine
area at the rear of the tank. It was the size and sheer weight that made the Tiger
intimidating and made it stand apart from other tanks. It was used in all theatres
of war from 1942 onwards and yet, despite its almost ubiquitous presence, only
1,357 vehicles were actually produced. This relatively low production number
was due to the fact that it was a complicated design, with each vehicle requiring
some 300,000 hours' assembly time. It would be the audacious manner in which
it was handled by commanders that could turn the course of a battle. For example,
during the Normandy campaign on 13 June 1944 Michael Wittmann, joined by
other Tiger tanks, surprised elements of the British 7th Armoured Division and
left in their wake twenty-five tanks destroyed along with a further twenty-eight
other armoured vehicles destroyed in an action lasting only minutes. It was originally intended that thirty Tiger I tanks would form special battalions and come
under command of either army or corps headquarters and, indeed, this was often
the case, but some regiments such as SS units had their own battalions formed
with Tiger tanks.

The Tiger I weighed 55 tons and was a very powerful weapon platform to carry
a powerful weapon in the shape of a KwK36 L/56 88mm gun and two MG34
machine guns. The machine guns were mounted one in the hull and the other
was co-axially mounted next to the main armament. The Tiger could carry up
to ninety-two rounds of ammunition for the 88mm gun and these could pierce
4in of armour at ranges up of over 500yd. A standard complement of five men
formed the crew operating in the usual roles of driver, gunner, loader, commander
and radio operator, which could make a formidable team. It was powered by a
Maybach HL230P45 V-12 water-cooled inline petrol engine that developed 700bhp

It was in a Tiger tank such as this that Michael Wittmann earned his reputation in France and finally met his end. The Tiger I was first encounterd on the battlefield by the Russians who had to develop more powerful weapons to deal with it.

at 3,000rpm, giving it a road speed of over 23mph, cross-country speeds of around 12.5mph and an operational road range of 62 miles.

Today there are only a handful of examples of the Tiger I tank surviving in museums around the world with a few more believed to be in private hands. They are all in various states of repair or running conditions. The French Tank Museum at Saumur has an example and the vehicle held by the Aberdeen Proving Ground in the United States is understood at present to be undergoing an extensive restoration project. There is an example by the roadside just outside the French village of Vimoutier, having been recovered and put on display. This example is missing many components, is far from being anywhere near complete and is certainly not

The Tiger tank was feared and respected by all the Allies who met it on the battlefield. The 88mm was the powerful punch of the Tiger and it could penetrate more than 4in of armour at ranges of almost 500yd. Whether moving or static the Tiger is always impressive.

roadworthy, but even so its sheer size remains very impressive. The museums at Kubinka in Russia and Koblenz in Germany each have an example of the giant 65-ton Sturmmorser variant of the Tiger. There are tantalising rumours of other examples of Tigers, but only two others are known to be definitely in private hands and in the course of restoration projects.

Unarguably one of the best-preserved surviving examples of a complete Tiger I is that held by the Bovington Tank Museum in Dorset, England, where it forms part of the permanent display. This exhibit is known as Bovington Tank Museum Accession Number 2351. The full provenance of this particular vehicle is well known, as is its production and service record. According to the files of Henschel, the company that built the Tiger I, the chassis records for the production run of the Tiger tank numbered from 250001 to 251357. The *Fahrgestell* or chassis number for the Tiger at Bovington is 250112, from which record one can place it as being one of the earliest vehicles to come off the assembly lines at Kassel. In fact, it is believed that the vehicle may have been completed around February 1943. The turret that houses the 88mm KwK36 L/56 main armament was built by Wegmann A.G., also based in Kassel. It is understood that the Bovington Tiger arrived in Tunisia sometime between early March and April 1943. It was given the unit numbering '131', which indicates that it served with No. 3 Platoon of No. 1 Company of the 504th *Schwere Heeres Panzerabteilung* (army heavy tank battalion).

The Bovington Museum Tiger went into action on 21 April 1943 at Medjez-el-Bab where it encountered Churchill tanks of No. 4 Troop, A Squadron of the 48th Royal Tank Regiment. It was a fierce engagement and one of the Churchill tanks, probably a Mk III armed with a 6-pounder gun, made a chance hit on the Tiger and disabled it. With no other choice, the crew evacuated the vehicle, which was abandoned on the battlefield. The British Army consolidated the area and the 'knocked out' Tiger was recovered from the battlefield by 104 Army Tank Workshops and the 25th Tank Brigade Workshops of the REME. It was removed back to Tunis on 24 May 1943, having been in the theatre of operations for barely two months. On 2 June Prime Minister Winston Churchill and Anthony Eden inspected the captured tank and on 18 June King George VI visited the area and took a keen interest in the Tiger. It was then decided to take the tank back to Britain as an exhibit, where it was displayed briefly at Horse Guards Parade in London. The damage inflicted to Tiger 131 on the battlefield was great because it was able to manoeuvre under its own automotive power at La Goulette Harbour as it was being prepared for transportation. After it had been displayed the tank was closely examined and taken apart for in-depth analysis and study into enemy tank technology. Six years after the end of the war the Tiger I was officially handed over to the Bovington Tank Museum in September 1951, where today it remains one of the 'star' attractions with visitors from all over the world.

The Battle of Kursk

The German attack against the Kursk salient was finally timed to begin at 5.30 a.m. on 5 July. Hitler had given his authority for the attack on 1 July and the days in the countdown to the commencement of the attack were used to bring in more armour to counter the build-up of Russian armoured forces that the Germans had learnt of. What their intelligence forces could not tell them, however, was the extent of the weight of the Russian forces facing them. The Lucy spy ring had got most of the details concerning the planned German attack correct except for the time at which it was due to start, which the agents had reported as being 3.30 a.m., two hours earlier than actually planned. The Russians decided to act first and unleashed a massive pre-emptive artillery barrage, which began at 2.20 a.m. with 3,000 guns firing half the ammunition supply allocated for the entire battle. The Germans endured this for just over an hour and then launched a series of infantry attacks beginning at 3.30 a.m. The Russians had prepared a series of eight defensive lines up to 100 miles deep and these were divided into three defensive areas. The Germans were unable to clear the minefields for the following tanks to move through but the Russians had laid the mines in such a fashion that they left pathways through the minefields that effectively channelled the German tanks into the firing line of the anti-tank guns. These positions were known as PaK Fronts from the German tactic of placing anti-tank guns, Panzer Abwehr Kanone or PaK, to engage tanks with intense firepower. Now it was being used against them. They had hoped to penetrate the defences in a day but Russian resistance slowed them down to a crawl. What developed over the next three weeks has gone down in history as the largest tank battle ever fought.

Hitler realised that he had to try to eliminate either the Western Allies or the Russians if his armies were to stand any chance of winning the war. The Americans and British were still flushed with their success in North Africa and growing stronger for the next phase of their operations, while in the east the Russians were being held for the time being at least. He also realised that the Americans and British were planning an invasion of Europe but he knew that would mean an amphibious assault, which would take time and careful planning. The Russians, on the other hand, were a more pressing question because they could simply batter their way forward and drive across Europe, bringing all their supplies with them. This made him decide to attack Kursk and pinch out the bothersome salient that posed a threat to the stability of his Eastern Front.

The Germans moved troops, trucks and tanks and artillery into a concentrated area in a build-up for the operation. In the north Colonel General Walther Model had the Ninth Army, XX and XXIII Corps along with the XLVI, XLVII and XLI Panzer Corps with air support. In the south Field Marshal Eric von Manstein had the 4th Panzer Army under Colonel General Hoth along with II SS and XLVIII Panzer Corps. (Army corps are always identified with Roman numerals in unit histories, such as the British XXX Corps, and this applied to all armies.) Other armoured units took the number of AFVs deployed to 2,700, but Colonel General Heinz Guderian, by now appointed to the position of inspector general of armoured forces, was concerned about the capability of some of these vehicles, in particular the Panther, armed with a 75mm-calibre main gun but untried and unproven in battle. The Ninth Army had over 100 Tiger I tanks with the 88mm gun and sixty-six versions of the Tiger known as the Brummbar, which mounted a 150mm gun; these were also serving in battle for the first time as SPGs. The Germans had 900,000 troops, 10,000 pieces of artillery and air support from 2,500 aircraft. Between the two Russian field commanders, General Konstantin Rokosovski, commanding the Central Front in the north, and General Nikolai Vatutin, commanding the

Mounted on horseback Cossack cavalry troops could scout fast and relatively quietly.

Veronezh Front in the south, they had a total of 1,357,000 troops, 22,000 pieces of artillery, including rocket batteries known as *Katyushas* ('Little Kates' but known to the Germans as 'Stalin's Organs'), 3,306 tanks and air support of 2,650 aircraft. In total, the strength of forces deployed by Zhukov represented almost 40 per cent of the entire force available for the defence of Russia. While the German Army was still struggling to maintain its strength and supply lines the Russians held a reserve force of 500,000 troops and supplies, which could be transported along secure routes. The perimeter of the Russian salient extended over 360 miles and with the elaborate defences created Zhukov hoped to blunt the powerful blitzkrieg tactics that usually skirted around strongpoints of defence. Here, before Kursk, he was hoping that by allowing the Germans to wear themselves out by trying to blast through these defences he would then be able to counter-attack.

Operation Citadel (*Zitadelle* in German) was forced to begin early due to the opening Russian artillery barrage, with infantry forces leading the way to open up routes for the tanks to follow. The action throughout the day was long and hard, and achieved a penetration of 4 miles deep, 7 miles at its furthest. The two German commanders were still separated and there was a long way to go before the blitzkrieg pincers could meet and surround the Russians. The Panther tanks were not proving as battleworthy as was hoped and the tactic of *Panzerkeil* (armoured wedge) designed to destroy the Russian anti-tank guns was not as successful as had been hoped either. Fighting continued with the Russians withdrawing, which encouraged the Germans to move deeper forward, but it was a subtle and well-planned trap. Between 6 and 11 July it looked as though Hitler's doubts about the operation were unfounded and it appeared that they may have succeeded even if the cost had been high. Then, on 12 July just outside the village of Prokhovka, a force of 800 Russian tanks, mainly T-34s, attacked the German armoured units, including SS panzer divisions, amounting to 450 tanks. This was the Russian counter-attack, Operation Kutuzov, which had been initiated by the code word 'Steel'. By the time darkness fell there were more than 350 German tanks burning on the battlefield and around 10,000 men had been killed. Further losses to the German tanks had been caused by the minefields and a figure has been suggested that for every tank lost to Russian tanks or anti-tank guns two more were destroyed by mines. Russian losses are believed to have been comparable to German losses but they had more vehicles to replace those destroyed and a massive reserve of manpower to draw from. In view of this action, on 13 July Hitler ordered his commanders to break off Operation Citadel. Fighting continued over the next two days as the Germans withdrew back to the original positions they had held before the battle started.

The Russian success forced the Germans to begin a massive withdrawal across a frontage of 400 miles wide, retreating over 200 miles in some places before estab-lishing new defensive lines along the Dnieper River from August onwards. The whole Battle of Kursk and fighting retreat cost the German Army over 200,000 killed, wounded and captured. Around 720 tanks and SPGs had been lost and the figure for the amount of artillery lost is not precise, but it is known that during the engagement at Kursk they lost some 500 guns. The Germans now implemented an action called *Verbrannte Erde* (Scorched Earth), which described the policy to the letter. Two years earlier the Russians had used the tactic to deny resources to the Germans and it was being repeated to try to slow down the pursuit by the Russians. In their wake they left a trail of destruction as the Germans herded up 350,000 cattle and killed 13,000 more. They transported over 250,000 tons of grain and destroyed a further 1 million tons. Factories, bridges, railways and anything else considered to be of use to the advancing Russians was destroyed and young Russian men of military age were rounded up to be taken for forced labour in the west. In this year of reversals on the battlefield for the German Army the factories were able to produce 14,400 pieces of artillery and 11,800 tanks and other AFVs, which was a great increase over the previous year when just over 5,000 armoured vehicles had been built. In 1944 this figure increased, despite Allied bombing, to produce 17,843 armoured vehicles of all types and 56,000 pieces of artillery. The one thing the German Army did find difficult to maintain was the level of trained and experienced crews to operate these tanks on the battlefield.

The Russians had lost over 863,000 men killed, wounded and captured in the fighting and more than 6,000 tanks and other fighting vehicles had been destroyed, along with 5,244 pieces of artillery. But now they were in a position to absorb these losses and even make good the deficiencies with replacements from factories geared up for production that were no longer being threatened by enemy action. At the start of the Battle of Kursk the Russians had over 5.5 million trained and armed men under arms and their tank force stood at around 10,000 of all types, but mainly the superb T-34. Factories were now producing tanks at a rate of 2,000 per month and, with the Americans still sending aid, Russia was in the ascendancy. In their pursuit of Manstein's 750,000 men the Russians recaptured the towns of Belgorod and Orel on the same day, 5 August. The city of Kharkov, which both sides had fought so hard for, was recaptured on 23 August and a month later, hundreds of miles to the north, the city of Smolensk was liberated on 25 September. Four days earlier the Russians had established a small bridgehead across the Dnieper River at Kanev, thereby keeping up the pressure on Manstein. By December the Russians had entered the Crimea and cut off the entire German Seventeenth Army of 65,000 men with all their equipment, weapons and vehicles.

Allied Invasion of Europe

The Western Allies were also making plans and their planners used the time after the Italo-German surrender in North Africa to consolidate their forces in readiness for the next move. One thing about which they were certain was the fact they had to get back into mainland Europe, but the question was, how was this to be achieved? It had already been decided at the Arcadia Conference between Churchill and Roosevelt in Washington that Germany would be treated as the priority enemy to be beaten at all costs. The Allied Conference at Casablanca reaffirmed this decision and Churchill took the opportunity to use the meeting to convince the Americans that a start to invade Europe should be made through Italy, which he described as 'the soft under belly'. In the event, the invasion of Europe by the back door would prove to be a 'tough old gut'.

The first step would be to make initial landings on the island of Sicily at the southern end of Italy, and from there the Allies could 'springboard' into mainland Europe. The operation would receive air cover from the RAF flying from Malta, and the Royal Navy and US Navy had dominance of the Mediterranean, ensuring the safety of the campaign. Code-named Operation Husky, the Allies had done a thorough job of amassing intelligence concerning the enemy dispositions on the island and even conceived an elaborate deception plan to fool the Germans into believing that they planned to attack through Greece. When everything was in place, the invasion fleet set sail. It had taken the Allies six months to build up the invasion force of 2,590 vessels required to transport and support the force of 180,000 troops along with 14,000 vehicles, 600 tanks and 1,800 pieces of artillery. The British troops were the most battle experienced, having seen action in the North African campaign, but most of the vehicles and supplies were provided by America. All the supplies, fuel, ammunition, food and medical stores were loaded aboard the ships to make this the largest amphibious landing of the war to

Arming shells for the 5.5in field gun probably in Italy

date. The Allies knew that facing them on Sicily there were 315,000 Italian troops along with 50,000 German troops and a further 40,000 German troops in reserve. In terms of manpower the Allies were outnumbered but in terms of equipment, tanks and artillery they were superior, and they had massive air support. Italy had already lost over 200,000 men killed, wounded or captured during the North African campaign and on the Eastern Front there were 217,000 Italian troops fighting alongside the Germans and other troops such as Romanians. In addition there were another 580,000 Italian troops fighting in Yugoslavia and engaged in conducting anti-partisan operations in the Balkans. This coming battle would be a testing time for Italy as Germany's ally.

The island of Sicily measures 9,927 square miles and the mountainous terrain in the interior is made up largely of volcanic rock, as the island is dominated by the active Mount Etna volcano, which rises to a height of more than 10,900ft. The Allies planned to land on two separate beachheads, together having a combined frontage of 40 miles. The American Seventh Army under Patton made its first landings under cover of darkness at around 2.45 a.m. at Licata where the Italian defenders soon surrendered. The Italian defenders at Gela, further east along the coast, were supported by Germans of the Herman Goering Division with Tiger tanks. The warships in the bay provided covering fire and the ships' guns' targets included the tanks. Along the south-west corner of the island the British Eighth Army under Montgomery included Canadian troops going into battle for the first time, like many of the American troops. Although separate landings had been achieved the operation was designed to be mutually supportive. On the ground,

however, each commander had his own ideas. Timings for the landings were crucial for the ships in the armada because they had to rendezvous precisely after
some had sailed directly from ports in America, others from Scotland and more
from ports in North Africa and Malta. The planned airborne landings by glider
and parachute went badly wrong but the amphibious landings assaulted inland
with the Americans fanning out to the west of the island whilst the British and
Canadians battled their way northwards up the east side of the island.

The American ranger units showed themselves to be remarkably adept at anti-
tank tactics almost from the moment they landed. On 11 July units of the 1st and
4th Rangers found themselves being attacked by the Italian Gruppo Mobile E
using thirty-two captured French tanks at Gela. During close-quarter fighting
the rangers destroyed three of these tanks and made the others withdraw. Some
seventeen Tiger tanks of the Herman Goering Division were sent in to attack the
rangers who managed to get some abandoned Italian anti-tank guns into action. It
was these tanks that the warships fired on, and between the navy and the rangers
they managed to destroy a number and force the remainder to withdraw. During
the course of three days of such fighting, sixteen Tiger tanks were destroyed. The
Americans then made a rapid advance inland and by 18 July had reached a point
about a third of the way across the island. By 22 July they had captured the town
of Palermo on the north coast and forces farther east were moving along the coast
road to capture San Stefano on the same day. The British were having a hard time
of it as the Germans mounted stiff resistance and fought fierce rearguard actions.
In fact, by 20 July the British had only reached the town of Enna in the centre of
the island. Patton was able to hurry ahead as Italian resistance collapsed and he
captured the port town of Messina, from where he could look across the Strait of
Messina to the Italian mainland. The Germans instigated an evacuation plan and
between 11 and 17 August they managed to get 40,000 German and 60,000 Italian
troops across the water to Italy.

On 17 August, after thirty-eight days of very difficult fighting, the Sicilian campaign was over and the Allies had either killed or captured 130,000, including
30,000 Germans. The British had suffered 9,000 casualties and the American
7th Army had sustained 7,000 casualties. At the peak of the campaign the Allies
had 467,000 men to support the operation. The way ahead was now clear to cross
the Strait of Messina, which at its narrowest point is only 2 miles across, but with
heavy concentrations of artillery to defend the crossing points it would have been
suicidal to cross here, for the time being at least. Instead plans were laid for more
ambitious landings at Salerno on the Italian coast. The Sicilian campaign had been
supported by a new type of vehicle called DUKW (termed 'Duck' by the troops)
which was an amphibious design.

US Amphibious Vehicles

Most fighting countries developed amphibious vehicles for lesser roles on the battle-field but the US Army saw these as having a wider role and for that reason requested a heavier design, comparable to a standard truck. What they got was exactly that: an amphibious version of the GMC Jimmy (also known as the 'deuce-and-a-half' from its weight of 2.5 tons) which was designed and built for the army by GMC. The acronym came from the code letters to designate the vehicle with D standing for the year 1942, when the first request for an initial order of 2,000 such vehicles was posted. The letter U designated it as amphibious. The letters K and W denoted all-wheel drive and

The driver's position on the DUKW which had additional controls for use in the water.

The boat-like shape to the hull helped the vehicle in the water but it had a low freeboard and it could not operate in 'choppy' water.

dual rear axles respectively. The DUKW was essentially a six-wheeled CCKW 353 truck fitted with a boat-like hull to make it amphibious along with a rudder and propeller, which was powered by the GMC 270 six-cylinder main engine, rated at 104hp. The vehicle was thus able to propel itself under its own power to a speed of 6mph when afloat and drive directly on to land where it was capable of reaching speeds of over 45mph. The first operational use of the DUKW came in March 1943 when it was used to support the landing in New Caledonia, and by the end of the war some 21,147 had been built by the Yellow Truck and Coach Manufacturing Division of GMC, based in Pontiac, Michigan.

The DUKW could drive directly out of the water onto dry land to deliver its load inland.It was essentially an amphibious version of the Jimmy and provided a vital service in supplying the troops; it was fitted with a winch for towing or helping to recover vehicles.

Vehicle Name	Manufacturer	Production Date	Armament	Weight	Max. Speed
Jimmy (DUKW)	GMC	1943 onwards	.50in-calibre machine gun (some vehicles only)	8.7 tons	6mph (water) 45mph (land)

The DUKW weighed 8.7 tons and measured 31ft long, almost 8ft 3in wide and 7ft 1in to the top of the hull. It had an operational road range of 400 miles but when operating in water this dropped to 50 miles. It had a large rear cargo area that could take loads of up to 2.5 tons or twenty-five fully equipped troops but in an emergency more troops could be carried. The amphibious capability of the DUKW meant it could be loaded at sea from a supply ship and on reaching land it could drive straight to the delivery point. During Operation Husky the landings were supported by 1,000 DUKWs, with some 230 being used by the British Army. The DUKW could be fitted with a canvas screen to cover the rear area but when erected it hampered the loading and unloading so it is rarely seen in wartime photographs. During the Burma campaign in the Far East DUKWs were used as ferries to cross the massive Irrawaddy River and in seventy-two hours they transported 6,000 men and 200 vehicles across the great waterway. During the Normandy Landings in June 1944 some 2,000 DUKWs carried around 40 per cent of all supplies ashore on D-Day itself. Those used by the British Army ferried 10,000 tons of stores ashore each day and it is estimated that they were responsible for carrying some 18 million tons of supplies ashore over a three-month period in support of the landings. The basic DUKW was not armed but at least one in four was equipped with a .50in-calibre machine gun for self-defence, but some vehicles were used as platforms for other weapons including trials with 105mm howitzers and 4.5in rocket launchers.

The Development of the Jeep

Another vehicle that had made an appearance by this time was a design called the Willys Jeep, the story of which began in 1940 when the war in Europe was spreading out across the globe and threatening to drag in other nations. Despite its official non-involvement stance there were some in America who realised that it was only a question of time before an incident occurred that would force this great industrialised nation to take action. It was realised that reliable, sturdy vehicles would be required in great numbers to suit a variety of roles for the military and in 1940 the US Ordnance Technical Committee produced a specification for a new military vehicle that had to meet a certain level of criteria for what was termed a 'utility car'. The specifications called for the new vehicle to be four-wheel drive, light with an upper weight limit set at 1,300lb and capable of carrying a payload of 600lb.

The request for the new vehicle was sent out to an incredible 175 specialist engineering and automobile companies. However, the request set a delivery date with a lead-time of almost eleven weeks in which each company could submit their

Jeep with 75mm howitzer and
ammunition trailer, as used by
British airborne forces at Arnhem.

Driver's position on the Jeep
which allowed it to cope with all
terrain and conditions.

models for consideration; this meant that in the end only two manufacturers actually
responded and even then only one managed to meet the deadline. The two companies
that showed an interest in competing for the contract were the American Bantam Car
Company and Willys-Overland Motors. The Bantam prototype design, known as the
Bantam Reconnaissance Command, was delivered in September 1940 and was put
through a series of trials at Fort Holabird. These field tests showed that the vehicle
had potential but lacked power and was not nearly rugged enough to withstand the
rigours of use and abuse on the battlefield. At Willys-Overland Motors, the chief engineer, Barney Roos, believed the specifications laid down were not realistic and any
design would be too constrained by them, especially when it came to the question of
the overall weight of the finished vehicle. Roos began working to design a vehicle that

Jeeps were flown into the Arnhem area during Operation Market Garden where they were used as radio vehicles, medical service and liaison vehicles. The British used thousands of Jeeps which they armed with weapons such as Vickers 'K' machine guns.

he felt was more suited to the needs of the US Army and decided to ignore the weight limits. He worked closely with the engineers from the US Army Quartermaster Corps and between them produced a vehicle ready for testing in November 1940. Early trials showed it to be successful in every instance and it looked promising.

Meanwhile, the Ordnance Technical Committee had made some concessions regarding the new 'utility car', including the weight limit, which was now raised to an upper limit of 2,160lb. Invitations for a new design with the amended specifications were sent to the companies of Ford, Willys-Overland and Bantam asking for their vehicles. In the end the Ford and Bantam designs were found to be inadequate, while the Willys design exceeded the new weight limit by some 120lb, but was more mechanically powerful, giving over 50 per cent more engine capability than the other designs. Again it

The Jeep was used in all theatres of operations by all services including airborne forces.

The LRDG used Jeeps and equipped them with German weapons and Americans as seen here during a display.

looked promising for the Willys design, but the weight factor remained a problem. Roos returned to examine the vehicle and stripped out all unnecessary items to bring it to just within the set limits. The hard work paid dividends and the new 'utility car' was accepted into service in 1941, in time for America entering the war following Japan's bombing of Pearl Harbor that December. An initial order for some 16,000 vehicles was placed and these were referred to as model MA. However, as production proceeded, so small modifications were made, such as fitting a larger-capacity fuel tank. These changes were reflected in a new nomenclature and these vehicles became the Willys Model MB with production commencing in December 1941. The Ford Motor Company was also contracted to build the vehicle to the Willys design and these were called Truck, Command and Reconnaissance, 0.25-ton, 4x4 Ford Model GPW.

The new vehicle soon acquired the term 'Jeep', a nickname that all reference sources agree was a contraction of the initials 'GP' which denoted the vehicle as being general purpose. Whether the story is simply apocryphal does not matter much, because the name stuck and is still used today. The Jeep proved itself to be invaluable in all roles from cargo carrier to medical support, capable of towing a trailer load of 1,000lb and carrying loads of 800lb on the vehicle itself. It was versatile enough to serve as a weapons platform on to which heavy machine guns could be mounted and even recoilless rifles for anti-vehicle roles and destroying bunkers. The Jeep's application to the army was obvious and proved useful to infantry, artillery and medical services, along with the marines and air force. It was also versatile enough to be used by airborne forces and the British LRDG and Special Air Service, who fitted them with a range of machine-gun configurations including twin Vickers 'K' guns, Bren guns, .30in-calibre and .50in-calibre machine guns. Jeeps were also capable of being directly driven ashore from landing craft during amphibious assaults such as North Africa, Salerno, D-Day and in the Far East during the landings at New Guinea.

The Jeep was used by Allied commanders such as Montgomery and Patton, and even Rommel ordered that captured vehicles be pressed into service. In the ambulance role the Jeep could carry up to three stretcher cases. For airborne operations where they were carried into battle by gliders, Jeeps were often stripped down to reduce

Looking like a hybrid between the DUKW and the Jeep, the GPA was an amphibious Jeep, but it was never popular.

The GPA could tow a trailer because the propeller was recessed into the hull and did not interfere with the tow-bar hook. The driver's position had controls for land and water propulsion but its role was limited (above). The exhaust had to vent out over the engine cover at the front (left).

weight and as such were able to be flown straight into battle during campaigns such as Normandy and Arnhem. The Jeep was used for a range of experimental trials including a half-track version and long wheelbase. The American 82nd Airborne Division are known to have modified some of their Jeeps by fitting armour plates for improved protection when in battle.

Under the terms of the Lend-Lease Act, which came into effect on 11 March 1941, America supplied Britain with thousands of vehicles, including many Jeeps. Russia too benefitted from a similar plan and in 1943 alone received over 210,000 vehicles, not including tanks, but including Jeeps. The vehicle was used to tow 6-pounder anti-tank guns, 75mm howitzers and a range of other artillery of ammunition trailers and gun crews. The thousands of shipped Jeeps were transported in versions known as either 'Partly Knocked Down' or 'Completely Knocked Down' and had to be assembled on delivery. In Britain the vehicles were assembled for use at locations all across the country and after D-Day Jeeps were even assembled in hastily prepared barns on recently liberated farms. The basic MB version weighed 3,254lb (1.5 tons) and measured 11ft long and 5ft 2in wide. It was powered by a four-cylinder side-valve engine, which gave a top speed of over 60mph and an operational range of 300 miles. Depending on the role, a typical Jeep could carry four men plus the driver along with personal equipment and heavy machine gun. Although Jeeps look essentially alike, there were actually four different types, not counting those converted to amphibious roles. By the end of the war over 639,000 Jeeps had been built, a figure almost forty times greater than the original production order of 16,000. Many more companies were involved in the production of the Jeep and there were a number of experiments conducted using the Jeep as the basis for this work. One such trial produced the GPA or amphibious design, which looked like a scaled-down version of the DUKW. Sometimes known as the 'Seep' (Sea-going Jeep) it was never a popular vehicle, being difficult to handle in the water and prone to being swamped. Around 12,778 were built, measuring just over 15ft long, 5ft 4in wide and 3ft 9in high. It weighed 3,665lb (1.6 tons) and was powered by a four-cylinder 154 cid 54hp engine to give road speeds of up to 50mph, while the propeller allowed it 5.5mph in the water.

Even before the campaign in Sicily had been concluded, events were unfolding in Italy that would have a profound effect on the Allies. On 24–25 July the Fascist Grand Council voted a massive no confidence in Mussolini as a wartime leader. In the evening of 25 July Mussolini had an audience with King Victor Emmanuel of Italy and was replaced by Marshal Pietro Badoglio, thereby ending twenty-one years of Fascist dictatorship. Mussolini was led away under armed escort, effectively military arrest, to be held first in Podgora Barracks before more permanent arrangements could be made. Italy now found itself in an almost impossible position: some troops deserted, others remained fighting alongside their German allies and some wanted to join the Anglo-American forces to fight the Germans. The Allies mounted a two-pronged attack on Italy, with the British launching Operation Baytown on 3 September by crossing the Strait of Messina. Naval bombardment and air support meant that the Eighth Army under Montgomery landed virtually unopposed at Reggio di Calabria and then moved inland along two axes of advance up the peninsular, with the left flank heading for Pizzo and the right flank heading for Catanzaro. By 9 September the right flank had reached the outskirts of Taranto where the harbour town was captured by an airborne assault by the British 1st Airborne Division and the Royal Navy during Operation Slapstick. That day a fleet of 450 vessels carrying 69,000 American troops with 20,000 vehicles, commanded by General Mark Clark, landed at Salerno. This was Operation Avalanche and men of the Fifth Army were hoping that things were going to be easy, after all Italy had capitulated six days earlier. General Clark was one of them and he hoped to be in Naples by 14 September. Salerno was not the best landing place and Clark had refused air cover or naval bombardment to support his landings, hoping he would achieve total surprise by landing under cover of darkness.

The Germans were well prepared, and firing from defensive positions, they took a terrible toll on the men coming ashore. The German Luftwaffe sank Allied transport vessels using radio-controlled bombs, and the troops faced a tough fight. At one point Clark seriously considered evacuating the beachhead. During one period of fighting the Americans fired 10,000 artillery shells and held the line. At last the Allies managed to link up at Auletta on 20 September, but it would be another two weeks before they finally broke out of the beachhead in force. On 10 October, a full month after the landings at Salerno, the position was secure and 200,000 troops had been landed, along with 35,000 tanks and other vehicles and 15,000 tons of supplies. The Germans made a fighting withdrawal northwards, first behind the Barbara Line of defensive positions before establishing themselves on the formidable Gothic Line, which stretched across the breadth of Italy barring the Allies' advance. One Allied soldier remembered advancing towards these positions in November: 'We piled into trucks and drove through the rain ... Dozens of 105mm howitzers and 155mm Long Toms and other breeds of howitzers were all round, firing day and night.' On the east coast of Italy the British Eighth Army penetrated the left flank of the Gothic Line and captured the town of Ortona on 27 December. In the west things were much different and the seemingly impossible task of capturing Monte Cassino, from where the Germans could direct artillery fire, lay ahead. Even so, the Allies had come a long way but they had achieved a great deal. Italy was ineffectual as Germany's ally, they were back in Europe and troops were being siphoned away from France and Russia along with their equipment and weapons.

The War in the Pacific

On the other side of the world the war in the Pacific was being defined by naval engagements supported with aircraft and conducted over vast distances of the ocean. The larger land masses of Burma and the Malay Peninsula did allow for mechanised strategy but the density of the jungles and the remoteness of the islands precluded armoured battles approaching anywhere near the scale of those in Russia and Europe. That is not to say that tank actions were not engaged in but it was only by armoured vehicles deployed in support of amphibious landings. Each island taken had to be consolidated and airfields established and built from where aircraft could operate to support operations. The strategy had been developed so that American forces would advance stage by stage in an inexorable move towards the Japanese homeland. In May 1943 the Allies had agreed to expand the war in the Pacific and build up forces in readiness to invade the Gilbert Islands, many of which were tiny fragments such as Betio, which measures only 2.5 miles long by 0.5 miles wide, or Tarawa, which covers only 14 square miles. Supporting these operations across the islands was to prove costly to both sides because everything had to be taken to them in turn in order to cope with any eventuality. For the Japanese, once the garrison was established they were at the mercy of re-supply convoys and if these were intercepted they did not receive food, fuel or other vital stores. The Americans left nothing to chance and each amphibious assault carried everything and each landing taught vital lessons required for subsequent operations. Each amphibious landing required logistical build-up and the actual assaults went in only after massive naval and aerial bombardment. Even so, the US marines found themselves confronted by fanatical troops. For example after a naval bombardment lasting 2.5 hours and dropping 3,000 tons of bombs on Betio, the US 2nd Marine Division found themselves fighting 500 Japanese supported by tanks dug into defensive positions and artillery. For the actual assault on Tarawa the US marines used 27,000 troops with a further 7,600 held in readiness for garrison duties and supported with 6,000 vehicles. The tanks were unable to land in support of the initial assault because of the coral reef surrounding the island

Bulldozers were essential in the construction of airfields.

Bulldozers and graders were used on the Pacific islands to create airfields and also in Europe.

but those landed later dealt with points of resistance and Japanese tanks. Once the island had been secured bulldozers and earth-moving equipment was landed to prepare airfields, from where American aircraft could fly support missions to cover the next assault. It was a slow, grinding process, but it was rolling the Japanese back. The fighting on Tarawa had cost the Americans 3,000 killed and wounded, while the Japanese force of 4,700 troops fought so desperately that only 100 were taken alive.

7

THE RISE OF THE MACHINES: THE CAMPAIGNS OF 1944

Logistics

The Western Allies had been building up their forces throughout 1943 when an average of 750,000 tons of supplies were arriving in Britain each month as they prepared for the invasion of Europe. By 1944 the monthly average of supplies being shipped was 2 million tons, requiring the US Army to establish an administrative force of 31,500 officers and 350,000 men to handle the transport and distribution. Fast ocean-going passenger liners were requisitioned to transport the troops across the Atlantic from America. For example, the RMS *Queen Mary* and her sister ship the RMS *Queen Elizabeth* were both conscripted for the duration. The 82,000-ton *Queen Mary* had an overall length of 1,019ft and could sail at speeds of up to 28.5 knots (32.8mph) and on each transatlantic crossing carried an average complement of 15,000 troops. In December 1942 she exceeded this figure and on one crossing she carried 16,000 troops. The 83,000-ton RMS *Queen Elizabeth* is estimated to have transported some 750,000 troops and sailed 500,000 miles for the war effort. The numbers of troops based in Britain would eventually reach 1.5 million men with more in training in America. Thousands of tanks, armoured cars and SPGs arrived in Britain including specialist vehicles such as the recovery trucks, along with transporters for tanks such as the M25 Dragon Wagon.

Ships, railways and aircraft can only take supplies so far, after which point they have to be transported to the front-line troops by trucks, and there was a limit to how much could be moved before the sheer weight overwhelmed the infrastructure. Reports by the German chief of Transportation Corps in the early stages of the war reported that the Reich railroads could not handle any additional burden. The report stated that the railroads were not ready for war and that 'they cannot supply the domestic economy right now'. Fleets of lorries were built and in the case of Germany, General Gerke, chief of transport, was informed in mid-May 1940 that all lorries in Germany were needed because of the strain of the campaign in France and Belgium. In his 1977 work *Supplying War*, the Dutch-born military historian Martin van Creveld has stated that in his opinion 'no less than 1,600 lorries were needed to equal the capacity of just one double-tracked railway line'. Germany would have to work hard to remedy the breakdown rate of 50 per cent that inflicted the vehicle fleets in some units. The standard European gauge of railway was based on a track width of 4ft 8.5in. The Russian standard gauge for railway track width was 5ft. On the Eastern Front when one side had to use the

The Royal Army Service Corps

The unit responsible for handling logistics in the British Army was the Royal Army Service Corps (RASC). During the First World War the regiment had been the Army Service Corps (ASC) but was granted the 'Royal' prefix in 1918 in recognition of the duties it had performed. Before the outbreak of the First World War the strength of the ASC was 500 officers and 6,000 other ranks. Four years later the ASC had 320,000 all ranks serving with some 165,000 vehicles. The regiment could trace its origins back to earlier transport units such as the Royal Waggon Corps in 1799, which then became known as the Royal Waggon Train between 1802 and 1823. During the Crimean War, 1855–56, the unit was given the new title Land Transport Corps and then the Military Train between 1857 and 1869, and finally the Army Service Corps in 1888. During the Second World War the numbers serving in the ranks of the RASC increased dramatically as it had in the First World War. In 1939 there were only 10,000 serving in the RASC but by 1945 there were some 135,000 men supplying ammunition and stores to an army of almost 3 million men with fourteen armoured divisions and sixty-four regiments of infantry alone.

other's system they had to either relay the railway track to their standard gauge or hope they could capture sufficient rolling stock. When the Russians invaded Germany, whole armies of engineers were engaged in relaying the railway track to the Russian 5ft gauge, which was seen as the most expedient solution to the problem, especially as the Germans had retreated with the rolling stock or destroyed carriages and ripped up the tracks in their retreat.

When the Second World War broke out in 1939 the US Army had only 300 light tanks in service, but as the country was not involved in the fighting this was believed to be sufficient for the country's needs at the time. However, three years later, America was in the war and the situation regarding tanks could not have been much different, with around 20,000 tanks of all types being produced in 1942. This figure increased by almost 50 per cent the following year when American factories built 29,500 tanks. Not all of these vehicles were intended for use by the US Army as some were supplied to Britain and Russia, and later France would also benefit from this military aid under the Lend-Lease Act.

US Army Transporters

The US Army learned how to move tanks over long distances by rail and special transporter vehicles were developed in order to reduce unnecessary wear on them as they moved to the battle area. Britain and Germany built a range of such vehicles to move tanks and the US Army also used a number of designs, such as the heavy tank transporter, known as the M25 but nicknamed the 'Dragon Wagon' by the troops. The whole rig comprised the M26 6x6 tractor unit, protected by .75in of armour plate fitted to the front and .25in of armour plate fitted to the sides and rear of the driver's cab, and the M15 trailer rated to carry loads up to 40 tons. It originated in 1942 and was designed by the Knuckey Truck Company of San Francisco, which had experience in designing heavy-duty trucks for mining operations and actually based the M25 on one of these vehicles. The vehicle was built by the Pacific Car and Foundry Company of Renton in Washington, which designated it the TR-1, and the M15 trailer was built by the Detroit-based company of Fruehauf. It was a recovery vehicle as well as a transporter and in all roles it exceeded the capabilities of other similar but lighter vehicles serving in the same roles. Numbers built vary according to sources used as reference with some stating a figure of 1,270 and others stating 1,300, but the low discrepancy is surely an academic point. The Dragon Wagon was powered by a Hall-Scott 440 six-cylinder petrol engine of 17.85-litre capacity to produce 230hp at 2,100rpm, which gave road speeds of up to 28mph.

Vehicle Name	Manufacturer	Production Date	Armament	Weight	Max. Speed
M25 'Dragon Wagon'	Pacific Car and Foundry Company	1942	.50in-calibre machine gun	12 tons	28mph
M26	Knuckey Truck Company	1943	.50in-calibre machine gun	20.5 tons	28mph
M26A1	Knuckey Truck Company	1943	.50in-calibre machine gun	19.5 tons	28mph

The M26 tractor unit weighed 20.5 tons and the M15 trailer just over 17 tons to give a combined weight of 37.6 tons and the whole combination measured 57.34ft long. Although rated to recover vehicles of up to 44 tons it often exceeded that load capacity and wartime photographs show the Dragon Wagon carrying loads of up to 57 tons. The fuel capacity was 120 gallons and, with fuel consumption at 1 mile per gallon, this gave the Dragon Wagon an operational range on roads of 120 miles. It was served by a crew of seven men to operate all the on-board equipment such as the front-mounted winch, which was rated at 35,000lb (15.6 tons) and the two rear-mounted winches rated at 60,000lb (26.8 tons). On board the vehicle carried all the tools required to effect repairs in the field, including oxyacetylene-cutting equipment. Towards the end of the war a lighter unarmoured version known as the M26A1 was developed. The vehicle was never intended to go into battle but nevertheless it was armed with a single .50in-calibre machine gun mounted on a race-ring fitted to the roof of the vehicle cab for self-defence in an emergency.

The armoured screens could be lifted into place to protect the crew from small arms fire and mounting on the roof of the cab allowed a machine gun to be fitted for self-defence. The Dragon Wagon could transport all types of tank to the combat area and could transport tanks forward to help ease the wear and tear and also speeded up mobilisation.

Mortar-Carrying Vehicles

The British Army was also making changes by forming specialist units and accepting into service a range of different vehicles including American-built designs such as half-tracks produced by companies such as International and White, along with versatile M3 scout cars armed with machine guns. The half-track range was versatile and each had its own 'M' designation prefix. For example, the mortar-carrying vehicle was the M21, the anti-aircraft version equipped with quadruple-mounted .50in-calibre machine guns was the M16 and the M14 and M3 were personnel carriers. A number of these were used by the British Army, but some, such as the M21 mortar carrier, were not.

The British Army used the M3 scout car as an infantry carrier and it served with XXX Corps during Operation Market Garden to try to reach Arnhem. The M3 scout car was popular with the American troops who used it to provide fire support as it could be fitted out as a machine-gun platform.

Vehicle Name	Manufacturer	Production Date	Armament	Weight	Max. Speed
M21 Mortar Motor Carriage	White Motor Company	1943	M1 81mm mortar and .50in-calibre machine gun	9 tons	45mph
M4A1	White Motor Company	1943	M1 81mm morta, .50in- and 30in-calibre machine guns	8.2 tons	45mph

There were two main types of mortar-carrying vehicle developed but neither was built in great numbers. For example, only around 110 models of the M21 mortar-carrying version of the White half-track were built and perhaps only 600 vehicles of the similar M4A1 mortar carrier. The M21 and M4A1 mortar carriers were both based on the M3 half-track, of which some 43,000 vehicles were built, serving in various roles including SPG, anti-aircraft gun platform and communications

Half-tracks could be equipped to carry mortars and 75mm field guns to support operations.

Half-tracks made useful mobile cover from behind which the infantry could fight.

A 5.5in field gun opens fire in the Normandy campaign, July 1944. All the shells had to be transported by trucks.

vehicle. The White Motor Company built the prototype of the M21 in early 1943 as the T-19 and following successful trials it was standardised as the M21 Mortar Motor Carriage in July the same year. It was accepted into service in January 1944 and among the actual units to receive the vehicles was the 54th Armoured Infantry Regiment of the 10th Armoured Division, which later saw heavy fighting during the Battle of the Bulge in December 1944. The M21 had a crew of six to operate the vehicle, mortar and other weapons, and frames on the side of the vehicle allowed mines to be carried, so the crew would have had to be familiar with the use of these also. The vehicle had a combat weight of almost 9 tons with an overall length of almost 19ft 6in. The height was 7ft 5in with a width of almost 7ft 5in over the mine racks on the sides. The main weapon was the M1 81mm mortar with bipod support and special baseplate mount, which allowed it to be fired from the rear of the vehicle. A total of ninety-seven rounds of ammunition was carried and included smoke, illuminating and high-explosive rounds. The ammunition was stored in lockers on either side of the hull where the crew could access it easily.

The mortar fired forward over the front of the vehicle and could be traversed 30 degrees left and right, and for greater changes the vehicle would have to be manoeuvred in the direction of the target. The mortar had a rate of fire of eighteen rounds per minute with a range of almost 3,300yd with the high-explosive rounds. The barrel could be elevated between +40 and -85 degrees to alter the range. The

The M3 half-track carrying infantry into a battle re-enactment. The soldier on the left is holding a Bazooka anti-tank rocket launcher (top left). The M16 half-track quadruple .50in-calibre machine gun vehicle (top right). The M14 version half-track in the colours of the Guards Armoured Division as serving with the British XXX Corps in 1944 (above).

.50in-calibre machine gun was fitted on a pedestal mount to the rear of the vehicle and a total of 400 rounds of ammunition were carried. From there the firer could traverse through 360 degrees to provide all-round fire support. The vehicle was only lightly armoured up to a maximum of 13mm thickness. The M21 was fitted with a White 160AX six-cylinder petrol engine that developed 147hp at 3,000rpm to give speeds of up to 45mph on roads. Fuel capacity was 60 gallons and this allowed an operational range of 200 miles on roads. The front wheels were operated by a standard steering wheel and the tracks were fitted with double sets of twin bogies as road wheels, larger idler-type wheels at the front and rear of the track layout and only one return roller. The open top of the vehicle could be covered by a canvas tarpaulin during inclement weather and this could be thrown off quickly when going into action. Although only few in number, together with the more numerous M4A1 mortar carrier, it would have provided excellent mobile fire support to infantry units wherever required. The vehicle was equipped with a radio set to communicate and receive orders as to where to deploy if needed to fire against targets. There were plans to develop a similar vehicle to carry the larger 4.2in-calibre mortar but it never entered service.

British Army Motorcycles

New British designs were also being produced and changes were being made, with new motorcycles for use by their dispatch riders, known as 'Don Rs', which included female riders of the Auxiliary Territorial Service (ATS) who were already used to driving trucks in convoys. In 1940 the army had been using machines such as the Ariel WMG 350cc but following the retreat from Dunkirk those machines still in service were issued to the RAF because the army required more powerful motorcycles. The new models included the BSA WD M20 design, rated at 500cc, from around 1942, but some of these were replaced by the Jeep when they came into service in numbers. Some lighter motorcycles remained in service such as the Matchless 350cc, while for the specialist role with the airborne divisions the James ML, rated at 125cc, was developed and nicknamed the 'Clockwork Mouse' by the troops; these could be dropped by parachute or carried inside aircraft such as the Hamilcar or Horsa gliders and used during operations such as Market Garden at Arnhem in Holland in September 1944.

British Army BSA WD M20 500cc motorcycle.

BSA 500cc M20 motorcycle combination of
the British Army in REME colours and BSA
WD M20 1942 500cc with dispatch rider in
full clothing of period.

ML Airborne, 1943 125cc
'Clockwork Mouse' as flown
into the Arnhem bridgehead by
glider in September 1944.

RAF motorcycle, Ariel WMG
350cc 1940. Originally army
then RAF after Dunkirk.

Vehicles of the 79th Armoured Division

The Churchill tank was fitted with a spigot mortar to launch a powerful demolition charge of 40lb to destroy obstacles. The vehicle was called the 'Petard' and the projectiles it fired were called 'Flying Dustbins' due to their size and shape. Flail tanks based on the Sherman, known as 'Crabs', were designed to beat a path through minefields in the same manner as the Matilda Scorpions used in North Africa. The 'Bobbin' was a massive reel of canvas matting that was carried on a drum mounted on a Churchill tank and was designed to unroll in front of the vehicle as it advanced. This system was to permit light-wheeled vehicles such as Jeeps and trucks to drive over soft sand without becoming bogged down. Another design developed by the 79th Armoured Division was the duplex drive, which was an amphibious tank based on the Sherman. The method of making the tank float for amphibious operations consisted of fitting a canvas screen inflated by a cylinder of compressed air and kept rigid by a series of wooden slats. A propeller was fitted at the rear and operated by power take-off from the main drive shaft. The concept had been trialled on the Valentine but the Sherman had been chosen because it was more numerous in service and a modern design. Together, all of these designs and many others were built and prepared in readiness for the D-Day landings at Normandy in June 1944. Other designs were quite simple, such as the Universal Bren gun carrier which was fitted with higher sides to cope with the deeper water. The Bren carrier was also used as the carrier vehicle on which to mount a structure containing two Bren guns, which could be elevated in order to fire over hedgerows. Trials were conducted but it was decided not to pursue it to the development stage and only a few prototypes were built. For the most part these vehicles of 79th Armoured Division worked well but there were some occasions when they failed but this was largely due to misunderstanding how they should be used and their limitations.

British Army Specialised Units

The British Army was also forming yet more specialised units in 1943 such as the 79th Armoured Division. This unit had originally been formed in 1942 but it was reorganised and its composition was changed in April 1943 with the specific intention of creating specialist armoured units after lessons learned in the aftermath of the disastrous Dieppe raid in August 1942. It was realised that specialist vehicles had to be developed based on existing tank chassis to cope with certain difficulties on the battlefield, including the clearance of obstacles such as anti-tank walls and ditches, bunker emplacements and minefields. The 79th Armoured Division had originally been intended to serve as an ordinary unit equipped with a standard range of AFVs and in March 1943 it was about to be disbanded due to lack of equipment. Field Marshal Sir Alan Brooke CIGS intervened, however, and suggested that the division be turned into a specialist unit to develop equipment and vehicles to deal with obstacles. Command of the new unit was given to Major General Sir Percy Hobart who had seen service in France and the Middle East during the First World War, winning the Military Cross. He was very much influenced by the writings of Basil Liddell Hart, and it would be under his direction that many useful vehicles would be developed, such as the Churchill 'Ark' which could lay a bridge to span gaps and natural water obstacles. The Churchill proved ideal for this type of work and other designs based on the Churchill included a flame-thrower called the 'Crocodile' and another which could unload a tightly bound roll of wooden staves known as a fascine, which could be dropped into tank traps to fill the gap quickly and easily so that vehicles following after could drive over the obstacle unimpeded.

Wrecker and Recovery Trucks

All armies during the war came to realise that it was usually best to have more than one vehicle to operate in specialised roles and the policy applied to armoured vehicles, liaison vehicles and even trucks used for transportation. For example, the US Army developed a range of vehicles known as 'wreckers' that were used for the recovery of vehicles and for lifting heavy loads using cranes on board the vehicle. One particular design of this type of vehicle was the Diamond T 969 wrecker truck, which was also built in two other versions known as A and B. The vehicle was basically a standard truck body built by the Holmes Company but configured to the role of recovery or wrecker truck. It initially entered service with the US Army in 1941, having been designed and developed in 1939, but later it went on to be used by the British and Canadian armies and by the end of the war a total of 31,245 vehicles in all models were produced, including variants known as 970, 972 and 975, of which some 6,420 were wreckers.

Vehicle Name	Manufacturer	Production Date	Armament	Weight	Max. Speed
Diamond T 969	Holmes Company	1941	Some fitted with a .50in-calibre machine gun	9.6 tons	40mph
969 A	Holmes Company	1943	Some fitted with a .50in-calibre machine gun	9.6 tons	40mph
969 B	Holmes Company	1943	Some fitted with a .50in-calibre machine gun	9.6 tons	40mph
M1A1	Ward La France/ Kenworth	1943	Some fitted with a .50in-calibre machine gun	15.5 tons	40mph

The Diamond T 969 was 24.3ft long, 8.4ft wide and 9.25ft high to the top of the driver's cab. It was a heavy vehicle weighing 9.6 tons and it had to be in order to deal with the heavy duties it was expected to cope with. It was fitted with a

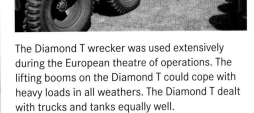

The Diamond T wrecker was used extensively during the European theatre of operations. The lifting booms on the Diamond T could cope with heavy loads in all weathers. The Diamond T dealt with trucks and tanks equally well.

Hercules RXC six-cylinder 8.7-litre side-valve engine rated to 131bhp mounted to the front and covered with a curved bonnet, which was distinct from other wrecker designs. It had a five-speed gearbox with a two-speed transfer, allowing road speeds of almost 40mph, which was sufficient to move in convoy. The front set of wheels were basic truck tyres, with the two sets of rear axles fitted with double tyres in keeping with other truck designs. It had a fuel capacity of 50 gallons and this allowed an operational range of over 130 miles. The vehicle was never intended to operate off-road but sometimes road conditions were bad due to artillery and the 969 could wade through water obstacles of up to 24in deep.

The first version of the 969 to enter service was the closed cab type, but after 1943 the open cab version, which was actually a canvas-topped model, was introduced. These were also built in the variants known as the 969A and 969B. The first production vehicles in the 969 range had been built using civilian components but later it was decided to change over to military standard components, and this became the standard 969A. The 969B version was the design supplied to overseas armies and was not used by the US Army. However, they did retain certain distinguishing features such as the drop-down tailgate and the 'rounded-off' mudguards over the front wheels. One in four vehicles were fitted with an M36 'race-ring' mounting on top of the cab so that a .50in-calibre machine gun could be fitted to provide self-defence against low-flying aircraft and as protection in case of attack by ground troops.

Mounted on the rear of the vehicle was a Holmes W-45 crane with a twin boom design with each one rated for a 5-ton lift capacity, giving a combined lift capability of 10 tons. This was useful for many duties, including being used to lift disabled aircraft on to trailers for removal. A large number of 969 vehicles were fitted with front-mounted winches, which were useful for recovery duties where a vehicle had simply skidded off the road and got stuck. The winches were rated for 6.6 tons and could haul damaged vehicles into a position where the vehicle's on-board crane could be used either to lift it on to a recovery trailer or tow it away for repair. The vehicle could tow loads of over 11 tons, which meant that it could cope with all but the heaviest armoured vehicles. The vehicle was equipped with a range of tools and equipment to allow the crew to complete vehicle maintenance in the field and this range of equipment included an air compressor for the workshop.

Another design of wrecker truck was developed by the company of Ward La France, which already had a pre-war reputation for providing specialist 6x6 trucks fitted with cranes that could be used for heavy recovery duties. This manufacturer, along with others such as Kenworth, increased their production of vehicles of all types, especially recovery vehicles, which the armies would need in order to tow abandoned vehicles back to base for repair. From 1943 onwards this included a series of recovery trucks called the M1A1, also known as a 'wrecker', which was standardised for the vital role of retrieving tanks and other damaged heavy equipment such as artillery from the battlefield. Like other American-built trucks this too would enter service with the British Army and serve with the light aid detachments of the REME and be used in Italy and the Middle East.

The M1A1 had a number of features that set it apart from other similar vehicles, such as 'squared' mudguards and lacking full doors, which led to the term 'open' cab, the roof of which was fitted with a folding canvas cover. Some vehicles had a race-ring fitted above the cab to permit a .50in-calibre machine gun to be mounted for self-defence. Between them the two manufacturers, Ward La France and Kenworth, built 3,735 M1A1s, producing 3,425 and 310 respectively,

The crew of the M1A1 and other specialists could work in the caravan in all weathers to repair vehicles.

but some sources put this figure much higher. It was operated by a two-man crew, driver and co-driver, and the vehicle was equipped with all the tools necessary to undertake repairs in the field or to tow badly damaged vehicles back to a base workshop where there were the facilities to deal with them. Some wreckers towed trailer workshops for repairs in the field, complete with all the tools essential for maintenance including cutting and welding equipment. In addition to the rear-mounted crane, which had a 9.75-ton rating, winches were fitted front and rear. The front winch had a rating of 13 US tons while the rear winch had a rating of 22 US tons, making it suitable to recover most armoured vehicles and field guns.

The M1A1 wrecker was fitted with a powerful 8.2-litre six-cylinder Continental Model 22R petrol engine, which gave 145bhp at 2,400rpm to provide road speeds over 40mph. Its massive weight of over 15.5 tons helped with tackling heavy loads but it came at a price, with the fuel capacity of 84 gallons allowing an operational road range of only 250 miles. The transmission was a five-speed Fuller 5A620 and the 6x6 drive featured double tyres on the two sets of rear wheels as standard. The overall length of the M1A1 was almost 26ft, and it was just over 10ft high and 8.2ft wide. Along with the Diamond T 969 and the British vehicles, they provided the Allies with a fleet of recovery vehicles to keep the armies on the move.

The recovery of vehicles from the battlefield had been developed properly during the fighting in the desert and was continually being improved, which in turn led to the development of one of the best specialist recovery vehicles in late 1944. This

The driver's position with all the controls to drive the vehicle over the roughest terrain (top left).The M1A1 wrecker served in the same role as other similar vehicles but was an entirely different design. The M1A1 booms could be used to lift aircraft fuselages to clear crash sites on airfields.

The M1A1 wrecker towed a trailer which served as a field workshop to repair vehicles without the need to return to base depots.

The M1A1 wrecker was powerful enough to tow tanks such as this example seen at a military vehicle show.

was based on the Churchill Mk III tank and was known as the ARV (Armoured Recovery Vehicle) Mk II. It was fitted with a winch rated to a 25-ton pull capacity and a rear-mounted jib with a 15-ton lift capacity; another jib, which could be dismounted, was fitted forward and this had a lift capacity of 7.5 tons. The Americans assessed that an average of at least 60 per cent of vehicles damaged in battle could be repaired using resources such as these. The British 21st Army Group believed that 30 per cent of repairs undertaken in field workshops were completed on vehicles that had sustained battle damage and the other 70 per cent of work was to vehicles that had sustained mechanical failure. In one particular operation a division lost forty-eight Sherman tanks damaged while negotiating a minefield. The

REME recovered and repaired thirty-two of them, returning the tanks to their unit within forty-eight hours. This represents a two-thirds recovery and repair rate, something that was not thought possible in the early days of the war. Such capabilities were as a result of lessons learnt during the early campaigns of the war, such as Operation Battleaxe during the North African campaign in 1941 when 135 Matildas had been overhauled in field workshops in forty-eight hours and many other vehicles were also repaired and maintained to continue operating in the battle.

Prime Movers and Anti-Aircraft Gun Towing Vehicles

All armies also used vehicles known as prime movers to tow artillery. This series of vehicles was very versatile but perhaps the most diverse range was that used by the German Army throughout the Second World War. The vehicles that operated in this role proved themselves to be highly useful in a range of roles other than that for which they were originally intended. The most versatile of all these were the half-tracks, such as the SdKfz 251, which was configured into no fewer than twenty-three separate roles, with further designs planned, but the war ended before they could enter service. Half-tracks came in a variety of sizes and were produced throughout the entire war, being among some of the last vehicles still being built by German factories right up to the time of the surrender. Because of their adaptability to serve in any role they could be seen as the workhorses of the German Army and were deployed to all theatres of fighting and engaged in all campaigns.

German Vehicles

Vehicle Name	Manufacturer	Production Date	Armament	Weight	Max. Speed
SdKfz 7	Krauss-Maffei, Borgward, Saurer	1939	N/A	11.3 tons	30mph
SdKfz 7/1	Krauss-Maffei, Borgward, Saurer	1943	4x 2cm FlaK 38	12.8 tons	30mph
SdKfz 7/2	Krauss-Maffei, Borgward, Saurer	1943	3.7cm FlaK 36 L/98	13.2 tons	30mph

One of the most important types of the prime mover series of vehicles was the SdKfz 7, not because of the number of variants made, but for the fact that it was used to tow the formidable 88mm gun in either its anti-aircraft or anti-tank role. Development of the SdKfz 7 began in 1934 when Germany started its rearmament programme in earnest. The vehicle was designed in response to the army's need for an 8-ton half-track for towing and supply transportation purposes. The first model appeared in 1938 and during the war three main companies became involved with either its direct production or one of the variants derived from the basic version. These were Krauss-Maffei and Borgward, who were joined later by Saurer. Almost from the beginning the SdKfz 7 was seen as a *Gepanzerte Zugkraftwage* (armoured gun tractor), and became the main half-track prime mover of the German Army. It was used to tow not only the 88mm gun, but also much larger and heavier guns such as the 150mm-calibre sFH18 howitzer. The first SdKfz 7 vehicles were issued to the *Schwere Panzerjäger Abteilungen* (heavy anti-tank gun battalions) of the Wehrmacht in 1939 and were ready to participate in the Polish campaign in September that year. The vehicle would also be used by the Waffen-SS for its artillery and the Luftwaffe would use it for its anti-aircraft units with 88mm guns. Apart from being able to tow all main types of 88mm gun the vehicle could also transport the gun crew of up to twelve men with their personal kit and a supply of ready-to-use ammunition. Further supplies of ammunition were transported by other accompanying vehicles.

The driver was seated to the left with his co-driver alongside and the rear seating layout for the gun crew arranged in rows facing forward. A space behind the driver's position was provided for the storage of personal kit, weapons and ammunition. The SdKfz 7 had a soft canvas top that could be erected during inclement weather but it is more usually seen in wartime photographs without this fitted. The vehicle was open-sided, which allowed the crew to deploy quickly, but it also meant that they were exposed to enemy fire. Some vehicles did have armoured superstructures added to the sides for protection, but apparently this was not standard and may have been fitted by field workshops. The driver's cab and engine compartment were the only parts to be fitted with standard armour protection and even then only to 8mm thickness. As the war progressed production was modified to contend with the shortages in raw materials and reduce the use of metal, and a simplified version of the SdKfz 7 was developed. This used wooden side frames, which gave it a truck-like appearance. The seats were wooden and the crew had to board and leave by means of a drop gate at the rear.

The SdKfz 7 was 22.4ft long, 7.7ft wide, 8.6ft high and weighed 11.3 tons. It was capable of towing loads of up to 8 tons and when towing an 88mm gun the barrel always faced forward, as is evidenced in all wartime photographs and film footage. It was this capability to tow heavy loads that led to the SdKfz 7 being used as a recovery vehicle when it was available, and some were fitted with integral winches to improve this capacity. Powered by a Maybach HL62TUK six-cylinder petrol engine developing 140hp, the SdKfz 7 could reach speeds of up to over 30mph on roads with an operational range of 155 miles on roads and around 75 miles cross-country. It was fitted with a gearbox layout that gave 4x2 forward gears and 1x2 reverse gears. The front wheels were fitted with hydro-pneumatic tyres, which provided steering through a conventional steering column and wheel configuration. Torsion bars provided the suspension to the track layout, which comprised seven pairs of double wheels overlapping with the drive sprocket at the front on either side. From the desert wastes of North Africa to the sub-zero steppes of Russia and all across Europe the SdKfz 7 was to be found serving in the role of prime mover for artillery. Three main variants of the SdKfz 7 were developed, two of which were configured into the self-propelled anti-aircraft role. The third was fitted with

Fully restored SdKfz 7 half-track prime mover used to tow the 88mm anti-tank gun.

Prime mover SdKfz 7 towing a PaK43 88mm anti-tank gun on the Eastern Front.

The SdKfz 7 prime mover towing an 88mm anti-tank gun at a vehicle display.

The SdKfz 7 carried the gun crew and all their kit on the vehicle and some ammunition as well.

an all-enclosing armoured superstructure and used in the highly specialised role of launching the mobile versions of the long-range V2 rocket. This variant was called the Feuerleitpanzerfahzeug Fur V2 Raketen auf Zugkraftwagen 8t and little resembled the original SdKfz 7 on which it was based. These vehicles served as the towing unit for the massive rockets but they also provided the command, control and communications centre for firing instructions.

The anti-aircraft gun platform vehicles were termed the SdKfz 7/1 and SdKfz 7/2 and were armed with four 2cm FlaK 38 and a single FlaK 36 of 3.7cm calibre respectively. The SdKfz 7/1 was referred to as the 2cm Flakvierling 38 auf Fahrgestell Zugkraftwagen 8t. A total of 319 were built between mid-1943 and October 1944 and used exclusively by the FlaK units of the Luftwaffe. Everything about the basic vehicle remained the same except the rear seats were stripped out to permit the fitting of the gun mounting for the quadruple 2cm FlaK 38. A full 360-degree traverse by hand was permitted and the guns could be elevated between -10 degrees and +100 degrees to allow ground and aerial targets to be engaged. The SdKfz 7/2 was fitted with a single FlaK 36 L/98 3.7cm calibre on a mounting in place of the rear seats. This was termed the 3.7cm FlaK 36 auf Fahrgestell Zugkraftwagen 8t. The gun could be traversed through a full 360 degrees by hand and elevated between -8 degrees and +85 degrees to permit both ground and aerial targets to be engaged. About 123 examples of this version were built from around 1943 until February 1945, again being used exclusively by the FlaK units of the Luftwaffe. Both versions were fitted with the Flakvisier 40 for aiming and each appeared with either an armoured and unarmoured cab for the driver. The SdKfz 7/1 towed a special trailer called the Sonder Anhanger 56, which carried extra ammunition. The SdKfz 7/2 towed a similar trailer called the Sonder Anhanger 57 for its ammunition supply. Development of a third self-propelled anti-aircraft gun version of the SdKfz 7 was started and this would have been the fourth variant of the basic vehicle. This was to have been armed with the 5cm FlaK 41 gun to become the *Sonderfahrgestell* (Special Purpose Chassis) auf Zugkraftwagen 8t. It is understood that only a very few pre-production vehicles were made in this series in 1942 and evidence points to the fact that it is unlikely the version ever went into production and the few pre-production models almost certainly never entered service. Photographs of the version exist and show it to be a well-designed vehicle with a gun capable of engaging both ground and aerial targets like the other anti-aircraft versions.

Allied Vehicles

Vehicle Name	Manufacturer	Production Date	Armament	Weight	Max. Speed
Mack 7 (G532)	Mack	1943	.50in-calibre machine gun	14.4 tons	
AEC Matador	Leyland	1930s	N/A	7.5 tons	30mph
Retriever	Leyland	1930s	N/A	7.7 tons	30mph
The Quad	Morris	1937	N/A	3.3 tons	50mph

The US Army often used wheeled trucks as prime movers and one of the manufacturers to produce these kinds of trucks for this role was the North Carolina-based vehicle manufacturer Mack, which between 1941 and 1945 used its pre-war experience of producing heavy trucks for the civilian market to supply a total of more than 35,000 trucks to the US Army, along with the British, Canadian and French armies. These were mainly the 'N' series, which made up almost 27,000 vehicles of that figure alone. Some 2,053 'NO' 6x6 models were built up to 1945 with the Mack NO 7yd (21ft) 2-ton vehicle being used for towing large pieces of artillery such as the M1 155mm-calibre Long Tom field gun, capable of firing shells weighing over 90lb out to a maximum range of 14.5 miles. The Long Tom in its basic M1 version had a barrel length of 22.8ft and was served by a crew of fourteen, who travelled in the rear of the truck, and it could fire forty high-explosive shells an hour.

The Mack 7 vehicle had been developed specifically as a prime mover for the role of towing such large and heavy artillery and the 'NO' series ran through models 1 to 7. The vehicle was operated by a five-man crew and to help manoeuvre the Long Tom into and out of its firing positions a Gar Wood 5MB winch with a 40,000lb capacity was fitted to the front of the Mack 7. In the rear area a hoist was mounted and this was used to lift the trail arms of the Long Tom. The vehicle had a canvas cab and the cargo body was sometimes made from wood, but even so the Mack 7 (G532) still weighed 30,000lb when empty. It could carry loads of up to 10 tons and pull loads of up to 25 tons, so the 30,600lb load of the Long Tom was well within its capacity. The Mack 7 was powered by a Mack EY six-cylinder 707 cid engine, which produced 159hp at 2,100rpm. It had a five-speed transmission and for self-defence an M36 race-ring mount for a .50in-calibre machine gun was fitted over the roof of the driver's cab.

The British Army had its own version of the Mack – the AEC Matador. This 7.5-ton heavyweight truck could be used to recover abandoned vehicles but more commonly it was used as an artillery tractor for the 5-ton 5.5in-calibre field gun. Some 11,000 of these were built and they were equipped with a winch rated at 5 tons with 250ft of steel cable for the purpose of recovering guns or vehicles. In the artillery role the Matador could be used to carry the entire gun crew and all their kit. It was powered by an A187 7.7-litre diesel engine delivering 95hp to give road speeds of up to 30mph. Another British truck that could be fitted out for a range of tasks on the battlefield was the Retriever, of which some 6,500 were built by Leyland Motors. Originally produced from 1933, the vehicle was beginning to show its age by the time war broke out but nevertheless it was still service-able and could be fitted out for use as a field workshop complete with breakdown gantry. Powered by a 6-litre, four-cylinder Leyland engine rated at 73bhp, it had a standard road range of 195 miles with a fuel tank capacity of 31 gallons. Retrievers were also used to transport pontoon boats for river crossings and even as mobile platforms for searchlights, but perhaps the most famous role was the vehicle in this range which served as the campaign caravan for General, later Field Marshal, Montgomery.

During the rearmament period of the mid-1930s the British Army began experiments to use wheeled vehicles in a wide variety of roles, including as platforms on which to mount light anti-aircraft guns such as the 20mm-calibre Polsten. As war approached the army's fleet of vehicles was stretched to its capacity to meet demands and so it was essential that manufacturers produced as many vehicles as possible. Sometimes demands actually exceeded output, as was the case with the vehicle that would come to be universally referred to throughout the British Army simply as the 'Quad', and other manufacturers had to come in to help the main producer maintain production. When war was finally declared in September 1939 the Guy Motor Company was already producing the design of a 4x4 Field Artillery Tractor (FAT) vehicle, which became the Guy Quad ANT and had been unveiled in prototype form in 1937.

The 155mm Long Tom field gun was a heavyweight piece of artillery used in Italy and Europe. The Mack 7 and Long Tom combination took up its fair share of space on the road but they were essential in supporting operations. The Mack 7 truck was used to tow the heavyweight artillery and could also carry ammunition and the crew.

The 25-pounder field gun in North Africa camouflage and Eighth Army badge (top). Interior of the Quad showing the basic controls in the driver's position (above left). The limber used to carry ammunition for the 25-pounder field gun and towed by the Quad (above right). The Morris Commercial Quad used to tow the 25-pounder field gun seen here in Eighth Army colours for the North Africa campaign (left).

The AEC Matador was a heavyweight truck used to tow the large guns for the Royal Artillery such as the 5.5in field guns.

It was designed specifically for use as the prime mover or tractor for the new 25-pounder field gun just beginning to enter service. By coincidence the Morris Motor Company was also producing a similar vehicle, the Commercial C8. As demands for these specialist towing vehicles increased so it was that Morris took over production of the new FAT and so is synonymous with its wartime output. The Quad would go on to be built by other manufacturers and large numbers were even built by General Motors in Canada. In total some 10,000 Quads were built during the war and were used by British and Commonwealth troops including Canadian and Australian forces.

The Quad had a distinctive shape with the rear portion from the roof dropping away in a marked manner that identified it from other vehicles and especially artillery tractors. In fact, it was this feature in the design that allowed the Germans to know when artillery was about to be directed against them for they had come to associate the shape of the vehicle with artillery. To counter this a canvas screen was developed to disguise the characteristic shape. The Quad was associated with the 25-pounder gun but it could also tow the 17-pounder anti-tank gun and the hybrid 17/25-pounder gun known as the 'Pheasant', which was produced in limited numbers. On the battlefield the Germans learned to identify the Quad coming into action and they would either take cover from the artillery barrage they knew was imminent or, if they could engage first, would direct their own guns against the Quads in a counter-battery barrage.

The Quad in all its forms, and there would eventually be three variants, was unarmoured even though the Mk I had an all-metal body design including the roof. The Mk II had a canvas top that could be rolled back and the Mk III was the C8 GS. In addition to the tow hook for the gun and ammunition limber, the vehicle was fitted with a winch that could be useful in hauling artillery and recovery purposes. The interior was cramped but the crew always managed to store their kit and personal weapons, even if it meant hanging excess baggage on the outside of the vehicle.

The basic Quad measured 14.7ft long, 7.2ft wide and 7.4ft to the top of the roof. It weighed 3.3 tons and had the seating capacity to take five men in addition to the drivers, who served as crew for the 25-pounder gun. It was powered by a Morris EH four-cylinder 3.5-litre petrol engine that developed 70bhp, giving road speeds of up to 50mph and a range on roads of over 150 miles. It pulled the ammunition limber and the 25-pounder field gun, which weighed almost 1.8 tons alone, and could cope with most cross-country conditions. Britain did not follow the route taken by America or Germany and develop a half-track vehicle for towing artillery, and instead relied almost entirely on wheeled vehicles such as the Quad to do the job. Despite not being armoured its reliability on the battlefield in all theatres, from the blazing heat of North Africa to the damp muddy fields of Europe and the humid tropics of the Far East, meant that the Quad could always be depended on to give service.

Stalemate in Italy

The year 1944 began with the Allies facing stalemate in Italy. The troops in the line looked at the foreboding Monte Cassino rising to an elevation of over 1,700ft. This was not tank country in the true sense of the word and although the Allies committed 1,900 AFVs to the coming battle it would be the infantry, artillery and massive air support that would win the battle. Four distinct battles would be fought before the positions held by the Germans were finally taken and the western end of the Gothic Line penetrated. The first attack was made by American troops on 20 January and proved to be a disastrous engagement with 1,000 killed out of 6,000 men in the fight. The Allies had a plan to help take the pressure off Monte Cassino by making an amphibious landing over 50 miles behind German lines at Anzio, which, it was hoped, would make the Germans divert troops away to respond to the landings. The Anglo-American operation was known by the code name Shingle and was under the command of US Major-General John Lucas, whose forces included the US VI Corps. British Intelligence believed the landings would be unexpected and therefore resistance would be very light. On the other hand, Lucas' commanding officer, Mark Clark, thought it would be as bad as Salerno, if not worse.

The landings were made under cover of darkness at 2 a.m. on 22 January. The force of 40,000 men with 5,200 vehicles had been transported to the beachhead by a convoy of 289 vessels, which also provided a covering naval bombardment to suppress defences. Lucas shared Mark Clark's worries, and believed he faced a very real threat of a strong counter-attack. No commander ever feels he has sufficient troops or resources for the battle ahead and Lucas wanted to wait until his reinforcement force of 60,000 troops, thousands of vehicles and supplies had arrived before making a concerted breakout. On the day of the landings the Allies consolidated their positions and landed 36,000 troops and 3,200 vehicles, and the British 1st Division had moved 2 miles inland, facing little opposition. The Americans had also moved inland and a defensive perimeter was established, all for the cost of 154 killed, wounded and missing. The way to Rome appeared open, but Lucas did nothing to break out of the beachhead, leading Churchill to comment: 'I had hoped we were hurling a wild cat on to the shore, but all we got was a stranded whale.' Field Marshal Albert Kesselring, commander-in-chief of German forces in Italy, ordered units from locations across Italy to move on Anzio and these were reinforced by troops from France and Germany. By 24 January he had 40,000 troops to deploy against the Allied beachhead, which now measured 16 miles wide and 7 miles deep. The Allies continued to land at Anzio so that by 29 January there were 69,000 troops crammed into the beachhead along with 508 pieces of artillery and more than 200 tanks, as well as thousands of other vehicles. The German Fourteenth Army, commanded by General Eberhard von Mackensen, had built up their numbers to 90,000 men with armoured support and long-range artillery to fire on the landing beaches. These massive weapons were of 210mm and 240mm calibre, with one of 280mm capable of firing a shell weighing 560lb from its position 40 miles away. The Allies famously nicknamed this gun 'Anzio Annie'. The first real clash of forces came on 30 January as Lucas attempted to break out, with the British initially making good progress towards Campoleone. The Americans attacked Cisterna where the 1st Armoured Division became a victim of minefields. US rangers were caught by German forces in an ambush using tanks that was so effective that only six men out of a force of 767 made it back to the beachhead. The British were being badly assaulted but the Allies were determined to hang on because having come this far they were in Italy to stay and were not going to be pushed out.

The German propaganda machine made much capital of the Allies' progress with reference made to it as being slower than a snail's pace. The weather had turned and washed away roads, and rivers burst their banks causing flooding. The mountainous terrain also caused delays and destroyed bridges had to be repaired. Italy had become a 'tough old gut' but the Germans were in retreat. Fighting was fierce at Anzio and Monte Cassino; with no headway being made, Lucas was relieved of his command by Mark Clark, who replaced him with Major General Lucien Truscott Jr, who was a 'fighting' general in the true sense of the word and well liked by the British. Even so, he had a tough battle ahead of him. There was an Allied air raid on Monte Cassino on 15 February that dropped 450 tons of bombs on the site. It made no difference and the Germans continued to hold the position and repulsed all attempts to take it. Exactly a month later, on 15 March, another air raid attacked the position and surrounding area, dropping 1,000 tons of bombs, and the artillery fired 195,000 shells. Finally, on 13 May, Truscott was able to begin breaking out from the beachhead and by 18 May they were advancing on the Italian capital of Rome. That day the Polish forces fighting at Monte Cassino made it to the summit and the western end of the Gustav Line was penetrated. Rome had been declared an 'open' city by the Germans, which is to say that they had evacuated and were not going to defend it.

On 26 May troops from the Anzio beachhead and those who had fought at Monte Cassino met up. The German Tenth Army pulled back, heading northwards to new defensive positions. Mark Clark entered Rome on 4 June but the Allies did not let this prize prevent them from keeping up the pressure on the retreating enemy and they pursued the Germans over a distance of 90 miles in twelve days. The pace then slowed until finally they came face to face with the Gothic Line, which extended 200 miles across Italy. It had been started when Sicily had been evacuated in August the previous year and now comprised anti-tank obstacles, minefields and belts of barbed wire that extended up to 10 miles deep in some places. Fortified defences included the turrets of some thirty tanks that had been removed, complete with their 88mm guns, and positioned in concrete foundations, almost 2,400 machine-gun positions, 479 artillery positions, 100 steel-lined shelters and miles of tunnels and trenches for the infantry defenders. The Allies

Polish troops moving 5.5in artillery forward in Italy; probably heading for Monte Cassino. They are escorted by motorcyclists.

eventually stormed the position in September using 80,000 vehicles, artillery and overwhelming air support, and the US Fifth Army and 8th Division from the British Eighth Army. By late October, Mark Clark was deep into north Italy and holding secure positions.

German Vehicles

The HK Half-Track Vehicle Series

By now the Allies had encountered a wide range of German vehicles, not all of which were equipped for fighting. These were liaison types such as the Kubelwagen, which was the Germany's equivalent to the Jeep, and an extraordinary design called the *Kleines Kettenkrad* (little chain cycle), a handy machine developed and built by NSU and Stoewer Company and officially designated the SdKfz 2. As the German Army re-equipped with a range of modern vehicles, the fleet included wheeled and half- and three-quarter-tracked designs, one of which was a very compact half-track vehicle, introduced in 1939, with the designation HK 101. It was proposed that it would serve as a utility vehicle capable of operating in a variety of roles, including liaison and communications. The HK 101 was only 9ft 10in long, 3ft 3in wide and a mere 3ft 11in high. Despite this compact design it could still tow loads of almost 0.5 tons, which meant it was ideal for roles such as the re-supply of ammunition or the transportation of medical stores. It weighed 1.5 tons and comprised a small tracked unit, between which was the engine and what amounted to the front half of a motorcycle. The driver's position was fitted with a motorcycle saddle and was steered through the front wheel by means of motorcycle handlebars, which were linked to the transmission to control the differential movements of the tracks as in conventional tracked vehicles. The HK 101 was fitted with a water-cooled Opel Olympia four-cylinder petrol engine of 1,478cc, which developed 36bhp at 3,400rpm to give a top speed of 40mph. However, it was only in service between 1939 and 1940, after which an improved version was introduced in 1941.

The improved version was designated the HK 102, and, apart from being slightly larger, basically looked the same as the earlier HK 101, and still retained the designation of SdKfz 2. This model was slightly larger overall with a fully laden weight of 2.2 tons. Internally it differed from its predecessor in having a larger engine: a water-cooled, Stump K-20 four-cylinder petrol engine of 2,000cc, which developed 65bhp at 3,500rpm to give a top speed of 50mph. Apart from the slightly longer track there was virtually no external difference between the two versions. It was the HK 102 version that gave service throughout the rest of the war, being employed extensively on the Eastern Front. There were two radiators mounted between the driver and the two passengers it carried in rear-facing seats, through which cooling air was drawn. Warm air from the engine could be ducted towards the driver, which was very useful in the Russian theatre of operations where the temperatures could plunge to extreme lows.

The Kettenkrad

Vehicle Name	Manufacturer	Production Date	Armament	Weight	Max. Speed
SdKfz 2 Kettenkrad	NSU Werke, Neckarsulm, Stoeuer Werke	1941	N/A	1.5–2.2 tons	50mph

The Kettenkrad was usually steered in normal operations by means of motorcycle-type handlebars, which permitted standard road use. For more severe terrain and cross-country use the driver changed direction by varying the speed of the tracks, but this could only be achieved at low speeds. The vehicle was fitted with torsion-bar suspension and the drive was through a six-speed gearbox. The track drive sprocket was mounted at the front with the idler wheel at the rear, and four over-lapping road wheels on either side, to provide extremely good traction. Although the vehicle was credited with road speeds of 50mph, it was almost impossible to control at speeds greater than 40mph. However, when towing any load the driver kept the speed even lower for better control. It could transport two fully equipped infantrymen in rear-facing seats, but the position was very cramped. They had

clamps for their rifles, which meant that if they had to deploy as part of an anti-tank gun team, if necessary they could leave their weapons on the vehicle and move straight into action. The Kettenkrad was sometimes used for towing light anti-tank guns, Nebelwerfer rocket launchers and troops in airborne units operating as infantry used it to haul their recoilless guns. Under certain conditions and at reduced speeds, it was possible for the Kettenkrad to pull loads of up to 4 tons over short distances, but such

Kettenkrad in use towing a small trailer to move supplies.

feats put a severe strain on its capabilities. The SdKfz 2 Kettenkrad was a vehicle design unique to the German Army. It served throughout the entire war in all theatres with all branches of the army, including armoured units, and airborne formations. In total some 8,345 examples of the Kettenkrad were built, and in post-war use were employed in a variety of roles including forestry work, where its cross-country capability was greatly appreciated.

The Kettenkrad could tow light anti-tank guns or trailers with supplies over short distances to move essential loads. It also had a number of functions on the battlefield including laying cables for telephones. The vehicle could carry two men on the rear such as medics or signallers with their equipment in a trailer.

Volkswagen

When Adolf Hitler came to power in 1933 he asked manufacturers to begin production of trucks and cars that would have a military application as well as civilian use. One such manufacturer was Ferdinand Porsche, whom Hitler asked to develop a *Volkswagen* or 'People's Car' that was inexpensive and easy to manufacture. It was intended to be a mass-produced family vehicle, but what resulted was ideally suited as the basic vehicle for military use. In the 1930s the German motor industry underwent a radical change in an attempt to reduce development and production costs. For example, four companies, Audi, DKW, Horch and Wanderer, combined to form the Auto Union AG in November 1931, with the government of the Weimar

All branches of the German armed forces used the Kubelwagen for liaison duties. This reproduction version of the Kubelwagen built for the film *Where Eagles Dare* shows how it could be armed with a machine gun for self-defence (above right).

Republic at the time investing financial backing into this amalgamation. Two years later, when Hitler and the Nazi Party was elected, even more money was ploughed into developing the motor industry and it has been estimated that investment more than doubled in two years from 5 million marks in 1933 to some 11 million marks by 1935, at a time when around thirty-six companies were producing vehicles.

With the *Anschluss*, or annexation of Austria, in 1938, Germany acquired the motor industry of Czechoslovakia, which provided a huge manufacturing base with the capacity to produce all types of motor vehicles. Thousands of Czechoslovakian factories produced millions of tons of chemicals, textiles, steel, ammunition and leather for boots. The tanks were used to equip the newly formed 7th and 8th Panzer Divisions which would serve in the campaigns of 1940 and the rail network would be vital, also. There were 1,500 aircraft in service with the air force in 1938 and the Czechoslovakian Army had thirty-five divisions. Some troops would continue to fight as German allies until May 1945.

By now there were over 100 different types of trucks being produced, some fifty-five types of cars and 150 forms of motorcycle. It was obvious that streamlining had to be introduced and this number was reduced to create a more efficient industry. The number of truck designs was reduced by a massive 80 per cent so that only nineteen types were produced. The different types of cars were reduced down to thirty, from which Ferdinand Porsche's Volkswagen would emerge. It was a radical move but it reduced waste and introduced a range of commonality in parts. When war broke out the Type 62 car was already being used in a range of liaison roles. However, following experiences in the Polish campaign, the army asked for a more refined vehicle with better off-road capabilities. This resulted in the Type 82 or *Kubelwagen* (bucket-seat car). It was a very basic vehicle with no frills, which lent itself to a range of duties and was even developed into some variations, not all of which were successful. There were types of vans and even an ambulance version, while the Type 82/1 was a radio vehicle with three seats and the Type 82/7 was a command car. Production of the Type 82 commenced in February 1940 and continued until 1945, by which time almost 50,500 vehicles had been built.

The Type 82 Kubelwagen

Vehicle Name	Manufacturer	Production Date	Armament	Weight	Max. Speed
Type 82 Kubelwagen	Ferdinand Porsche	1940	7.92mm machine gun	0.7 tons	50mph

It was a basic 4x2, four-seat vehicle fitted with a four-cylinder, air-cooled engine rated at 985cc, 23bhp, to give speeds of up to 50mph. In 1943 a larger engine of 1,131cc, 25bhp was fitted which gave more power. The vehicle was highly successful in service, especially in Russia. The Kubelwagen measured 12ft 6in long, 5ft 4in wide and the height with the canvas roof erected was 5ft 6in. The windscreen could be folded down and the driving controls were very simple. It weighed

0.7 tons in its basic form but weights varied according to the role and the version. For example, the Type 276 Schlepperfahrzeug version, produced in 1944, was fitted with a tow hook that allowed it to tow the 3.7cm-calibre PaK35/36 anti-tank gun and carry the gun crew and ammunition.

The Volkswagen Schwimmwagen

Another liaison vehicle used by the German Army was the Volkswagen Schwimmwagen, of which more than 15,500 were built between 1941 and 1944. The Schwimmwagen used many of the same automotive and electrical systems as the Kubelwagen and the Type 87 command car, having a rear-mounted VW Boxer four-cylinder air-cooled petrol engine rated at 1,131cc to give 25hp at 3,000rpm. This allowed the vehicle to be driven at speeds of up to 50mph off-road, while its fuel capacity of 11 gallons, stored in two separate tanks of 5.5 gallons each, gave it an operational range of over 320 miles. Initially it was intended that the vehicle would serve as a replacement for motorcycle combinations and indeed the term *Kradschützen Ersatzwagen* (motorcycle troops replacement vehicle) was given to the first production models. These early vehicles had a wheelbase length of 7.8ft and were referred to as the Porsche 128. The design was almost certainly the creation of Erwin Komenda, a leading design engineer at Porsche. The first vehicles proved the feasibility of the amphibious design, but they also showed up a structural weakness in the hull that caused stress fracturing during cross-country operations.

This problem was overcome by reducing the length of the wheelbase to 6ft 6in exactly and this became the most commonly produced version, known as the Volkswagen Type 166 or Schwimmwagen. The German Army had never really seen a need for light amphibious vehicles and although an earlier design called the Trippel had preceded the Type 166 by a few years it was never built in the same numbers as the Volkswagen vehicle. The Schwimmwagen was a 4x4 and entered service with the German Army and Waffen-SS units, who deployed it to units across Europe and into Russia where its fording capabilities made it valuable in crossing the many rivers. In the freezing winter conditions of the Russian steppes a special cold weather starting fluid had to be used on the vehicle and this was kept in containers in the engine compartment, but the engine's air-cooled design meant that it suffered less in the sub-zero conditions than the conventionally liquid-cooled engines on heavier vehicles.

The four-speed gearbox provided 4x4 drive but only when driven in first gear. There were no doors for the obvious reason that they would have compromised the watertight design. The body was made of an all-welded design known as a unitised 'bodytub' structure, which gave it the appearance of a cross between a bathtub and a dinghy fitted with wheels. The body had a sharp incline to the front end that permitted it to be driven directly into the water smoothly and to exit most riverbanks. The Schwimmwagen was approximately 12.5ft in overall length and measured

Owner of a restored Schwimmwagen testing it
in the water (top). The Schwimmwagen was a
useful liaison vehicle on the land as well as being
amphibious.

4.8ft wide and 5.2ft high. It weighed just over 2,000lb and, while it could be armed
with a machine gun such as an MG34 or MG42, the vehicle did not always carry
armament, apart from the personal weapons of the crew. It was usually operated
by two men but four could be carried to operate in the liaison role, although this
would have been a very tight squeeze. A canvas cover could be erected in inclement
weather, but most wartime photographs show it without the cover.

The vehicle's propeller system, for movement in the water, comprised a triple-
bladed propeller that was stored upright when driving on roads and manually

Under its own power in the water just as it would have been when in service (left). Very basic driving controls of the Schwimmwagen (right).

lowered only on entering water. Power take-off came from the engine crankshaft and through the mechanism, which engaged in a dog clutch. The propeller provided forward motion only and the driver turned the steering wheel to turn the front wheels to guide the vehicle in the direction required, the same as driving on the road. If the vehicle had to reverse in the water or if a river crossing had to be completed in silence, paddles were provided. An alternative method of reversing in the water was for the driver to engage reverse gear and simply drive the vehicle with the rotation of the wheels providing momentum. Due to the propeller design the Schwimmwagen could never be used to tow trailers because a tow hook would have got in the way, so it was restricted to liaison duties.

Preparations for the Normandy Landings

At the beginning of 1944 Germany had 320 divisions either fighting or serving as occupation forces. Of this figure there were 206 divisions fighting in Russia, fifty in France and the Low Countries, twenty-two in Italy, twenty-four in the Balkans and eighteen in Norway and Denmark. In June 1944 the Russian offensives were in danger of running out of supplies because of the rapidity of their advance, which meant the supply columns could not keep up with the tanks and troops. This was what the Germans had experienced three years earlier as they advanced on Moscow, Stalingrad and Leningrad, but following their failure at Kursk in 1943 General Manstein stated that 'the initiatives in the Eastern Theatre of war finally passed to the Russians'. But unlike the German Army, which was always short of provisions, the Russians had plenty of supplies, manpower and, above all, time. At the same time that Mark Clark was entering Rome, decisions were being made in England that would affect the entire course of the war in Europe. Supreme Allied Commander General 'Ike' Eisenhower was about to give the word to launch the invasion of Europe. On the evening of 5 June, ships from ports all along the south coast of England and up the west coast to Wales set sail to rendezvous in total darkness in the middle of the English Channel at a point code-named Piccadilly Circus. An elaborate deception plan known as Fortitude South had led the Germans to believe the invasion would be directed against the Pas de Calais coast, the shortest crossing point between England and France. The deception created a phantom force called First US Army Group (FUSAG), but beyond some vehicles pouring out radio signals there was no such unit. The Allies knew that the Pas de Calais area was heavily defended and Brittany was too far away, which only left the Normandy coast as a credible landing point. Over many months the Allies had been building up a detailed picture of the landing points where their invasion force, larger than anything seen before, would go ashore.

The build-up for the invasion turned Britain into one gigantic airfield and vehicle parks sprang up all over the place such as Saltram Park in Devon where elements of the US 4th Infantry Division were based along with other units such as the 75th Medical Battalion (Armoured), 858 Quartermaster Fumigation & Bath, Company M, Detachment M and the 4059 Quartermaster Service Corps, 389 Engineer General Service Regiment, 2nd Battalion, Company D. All across the country, lanes, roads and fields were all used to disperse tanks and hide artillery and trucks to prevent them from being spotted by German reconnaissance aircraft. The Americans arriving in Britain had a lot to learn when it came to understanding the ways of their Allies. First was the fact that they had to learn to drive on the left-hand side of the road, which, to them, was the wrong side. When they arrived in Europe it was back to normal for them and driving on the right-hand side. They also had to come to terms with phrases for everyday things such as petrol, for which they used the term 'gas' from gasoline. Part of a humorous poem penned to highlight these differences included the lines:

> I drive on the left here in England,
> By 'lorry' and not in a truck;
> And when I'm spending my money
> 'Five Shillings' is limey for buck.

> My auto won't run without 'petrol',
> And 'cheerio' I use for goodbye;
> A 'clippie's' a street-car conductor,
> I say 'bloke' instead of guy

The Tank Destroyer

One particular form of armoured vehicle that began to arrive in readiness for the invasion was the category known as the tank destroyer. The Americans would come to make good use of these powerful vehicles when they engaged German tanks in Europe. One design of tank destroyer that earned a very good reputation for total dependability in combat was the M18 Hellcat. The origins of this vehicle were chequered and the development of the concept was not without its fair

M18 Hellcat tank destroyer had a long development history and was a latecomer into the war.

share of problems. It was initially planned to arm the new tank destroyer with a 37mm-calibre gun, but when the poor performance of this calibre weapon was observed in combat it was revised and a larger weapon of 57mm calibre was called for. The development programme was designated the T-49 gun motor carriage and would still be subject to further modifications. For example, the suspension was originally to be Christie-style and the vehicle was to weigh around 11.8 tons. What resulted was a vehicle fitted with helical springs that were not of the Christie type and powered by twin Buick engines that gave an impressive speed of 50mph. It all seemed to be a promising start but even so there were those who believed that there was still room for improvement. Changes were made and further weapon-firing tests led to the recommendation that an M3 75mm-calibre gun, of the type being fitted to the M4 Sherman tank, be used in place of the 57mm gun. This resulted in the T-67 version of the tank destroyer and although approved by the Armoured Vehicle Board it would be modified even further. Tank Destroyer Command suggested increasing the calibre of the gun to 76mm and adding torsion-bar suspension and an air-cooled Continental R-975-C4 nine-cylinder petrol radial engine. This developed 400hp at 2,400rpm to produce road speeds of 55mph, making it one of the fastest vehicles of its type to see service during the Second World War.

What the many changes had produced was in effect an entirely different vehicle from the original idea. In all, six pilot vehicles were prepared for trials in the programme, which was now designated T-70. These trials met with favourable comments despite the fact that the vehicle now weighed almost 19 tons, a big

The M8 armoured car, known to the British as the Greyhound, was a fast, useful reconnaissance vehicle. The .50in-calibre machine gun could be fitted on a race-ring or pintel mounting. The M8 was armed with a 37mm main gun, a .30in co-axial machine gun and a heavier .50in machine gun. Weapons had to be cleaned using rods fitted with brushes (above).

difference compared to the original design limit. The new M1A1 76mm gun with its muzzle brake was fitted in an open-topped turret with a full 360-degree traverse capability with elevation between -10 degrees and +19 degrees, and would prove to be highly effective against enemy armour. For example, the M62 armour piercing ammunition had a muzzle velocity of 2,600ft per second and could penetrate 102mm of armour. A total of forty-five rounds were carried for the main armament and almost 1,000 rounds for the .50in-calibre heavy machine gun mounted on a race-ring in the top of the turret, which was used for close support.

The Army Service Forces were impressed enough by this version that they placed an order for 1,000 vehicles of the T-70 design. The bow machine

The M8 was used from 1943 onwards and used throughout the European campaign in 1944–45.

gun, which was a feature on other US tank designs such as the M4 Sherman, M24 Chaffee and M3 light tank, was omitted on the T-70 thereby removing a man from the vehicle's crew. The new tank destroyer was operated by a five-man crew in keeping with tank crew numbers. By February 1944, as the final plans were being drawn up for the D-Day invasion and the build-up of equipment continued, the T-70 was officially designated the M18 tank destroyer with the term 'Hellcat' being applied. The Hellcat was 21ft 10in long, 9ft 5in wide and 8ft 5in high to the top of the turret. Savings had reduced the combat weight down to 16.8 tons and, with tracks slightly wider than usual, it had a very low ground pressure. The new vehicle had five road wheels and four return rollers with the drive sprocket at the front and the idler wheel at the rear. It had an operational road range of 104 miles, which may not sound a lot, but it was comparable to the Sherman and Chaffee tanks, although less than the M10 tank destroyer. The Hellcat was an ideal ambush vehicle and could be manoeuvred into position to catch enemy tanks unawares, which was just as well because in a fire-fight against, say, a Panzer IV, it would not have survived due to the fact that the armour protection was only between 7.9mm and 25.4mm in thickness. The Hellcat could negotiate vertical obstacles of up to 3ft, span trenches of more than 6ft wide and cross water obstacles up to depths of 4ft.

Vehicle Name	Manufacturer	Production Date	Armament	Weight	Max. Speed
M18 Hellcat	Buick Motor Division of General Motors	1943	57mm-calibre gun	16.8 tons	50mph
M10	General Motors	1942	76mm M7 gun or M36 90mm-calibre gun	29.5 tons	30mph
Achilles	Royal Arsenal Woolwich	1943	17-pounder anti-tank gun	29 tons	32mph

The crews who served in tank destroyer units liked the Hellcat, and its usefulness on the battlefield was recognised. Indeed, by October 1944 more than 2,000 M18s had been built by the Buick Motor Division of General Motors and plans were on the drawing board to develop a series of variants from the basic vehicle. In August 1944, for example, the Ordnance Department planned to produce a version armed with a T-12 105mm howitzer in a programme called T-88. In the end only a prototype was produced and the project was dropped in August 1945. As early as June 1944 the idea of developing the M18 into a prime mover known as the M39 Armoured Utility Vehicle was considered for towing the M6 3in anti-tank gun, and another idea was to develop a reconnaissance version, the T-41E1, followed by an APC vehicle. In each case the turret, with its distinctive bustle, would have been removed, the internal layout modified and the number of crew reduced to three men. By the end of the Second World War, 640 versions had been produced for other roles including reconnaissance and command vehicles. Other tank destroyer designs were also developed such as the 29.5-ton M10 armed with 76mm M7 gun, which entered service in 1942 and was also used by the British Army. The British Army also used the British-developed 'Achilles' armed with the 17-pounder anti-tank gun. The M10 had a road speed of 30mph and an operational range of 200 miles on roads. By the time of the Normandy campaign some M10 tank destroyers had been produced armed with the more powerful M36 90mm-calibre gun. It was these types of vehicles and others such as the M8 armoured cars, known to the British Army as the 'Greyhound', M7 SPG, half-tracks and M5 light tanks that were all being assembled for the invasion of Europe.

Harley-Davidson

Vehicle Name	Manufacturer	Production Date	Armament	Weight	Max. Speed
Model 50 WLA	Harley-Davidson			562lb	65mph

Lighter vehicles such as the Jeep became a familiar sight on the roads all across Britain and were joined by other wheeled vehicles including the heavy, powerful military motorcycles built by Harley-Davidson. The most widely used type was the Model 50 WLA fitted with a 45 cid flat-head side-valve engine, which could reach speeds of up to 65mph and was used for duties such as convoy escort, traffic control, liaison and for dispatch riders. The machine weighed 562lb and the fuel

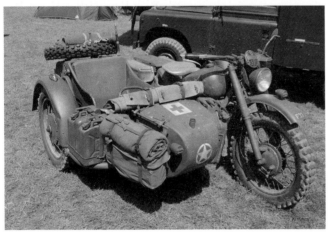

Harley-Davidson combination equipped as a medical support vehicle. It also carries spare fuel cans for extended operations.

tank had a capacity of over 3 gallons, giving it an operational range of 120 miles. It could ford water obstacles of up to 16in deep and panniers or saddlebags were fitted over the rear wheel for carrying various items of kit. A holster for the rider's personal weapon was fitted by the front wheel for easy reach.

It was in 1903 that two friends, William S. Harley and Arthur Davidson, both motorcycle enthusiasts, set up the company that bore their name in Milwaukee in Wisconsin. Their machines soon gained a reputation so that by 1916 the US military were using them for patrol duties during the Mexican Border War. When America entered the First World War in 1917 Harley-Davidson supplied the military with 15,000 machines. Between the wars times were hard, but sales to the military still remained, albeit in reduced numbers. When America entered the Second World War in 1941 it was only natural that Harley-Davidson should supply motorcycles to

The Harley-Davidson was a powerful machine able to cope with most conditions. Here it is fully equipped for dispatch-riding duties. It is also fitted with a holster for the rider's personal weapon.

the army. This was the 740cc WL design, which was given a suffix letter 'A' to denote army; while the US Navy also used the motorcycles the army used the greatest number of the 90,000 machines supplied. Harley-Davidson also built machines for the Canadian forces, known as 43 WLC and even supplied 30,000 more to the Soviet Union under the Lend-Lease Act from 1941. In 1942 the company built the XA model, which was a copy of the German BMW R71 motorcycle but it proved too expensive to produce and only around 1,000 were ever built.

Operation Overlord

Training in preparation was conducted in areas around Britain where locations were found that were similar to those facing the Allies in France. For example, US rangers trained with Royal Marine Commandos on the cliffs in Swanage

Bay, Dorset, where the chalky rock face resembled the feature at Pointe du Hoc, which the rangers would have to climb to attack a gun battery. Villages such as Castlemartin in Wales and Imber in Wiltshire were evacuated to allow the troops to practise firing and vehicle tactics. Villages in Devon were also evacuated, including Blackanton, Chillington, East Allington, Sherford, Slapton, Stokenham, Strete and Torcross. As the invasion date approached so the intensity of the training increased. British airborne forces practised on a specially constructed site at Inkpen, near Reading in Berkshire, and in Devon some 30,000 US troops began to arrive from December 1943 along with 16 million tons of stores and equipment to train for amphibious landings. For five months one major exercise after another was conducted, culminating in Exercise Tiger, which was scheduled to last for eight days. On the night of 27/28 May 1944 a convoy of several vessels left Plymouth and headed towards Slapton Sands in Lyme Bay, where the landings were to take place including vehicles and infantry. A chance encounter by German *Schnellboots* (torpedo boats) intercepted the convoy in the dark and fired a number of torpedoes that hit some of the vessels. A total of 749 soldiers and sailors were killed and many vehicles were lost including Sherman duplex drive (DD) 'Swimming' tanks, which had been developed for the actual invasion. There is discrepancy in the total figures and some sources put the figure higher. A memorial has been established to commemorate the tragic loss and the figures quoted here are taken from the roll of honour, which lists the names of those killed.

The incident did not affect the decision to mount Operation Overlord, as the invasion plan to land along the Normandy coast was designated. The Allies had learned many valuable lessons from operations such as Dieppe in 1942 and other raids had added to this and also helped them to build up a comprehensive intelligence picture concerning German defences and dispositions. They had also developed a whole range of specialist vehicles and a series of massive floating pontoons code-named Mulberry harbours, which would be towed across to the landing beaches where they would be assembled to allow vehicles and supplies to be taken ashore to support the troops. These massive structures had been built because operations had shown how vital it was to have port facilities to unload supplies to maintain the offensive. There would be two such harbours, which were designed with roadways that floated up and down with the tide to allow unloading to continue regardless of the state of the tide. The 'A' Mulberry was the American structure for the landings on the Omaha beachhead and the 'B' British harbour was built at Arromanches. The operation was the largest ever undertaken by the Allies during the entire war.

On the morning of 6 June 1944 an armada of 5,000 vessels of all types assembled off the Normandy coast, preparing to land 160,000 troops at five separate beachheads at different times due to the state of the tide. Some were designated as 'LSIs' (landing ships infantry) and others with bows that opened to permit vehicles to be driven out were called 'LSTs' (landing ships tank), but nicknamed 'large slow targets' by the Royal Navy. During the night of 5/6 June, 24,500 British and American airborne troops were landed by parachute or glider but scattered over a wide area, causing the Germans to dispatch troops to search for and capture them. The first landings over the beaches were made following a massive naval bombardment with air support from 8,000 aircraft. The troops had been given specific targets that they were designated to capture by nightfall, including the city of Caen, but this was not achieved and only a few objectives were taken. This was the first phase of the operation – to break in. The second phase would be to hold and the third phase would be the breakout.

At the end of the first day of fighting during Operation Overlord, the Allies managed to land some 150,000 troops across a 50-mile-wide area. Of the five beachheads only the western flank of the Canadian beach at Juno succeeded in linking up with the eastern flank of the British Gold beachhead, but the other three would not link up properly for some days to come. The German 21st Panzer Division did attack between the eastern flank of Juno and the western flank of the British Sword beachhead, but anti-tank gunners drove them back. The Juno beachhead was designated to be assaulted by 21,500 troops, and so many vehicles landed that it became congested and the movement area was reduced by 25 per cent, which threatened to bring operations to a halt. Things were eventually sorted out by beach masters and traffic controllers. The landings were supported by DD tanks and other specialist vehicles of the 79th Armoured Division. At some points the DD tanks were landed 'dry', which is to say that they were not launched at sea but were brought directly to the beaches and driven ashore. At the American beachhead code-named Omaha, the landing craft bringing the troops ashore were launched 12 miles out to sea. There were thirty-two DD Sherman tanks designated to support the landings here and these were launched 3.5 miles out from the beach, a distance they were never designed to cover. They became caught in a cross current and, not being able to cope with such conditions, twenty-seven sank. The Americans also turned down the use of specialist vehicles from the 79th Armoured Division and the landings were fiercely contested with over 2,000 casualties by nightfall. At the second American beachhead, code-named Utah, the landings were opposed but casualties were relatively light with only 214 men killed. But problems did arise and the landings here fell behind schedule and two days after the landings 32,000 men of a planned 39,722 had been landed, along with 3,200 vehicles out of a planned 4,732. The level of supplies was also greatly reduced, with only 2,500 tons landed out of a planned 7,000 tons. Nevertheless, Utah beach would come to be more important later in the campaign and the numbers of troops, vehicles and supplies passing through the area would be staggering.

The Germans mounted stiff resistance but the Allies continued to land and managed to get some 900 tanks and other AFVs ashore. Over the next forty-eight hours 1,500 tanks were landed across the beaches, which would be the number

Mulberry Harbours

The first parts of the massive Mulberry harbours were brought into place on 7 June and the construction of the whole operation was undertaken by a workforce of engineers. It was planned to use the structures to bring 7,000 tons of supplies ashore each day by D+4 (or 10 June). By D+8 (or 14 June) the average daily rate of supplies being unloaded through the Mulberry harbours was 12,000 tons and the British Mulberry at Arromanches allowed 16,000 troops to be brought ashore. At the American Mulberry harbour, 20,000 reinforcement troops were being landed and by D+11 (or 17 June) 22,000 tons of supplies were brought ashore being driven directly from ships on trucks and DUKWS, which could drive inland to supply depots. On D-Day, 6 June, a fleet of 2,000 DUKWs were used to bring supplies directly to the shore and delivered an estimated 40 per cent of all supplies on the day of the landings. On 18 June a powerful storm hit the Normandy coast, badly damaging the Mulberry harbours and destroying around 100 landing craft at the American Mulberry, which was declared irreparable but was still used. About 850 other vessels were destroyed or damaged along the landing area, but troops and supplies were still landed even if the levels did drop until repairs were completed. The British Mulberry continued to be used, allowing 12,000 tons of supplies to be landed even during the storm. The Mulberry harbours were only intended to be used for 100 days or until a deep-water port was captured, but this was not achieved until the port of Antwerp in Belgium was captured several months later, meaning that all supplies to support the Allied advance had to be brought over the Utah beachhead and through the British Mulberry harbour at Arromanches. The capture of the port at Cherbourg did help the situation but the facilities there had been badly damaged by the Germans, which limited the services it could provide. By late 1944 the Allies had brought 2.5 million men into the European theatre of operations this way, along with 500,000 vehicles and 4 million tons of supplies.

of tanks the Germans would lose during the Normandy campaign. Germany once again now found itself fighting a war on three fronts: in Italy, Russia and now France. The pressure on the fighting forces of the German Army was relentless and they were being squeezed by armies that between them had more than 20,000 tanks and thousands more other types of AFVs including SPGs, and vast fleets of trucks to haul supplies and artillery. The Allies had unrestricted access to oil for fuel while Germany by contrast was running out and having to resort to other means of obtaining fuel for the tanks and trucks. Germany, for example, had vast reserves of coal and scientists developed a method of extracting synthetic oil from the coal to keep the vehicles moving. In 1938 Germany had been producing around 3.8 million barrels of synthetic oil annually but by 1944 this had been increased to 12 million barrels to supplement the oil still coming

Top: Memorial dedicated to the villagers of Devon who gave up their homes to allow training for D-Day to take place.

Left: Memorial to the tragic loss during Exercise Tiger at Slapton Sands in Devon.

Below: Sherman tank memorial at Slapton Sands.

from the Romanian fields. The crisis could only deepen as the war continued and by November 1944 it was reported that the army 'had become virtually immobile because of the fuel shortage'. It was all very well with the factories still producing vehicles and tanks and ammunition and guns, but without fuel to power them and no crews to drive them they were completely useless. Between the shortage of fuel and the effects of the bombing campaign, the level of supplies required could not get through to the front-line units; the war had entered a stage of attrition and

it was only a question of time before Germany ran out of everything from troops to trucks and could no longer fight. That would take time, which was something the Allies had, but it would be in their interest to finish the war sooner rather than later. In the period leading up to the invasion of France, the Allies had bombed bridges, railway depots and roads, the loss of which would disrupt lines of supply.

Example of the beach obstacle facing the tanks on D-Day and which had to be dealt with by specialist armour or engineers (left). View across Omaha beachhead, where twenty-seven of the Sherman DD 'Swimming' tanks sank on their way to the shore (below).

In fact, of the 2,000 locomotives in France at the time, it is estimated that air attacks destroyed 1,500 and reduced the rail capacity to 40 per cent of its full capability. To make good these deficiencies the Allies also brought replacement locomotives with them.

Rommel was absent in Germany, where he had been asking for more armour to be released to the Normandy area but Hitler was adamant that those divisions in the Pas de Calais region would remain where they were. On the night of the invasion, Hitler had taken medication to sleep and although the alert was sounded, no one wanted to wake him. The result was crucial to the German Army and favourable to the Allies. It had been Montgomery's intention to draw as much German armour on to his Anglo-Canadian beachheads as possible in order to give the Americans some respite. His tactics worked and by comparison only a fraction of armoured units faced the Americans, but they would encounter strong resistance as they moved inland into the part of the countryside known as the Bocage. This terrain consisted of farmers' fields fringed by dense hedgerows, which made ideal camouflage for tanks to conceal themselves behind. To overcome this problem Sergeant Curtis Culin, serving with the 102nd Cavalry Reconnaissance, devised an attachment that could be fitted to the front of tanks to rip through the hedgerows. He suggested that metal girders that had been used as obstacles by the Germans be cut up and welded to form 'teeth-like' frames that could be mounted on the front of tanks such as the M5 Honey or M4 Sherman. The conversion could be made in the field using equipment and material to hand so there was no delay. The idea was an instant success and the device was referred to as the 'Culin Cutter'.

The M5 Stuart Light Tank

Production of the M5 Stuart light tank started in March 1942 on the Cadillac assembly line in Detroit. Its design from the earlier M3 Honey was apparent in the style but it was built using welded construction as opposed to rivets. There was no real difference between the M5 and M5A1 version, except that the latter was heavier by some 300lb and the fuel capacity was 3 gallons less, which reduced its combat range by several miles. Both versions were 14ft 6.75in long, 7ft 4.5in wide and 7ft 6.5in high. The main armament was a 37mm gun for which 123 rounds were carried, including high explosive, armour-piercing and canister, which could be used against infantry and soft-skinned vehicles. Top speed was 40mph and vertical obstacles up to 2ft high were not a problem to this vehicle, which weighed less than 15 tons in either version. One .30in-calibre machine gun was mounted co-axially in the turret, a second was fitted in a ball mounting in the bow and a third dismountable machine gun could be fitted to the roof of the turret. The M5 was used in combat for the first time during

Equipped with the Culin Cutter, the M5 could break through hedgerows to surprise the enemy.

The command version of the M5 Stuart light tank lacked a turret and carried a .50in-calibre machine gun and a .30in-calibre machine gun

Operation Torch and they were deployed to the Pacific to combat the Japanese tanks and bunkers on the islands. During the Normandy Landings some were fitted with extensions to their exhaust for deep-water wading. Three other variants were also built including the command vehicle, which lacked a turret and was armed with only a .50in-calibre machine gun. The M5 Dozer also lacked a turret and blade for moving earth was fitted to the front. The M8 howitzer motor carriage was armed with a 75mm howitzer for which forty-six rounds were carried. In all some 1,800 of these were built and used in action in Europe.

The command version of the M5 Stuart light tank was one of several variants. The gunner's position inside had a cramped interior (top right). The M5 Stuart light tank saw service in North Africa (above).

Vehicle Name	Manufacturer	Production Date	Armament	Weight	Max. Speed
M5 Stuart light tank	Cadillac Division, General Motors	1941	37mm gun and 2x .30in-calibre machine guns	15 tons	40mph

The M5 Stuart light tank was a useful vehicle for reconnaissance roles and was used during the Normandy Landings in June 1944. For wading through deep water it was fitted with extensions to the exhaust.

During the Normandy campaign the Germans lost men and equipment at an alarming rate and at one point Rommel received only 6,000 troops to replace 29,000 casualties. Vehicles could not be easily replaced and his men were fighting hard actions such as that conducted by SS-Obersturmführer (Lieutenant) Michael Wittmann at the town of Villers-Bocage on 13 June. Wittmann was serving with Schwere SS Panzer-Abteilung 101 and was a veteran of the fighting in Russia, where his personal score of enemy tanks was eighty-eight destroyed, along with numerous other vehicles. On 13 June Wittmann was in his Tiger tank when he encountered a column of vehicles of 22nd Armoured Brigade of the 7th Armoured Division parked up and not fully alert. Wittmann engaged the convoy and destroyed five Cromwell tanks, one Sherman Firefly, three M5 Honey light tanks, two observation tanks and several other vehicles including half-tracks. His attack was only ended when his tank was knocked out by a 6-pounder anti-tank gun, but Wittmann survived. By July the Allies had achieved two phases of the invasion by breaking in and succeeded in holding the gains they had made. Now they had to break out, and Montgomery had plans to do just that; Patton, who did not arrive in France until 6 July, would be part of the breakout. On 26 June Montgomery ordered the start of Operation Epsom, which was to penetrate to the west of Caen. Four days later, after encountering fierce opposition, the attack was called off with 4,000 casualties, but they had inflicted at least 3,000 casualties on the Germans and destroyed 126 tanks. Montgomery tried again on 18 July by ordering Operation Goodwood to attack east of Caen with more than 1,100 tanks available to the attack. Again the Germans mounted fierce resistance and destroyed or seriously damaged 400 tanks and inflicted 4,000 casualties. The Germans had sustained high losses, which have never been accurately computed, but they had lost 2,500 taken prisoner and 100 tanks destroyed by the time the attack was suspended on 20 June. Over to the west the Americans, commanded by Patton, were planning their own operation, code-named Cobra, which began on 25 July with the support of 2,451 tanks and tank destroyers. Facing them the Germans had deployed 190 tanks and assault guns including the Sturmgeschütz III, often abbreviated to simply StuG. III and being a specialised vehicle it was given the Sonderkraftfahrzeug title of SdKfz 142.

The StuG. III

The StuG. III was developed between 1935 and 1936 following the specifications as laid down by the German Army Weapons Department. The armaments manu-facturer Daimler-Benz was responsible for providing the chassis, which was based on the design used on the Panzer III tank. The engine was a Maybach HL120TRM V-12 water-cooled petrol engine, of the same type as fitted to the Models E to N of the Panzer III, which developed 300bhp at 3,000rpm to give a road speed of 25mph and a cross-country speed of 15mph. The gun chosen to arm the StuG. III was of 75mm calibre and as an assault gun the design of the new vehicle was a departure away from conventional tank design lacking, as it did, a turret and upper superstructure. The StuG. III had an extremely reduced silhouette which meant that the gun was mounted very low down in the hull. The overall height was kept down to 9ft 6in, making it one of the lowest vehicles in the war. The main armament was a short-barrelled StuK 37 L/24 of 75mm calibre, for which at least forty-five rounds were carried, fitted into a fixed mounting, slightly offset to the right with the fighting compartment accommodating the crew with the driver's position to the left of the gun.

Vehicle Name	Manufacturer	Production Date	Armament	Weight	Max. Speed
StuG. III Ausf. A	Daimler-Benz	1940	75mm-calibre StuK 37 L/24	19.6 tons	25mph
StuG. III Ausf. B	Daimler-Benz	1940–41		20.2 tons	25mph

The first examples of the StuG. III were given the Ausf. A designation and only thirty production vehicles of this design were built before modifications were introduced. This led to the Ausf. B version, of which 320 were built. The first StuG. III vehicles entered service in January 1940, which according to some sources were five prototypes that participated in the blitzkrieg into France in May that same year. Production did not begin in earnest until July 1940, and even so deliveries were slow and by the end of the year only 184 had been built, with an average monthly production rate of only thirty vehicles. However, once production was up and running, factories built over 9,400 between 1940 and 1944 with models A to G. Units equipped with the StuG. III recorded 20,000 enemy tanks destroyed using this one type of vehicle alone and the vehicle was deployed to actions such as Kursk.

German Resistance and Allied Tactics

By the time Operation Cobra was concluded on 31 July the Germans had lost 100 tanks in the fighting along with more than 250 other types of AFV. The Allies were becoming more secure each day and although progress was slow they were pushing the enemy back, and the capture of three bridges intact at Avranches gave them a route across the River Sèe. Aircraft were destroying German armour and Panzer Lehr was 70 per cent ineffective and virtually finished as a fighting force. Between 6 and 8 August the Germans mounted a counter-attack, code-named Operation Luttich, aimed at Mortain, but after initial gains the attack faltered. On the day Luttich was halted, the Germans suffered another blow to morale when their tank ace Michael Wittmann was killed during a counter-attack near the village of St Aignan de Cramesnil in an attempt to recapture a feature known as Hill 112, which had been captured during the opening stages of the Anglo-Canadian attack, Operation Totalise. Several Tigers from SS Panzer Abteilung 101 supported by a number of PzKw IV tanks and other vehicles were engaged by a squadron of Sherman Fireflys from the 1st Northamptonshire Yeomanry of 33rd Armoured Brigade. Close to the wooded area of Delle de la Roque a Firefly opened fire with its 17-pounder gun and destroyed Wittmann's tank.

German resistance was crumbling but they kept fighting even though they were receiving almost no reinforcements. Fighting had moved inland and in the small town of St Lambert a single PzKw V known as the Panther, with the designation SdKfz 171 and armed with a 75mm gun, halted the Canadian advance. Weighing 44.8 tons, the Panther had been the bane of Russian tank crews and in Normandy

A real StuG. III showing it was an efficient tank killer from Russia to France.

The StuG. was a tank killer with over 20,000 victims to its credit according to some sources.

it had given the Allies an equally difficult time. It had been developed specifically to combat the Russian T-34 tank and between 1942 and 1945 5,508 were built. The Maybach HL230P30 twelve-cylinder was rated at 70hp to give a speed of 29mph on roads with a combat range of 124 miles. The first models were not reliable, being overweight and underpowered, and of the 200 deployed at Kursk, 160 were out of action due to mechanical failure. Even when repaired and sent back into action they were not improved and at the end of the battle only forty-three were still effective. In Normandy it was the powerful gun and the thickness of the armour, up to 100mm, that gave them a true edge over the Allies. After destroying fourteen Sherman tanks in succession, the Canadians approaching St Lambert decided on a different tactic. The next morning the aptly named

Lieutenant Armour led a section of his men to attack the tank. They took it by surprise and, finding the hatch open, Lieutenant Armour dropped a grenade inside and the tank was destroyed. On the same day the Allies landed in the south of France in Operation Dragoon. With air support and airborne landings, a fleet of 880 vessels and 1,300 landing craft, a Franco-American army that would eventually build up to a force of 200,000 men was landed at points along the coast such as St Tropez and St Raphael. German resistance to the landings was relatively light and it was only when the fighting moved inland that the battle

Recreated StuG III. during a battle re-enactment showing how infantry rode into battle on its hull.

Looking very realistic this recreated StuG. III enters a battle re-enactment carrying infantry. The side plates are to protect it against anti-tank weapons.

intensified. The campaign lasted until 14 September, during which time the Allies suffered around 20,000 killed, wounded and missing. The Germans lost 7,000 killed, 20,000 wounded and eventually the 130,000 trapped in the area would be taken prisoner. On the first day of the landings 11,000 vehicles were put ashore and the port facilities were intact, unlike those in the north of France which had been badly affected by the fighting. Indeed, so good were they that the Allies could unload 17,000 tons of supplies each day to support the campaign. Dragoon was a victory but it was also a victim of priority as the bulk of supplies still went to northern France.

Bombing the French railway system had served to make it difficult for the Germans to move reinforcements and supplies forward but as they retreated the advancing Allies came to face the same problem, caused by their own air forces. The solution was to create a special convoy system of trucks to move the mass of supplies forward. Supplying fuel to so many vehicles would be a problem and tankers would not be able to cope with demand. Instead a solution was devised whereby an underwater pipeline would be laid through which fuel would be pumped from England to depots in France. Being underwater it was safe from damage by enemy action. Called 'Pipe Line Under The Ocean', or 'PLUTO' for short, the first pipes were laid in August 1944 covering a distance of some 70 miles from Shanklin on the Isle of Wight to Cherbourg, and this was joined by other pipes as the Allies moved eastwards. Eventually there would be four pipes laid between Shanklin and Cherbourg. By January 1945 around 300 tons of fuel was being pumped through the pipes each day and this increased to 3,000 tons per day by March 1945. In total around 172 million gallons of fuel had been pumped by the time the war ended in May 1945.

Casualties and Ambulances

In England thousands of beds had been prepared at hospitals in readiness to receive the wounded coming back from France. Casualty clearing stations would have already treated the wounded, but they had to be evacuated from the battle area. The wounded were put into ambulances such as the American WC54 or the British-built Austin K2Y, nicknamed 'Katy' by the troops and RAMC staff that drove them. More than 13,000 of these useful ambulances were built between 1939 and 1945 and they served in all theatres and were capable of 50mph. They could carry four stretcher cases or ten seated or 'walking' wounded under normal conditions, but one exceptional account reports a K2Y ambulance carrying twenty-seven wounded during the North African campaign. The vehicle weighed 3 tons, was 18ft long, 7ft 5in wide and 9ft high. As part of the preparations in readiness for war the British Army formed a female unit called the Auxiliary Territorial Service (ATS) in September 1938. This was not an entirely new idea because the Women's Auxiliary Army Corps had been created in 1917 for women serving as clerks, cooks and telephonists, but this had been disbanded in 1921. Now there was a very pressing need for more service personnel to fill these roles once again and even branch out into other duties. By 1940 there were 65,000 women serving in the ATS and by the end of the war this figure was 190,000. They were serving in mixed batteries of anti-aircraft defence units and thousands had been trained as drivers and some even as dispatch riders on motorcycles. Winston Churchill's daughter, Mary, served in the ATS and Princess Elizabeth, the future Queen Elizabeth II of Great Britain, qualified as a driver on the K2Y ambulance.

Austin K2Y ambulance, nicknamed 'Katy', in colours of British Army 21st Army Group in Europe.

Restored Austin K2Y ambulance seen here in RAF colours.

Fuel

It became apparent to the military planners that the amount of collateral damage caused to the railway infrastructure by strategic bombing would create problems in supplying the armies with provisions and reinforcements, including replacement tanks for those destroyed in the fighting. The railway tracks and rolling stock were smashed and the only alternative was to transport everything by road using trucks until the railways could be brought back into proper service. Major General Frank A. Ross, the US Army's transportation chief, devised the 'Red Ball Express', which soon became a byword for re-supply. The rapidity of the German retreat and the speed of Patton's advance meant that supplies could not be moved forward

Tankers, supply trucks and recovery vehicles were part of the Red Ball Express, which moved everything the army needed to keep fighting. Jimmy fuel tankers could fill the jerricans for individual vehicles.

All Jimmys could be covered at the rear with a canvas tarpaulin to protect the cargo. Driver's position of the Jimmy seen from the left hand side showing simple driving controls (above left). As well as loads they also towed trailers for water or fuel.

fast enough by normal methods if they were to keep pace with the advancing units. The term 'Red Ball Express' was derived from the US railways, which were known for their fast delivery of freight. It was the only way planners could see of solving the problem of delivering supplies. It operated a one-way road system, which by August ran from St Lô in Normandy to Versailles just outside of Paris. There the vehicles branched either north to Soissons to supply the US First Army commanded by General Courtney H. Hodges, or to the south towards Sommesous to supply the US Third Army under Patton. The system proved itself by supplying

Jimmys could be used to carry extraordinary loads to supply the troops.

400,000 tons of materiel in just over eleven weeks using an armada of almost 6,000 trucks, which were driven day and night. In one twelve-day period between 25 August and 6 September, the Red Ball Express delivered more than 81,500 tons of supplies, by which time the route extended some 300 miles. The drivers were reckless in delivering their cargoes and infantry marching on the roads risked being run down by the trucks passing non-stop. Soldiers tried to avoid the trucks and as one British soldier commented, the only way to avoid being killed by these trucks was to 'not only get off the road but climb a tree'. Operating a fleet of trucks of this size was costly in fuel and the vehicles consumed 250,000 gallons each day, but the army had to be kept moving. For the Germans fuel was a scarce commodity, but for the Allies it was in plentiful supply.

Vehicle Name	Manufacturer	Production Date	Armament	Weight	Max. Speed
CCKW	General Motors	1941 onwards	Some equipped with .50in-calibre machine gun	5.3 tons	45mph

The trucks used in this convoy system were CCKW, built by GMC, and known by the troops as either the 'Deuce-and-a-half' or the 'Jimmy'. They were capable of carrying payloads of up to 2.5 tons but in reality many were greatly overloaded due to the emergencies during battle. All could tow trailers and some were also developed for specialist roles such as the 750-gallon capacity fuel tanker and

700-gallon capacity water tanker, while others were converted to be used in bomb disposal, as medical support vehicles and fire trucks; the famous DUKW ('Duck') amphibious truck was also developed from the CCKW design. There were two basic types of these 6x6 trucks, the Short Wheel Base 352 and the Long Wheel Base 353 and either the closed cab or open cab versions. The CCKW lettering designated the year 1941 (C), conventional cab (C), all-wheel drive (K) and tandem rear axles (K). The basic version weighed 5.3 tons and measured 21.36ft long, 7.35ft wide and 9.19ft high. Between 1941 and 1945 General Motors produced over 562,000 of these trucks and other manufacturers took the production figure to more than 812,000 vehicles. The Jimmy was fitted with a GMC six-cylinder 269 cid 91.5hp engine, which gave road speeds of up to 45mph. It was thirsty on fuel and a 40-gallon fuel capacity would allow an operational range of 300 miles (7.5 miles to the gallon). Some Jimmys had provision for a .50in-calibre machine gun to be mounted above the cab roof for use in self-defence in case of attack.

The route being followed by the British Twenty-First Army commanded by Montgomery was considerably shorter but they were hit by a crisis when the fleet of 1,400 trucks capable of transporting 800 tons of supplies per day had to be taken out of service because they had been fitted with the wrong parts, which caused gearbox failure and led the vehicles to be withdrawn. The British Army operated a supply system called 'Red Lion Express', which was similar to the American system. This could have been a problem but the Allies were able to replace their losses from the huge stockpile of equipment that had been built up in Britain since 1942.

On 20 August the British and Americans finally linked up at Chambois, just south-west of Falaise, to where many Germans had managed to escape on foot. In their wake they left behind the debris of an army in full retreat. It was reminiscent of the British Army's retreat to Dunkirk four years earlier and just like that army, the Germans had abandoned all their heavy equipment, including tanks, artillery and trucks because they were out of fuel and other non-essentials. They resorted to horses in many instances, which they commandeered from farms. Five days later the French capital Paris was liberated and the Normandy campaign was over. The city had been prepared for destruction, but the commandant, Major General Dietrich von Choltitz, declared it an open city to prevent destructive fighting. The fighting had cost the Germans 500,000 men killed, wounded or captured, the loss of 1,500 tanks, 3,500 guns and 20,000 other vehicles. The Allies had lost almost 210,000 killed, missing and wounded, and in terms of materiel the losses were great, but could be replaced. To supply the great city 2,400 tons of supplies had to be delivered daily by a fleet of military trucks until things began to return to some semblance of normality.

Jimmys were built with hard-topped cabs or canvas cabs as seen in the top image. Some were fitted with a mounting to be armed with a .50in-calibre machine gun (above left). Some were also fitted with front-mounted winches which could be used to help in the recovery of other vehicles (above). Others came with canvas roofs and no doors, but they could still carry a useful payload (left).

The Russian Front

On the Eastern Front the Russians had been biding their time and building up their resources in readiness for a series of massive offensives, but had been engaging the Germans to prevent them from guessing that anything was in the offing. News of the Allied landings in Normandy was delayed until 14 June because Stalin wanted to be sure the attack was a success. On 22 June, three years to the day since Germany had attacked them, the Russians launched an offensive on an unprecedented scale. This was Operation Bagration, which had been planned since April 1944 but the Russians had been conducting other operations since the end of 1943 and kept up a relentless pressure on the Germans. For the Russians, 1944 would become known as 'The Year of Ten Victories'. The prelude to the first of these came on 14 January 1944 when a massive artillery barrage of 100,000 shells was fired on German forces, investing the city of Leningrad in just over an hour. The following day an even more intensive barrage lasting 105 minutes poured out 200,000 shells. The Germans were shattered and had nothing to respond with. The full

The T-34 was used to fight all the way into Berlin in April 1945. The T-34 was the mainstay of the Russian armoured divisions first with the 76mm gun and the more powerful 85mm seen here.

weight of the Russian attack forced the Germans to pull back and after only twelve days of fighting the city was finally relieved after a siege lasting 890 days.

On another part of the front the Russians attacked the German pocket at Korsun, where 60,000 troops were surrounded. Their armoured vehicles were low on fuel and had to crawl slowly over the ice in sub-zero conditions. Supplies had to be pulled on horse-drawn sledges and everything was running out. The Luftwaffe tried to supply the group by airlift, but it was useless and many aircraft were lost as they attempted to drop provisions. By 17 February this outpost was destroyed. At least 30,000 men did escape, but they had to abandon all their equipment. The Russians continued to advance at all points along the front and forced the Germans back to Romania, Poland and Norway. In preparation for Bagration, which concentrated on the region of Minsk, an area held by the German Army Group Centre, the Russians assembled an artillery force of 285 guns per mile. When they opened fire at first light, the T-34 tanks supported by SU-122 assault guns rumbled forward. The Germans held a position called a salient, which bulged forward and allowed the Russians to attack from three sides: north, south and centre. Within three days the Germans had lost 20,000 killed and 10,000 captured, along with all their equipment and vehicles. Operation Bagration itself was completed on 3 July and had inflicted 350,000 casualties on the Germans. The Russians committed 2.3 million troops to the offensive along with 80,000 Polish troops supported by 2,715 tanks, 1,355 assault guns, 24,363 pieces of artillery and fleets of trucks. The Germans had 118 tanks, 377 assault guns and 2,589 pieces of artillery. The overall offensive lasted until 29 August, by which time the Russians had lost 2,957 tanks and assault guns and 2,447 pieces of artillery, and had only thirty-three divisions to face 133 Russian divisions.

Russian Vehicles

Vehicle Name	Manufacturer	Production Date	Armament	Weight	Max. Speed
T-26 light tank	Stalingrad Tractor Factory	1928–31	45mm-calibre gun	7.8 tons	14mph
BT-7 fast tank	KhPZ	1932–41	45mm-calibre gun and 2x 7.62mm DT machine guns	13.6 tons	46mph
T-40 amphibious tank	State factories	1941–42	12.7mm DShK and 7.62mm DT machine guns	4.8 tons	28mph
T-70 light tank	Factory 37 Kirov, GAZ Gorky	1941–42	45mm-calibre gun and 7.62mm DT machine gun	9 tons	28mph
BA-64 armoured car	GAZ	1942 onwards	7.62mm DT machine gun	2.3 tons	50mph
KV-1 heavy tank	Chelyabinsk Tractor Factory, state plants incl. Kirov Factory	1939 onwards	76.2mm main gun and 3x 7.62mm DT machine guns	46.3 tons	22mph
KV-2 heavy tank	Kirov Factory, ChTZ	1939–45	152mm howitzer and 2x 7.62mm DT machine guns	52.2 tons	26mph
T-34	Stalingrad Tractor Factory, state plants	1939 onwards	76.2mm main gun and 2x 7.62mm DT machine guns	27.6 tons	31mph

The KV-1 heavy tank was armed with the 76.2mm main gun.

Russian T-26 light tank was used during the Russo-Japanese War in Manchuria and also against the Germans throughout the war.

The Russian Army had entered the war with a massive tank force calculated to have been 24,000 vehicles strong, but most of these were obsolete and no match for the fast, modern German tanks. The tactics they employed meant that they did not stand a chance against the massed forces of the panzer divisions. Following one defeat after another, the Russians finally managed to stabilise their position and

Seen here in post-war colours of the Egyptian Army, the Russian-built SU-100 was used by the Russians to destroy heavy German tanks such as the Tiger I and II. The SU-100 was introduced in 1944 and its 100mm gun could destroy the most powerful German tanks. It was used by several armies after the war.

the hundreds of relocated factories began to produce more modern designs in large numbers. The Russians used vehicles such as the 7.8-ton T-26 light tank and the 13.6-ton BT-7 fast tank, capable of speeds of up to 46mph on roads, both armed with the 45mm-calibre gun. These served in many battles along with other AFVs such as the T-40 amphibious tank and T-70 light tank and BA-64 armoured car, but it is the heavier vehicles that the Russian tank force came back with to counter the German vehicles for which the country is best remembered. The KV-1 and KV-2 heavy tanks were armed with 76.2mm-calibre guns that were later replaced on some versions with more powerful weapons and it was these that were available for the defence of Moscow in late 1941. The chassis of these vehicles also served as the basis for SPG designs and the Tankograd factory produced 13,500 KV tanks. One of the SPG designs based on the KV-1 chassis was the ISU-122, armed with a 122mm-calibre gun and later an even heavier version armed with a 155mm gun was developed. These were used at Kursk in 1943 and continued to be used to the end of the war. The smaller SU-76 SPG entered service in 1943 and was armed with a 76.2mm calibre gun. Like other vehicles of this type it went through a series of variant designs including anti-aircraft versions and by the end of the war some 12,600 had been built.

The 29.1-ton SU-85 appeared in 1943 and the heavier 31.1-ton SU-100 appeared a year later. They were so called from the calibre of their guns, and forced the Germans to build more powerful tanks and develop heavier anti-tank guns. Together with the T-34 tank, which originated from a design in 1939, they helped swing the balance of armoured power in to Russia's favour. The T-34 would come to form the backbone of the Russian tank forces. By 1941 2,810 had been built and when deployed in the defence of Moscow its appearance shocked the Germans. The T-34 weighed around 28 tons but variants meant that this changed accordingly. The basic version was armed with the M40 76.2mm-calibre gun and was 21ft in length over the hull, 9ft 7in in width and 7ft 10in in height. Fitted with a V-2-34 twelve-cylinder engine delivering 500hp at 1,800rpm, it could reach road speeds of up to 31mph and had an operational range of 188 miles. Served by a crew of four, the T-34 was committed to battle along all sectors of the front. It was developed for mine-clearing roles and in bridging models as well as a flame-thrower. It was even fitted with a more powerful 85mm-calibre gun and fitted with long-range fuel tanks to extend the operational range to 220 miles. The original T-34 carried seventy-seven rounds for its 76.2mm gun, and the version armed with the more powerful 85mm gun carried fifty-five rounds. The T-34/85 version began production in 1943 and by the end of the war 11,000 had been built. It was these vehicles along with the SPGs that entered Berlin in April 1945 to finish the war.

The Katyusha (little Kate) rocket artillery system was used extensively by the Russian Army and developed into several versions mounted on vehicles such as the ZIS or GAZ trucks for mobility. They were built in calibres ranging from 82mm to 300mm and range varied accordingly, but the middle-range calibre of 132 was also widely used. Depending on the calibre of the rocket, the system could fire twelve or sixteen rounds in only seconds. The M31 300 version fired thirty-six rockets from rail launchers on the rear of the transporting truck to saturate an area and whole batteries could pulverise enemy positions. The Germans were also using their trucks as mobile platforms for weapons, most often 2cm guns such as the FlaK 36 2cm light anti-aircraft gun, which could be depressed low enough to engage ground targets. These would carry their own supply of ammunition on board with re-supply coming from vehicles accompanying the gun vehicles.

British Light Armoured Vehicles

The British Army had used tanks designed and produced by British companies in the early days of the war but by 1941, after the Lend-Lease Act with America and with its shortfall in armoured vehicles following the losses during the Dunkirk campaign, it began to benefit from American-designed tanks. Three of these designs, the M3 Honey, M3 Lee-Grant and M4 Sherman, had been battle tested by the British Army before America entered the war. With these vehicles being made in quantity, some British tanks were turned over to other roles such as with the 79th Armoured Division, but designs such as the Churchill remained very good gun tanks and the Cromwell gave excellent service in the Normandy campaign. During the European campaign through Belgium, Holland and into Germany the range of light British armoured vehicles proved themselves in many actions.

The Dingo

The Dingo, a very compact vehicle measuring 10ft 5in long, 5ft 7.5in wide and only 4ft 11in high, was fitted with a rear-mounted 2.5-litre six-cylinder Daimler petrol engine of 55hp to give road speeds of up to 55mph, which made it extremely useful in the reconnaissance role. It had five forward gears and five reverse gears to maintain speed in all situations and the operational range of 200 miles was very useful for extended operations in the scouting role. A two-man crew comprising driver and commander operated the little vehicle, which was usually armed with a single Bren gun, although some vehicles were armed with a Boys .55in-calibre anti-tank rifle. A very few Dingo scout cars were armed with Vickers 'K' machine guns. All this, including a No. 11 or No. 19 radio set and personal kit and rations, was packed into this tiny 3-ton vehicle. It was protected by armour up to 30mm in thickness, which was sufficient against some small arms fire but its light weight and low ground clearance of around 200mm left it extremely vulnerable to mines.

Vehicle Name	Manufacturer	Production Date	Armament	Weight	Max. Speed
Dingo	BSA, Daimler	1939	Bren gun or Boys .55in-calibre gun or Vickers 'K' machine gun	3 tons	55mph

The Dingo dated back to 1937 as a result of specifications for a new scout car for the British Army that were placed before the Coventry-based company Alvis by the Mechanisation Board. It was met with a speedy response and Alvis produced a prototype vehicle termed the Dingo, which was a 4x4 wheel drive, served by a crew of two men and armed with a single .303in-calibre Bren gun, which as a weapon itself was just beginning to enter service with the British Army. By coincidence, at the same time as Alvis was undertaking this development work, two other manu-facturers were developing their own separate designs for vehicles to operate in the role of scout car. The first was Birmingham Smalls Arms (BSA) whose vehicle was also a two-man design armed with a Bren gun. The other design was by Morris Commercial Cars, which although interesting enough did not match either the Alvis or the BSA vehicles. During 1938 a series of trials was conducted between all vehicles and it was decided that after some modifications the BSA design would be the vehicle for the British Army. At this time BSA was in the process of being acquired by Daimler and so it was that when the vehicle went into production in

The Daimler Dingo had a very low silhouette which was ideal for reconnaissance roles. Indeed, the Dingo served in North Africa as a reconnaissance vehicle for armoured units.

1939, under a design team of engineers headed by Sidney Shellard, it was known as Car, Scout, Daimler Mk I, or Dingo for short, which was the name applied to the Alvis design. By the end of the war the vehicle had been produced in five different marks with a total of 6,626 being built – an incredible number considering the original order placed in 1939 had been for 172 vehicles.

The first version to roll off the production was the Mk I in 1939 and this was fitted with 4x4 steering and a sliding roof. The tyres were of the run-flat type and still allowed for a very smooth ride. This was followed by the Mk IA which had a folding roof and improved suspension. The Mk IB appeared with a reversed engine-cooling fan, but in almost every other aspect differed very little from the original version. The Mk II Dingo was fitted with slightly different radiator grilles and the 4x4 steering was replaced by front-wheel steering only, in order to make it easier for inexperienced drivers to control. The final version was the Mk III and this had a waterproof engine fitted and no overhead cover.

The compact design still allowed for a good range of storage lockers to be provided to stow tools, personal kit and a small cooker for the crew to heat food and make hot drinks when operating far ahead in the scouting role. In the desert, sand channels were carried to help recover the vehicle if it became bogged down in the sand. The Dingo did remarkably well throughout the war and proved itself to be a most resilient vehicle from the early engagements in France in 1940 to the beaches of Normandy in 1944 and beyond.

The Humber Scout Car and Humber LRC

The Humber scout car appeared in 1942 and was not too dissimilar to the appearance of the Daimler Dingo, but was slightly larger and heavier. The company of Rootes built over 4,100 scout cars in two different variants and has been described as being less 'mechanically sophisticated' than the Daimler scout car, but it went on to prove popular with crews. The first vehicles were known as the Mk I, of which some 1,698 were built and went into service, followed by the Mk II, which differed by having an improved transmission. The Humber scout car was used by the Guards Armoured Division, Canadian troops, the 1st Czechoslovakian Armoured Brigade and the Polish II Corps, the last two of which were fighting with the Allies as free forces in exile. The 11th Armoured Division, with its distinctive emblem of a black bull on a yellow background, landed on the beaches at Normandy a week after the initial assault and was involved in the Goodwood and Epsom 'breakout' operations around the city of Caen as the British Army forced its way inland. The 11th Armoured Division used the Humber scout car and later saw action during the Battle of the Bulge in December 1944 when they fought German units on the Maas in weather conditions which, according to the historian Charles Whiting, '... would have undermined the morale of any but the staunchest soldiers ...'

Vehicle Name	Manufacturer	Production Date	Armament	Weight	Max. Speed
Humber scout car	Humber	1942	.303in-calibre Bren gun	3.4 tons	60mph
Humber LRC	Humber	1940	Boys .55in anti-tank rifle and .303in-calibre machine gun	3.5 tons	50mph

The Humber scout car was normally served by a crew of two, the driver and commander, but provision was made for a third person inside the small vehicle. This was usually someone serving in the role of forward observation officer (FOO) directing artillery fire. To keep in contact with other units and relay details back to the artillery positions, the vehicle was fitted with a No. 19 radio set. The scout car was fitted with a Rootes six-cylinder petrol engine of 87hp at 3,300rpm, which was mounted in the rear and meant a power-to-weight ratio of 25.6hp per ton and gave a top speed of 60mph on roads, which was better than the Dingo. The Humber scout car was fitted with a four-speed gearbox, plus reverse, and the Mk II was fitted

The Humber LRC could be fitted with a turret to carry armament but those without turrets could be used for artillery observation. Like other LRC designs the Humbers could be used in the reconnaissance role to gather information. Reconnaissance vehicles carried all spares with them to remain operational.

with synchromesh to the second, third and fourth gears. It was a four-wheeled vehicle with heavy-duty tyres for good cross-country capability and had a maximum operational range of 200 miles, which, combined with its speed, was impressive and comparable to the Dingo. The Mk I vehicles utilised components from existing Humber designs such as the four-wheel light reconnaissance car, which helped with early production somewhat. The vehicle had a ground clearance of 10in, could scale vertical obstacles of 12in in height and ford water obstacles up to 3ft deep.

The armament was often a single .303in-calibre Bren gun mounted on the roof of the vehicle and fitted with a special Parrish-Lakeman mounting, which permitted it to be fired from within the vehicle. The design of this mounting resembled the handlebars of a bicycle, with the trigger mechanism operated in a manner similar to applying the brake lever. The Bren gun in this case was modified to be fitted with a drum magazine holding 100 rounds, which was more than three times the capacity of the standard magazine and meant that the firer did not have to expose himself to reload so often. An alternative armament layout was a pair of Bren guns mounted side by side on the roof, and these were more often fitted with the standard thirty-round capacity magazine, which was slightly curved to allow for the shape of the base of the bullets, which had a rim; it was the same type fired by the Mk IV Lee-Enfield rifle, which was the service rifle of the British infantryman. The Bren gun had a cyclic rate of fire of 500 rounds per minute and could be used to engage targets out to a range of 600yd. Additional ammunition capacity, up to 1,000 rounds, was stored inside the vehicle and because it was a standard .303in-calibre rifle round it was easily re-supplied. This allowed the vehicle to engage infantry in the open but beyond that it had to rely on speed and manoeuvrability to extricate itself from any unexpected situation that might arise. The Humber scout car weighed 3.4 tons and was protected by armour up to 14mm thickness with an open top and unarmoured floor. It was 12ft 7in long, 6ft 2in wide and 6ft 11in high. The hull was well angled to deflect light projectiles and the crew accessed it through hatches in the roof or by a single door on the left-hand side.

The terms 'scout car' and 'armoured car' described exactly what roles these vehicles served in, but the British Army came up with another name, the 'light reconnaissance car' (LRC), which was just another form of repeating what was already in service. The Canadians developed the Otter for this role and the British Army would take two principal designs into service. One was the Humber LRC, a design that would be produced in 3,600 models in four different marks, and the other was a design built by Morris. The first version of the Humber LRC was naturally termed the Mk I and entered service in 1940. This was nicknamed the 'Ironside 1' and, with the engine housing extending forward to accommodate the Humber six-cylinder petrol engine, it resembled an armoured car from an earlier age, an impression that was added to by the small turret sitting atop the vehicle, housing a single machine gun, which would appear on later models. It was based on the Humber heavy utility chassis and given a 4x2 wheel drive. Three of these Mk I LRCs

Building an airfield during the Normandy Camapign to receive flights of supplies.

were modified and, with the engine rated at 87hp to give road speeds of up to 50mph and an operational range of 250 miles, they were ideally suited to be used to drive members of the British War Cabinet. These were open-topped versions, designated 'Special Ironsides'. The Mk II soon followed and this also was a 4x2-wheel drive. It was fitted with a small turret with a full 360-degree traverse capability for all-round defensive fire. Armament was usually a single .303in-calibre Bren gun but some versions were armed with the much heavier .55in-calibre Boys anti-tank rifle. This was limited in use against vehicles other than light armoured cars or trucks. Over the next two years two further models of the Humber LRC would be produced. These were the Mk III and Mk IIIA, which were fitted with 4x4-wheel drive, and both entered service in 1942. The basic vehicle weighed 3.5 tons and measured 14ft 4in long, 6ft 2in wide and 7ft 1in to the top of the turret. Overall it was not greatly different from the Morris LRC in terms of armament and role on the battlefield.

A crew of three operated the Humber LRC and it would have been very cramped with all the personal kit, food, personal weapons and the radio equipment to be stored. The main role was that the vehicle should use the on-board No. 19 radio set to transmit observations back to the main force and try to avoid being engaged by the enemy. The vehicle had armour plating extending to a thickness of 10mm maximum which gave it some degree of protection against small arms fire and a smoke-grenade launcher could be used to screen the vehicle's movements for short periods. Changes were made to the different marks and by the time the Mk IIIA entered service in 1942 the vehicle was fitted with extra observation slits. The armour on the superstructure was well sloped, which added to its survivability, but the LRC was never intended to engage in heavy fighting and the turret armament was really for self-defence. Some LRCs had their turrets removed and served in the FOO role for the Royal Artillery and others were used by the Royal Engineers. The Royal Air Force Regiment used the Humber LRC for airfield defence duties after D-Day in 1944 as they advanced across France and Belgium.

Morris LRC

The second type of LRC to be used was the Morris design, which entered service in 1942 and was deployed with units to Tunisia and Italy and would later be used during the Normandy campaign and after as the Allies advanced across Europe.

Looking down into the firer's position for the Boys anti-tank rifle on the Morris LRC.

The Morris LRC seen here in the colours of the 43rd (Wessex) Division was armed with a Bren gun and a Boys .55in-calibre anti-tank rifle.

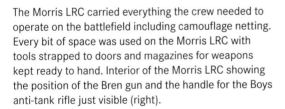

The Morris LRC carried everything the crew needed to operate on the battlefield including camouflage netting. Every bit of space was used on the Morris LRC with tools strapped to doors and magazines for weapons kept ready to hand. Interior of the Morris LRC showing the position of the Bren gun and the handle for the Boys anti-tank rifle just visible (right).

The design was never intended to replace other vehicles serving in the reconnaissance role, such as the Humber or Daimler scout cars, but rather to supplement them in their duties, first within the Reconnaissance Corps and then, when this unit was absorbed, with the Royal Armoured Corps. The Royal Air Force Regiment used around 200 Morris LRCs for patrolling forward airfields after the Normandy Landings and for security at other bases. Some Polish units used the vehicle for reconnaissance duties also. The Morris LRC was built in two versions, the Mk I and

the Mk II, and around 2,290 vehicles in both marks were built. The first version
of this four-wheeled design had two-wheel drive on the rear axle and was built by
the Nuffield Group, measuring 13ft 3in long and 6ft 8in wide. The height to the
top of the open-topped turret set to the right of the vehicle was 6ft 2in. It was fitted
with armour varying in thickness from 8mm to 14mm, which afforded some degree
of protection against small arms fire but not against larger calibres. The vehicle
weighed 3.7 tons and, with a rear-mounted Morris four-cylinder petrol engine
developing 71hp at 3,100rpm, it could achieve speeds of up to 50mph on roads. This
layout gave it an elongated rear deck area and a rather stubby bow-fronted appearance with a short glacis plate. A fuel tank holding 14 gallons of petrol gave it an
operational range of 250 miles and was operated by a crew of three.

Vehicle Name	Manufacturer	Production Date	Armament	Weight	Max. Speed
Morris LRC Mk I (2x4)	Nuffield Group	1942	Boys .55in-calibre anti-tank rifle and .303in-calibre machine gun	3.7 tons	50mph
Morris LRC Mk II (4x4)	Nuffield Group	1943	Boys .55in-calibre anti-tank rifle and .303in-calibre machine gun	3.7 tons	50mph

The crew sat in line abreast with the driver's position in the middle. This allowed
the man to his left to operate the radio and fire the Boys .55in-calibre anti-tank
rifle. The man to the driver's right operated the .303in-calibre Bren gun mounted
in the turret. By 1942 the Boys anti-tank rifle had little if any value against
armoured vehicles, but it could still be used against light trucks. It weighed 36lb
and measured 63.5in in length and was probably best used mounted in a vehicle because of these factors. It fired a steel-cored armour-piercing bullet with a
muzzle velocity of 3,250fps and could penetrate 20mm of armour at ranges of
over 500yd. The Bren gun fired 500 rounds per minute cyclic from box magazines
and was useful against infantry out to ranges of 600yd and gave the Morris a good
self-defence armament. The front of the turret had a long vertical opening and
veterans who operated the vehicle felt vulnerable to this because they believed
the opening allowed bullets to enter. The position for the Boys anti-tank rifle had a
pair of hinged covers that could be folded down to give some overhead protection
against shell splinters. The underside of the Morris LRC Mk I was flat and free
from any protuberances and a good ground clearance made it suitable for cross-
country operations. The front wheels were equipped with large coiled springs to
provide independent suspension, and semi-elliptical springs absorbed the shock
during cross-country operations. A variant of the Mk I was developed to serve in
the observation role, and was given the designation Morris Mk I OP. It was fitted
with a pair of range finders and was used for spotting the fall of shot for artillery
batteries. The radio operator would relay changes to be made direct to the gun
positions to engage enemy targets.

As useful as the Morris Mk I was it was felt that the two-wheel drive could be improved and calls were made to produce a four-wheel drive version for improved cross-country capabilities. This request was met in 1943 and resulted in the Morris LRC Mk II. There were no real external differences and only a slight increase in weight due to semi-elliptical leaf springs being fitted all round. Apart from that all operational abilities remained unaltered. The role remained the same and even saw the vehicle being used by other specialist units such as the Royal Engineers, who used it in reconnaissance roles and for liaison duties. It has been claimed in some areas that the Royal Armoured Corps did not rate the Morris LRC very highly, but then no vehicle ever comes up to all expectations and there will always be critics saying that a vehicle could be better. One cause for this criticism may have been the fact that the level of armour protection was never improved, not even on the Mk II, and that storage space for kit and extra ammunition was poorly thought out. Despite this the vehicle served well in its appointed role and supplemented other reconnaissance vehicles used by units such as the 43rd (Wessex) Division. The Morris LRC was never meant to be used in front-line action against armoured units, but rather to operate as covertly as possible, and this should be remembered when considering its overall wartime performance. Apart from the army units that used the Morris LRC, the Royal Air Force Regiment, which provided the security and defence for airfields, also used the vehicle. Among the first of its operational deployment roles was to provide security at an air base at Bradwell Bay in Essex. During the Tunisian campaign from March 1943 the RAF Regiment used their Morris LRCs alongside the British First Army at such locations as 'Tally Ho Corner' where they provided security. In January 1944 units of the RAF Regiment serving on the Azores deployed Morris LRCs to guard airfields. Although the Azores were and still are a Portuguese possession and the country was neutral during the war, the Allies were permitted to maintain bases on the islands. Despite this status the airfields still had to be guarded against possible saboteurs. After the Normandy Landings the RAF Regiment moved forward, with their Morris LRCs advancing around Bretteville in late June 1944, and were even involved with Operation Goodwood, the breakout action south-east of Caen on 18 July 1944.

The Remaining German Force

The Normandy campaign was still fresh in the minds of all who fought in the battles across France and the Allies had entered Belgium when Montgomery devised a new plan that he was sure would help win the war by the end of the year. His plan was a simple one in principle but in practice it was complicated, relying on too many 'ifs and buts' and making no allowance for unforeseen complications. The idea was to make a powerful thrust along a narrow front into the Ruhr, which contained the bulk of Germany's industrial capacity. He believed that if these facilities were seized the country could not fight, and secondly, once into the area the Allies would be able to swing round the northern flank of the Siegfried Line protecting Germany's border. The German Army may have been contracting back on all fronts but it was still capable of turning and making stands that turned into fierce pitched battles. Its armoured divisions were by now only a fraction of what they had been four years earlier but they still had powerful weapons in their armoury such as the Hetzer ('Baiter') also known as the Panzerjäger 38 (t) or Sdkfz 138. It appeared late in the war and was the result of combining the available industrial resources to produce a vehicle for use with the defensive anti-tank units serving with infantry divisions, which had requested that suitable weapons be made available to them in order to engage superior Russian armour.

The Marder III

The chassis of the Panzerjäger 38 (t) had Christie-type suspension, which gave good road speeds, but had very poor cross-country performance. However, this was more than made up for by the fact that it had excellent manoeuvrability and although it had performed well during the early campaigns of the war, by 1943 it was fast approaching the end of its useful service life, particularly when pitted against Russian T-34 tanks. Rather than phase the vehicle completely from service it was decided that the chassis would be used to form the basis of alternative fighting vehicles, one of which was the Marder III series armed with a 75mm gun to serve as an SPG. Between April 1942 and May 1944, 2,812 such vehicles were built using redundant chassis; they had a road speed of 25mph and an operational range of 118 miles. The Marder weighed 10.6 tons and was 20ft 3in long with armour protection between 5mm and 20mm, and it served on all operational fronts. The 38 (t) chassis was so versatile that it was used in a whole range of specialised roles including recovery vehicles and ammunition supply, SPGs and tank destroyers.

Vehicle Name	Manufacturer	Production Date	Armament	Weight	Max. Speed
Marder III	BMM	1942	75mm gun	10.6 tons	25mph

The Hetzer

In March 1943, General Heinz Guderian, in his capacity as inspector of armoured units, suggested the development of a light tank destroyer that could be used to break up enemy armoured formations. On his proposal all available 38 (t) chassis were given over to the production of tank destroyers. The result was the Hetzer, a light, but extremely well-armoured and effective tank destroyer specifically intended for use with the defensive anti-tank units of infantry divisions and would be the only vehicle based on the 38 (t) chassis to be adopted for use by the German Army after 1943. By the end of the war, and after only one year of being in production, more than 2,584 Hetzers had been built, which gives some idea of the degree of urgency placed in producing the vehicle. The company of BMM in Prague served as the controlling firm with Škoda producing all the automotive parts for the vehicle. The final design of the vehicle as it appeared was a low profile, only 6ft 5in tall, with well-sloped armour varying in thickness from 8mm to a maximum of 60mm over the frontal area. The Hetzer was 15ft 7in long, 7ft 2in wide and weighed 17.1 tons.

Vehicle Name	Manufacturer	Production Date	Armament	Weight	Max. Speed
The Hetzer	BMM and Škoda	1944	75mm PaK39 L/48 and either an MG34 or MG42 machine gun	17.1 tons	26mph

The Hetzer was fitted with a Praga AC/2 six-cylinder, water-cooled, inline engine, which developed 150hp at 2,600rpm to produce road speeds of more than 26mph and an operational range of 130 miles. The main armament of 75mm was the specialised PaK 39 L/48 mounted in the front of the well-slopped hull and set off slightly to the right. The mantlet had a distinctive shape, which was referred to as *saukopfblende* or 'pig snout' because it was thought to resemble the nose of a pig. The mounting method gave a limited traverse of only 5 degrees to the left and 11 degrees to the right, a total of 16 degrees. The gun could be depressed to -6 degrees and elevated to +12 degrees. The Hetzer carried forty-one rounds of ammunition ready to use and targets out to almost 2,000yd could be engaged, which made it deadly against a range of Allied tanks including the American-built Sherman and Russian T-34s.

Field trials were successfully concluded by December 1943 and the design was proven and production commenced in April 1944, continuing until May 1945. The first units to be equipped with the Hetzer were the 731 and 743 Panzerjäger Abteilungen and the 15th and 76th Infantry Divisions, which received their vehicles in July 1944. The Hetzer served successfully in all theatres of operation after its introduction, and in particular on the Russian front. For close support and self-protection against infantry attack, the vehicle was armed with either a single MG34 or MG42 machine gun, which was mounted on the roof of the vehicle. A small shield protected the firer and was a standard feature on several other armoured vehicles in the German Army.

The driver's position was to the left of the vehicle with the gun's breech mechanism to his right. Access to the cramped interior of the vehicle was through a roof hatch, with a further hatch for the machine-gunner. Had the war continued beyond 1945, and taking into account Germany's ability to stretch out vital war resources, it is quite possible that the Hetzer could have formed a greater part of the tank destroyer programme. In fact, plans were in place to produce 1,000 Hetzers per month by mid-1945, in which case it could have gone on to be used in special tank-hunting units moving rapidly from one zone of engagement to another. In fact, there were a number of proposed variants in the Hetzer series including plans to upgrade the main armament to a 105mm-calibre StuH 42 assault howitzer. The war ended before any conversions could be completed however. At least twenty Hetzers were converted to the Flammpanzer, a flame-throwing version, and were made available in December 1944 in readiness to participate in the Battle of the Bulge in the Ardennes sector. For this role the 7.5cm PaK39 gun was replaced by a Flammenwerfer 41, which had the same traverse and elevation as the standard gun and could fire twenty-four bursts from a fuel reserve of 700 litres. This produced the equivalent of a continuous flame jet of 87.5 seconds which could reach out to ranges of 60m. The vehicle recovery version was known as the Bergepanzer, of which sixty-four vehicles were produced, and these began to enter service from October 1944 onwards and served with anti-tank units operating with Hetzers.

Operation Market Garden

Montgomery's plans were finally approved and given the code name Operation Market Garden. They involved airborne landings deep behind German lines to seize vital bridges, and British armoured divisions racing down the corridor to secure the area. On 17 September men from the US 101st Airborne Division began to land in the area around Eindhoven to secure the bridges, while further on, men from the US 82nd Airborne Division eventually seized the bridge at Nijmegen and the British 1st Airborne Division landed around the town of Arnhem to seize and hold the bridge over the River Rhine until the British XXX Corps could fight its way up the road route. The airborne troops had taken off from airfields in England and the gliders carried anti-tank guns, motorcycles and Jeeps. The Germans had not expected such a daring, indeed reckless, assault, but by sheer coincidence they had moved the SS II Panzer Corps, 15,000 men and 250 tanks, into the area of Arnhem ten days before the start of Market Garden for rest and the refitting of their vehicles. The British XXX Corps, with 50,000 men and 23,000 tanks, AFVs and trucks, set off at 2.35 p.m. to cover the 60-mile route to reach Arnhem. The road was narrow and elevated, which silhouetted the vehicles and made them an easy target for anti-tank guns. Within twenty minutes of setting out, the column had lost nine tanks in two minutes through enemy fire. Self-contained with artillery, engineers and signals, XXX Corps with the Guards Armoured Division was experienced, having seen action in Tunisia, Sicily and all the way from the beaches at Normandy. Unfortunately the nature of the terrain they were passing over, known as polder, was too soft to bear the weight of tanks and, unable to spread out, the British armour was confined to the roadway. They would continue to be pounded as they advanced up the only route. The airborne drop experienced complications but finally, by 2 a.m. on 18 September, some 20,000 men had been landed along with 511 vehicles and 330 pieces of artillery, including anti-tank guns.

Bailey bridge built to replace destroyed original at Randazzo during the Sicily campaign 1943.

The Germans realised that the airborne troops at Arnhem were only lightly armed and were not equipped to deal with heavy armour. As the operation continued they brought the full weight of their Tiger tanks and other armoured vehicles to bear on the British forces and surrounded the parachute troops. The advance by XXX Corps was put further behind schedule and they did not reach Eindhoven until the following day, where they were informed that the bridge over the Son River was destroyed. Specialist equipment had to be driven forward and a Bailey bridge, designed by engineer Donald Bailey in 1940, was built over the river. Hundreds of Bailey bridges would be built across Europe to replace those destroyed by the Germans and some constructions could support weights of up to 70 tons. The troops referred to the route as 'Hell's Highway' and with good cause. The men at Arnhem were using PIATs to engage tanks and fighting was fierce at all points. Supply drops were being made by aircraft and by the end of the operation 20,190 men had been parachuted in, 13,781 men had been landed by 491 gliders along with 5,230 tons of supplies, and 1,927 vehicles and 568 pieces of artillery had been landed in the three drop zones. Almost 10,000 British troops of 1st Airborne Division would find themselves in defensive positions at the bridgehead at Arnhem and surrounded by Germans. This was an operation that should have been concluded in three or four days until relieved by XXX Corps, but the men at Arnhem held on for ten days until the order was given for them to get out as best they could. The German defences were too strong and they badly battered XXX Corps, making it almost impossible to reach Arnhem. The bridges captured by the US airborne divisions were secure but at Arnhem the position was evacuated and 2,163 men escaped; 1,440 had been killed, with the remainder including the wounded being taken prisoner. The fighting had cost the Allies eighty-eight tanks plus trucks and other AFVs, and XXX Corps had suffered 1,500 killed and wounded. The Germans had lost between 6,315 and 13,300 killed, wounded and captured, although estimates vary enormously, and thirty tanks and SPGs had been destroyed by anti-tank guns and PIATs. Some of these were ageing French tanks such as the Char B1 bis, remarkably still in service after four years, but these were destroyed by British anti-tank gunners in the fighting. It had been a bold plan but in the end all it left the Allies with was a long narrow salient and the prospect of fighting through another winter. It also proved that there was still a long way to go to beat the Germans in the field.

Maintaining the Allied Advance

The Allies had advanced hundreds of miles across Europe from the beachheads in Normandy but lacked the proper port facilities to unload the supplies necessary to maintain the advance, as all the fuel, stores, food and ammunition had to be transported 300 miles by road from ports such as Cherbourg. Each Allied division required a minimum of 520 tons of supplies each day if they were to keep at levels of combat readiness. To move this mountain of supplies the Allies had around 450,000 trucks being driven day and night to carry essentials and specialist items such as bridging equipment to span rivers. For the most part these were American Jimmys and British Bedford and Morris trucks, which could handle ammunition, fuel, medical stores and troops, but there were also 15,000 trucks that had long-distance capabilities for exceptionally heavy loads and for moving replacement tanks to the front. Even so, the drivers were finding it difficult to keep up with the advancing armies and Montgomery's 21st Army Group, which should have been receiving 12,000 tons of supplies per day, had only 6,000 tons delivered. In an effort to try to supplement this shortfall, 1,000 tons per day were airlifted, but often this method of transportation fell below this level. The problem was only partially alleviated when the deep-water port of Antwerp, lying 56 miles inland from the coast, was captured by the British 11th Armoured Division on 5 September. The facilities here had the capacity to allow the Allies to unload 40,000 tons of supplies each day, which would eliminate the need to transport everything long distance, but the problem lay in the fact that the Germans still held the area around the approaches to the port and these had to be cleared out. The supplies were there but they could not be delivered in quantity, which meant a slowing down of the Allied advance which, in turn, gave the Germans time to regroup and reorganise. But they were running out of men, and troops from naval units and Luftwaffe units were being redeployed to the front line to serve as infantry; as well, anti-aircraft gunners were now employed in the anti-tank role with their formidable 88mm guns.

The Western Allies continued to advance but were hampered by heavy rain, and roads, which had been badly damaged and weakened by the extra weight of so much military traffic, were washed away. German units were fighting rearguard actions, which delayed the Allies, but finally they pushed into the area of the Scheldt estuary, covering the entrance to the port of Antwerp and cleared it of the enemy. On 28 November the first convoy arrived to unload cargo. Supplies could now be brought close to the front line and replacement vehicles driven directly to where they were needed along with reinforcements. To the south in the mountainous region of the Vosges, the French First Army under the command of General Jean de Lattre de Tassigny, equipped with American-built vehicles such as the M8 armoured car armed with a 37mm gun and capable of road speeds of up to 55mph, in company with the American Seventh Army under Major General Alexander Patch, were closing in to trap the Germans in what would become known as the 'Colmar Pocket', close to the Swiss border. When the fighting finally ended there in February 1945 the French had lost 13,390 killed and wounded, and the Americans had 8,000 casualties. According to some sources the Germans lost 38,500 killed, wounded and captured, and those who escaped abandoned fifty-five AFVs and sixty-six pieces of artillery. By now Germany was losing its allies as they came to realise that the war was being won by the Russians and Western Allies. Bulgaria and Romania both changed sides on 23 August 1944 and on 20 January 1945 Hungary signed an armistice. The armed forces of these states had been supplied primarily by Germany, with standard weapons, equipment and AFVs, including tanks, as used by the German Army. They had fought together against Russia on the Eastern Front and supplying them had placed added pressure on the German supply lines. While the Western Allies were moving in from Belgium and the Netherlands, the Russians were keeping up the pressure from the east and their list of Ten Victories for the year of 1944 included the invasion of Estonia and Latvia in September and then moving into Hungary, Czechoslovakia and Yugoslavia in October. The Russians poured 450,000 troops into Finland along with 800 tanks and massive air support. On 19 September Finland signed an armistice with Russia and on 1 October attacked Germany. Germany was now fighting on its own, apart from some volunteer units still serving in divisions of infantry or armoured units.

Operation Wacht am Rhein

In mid-December 1944 the Western Allies had crossed the German border in several places and were advancing across a frontage 1,000 miles wide. In the depths of winter everything had slowed down and there was very little movement and certainly nothing to give cause for concern. In fact, military intelligence concluded that the Germans were not in any position to mount an offensive of a serious nature. Around the densely wooded area of the Ardennes Forest, considered to be impassable by tanks, 83,000 men of the US First Army, commanded by Lieutenant General Courtney Hodges, were looking forward to Christmas. The troops were largely inexperienced and the area was quiet and patrols reported nothing unusual apart from some isolated exchanges of gunfire. Suddenly at 5.30 a.m. on 16 December, German artillery opened fire with such intensity that it threw the Americans into disarray. The planned parachute drop that would have added to the confusion was abandoned when the trucks taking the troops to their aircraft ran out of fuel. This was Operation *Wacht am Rhein* (Watch on the Rhine) which had been in planning since October, and which Hitler was hoping would push the Allies back. The attack was launched across a 60-mile-wide front extending from the border town of Monschau in the north to Echternach in the south. The attack was supported by 275,000 troops, many experienced, along with 1,900 pieces of artillery and 950 tanks and other AFVs. Opposing them, the Americans had just 394 pieces of artillery and 420 tanks and AFVs.

The weather had closed in and Allied aircraft were grounded so there was no air support to break up the attack. The Germans advanced quickly and were in danger of becoming a victim of their own success. At one point a traffic jam of 100 tanks, PzKw IV and Panthers, built up, and used up precious fuel, which was in short supply, as the crews waited for the road to be cleared. Another type of vehicle committed to the operation was the Jagdpanther, a very powerful tank destroyer armed with the formidable 88mm gun capable of destroying targets of up to 3,000m range in ideal conditions. The first production models of the vehicle had been built in February 1944 with the first units entering service with 559th and 654th Panzerjäger Abteilungen in June 1944. Many Jagdpanthers were deployed to the Russian front, where they were used against T-34 tanks and the heavier vehicles and SPGs, and were operated within a separate heavy anti-tank battalion in a panzer division. The Jagdpanther inflicted severe losses against Allied armoured units in the later stages of the Normandy campaign. During one engagement in July 1944 three Jagdpanthers destroyed eleven tanks in only minutes before a squadron of Churchill tanks arrived destroying two and causing the third to withdraw. It was 32ft 10in in length with an overall height of 8ft 11in and armour thickness between 25mm and 80mm, and yet weighed only 44.8 tons with an operational range of 130 miles.

Vehicle Name	Manufacturer	Production Date	Armament	Weight	Max. Speed
Jagdpanther SdKfz 173 tank destroyer	MIAG and MNH	1944	88mm gun	44.8 tons	29 mph

The Jagdpanther served on the Russian front and the last units were still in action as the fighting fell back to the outskirts of Berlin in the final stages of the war.

Sherman tanks with the British Army over the Rhine and advancing into Germany.

In December 1944 the Germans had concentrated numbers of the Jagdpanther together in the Ardennes, but due to fuel shortages and a lack of air cover to protect them against air strikes by Allied attack aircraft, they were hampered, but not before giving good account of themselves in action. The Jagdpanther was developed using the Panther as a starting point, with the hull and chassis being kept and a new superstructure built on to the bodywork. The engine remained the same, which is to say it was a petrol-driven water-cooled Maybach HLP30 V-12, which developed 700bhp at 3,000rpm to produce road speeds of 29mph and cross-country speeds of 15mph. A wooden mock-up was prepared in October 1943 and the prototype was ready for inspection by Hitler in December the same year. Satisfied with the results, production of the new tank destroyer was approved and designated as the Jagdpanther SdKfz 173, with the contract being awarded to the company of MIAG in January 1944 with the order to produce 150 new vehicles per month. The company of MNH was also awarded a production contract in November 1944, but even so the monthly output of the new vehicle never reached anywhere near the stipulated production figures. In fact, by the time production ceased in March 1945 only 382 vehicles had been produced, with seventy-two vehicles being produced in January, just four months before the war ended.

The Americans fell back in disarray but it was not widespread panic, and pockets of resistance were established, such as at the town of Bastogne where men of the 101st Airborne Division held out against everything sent to attack them. Patton

The SdKfz 173 or Jagdpanther was a late design in the war and a very powerful weapon in the German army's arsenal. The Jagdpanther could reach speeds up to 28mph which was impressive for its size and was a tank destroyer which did not have a turret, reducing the number of moving parts.

with the Third Army moved northwards to attack the left flank of the salient that was forming due to the nature of the German attack. The Germans had been hoping to use captured stocks of fuel to keep their vehicles moving but destroyed bridges slowed them and prevented them from reaching these vital stocks. Slowly the front began to stabilise and the Americans began to deal with the Germans, such as at Remonville, where Patton's forces captured the town. By 26 December he had linked up with Bastogne, where the paratroopers of the 101st Airborne Division used bazooka shoulder-fired rocket launchers to destroy seven tanks. By that time the German attack was almost a spent force, having used up its last reserves of fuel and ammunition. The weather began to clear and the Allied aircraft were able to fly air-support missions that destroyed German vehicles as they moved. The operation had cost the Americans and British 7,000 killed, 33,400 wounded and 21,000 taken prisoner or missing, along with 700 tanks and other AFVs destroyed. For the Germans it was disastrous, with 120,000 men killed, wounded or captured. They had lost 1,600 aircraft, 600 tanks and 6,000 other AFVs and trucks. Over the next three months the Allies kept up a relentless pressure, all the time pushing the Germans back, albeit very slowly, but on 7 March 1945 they had a route over the Rhine River when the badly battered bridge at Remagen was captured. Ten days later the weakened structure collapsed, but the British and Americans were over the Rhine. The city of Berlin, the German capital, was not scheduled for attack by the Western Allies – that was to be left to the Russians.

The Russian Advance

The Russians had ended 1944 holding positions in eastern Poland, with a front line extending from the Baltic coast in Lithuania in the north and running down the Czechoslovakian border in the south. They held these positions, which extended for over 750 miles, for six months before making their next move. In the centre was the 1st Belorussian Front under the command of Marshal Georgi Zhukov, and to his left was the 1st Ukrainian Front with 2.2 million men commanded by Marshal Ivan Koniev. In the north on Zhukov's right flank was the 2nd and 3rd Belorussian Fronts with 1.6 million men facing the German Army Group Centre with only 400,000 troops. Army Group A, commanded by General Josef Harpe, was severely outnumbered at every level including tanks at a ratio of seven to one. On the morning of 12 January 1945 the Russian artillery opened fire with such ferocity that the Germans immediately began to fall back. Harpe's men could not stem the attack and within five days of continuous fighting, the 1st Ukrainian Front had advanced 100 miles across a front of 160 miles. By 31 January Zhukov had reached the Oder River near the town of Kustrin and had advanced his entire front 300 miles in less than three weeks.

In a desperate measure Hitler appointed Heinrich Himmler, head of the SS and with no formal military training at any level, to command Army Group Vistula in the north. The Russians were now only 40 miles from Berlin and Hitler responded by ordering operations to be conducted in the south, which only served to cost the army more troops lost and tanks destroyed. Further pressure by the Russians in the centre took the city of Berlin as their axis of advance as they pressed ahead 6 miles across the Oder River along a front 30 miles wide. The 1st and 2nd Belorussian Fronts and 1st Ukrainian Front now threatened Berlin directly. Fighting slowed the Russian advance down somewhat as the Germans put up a concerted defence, but it was only prolonging the inevitable. The Russians

scheduled the final push for 16 April and the 2nd Belorussian Front was ordered
north to deal with the German 3rd Panzer Army. Even so, this still left Zhukov with
2.5 million men, 41,000 pieces of artillery, 6,250 tanks and AFVs, with air support
from 7,500 aircraft. The Germans had 700,000 men, 9,000 pieces of artillery and
1,500 tanks and AFVs. The Volkssturm, a home defence unit comprising old men,
and the Hitler Youth, added another 70,000 to the strength. They managed to slow
the Russians but again they could not mount any credible defence given the poor
quality of the weapons and lack of real training. Zhukov began the final assault
with a massive bombardment from artillery positioned at the rate of one gun every
13ft along a front stretching over 55 miles. By 25 April the city was encircled
by the 1st Belorussian Front and the 1st Ukrainian Front. General Karl Weidling,
commanding the remnants of the LVI Panzer Corps, was put in charge of defending
the city. His own unit comprised 1,500 men and sixty tanks. Berlin was ringed by
anti-tank ditches, but these and other obstacles did not stand in the way of the
Russian advance. On 21 April the Russians had broken into the suburbs of the
city and street fighting began. Tanks by their very nature are wholly unsuited to
such tactics but the Russians pushed them in to deal with last remaining German
vehicles. They joined the SPGs in firing at buildings at point-blank range to crush
any resistance.

   On 28 April Heinrich Himmler made an attempt at striking the most extraordinary deal of the war when he entered negotiations with the Swedish Count
Bernadotte, when he tried to exchange Jews for trucks. He told Count Bernadotte
that he was prepared to release 100,000 Jews from concentration camps in return
for 10,000 trucks from the Americans. Exactly what he intended to use the vehicles for can only be guessed at and exactly what he intended to use as fuel given
there was nothing in Germany for a fleet of vehicles this size was anyone's guess.
In the end nothing came of the talks but it still showed how important vehicles
were in a modern war. Day by day the Russians continued to press in on all sides,
reducing the German pockets of resistance. On 30 April Hitler committed suicide
in his headquarters bunker in Berlin but diehard units still kept fighting. Two
days later, on 2 May, the Russians had complete control of the city and that day
German forces in Italy finally surrendered. Gradually the small pockets of resistance also surrendered, including in Denmark on 5 May. VE Day (Victory in Europe
Day) was declared on 8 May and was the end of the war. The garrison on the island
of Guernsey, part of 319th Infantry Division, surrendered, and the island was liberated. The neighbouring island of Jersey in the Channel Islands was liberated on
9 May without a shot being fired. Eventually, from this small island measuring
only 45 square miles, some 22,000 tons of ammunition of all calibres would be
removed along with tens of thousands of mines, trucks and tanks.

German Siebel Ferry seen in harbour at St Helier, Jersey, after the occupation. There were several versions of these and they could carry between 50 and 100 tons of supplies.

This truck has gone through a wall down by the harbour in St Helier during the clearing up after the occupation.

The End of the War in the Pacific

The war in the Pacific was still being fought but it would end very differently to the war in Europe. The Japanese had three tank divisions in 1942 but the tanks themselves were lightly armed and armoured and used in small 'penny packet' formations, usually acting in support of the infantry. In 1944 they produced only 400 tanks and in 1945 this figure was 141, such was the desperate need for raw materials, especially metal, to produce the vehicles. Allied armoured units in the early part of the war in the Far East were restricted by the terrain and the dense jungle, which vehicles could only traverse by defined routes that left them open to ambush tactics with anti-tank guns, a strategy the Japanese were extremely good at. Japanese tanks were largely obsolete designs but some development to improve them was undertaken such as the amphibious Type 2 Kamisha of 11 tons, while the Imperial Japanese Navy experimented with the 26-ton Kachisha amphibious tank. By and large though, the Japanese remained committed to what they had in service and preferred to fit heavier guns to them (such as the Type 97) and improve their armour. The Japanese tank force was never involved in campaigns or battles to the same degree as in Russia or Europe and the vehicles were used as mobile machine-gun posts. Despite this the British and Americans came to know the Japanese as tenacious defenders of even the most desolate places, who would fight almost to the last man. For example, when the 1st US Marine Division landed on the island of Peleliu, measuring just 6 square miles, they fought a hard battle against a garrison of 11,000 men. When the last Japanese soldier surrendered in February 1945 the fighting had cost them over 10,600 killed and barely 200 captured. The remainder were listed as 'missing' and had probably been cremated by the flame-throwers. To capture the island the Americans fired more than 15 million rounds of small arms ammunition, 150,000 mortar bombs, and had thrown over 118,000 hand grenades. It was later calculated that taking into account naval fire support it had taken an average of 1,500 rounds of artillery to kill each Japanese soldier just to capture one small island.

  The fighting on the mainland in Burma also had its own unique set of problems concerning re-supply because of the distances involved. The troops on the ground could only carry so much with them on mules and they had to be re-supplied by air drops, something that the Germans had tried and experienced mixed results. During the Imphal and Kohima battles, the British Chindit forces were kept supplied by the 3rd Tactical Air Force of the RAF, which flew hundreds of missions covering many thousands of miles over a four-month period in early 1944. The Chindits lost 17,000 mules and pack ponies during their campaigns and these had to be replaced and were flown in by air. The RAF flew in 1 million gallons of fuel, 6,250 tons of supplies, including food, ammunition and medical equipment, along with 12,000 replacement troops, and evacuated 13,000 casualties. That was just part of the overall total to support operations in Burma. Between 1943 and 1945 the combined efforts of the Allied air forces flew some 650,000 tons of supplies into airstrips that had been carved out deep in the jungle. They also flew in 315,000 men and evacuated 110,000 casualties, all of which kept the campaign moving.

The Japanese deployed 620,000 troops to China and the 10th US Air Force flew missions to supply the Chinese troops engaged in the fighting. The American pilots were based in Assam and flew a route that took them over the Himalayan mountain range with peaks rising to over 20,000ft. The pilots called it 'flying the hump'. In 1942 they were transporting 3,700 tons of supplies per month, but by late 1944 this figure had risen to exceed 35,000 tons per month. The Japanese could not compete with this level of re-supply and relied massively on their man-power levels, but even this resource was dwindling. While the Allies could fly in thousands of tons of supplies and troops, the Japanese were still being urged to attack with fanatical zeal that was as suicidal as their comrades fighting to almost the last man on the Pacific islands. After the fighting to capture Eniwetok, for example, the US marines took only sixty-four prisoners out of a garrison of 2,741. The same thing was repeated elsewhere, sometimes on a much higher scale, such as at Saipan, where only 2,000 men out of a garrison of 32,000 were taken prisoner. Movement of tanks under such conditions was ponderous and slow but the fire support they provided was invaluable in destroying bunkers and Japanese tanks when they appeared, but there were no pitched battles between the armoured units. Artillery played a large part in the campaigns along with mortars, all of which had to be moved by men or on mules. These animals were widely used in the Italian campaign but in Burma they proved vital to the British Chindits and Merrill's 'Marauders', going where no vehicle could move. The fighting in the Pacific ended when the atomic bomb was dropped on the cities of Hiroshima and Nagasaki. There had never been the full-scale armoured battles as in Europe but the tanks still had to be dealt with by anti-tank weapons.

The Vehicles Today

Today, many years after the end of the war, a large number of these vehicles are still operational and the owners take them to public shows. Some are used in documentaries and film productions, because people do like watching war films. Modellers enjoy making plastic kits and manufacturers produce many different types to keep this interest fresh. The museums where the tanks and trucks are on display attract good visitor numbers and some of these, such as Imperial War Museum Duxford in Cambridgeshire and the Tank Museum at Bovington in Dorset, have a full schedule of events throughout the year for public visits. There are similar museums in other countries, such as Saumur in France, where they also organise special displays. Re-enactment events also attract large numbers of vehicles and the owners' clubs and societies have a large number of members. It is to these dedicated people that we should be grateful that there are so many of these historical vehicles still in working order for us to appreciate.

WHERE TO SEE TRUCKS AND TANKS

Cobbaton Combat Collection, Chittlehampton, Umberleigh, North Devon
EX37 9RZ.
Tel: 01769 540740. Website: www.cobbatoncombat.co.uk

History on Wheels Museum, Longclose House, Common Road, Eton Wick, near
Windsor, Berkshire SL4 6QY.
Tel: 01753 862637. Website: www.historyonwheels.co.uk

Muckleburgh Military Collection, Weybourne, Norfolk NR25 7EG.
Tel: 01263 588210. Website: www.muckleburgh.co.uk

Imperial War Museum, Lambeth, London SE1 6HZ.
Tel: 020 7416 5374. Website: www.iwm.org.uk

Imperial War Museum, Duxford, Cambridge CB2 4QR.
Tel: 01223 835000. Website: www.iwm.org.uk

Tank Museum, Bovington, Dorset BH20 6JG.
Tel: 01929 405096. Website: www.tankmuseum.org.uk

REME Museum of Technology, Isaac Newton Road, Arborfield, Berkshire RG2 9NJ.
Tel: 0118 9763 480. Website: www.reme-museum.org.uk

The annual War and Peach Show in Kent: www.thewarandpeaceshow.com

The Royal Logistic Corps Museum, The Princess Royal Barracks, Deepcut, Surrey
GU16 6RW.
Tel: 01252 833371. Website: www.rlcmuseum.co.uk

Aldershot Military Museum, Queen's Avenue, Aldershot, Hampshire GU11 2LG.
Tel: 01252 314598.

BIBLIOGRAPHY

Arnold-Forster, M., *The World at War* (London: William Collins Sons & Co. Ltd, 1973)

Bacon, Admiral Sir R. et al. (eds), *Warfare Today* (London: Odhams Press Ltd)

Barker, A.J., *Japanese Army Handbook 1939–1945* (Surrey: Ian Allan, 1979)

Brereton, J.M., *The Horse in War* (Devon: David & Charles, 1976)

Campbell, C., *The World War II Fact Book* (London: Futura, 1986)

Chandler, D., *The Art of Warfare on Land* (London: Penguin Books, 2000)

Chamberlain, P. and Doyle, H., *Encyclopedia of German Tanks of World War Two* (London: Arms & Armour, 1999)

Davies, W.J.K., *German Army Handbook 1939–1945* (Surrey: Ian Allan Ltd, 1973)

Deighton, L., *Blitzkrieg* (London: Jonathan Cape, 1969)

Dyer, G., *War* (London: Guild Publishing, 1986)

Ellison Hawks, R.A., Captain, *Britain's Wonderful Fighting Forces* (London: Odhams Press Ltd)

Evans, M.M., *Retreat, Hell! We Just Got Here! The American Expeditionary Force in France 1917–1918* (Oxford: Osprey Publishing, 1998)

Fletcher, D., et al., *Tiger Tank* (Somerset: Haynes Publishing, 2011)

Forty, G., *US Tanks of World War II* (Dorset: Blandford Press, 1983)

Foss, C.F. et al., *Tanks and Fighting Vehicles* (London: Salamander Books Ltd, 1977)

Georgano, G.N., *World War Two Military Vehicles* (Oxford: Osprey Publishing, 1994)

Jukes, G., *Kursk: the Clash of Armour* (London: MacDonald & Co. Ltd, 1968)

Macksey, K., *Panzer Division: The Mailed Fist* (London: MacDonald & Co. Ltd, 1968)

Macksey, K. and Batchelor, J.H., *Tank: A History of the Armoured Fighting Vehicle* (London: Military Book Society, 1970)

Macksey, K., *The Guiness History of Land Warfare* (Middlesex: Guinness Superlatives, 1973)

Macksey, K., et al., *The Guinness Book of Tank Facts & Feats* (London: Guinness Superlatives, 1976)

Morris, E., *Tanks; Tank Weaponry and Warfare* (London: Octopus Books Ltd, 1975)

Perrett, B., *Knights of the Black Cross* (London: Grafton Books, 1990)

Perrett, B., *Tank Warfare, Arms & Armour* (London: 1990)

Quarrie, B., *Lightning Death: The Story of the Waffen-SS* (Somerset: Patrick Stephens Ltd, 1991)

Rutherford. W., *Kasserine Baptism of Fire* (London: MacDonald & Co. Ltd, 1970)

Smithers, A.J., *A New Excalibur* (London: Grafton Books, 1988)

Smurthwaite, D., et al., *Against All Odds* (London: National Army Museum, 1989)

Sutherland, J., *World War II Tanks and AFVs* (Shrewsbury: Airlife Publishing Ltd, 2002)

Townshend, C. (ed.), *The Oxford Illustrated History of Modern War* (Oxford: Oxford University Press, 1997)

Ware, P., *Military Jeep* (Somerset: Haynes Publishing, 2010)

Ware, P., *Sherman Tank* (Somerset: Haynes Publishing, 2012)

White, B.T., *Tanks and Other Armoured Fighting Vehicles of the World* (Dorset: Blandford Press, 1975)

Winter. J.M., *The Experience of World War I* (Oxford: Equinox, 1988)

INDEX

Italics indicate illustrations